CLASSIC
FAVOURITES

CLASSIC FAVOURITES

Traditional recipes from around the world

PUBLISHED BY THE READER'S DIGEST ASSOCIATION LIMITED
LONDON   MONTREAL   SYDNEY

CLASSIC FAVOURITES *Traditional recipes from around the world* was edited and designed by The Reader's Digest Association Limited, London and is based on Farmhouse Cookery, Copyright © 1980 The Reader's Digest Association Limited, London, and The South African Cookbook, Copyright © 1985 The Reader's Digest Association, South Africa (Pty) Limited, Cape Town.

First edition copyright © 1986 The Reader's Digest Association Limited 25 Berkeley Square, London W1X 6AB

Copyright © 1986 Reader's Digest Association, Far East Limited

Copyright ©1986 The Reader's Digest Association (Canada) Inc.

ISBN 0-276-39824-6

Filmset by MS Filmsetting Ltd, Frome Printed by Blantyre Printing & Binding Co. Ltd, Glasgow Bound by Hazell Watson & Viney Ltd, Aylesbury

ACKNOWLEDGEMENTS

Classic Favourites is based on *Farmhouse Cookery* to which the following made major contributions: Elizabeth Ayrton, Philippa Back, Peter Bailey, Michael Bateman, Frederick Bayliss, Brian Binns, Trudy Blacker, Richard Bonson, Leonora Box, Lizzie Boyd, Barbara Brown, Dorothy Brown, Caroline Conran, Sheena Davis, Philip Dowell, Alex Dufort, Caroline Elwood, Eric Fraser, Theodora Fitzgibbon, Antonia Gaunt, Jane Grigson, Christine Hanscomb, Molly Harrison, Moira Hodgson, Babs Honey, Robin Jacques, Margaret Leach, Margaret Mackenzie, Jeffery Matthews, Moya Maynard, Frederick Middlehurst, Dinah Morrison, Mary Norwak, Olive Odell, Jean Robertson, Carolyn Russell, Simone Sekers, Marika Hanbury Tenison, Tessa Traeger, Judy Urquart, C. Anne Wilson.

Additional material has been taken from the *South African Cookbook* to which the following contributed: Irma Barenblatt, Lynn Bedford Hall, Roger Bell, Phillippa Cheifitz, Renata Coetzee, Jac de Villiers, Gerti Easterbrook, Vivia Ferreira, Ian Gallie, Sonja Garber, Felicity Harris, Martine Israel, Anthony Johnson, Drexler Kyzer, Pamela Lassak, Vivien le Roux, Franz Lauinger, Susan Long, Wendy Malleson, Barbara Newman, Ina Paarman, Ramola Parbhoo, Alain Proust, Simon Rappaport, Sue Ross, Betsie Rood, Sylvia Sieff, Elizabeth Southey, Irna Turilli, Professor Leonie van Heerden, Magdaleen van Wyk, Peter Veldsman.

CONTENTS

HOW TO USE THIS BOOK

The food in this book reflects the diversity of the world in which we live, and the spirit of adventure which has awakened in the kitchen in recent years. This book explores many culinary boundaries and also includes those traditional dishes which have endured through changes in lifestyles and eating habits. The recipes, whether new or traditional, have been contributed by top cookery writers.

Before you begin preparing a dish, read the recipe through to ensure that you have all the ingredients and equipment required. If any of the techniques described are unfamiliar, try referring to The Practical Cook section, which contains basic recipes, useful tips on the preparation of different types of food, and a list of familiar and less familiar herbs and spices. There is also a glossary which explains the meaning of many commonly used cookery terms.

From time to time you will notice an asterisk marked next to an ingredient, a term, or recipe, for example *flaky pastry**, or *2 onions, peeled and chopped**. Asterisks indicate cross-references to other parts of the book, so that basic information is not constantly repeated. In the first example, the asterisk indicates that a recipe is given elsewhere in the book for flaky pastry; in the second example it means there is a description of the best way to peel and chop onions. In all cases, refer to the index to locate the relevant page. The following additional information, where applicable, is contained in the recipes themselves:

Preparation and cooking time Each recipe gives the time needed to prepare and cook it. Use this as a rough guide to plan your meal: the time taken can vary from one cook to another, depending on the speed with which they can tackle the particular steps and whether they use time-saving devices, such as electric beaters or food processors.

Standing and marinating time If a dish (or part of it) needs to be left for 30 minutes or longer, this time has been calculated separately to help you with planning. Where standing or marinating time is shorter than 30 minutes, this has been incorporated into the preparation time.

Chilling and freezing time Some dishes need chilling or freezing as part of the preparation. If this time should exceed 30 minutes, it will be listed separately from the preparation time. (The times stated are only rough guides, since some refrigerators and freezers are more efficient than others.)

Yield Each recipe indicates how many people can be served with the given amount or, where more appropriate, the yield in kilograms and grams (pounds and ounces) litres and millilitres (pints and fluid ounces) or quantities (for example, 20 brandy snaps).

Serving suggestions and variations Suitable accompaniments to a dish, and ways in which you can alter the dish to suit your personal taste, are given at the end of a recipe when appropriate.

MEASURES AND TEMPERATURES

Both metric and imperial measures have been used for volume and mass throughout the book.

The temperatures are given in degrees Celsius (centigrade), degrees Fahrenheit, and for those who use gas cookers, the mark or regulo reading. Other useful temperatures can be found in the charts for cooking meat (page 171) and poultry (page 174).

INGREDIENTS

Where ingredients are commonly referred to by more than one name, both names are given, for example aubergine (eggplant).

Sugar In recipes that specify only 'sugar', use granulated, white sugar.

Flour Where simply 'flour' is mentioned, use cake flour and not the stronger bread flour.

Cream Unless otherwise specified, the cream used should be thick enough for whipping.

STARTERS

THE CORRECT CHOICE of starter is crucial to the success of a meal, whether the occasion is formal or informal. If starting with a fish terrine or salmon mousse, for example, do not follow with a fish main course. Similarly, try to avoid serving too generous a starter with a substantial main course – it should complement rather than overwhelm the dish that is to follow.

You do not have to spend a lot of money to produce a tasty and attractive starter. Remember that it is intended primarily as an appetite stimulant – and visual appeal plays a great part in this. Be free with the use of fresh ingredients which provide a variety of tastes and textures.

Starters open up a whole new culinary world for the imaginative cook. Try stuffing avocados with cream cheese and caviar, or purée them for a Mexican guacamole. Create patterns on a large platter with sliced meats (Italian antipasti), and experiment with dips and pâtés.

DOLMADES

STUFFED VINE LEAVES is a popular dish world-wide with an intriguing combination of flavours. It is generally a starter for Greek meals but it may be served as a main course.

You can also make dolmades with cabbage leaves or spinach leaves. Try to choose young leaves with no holes.

Dolmades can be frozen successfully; drain and open-freeze them on a tray. Once they are hard, arrange them closely together in containers and separate the layers with freezer film.

PREPARATION TIME: 30 MINUTES
SOAKING TIME: UP TO 30 MINUTES FOR THE VINE LEAVES; 1 HOUR FOR THE CURRANTS
COOKING TIME: 30 MINUTES

INGREDIENTS FOR ABOUT 40 DOLMADES
40 fresh young vine leaves (or 1 jar or tin of vine leaves)
35 g (1½ oz) currants
2 tablespoons dry white wine
125 ml (4 fl oz) olive oil
2 medium-sized onions, chopped*
¾ teaspoon salt
¼ teaspoon pepper
200 g (7 oz) rice
375 ml (13 fl oz) water
Juice of 2 large lemons
4 tablespoons chopped parsley
40 g (1½ oz) pine nuts (kernels)
2 tablespoons chopped mint
¾ teaspoon dried oregano
¼ teaspoon allspice
¾ teaspoon cinnamon
A few sprigs of parsley

Choose fresh, young vine leaves about the size of your palm. Before cooking, tie them into bundles and dunk in boiling water for 2 minutes, then drain. If you are using pickled vine leaves, first soak for 30 minutes to reduce the briny taste.

Tinned vine leaves are very delicate, and must be handled carefully to avoid tearing. After removing the compacted leaves from the tin, stand them in a large bowl of cold water for 15-20 minutes; then gently separate the individual leaves. Any broken leaves can be used to line the cooking pan and patch holes.

Dry the leaves and spread them out on a large surface, with the undersides facing up and the stalks towards you. Cut off and discard the stalks. Soak the currants in the wine for about 1 hour.

Heat half the oil in a saucepan and gently fry the onions until tender and transparent. Add the salt and pepper, rice, water and half the lemon juice. Cover the pan and cook over a very gentle heat for about 10 minutes, or until the rice is tender.

Stir in the chopped parsley, pine nuts (kernels), currants, mint, oregano, allspice and cinnamon.

Spoon about 2 teaspoons of the mixture onto each leaf, and wrap them up securely. Place the dolmades side by side in a heavy-bottomed saucepan, interspersing them with sprigs of parsley.

Add the rest of the olive oil and the juice of the remaining lemon. Weigh the dolmades down with a large plate, cover the saucepan and steam gently for 20 minutes. Lift out the vine parcels with a perforated spoon, arrange them on a warm serving dish and serve immediately.

SERVING SUGGESTIONS Natural yoghurt or egg and lemon sauce* make good accompaniments.

VARIATIONS Dolmades can also be eaten cold. When they are cool, sprinkle them with a little lemon juice, olive oil and freshly ground black pepper, or simply serve with lemon wedges.

ANTIPASTI – AN ITALIAN TREAT

These Italian favourites should be arranged on giant eye-catching platters if you plan to entertain a crowd, or on attractive plates for individual servings. Serve with chunks of crusty bread to mop up the tasty marinades.

To make a cold marinade, mix together 160 ml (5½ fl oz) olive oil, 80 ml (2½ fl oz) wine vinegar, 1 large clove crushed garlic, 1 teaspoon oregano, salt and freshly ground black pepper to taste.

Pour the marinade over thinly sliced raw mushrooms, wedges of tomato, onion rings, quarters of fennel, julienne strips* of baby carrot, cooked butter beans, calamari rings (simmered in lightly salted water until opaque), chunks of tuna, ripe black olives, tinned artichoke hearts, anchovies and slices of skinned red, yellow and green peppers.

To make a hot marinade, simmer (for 5 minutes) 125 ml (4 fl oz) sunflower or olive oil, with 125 ml (4 fl oz) wine vinegar, 1 or 2 cloves crushed garlic, a few sprigs of parsley, 1 bay leaf, 1 teaspoon oregano, 12 coriander seeds (optional), 4 peppercorns and ½ teaspoon salt.

Pour the marinade over the following hot, lightly cooked vegetables: whole green beans, thick slices of courgettes (zucchini), strips or rounds of carrot, small whole mushrooms, florets of cauliflower and broccoli, cubes or slices of aubergine (eggplant) and quarters of freshly boiled artichokes. Leave the vegetables in the marinade for 2-3 days before serving.

Other good antipasti include paper-thin slices of prosciutto (Parma ham) wrapped around wedges of melon or peeled ripe figs, thinly sliced mortadella, and salami.

HOT SPINACH AND BACON SALAD

SPINACH HAS BEEN CULTIVATED for thousands of years and is eaten in many ways. It contains a high proportion of calcium and iron, and is rich in magnesium and potassium.

This popular spinach salad, garnished with bacon and croûtons, makes a tasty and attractive addition to the dinner table. Prepare as much of the recipe as possible ahead of time, then quickly complete the final stages before serving.

PREPARATION TIME: 40 MINUTES
COOKING TIME: 20 MINUTES

INGREDIENTS FOR SIX
2 slices stale bread
600 g (1 lb 5 oz) spinach
250 g (9 oz) rindless bacon, diced
125 ml (4 fl oz) olive oil
1 large clove garlic, crushed
Juice of 1 large lemon
Freshly ground black pepper
Salt

Lightly toast the bread, trim the crusts and cut into small cubes. Wash the spinach leaves very well and cut away any thick stalks. Leave small, young leaves whole or shred them coarsely. Dry the leaves thoroughly. Cook the bacon in its own fat until crisp, then remove with a slotted spoon.

Add the cubes of bread and fry in the bacon fat until golden, adding a little oil only if necessary.

Heat the olive oil in a clean pan and add the spinach. Cook gently until it turns bright green (it should be limp and glistening with oil). Add the crushed garlic and lemon juice and turn the spinach into a heated dish. Then add the bacon and croûtons and toss together. Add a grinding or two of black pepper and a little salt.

SMOKED FISH PÂTÉ

THE EXCELLENCE of smoked fish pâté depends primarily upon the quality of fish used, so choose a superior fish wherever possible.

Pâté made from kippers, smoked haddock or smoked trout is excellent as a first course (serve with Melba toast) or as a sandwich filling. Bland fish can often be

HOT SPINACH AND BACON SALAD *is an unusual flavour combination.*

improved by adding fresh grated horse-radish or a pinch of cayenne pepper.

PREPARATION TIME: 30 MINUTES
COOKING TIME: 15 MINUTES

INGREDIENTS FOR SIX
4 kippers, or 2 large smoked haddock fillets, or 2 smoked trout
125 g (4¼ oz) soft butter
Juice of 1 lemon
Freshly ground black pepper
Salt
Clarified butter* or ghee

Cook the kippers in water, or the smoked haddock in milk and water, until the fish is tender (about 10-15 minutes). The trout need not be cooked further. Remove the skin and bones. Small kipper bones will be well broken up when the ingredients are blended, so do not bother to remove these.

Put the fish and butter in a blender with half the lemon juice and pepper and blend until smooth. Check the seasoning and add salt (the trout may need a little). Beat in the rest of the lemon juice if needed. Pot the pâté, sealing with clarified butter or ghee. Do not keep too long before eating – fish pâté tastes best when eaten fresh.

POTTED SHRIMPS

THE TRADITIONAL MENU for an English 'shrimp tea' includes potted shrimps, thin slices of buttered bread, and a large plate of watercress.

Shrimps heated in butter and spices, then sealed in pots with clarified butter or ghee, make a delicious starter.

PREPARATION TIME: 20 MINUTES

INGREDIENTS FOR FOUR
450 g (1 lb) frozen cooked and shelled shrimps (or small prawns)
125 g (4¼ oz) butter
¼ teaspoon ground mace or nutmeg
¼ teaspoon cayenne pepper
Salt and freshly ground black pepper
Clarified butter* or ghee

Defrost the shrimps and pat quite dry. Melt the butter over a moderate heat. Add the shrimps, mace or nutmeg and cayenne pepper. Season with salt and pepper. Heat through but do not allow the shrimps to boil, as this makes them tough. Stir while heating them.

Put into small pots, seal with clarified butter or ghee, and leave them to chill in the refrigerator.

TARAMASALATA

TARAMASALATA, A FISH ROE PÂTÉ, is a popular Greek appetiser. Tarama, the main ingredient, is smoked fish roe (typically obtained from grey mullet or cod). It is bright orange and salty, and should be beaten with the other ingredients until pale pink, and light and creamy in texture.

PREPARATION TIME: 15 MINUTES
CHILLING TIME: 1 HOUR

INGREDIENTS FOR SIX
75 g (3 oz) smoked fish roe
    (tarama)
4 thick slices white bread, crusts
    removed
80 ml (2½ fl oz) milk
1 clove garlic, crushed
150 ml (¼ pint) olive oil
60 ml (2 fl oz) lemon juice
Freshly ground black pepper

Beat the tarama in a food processor or blender, or with an electric beater, until it is smooth. Soak the bread in the milk for a few minutes and add to the tarama with the garlic. Beat well together, then beat in the oil, alternating with the lemon juice, a little at a time. Add a grinding or two of black pepper. If the mixture is still salty, beat in a little milk. Chill the taramasalata until ready to serve.

SERVING SUGGESTIONS This dish may be accompanied by quarters of pitta bread* or hot toast and garnished with stoned black or green olives.

VARIATION Instead of using the white bread and milk, mix the tarama with 100 g (3¾ oz) cream cheese and 60 ml (2 fl oz) cream and use this as a dip.

The enormous variety of foods which are suitable for dipping into such a mixture ranges from raw vegetables to crackers and bread. If you plan to serve raw vegetables, first soak them in iced water in the refrigerator to make them really crisp. Fresh asparagus spears, and florets of cauliflower and broccoli should also be blanched*.

If possible, offer a selection of vegetables. Any of the following are ideal: whole baby carrots or sticks of carrot; sticks of celery; strips of cucumber; small radishes; strips of red, green or yellow peppers; baby mushrooms; wedges of fennel; young spring onions.

CAMEMBERT EN CROÛTE *Crisp pastry wrapped around ripe Camembert.*

CAMEMBERT EN CROÛTE

CAMEMBERT, AN INTERNATIONALLY popular soft cheese created by a French farmer's wife in the late 1700s, lends itself to combination with a large variety of ingredients. This recipe is for Camembert in a pastry shell, served hot.

PREPARATION TIME: 1 HOUR
FREEZING TIME: 1-2 HOURS
CHILLING TIME: 2 HOURS
COOKING TIME: 20 MINUTES
STANDING TIME: 30 MINUTES
PREHEAT OVEN TO 220°C (425°F, MARK 7)

INGREDIENTS FOR FOUR
A 125 g (4¼ oz) Camembert cheese
120 g (¼ lb) flour, sifted
A pinch of salt
60 g (2 oz) smooth cottage cheese
60 g (2 oz) butter
1 egg yolk, beaten

Place the Camembert cheese in the freezer for an hour or two before you make the pastry. Sift the flour and salt together, then add the cottage cheese and butter, and rub lightly together until the mixture resembles coarse crumbs. Knead the mixture very slightly, form the dough into a ball, and refrigerate (covered) for 1 hour.

Roll out the dough (not too thinly) on a lightly floured board. Cut out a circle large enough to enclose the base and sides of the cheese. Place the cheese in the centre of the circle and bring the pastry up around the side and 2 cm (¾ in) over the top of the cheese. Cut a circle of dough to fit the top of the cheese, moisten the edges with egg yolk and press to make a seal. Decorate the top of the cheese with leaf and rose shapes cut from the remaining pastry.

Refrigerate for about an hour, then brush with the remaining egg yolk and bake at 220°C (425°F, mark 7) for 20 minutes or until golden. Allow the baked Camembert to stand in a warm place for at least 30 minutes before serving.

SERVING SUGGESTIONS Serve on a platter with a radish and spring onion or garnish it with a sprig of parsley.

Prepare crunchy raw vegetables (such as celery stalks, young carrots, mushrooms, cauliflower florets, radishes and spring onions) for dipping into the melted cheese.

VARIATIONS Place frozen Camembert cheese on five layers of filo pastry*, first brushing each layer of pastry with melted butter. Fold the edges of the pastry up around the cheese, then cover the top with six sheets of pastry, once again brushing each sheet with melted butter. Tuck the ends of the pastry under the cheese, and freeze for 10 minutes or longer before baking. Brush all over with more melted butter and bake.

CHICKEN LIVER PÂTÉ WITH PORT

A HOMEMADE PÂTÉ, butter-smooth and well-matured, is one of the most delicious and successful ways of starting a meal. It is also one of the simplest dishes that one can make.

This pâté should preferably be refrigerated for two or three days before it is eaten. As long as it is protected from the air, it will keep in the refrigerator for several weeks. Fill several small pots rather than one large pot, because the pâté will stay at its best for longer if it is well sealed.

A pot of pâté makes a welcome gift, and – if served with pickles, mustard and puffy crisp rolls – it also makes an appetising lunch.

PREPARATION TIME: 1 HOUR
COOKING TIME: 20 MINUTES
CHILLING TIME: 12 HOURS

INGREDIENTS FOR SIX
500 g (1 lb 2 oz) chicken livers
250 g (9 oz) soft butter
½ medium-sized onion, peeled* and grated
2 tablespoons brandy
2 tablespoons port
1 clove garlic, peeled and crushed or finely chopped
1 teaspoon dry mustard
¼ teaspoon dried thyme
¼ teaspoon mace or nutmeg
Salt
Clarified butter* or ghee

Clean the livers very carefully, paring off any greenish parts, which may give an unpleasant bitter flavour to the pâté. Melt 50 g (2 oz) of the butter in a frying pan and sauté the grated onion until soft, then remove it from the pan and put it to one side.

Add a little more butter if necessary and then sauté the livers, whole, for about 5 minutes (they should be cooked on the outside but still pink in the centre). Remove the livers from the pan and pour in the brandy.

Heat the brandy until it bubbles, then add the port, garlic, mustard, thyme and mace, and cook for 1 minute.

Put the livers, onion, pan sauces and remaining butter into a food processor or blender and blend to a smooth paste, then add salt to taste.

CHICKEN LIVER PÂTÉ *A delicately flavoured pâté that makes a wonderful snack.*

Spoon the mixture into small pots and top with clarified butter or ghee to seal; the butter should be 3-5 mm (about ¼ in) thick. Cover the pots with foil and chill the pâté thoroughly before eating. You can freeze this pâté for about 6 weeks, but the texture may coarsen.

SERVING SUGGESTIONS Serve the pâté very cold with hot toast or warm, sliced French bread. Because this is such a rich pâté, you should not need to give your guests extra butter. Similarly, no butter is necessary if you serve the pâté on cocktail biscuits or crackers as a snack.

Otherwise, spread it thickly on toast and pop it under a hot grill until the pâté bubbles. Serve immediately, topped with a spoon of thick sour cream.

VARIATION If you do not have a food processor or blender, you can use a baby-food mouli or alternatively pound the various ingredients in a mortar.

15

MAKING THE MOST OF AVOCADOS

Avocado pears are used in a variety of dishes: they can be chopped for salads, puréed for mousses, used as a spread for sandwiches or even made into desserts.

Select 2-3 perfect ripe avocados. Split them lengthways, discard the stones and brush them with lemon juice in order to prevent discolouring of the flesh. Fill the centres with one or more of the following mixtures and serve with thin crisp slices of Melba toast*.

Mix 125 g (4¼ oz) cream cheese with 2 tablespoons sour cream. Pipe swirls or spoon into the centres. Top with a spoonful of Danish caviar (lumpfish roe) and serve well chilled.

Mix together two sliced stalks of celery, a thinly sliced (or chopped) green apple and 2 tablespoons chopped pecans or walnuts with 4 tablespoons mayonnaise* and 4 tablespoons sour cream or natural yoghurt, adding salt and freshly ground black pepper to taste.

Mix 250 g (9 oz) cooked and shelled prawns* or cubes of boiled crayfish or lobster with 4 tablespoons sour cream, 1 tablespoon tomato paste, ½ teaspoon Worcestershire sauce, a small dash of Tabasco and a squeeze of lemon juice. Add freshly milled salt and black pepper to taste, if you like your food well seasoned.

Fill the avocados with cooked and shelled prawns* or cubes of crayfish or lobster. Mix 125 ml (4 fl oz) very thick mayonnaise* with 50 g (2 oz) grated Gruyère cheese and fold in a stiffly beaten egg white. Spoon over the seafood and ensure that the avocados are completely covered. Bake at 200°C (400°F, mark 6) for 15 minutes or grill briefly until slightly puffed and pale golden. Dust with paprika and serve immediately.

Guacamole is a Mexican dip, best made with very ripe avocados. To make enough for 6 people, mash the flesh of 3 pears with ½ small grated onion and 2 crushed garlic cloves. Blend with 1 tablespoon of lemon juice and 1 tablespoon of olive oil. Season to taste with salt, freshly ground pepper, cayenne, Tabasco and ¼ teaspoon of Worcestershire sauce. Chill for 30 minutes and serve with mixed raw vegetables.

CHOPPED HERRING

CHOPPED HERRING (gehackte herring) is usually associated with traditional Jewish cooking, and at most Jewish parties or functions the menu would not be considered complete if this dish was not served.

Salt herring was a staple food of the Ashkenazi Jews of Poland and Russia, from where the dish's popularity spread throughout the world.

SOAKING TIME: OVERNIGHT
PREPARATION TIME: 35 MINUTES

INGREDIENTS FOR SIX
2 salt herring, cleaned and heads removed
5 hard-boiled eggs
1 medium-sized onion, finely grated
2 green apples, peeled and cored
10 semi-sweet plain biscuits
75 g (3 oz) sugar (or to taste)
80 ml (2½ fl oz) white vinegar (or a few drops tartaric acid)
A dash of pepper
A dash of cinnamon
Fresh parsley for garnish

Soak the herring overnight in cold water, changing the water once. Remove the herring skins and as many of the bones as possible, dry the fish well and mince them into a large mixing bowl with three of the eggs, onion, apples and biscuits. Slowly add the sugar and vinegar, tasting the mixture to achieve the flavour you desire (some people like it sweeter than others). Season with pepper and cinnamon and spoon it onto a flat serving platter. Grate the remaining eggs and use them to decorate the dish. Garnish with sprigs of fresh parsley, if available.

SERVING SUGGESTION Serve as an hors d'oeuvre with crackers or the traditional Jewish kichel (a thin, crisp biscuit).

VARIATION Try leaving out the onion: you will find that the mixture then becomes much firmer.

FISH TERRINE WITH SOUR CREAM SAUCE

THIS DISH MAKES a very pretty start to a sumptuous dinner. The array of colours in the multi-layered terrine is sure to delight your guests, as will its special combination of flavours.

The recipe calls for sufficient ingredients to make a substantial terrine, so you may choose to serve it as the first course rather than as an appetiser.

PREPARATION TIME: 45 MINUTES
COOKING TIME: 1¼-1½ HOURS
PREHEAT OVEN TO 180°C (350°F, MARK 4)

INGREDIENTS FOR TWELVE
For the terrine:
500 g (1 lb 2 oz) monkfish, bream or snapper, skinned and filleted*
250 g (9 oz) sole or flounder, skinned and filleted*
2 eggs
2 teaspoons salt
1 teaspoon white pepper
¼ teaspoon grated nutmeg
90 ml (3 fl oz) lemon juice
500 ml (17 fl oz) fresh white breadcrumbs
500-750 ml (17-26 fl oz) cream
125 g (4¼ oz) smoked salmon
250 g (9 oz) frozen spinach
Boiling water

For the sauce:
Cooking juices from terrine
250 ml (9 fl oz) sour cream
125 ml (4 fl oz) fresh cream
2 teaspoons horseradish
1 teaspoon mild mustard
1 teaspoon lemon juice
Salt and white pepper

Line a loaf tin or terrine (1.5 litre or about 2¾ pint capacity) with aluminium foil and butter it generously.

Place the monkfish (or bream or snapper) and sole (or flounder) together in a food processor and blend until smooth, then remove the lid and add the eggs, salt, pepper, nutmeg, lemon juice, breadcrumbs and 500 ml (17 fl oz) of the cream.

Mix these ingredients until they are thoroughly blended, then test for the right consistency: peaks should just hold their shape. If the mixture is too firm, add more cream until you achieve the correct consistency. Taste for seasoning and then assemble the terrine.

FISH TERRINE WITH SOUR CREAM SAUCE *A colourful combination of puréed fish with a savoury cream sauce.*

Process about 3 tablespoons of the mixture with the smoked salmon until smooth, adding more cream if the mixture becomes too stiff and dry.

Process another 3 tablespoons of the mixture with the spinach until it is well blended, then divide the remaining white fish mixture into three equal portions. Arrange the terrine in layers: first a white layer of the mousse mixture, then green, white, pink, and finally another white layer. Use a wet spoon to smooth down layers and achieve an even spread.

Butter a piece of wax paper and place it, buttered side down, on top of the terrine. Cover the terrine with aluminium foil and place it in an ovenproof dish. Pour in enough boiling water to come halfway up the baking dish. Bake at 180°C (350°F, mark 4) for 1¼-1½ hours, depending on the shape of the tin. If it is long and narrow, it will take the shorter time, but if it is short and deep, it can take up to 1½ hours. When it is almost ready, the mousse will start rising.

Remove the terrine from the oven, and pour off and retain the juices. Turn the terrine out onto a serving dish. It will keep in the oven for up to 10 minutes while you mix the sauce ingredients (keep it covered with the loaf tin or terrine). This dish may be cooked the day before serving and reheated in a *bain marie**. Serve the terrine with the sour cream sauce, made by combining the ingredients in a bowl and mixing well.

VARIATIONS Instead of spinach, use sorrel or watercress, or both, and add finely chopped watercress to the sauce.

To serve cold, remove the dish from the water. Pour off the juices and allow the terrine to cool. Cover it with plastic wrap and place it in the refrigerator. The terrine will keep for two or three days. A terrine which is to be served cold should be slightly over-seasoned, since it becomes less strong on cooling.

17

BLINI WITH CAVIAR *Freshly fried buckwheat pancakes are served with caviar, chopped onion, sour cream and lemon.*

BLINI WITH CAVIAR

Buckwheat pancakes, known as blini, have been made in Russia for over a thousand years. In western Russia, during a spring festival called 'Mother-in-Law's Day', it was the custom for every young husband to go to his mother-in-law's house to eat blini.

The inclusion of real or Danish caviar as an accompaniment makes this a particularly appealing blini dish and an ideal starter for a dinner party.

PREPARATION TIME: 25 MINUTES
RISING TIME: 1½ HOURS
COOKING TIME: 20 MINUTES

INGREDIENTS FOR SIX

¼ teaspoon sugar
300 ml (½ pint) warm milk
15 g (½ oz) fresh yeast
225 g (½ lb) buckwheat or
    wholemeal flour
A pinch of salt
25 g (1 oz) butter, melted
1 egg white, whisked until stiff
2 onions, coarsely chopped*
250 ml (9 fl oz) sour cream
1 small jar (about 100 g/3¾ oz)
    Danish caviar (lumpfish roe)
1 lemon
Sunflower oil for frying

Dissolve the sugar in the warm milk and use 2 tablespoons of the liquid to mix the yeast to a smooth, thin paste in a large, warmed mixing bowl. Stir in the remaining milk. Add about two-thirds of the flour and the salt and whisk to make a smooth batter. Cover with plastic wrap and leave to stand in a warm place to rise for about 1 hour.

Add the remaining flour and the butter to the batter, and beat well. The mixture should have the consistency of thick cream; if it is too stiff, add a little extra warm milk. Fold the egg white into the batter. Cover and allow to rise again for another 30 minutes.

Meanwhile, put the onions in a serving bowl. Spoon the sour cream and caviar into two serving bowls. Wash the lemon, cut it into segments and arrange them in another bowl. Chill until you are ready to serve the blini.

Brush the inside of a large, heavy-based frying pan with oil and heat it until it exudes a slight haze. Cook three blini at a time, allowing a full tablespoon of batter for each. Fry gently for about 2 minutes, until the surface has just dried out and is a mass of small holes, then turn the blini over to brown the other sides for about 2 minutes. Cover the cooked blini with foil and keep warm until you are ready to serve.

When serving, place two or three blini on each plate and pass around the bowls of onions, cream, caviar and sliced lemon.

VARIATIONS For different flavours, try the blini with thinly sliced smoked salmon or chopped hard-boiled eggs.

SMOKED SALMON BLINTZES

CRISPLY FRIED and served off the pan with a dollop of sour cream, savoury blintzes make a most delicious starter. You can also bake them in the oven with excellent results when you want to cook larger quantities.

Make these savoury blintzes a day ahead of time and refrigerate, or keep in a freezer for weeks. This recipe allows two blintzes per serving.

PREPARATION TIME: 1 HOUR
COOKING TIME: 20 MINUTES

INGREDIENTS FOR SIX
2 eggs
375 ml (13 fl oz) water
125 g (4¼ oz) flour
A pinch of salt
125 ml (4 fl oz) sunflower oil
60 g (2 oz) butter
Butter and sunflower oil for frying
250 ml (9 fl oz) sour cream

For the filling:
250 g (9 oz) smoked salmon, finely chopped
250 g (9 oz) smooth cottage cheese
¼ teaspoon dried dill or 2 teaspoons fresh dill (optional)
A squeeze of lemon juice
Freshly ground black pepper

Lightly beat the eggs, add the water, and then the flour and salt. Beat well until the mixture is smooth (you could also use a blender). If the mixture is too thick, add a little water very gradually until it has the consistency of thin cream. Strain the batter into a jug: this may be refrigerated for a few hours before making the blintzes but it is not essential.

Heat a buttered or oiled pan and pour in a thin layer of the batter. The pan must not be too hot as the blintz should set without browning. It is ready when the edges curl. Cook it on one side only and turn it out onto a clean tea towel to cool.

Combine the ingredients for the filling and place a spoonful of the mixture on the cooked side of each blintz. Fold the ends over the filling and roll them up. Fry the blintzes in a mixture of hot butter and oil until they are crisp and golden.

Drain on a paper towel and serve piping hot with dollops of sour cream.

VARIATIONS Try baking the blintzes instead. Place them in a buttered ovenproof

SERVING SMOKED SALMON

Many people consider smoked salmon to be the prince of smoked fish. Some believe the only salmon worth eating are those caught in Scottish waters, while others maintain those found in Norwegian waters are best. Whatever the origin, avoid any salmon with a darker than normal orange or red colour, because this usually indicates over-cured or dyed fish.

Use a very long, flexible knife to cut the salmon (it must be very sharp, with a serrated edge). Cut across the grain, working from the shoulder towards the tail. The slices should be as thin as possible.

Serve it generously, with finely cut slices of brown bread and butter. If you wish, season it with sprinklings of lemon juice and freshly ground black pepper. For a colourful presentation, try serving rolled-up salmon with radicchio leaves and twists of lemon.

Use the trimmings, pounded finely, as a filling for omelettes, little pastry cases and vol-au-vents.

dish and pour over 250 ml (9 fl oz) cream. Bake them (uncovered) at 200°C (400°F, mark 6) for 20 minutes, or until they are bubbly and browned.

Pour over 250 ml (9 fl oz) thin cheese sauce* before baking. Or use the cream, but sprinkle with grated Gruyère and Parmesan cheese before baking.

Use a tin of well-drained and boned salmon instead of smoked salmon. Combine the salmon and cheese with a fork, rather than a food processor, or the mixture will be too runny.

CUCUMBER AND PRAWN MOUSSE

CUCUMBERS BELONG to the gourd family of plants, and come in many shapes and sizes. They have been cultivated in the northwest of India for about three thousand years.

Prawns and cucumbers combined in a mousse make a very delicate, cool start to a lunch on a hot summer's day.

PREPARATION TIME: 30 MINUTES
CHILLING TIME: 2 HOURS

INGREDIENTS FOR FOUR
125 g (4¼ oz) cream cheese
175 ml (6 fl oz) natural yoghurt
½ green cucumber
100 g (3¼ oz) small cooked and shelled prawns*
1 tablespoon lemon juice
1 tablespoon gelatine
125 ml (4 fl oz) chicken stock*
Salt and white pepper

For the sauce:
250 ml (9 fl oz) natural yoghurt diluted with milk
2 tablespoons thick mayonnaise*
Salt and white pepper
2 tablespoons fresh chopped dill

Beat together the cream cheese and yoghurt until smooth. Reserve 4 thin slices of cucumber and a few prawns for the garnish. Peel and finely chop (or grate) the rest of the cucumber and add, with the prawns, to the cheese and yoghurt. Add the lemon juice.

Next, sprinkle the gelatine over the stock and heat, stirring until dissolved. Strain into the mousse mixture and stir well. Check the seasoning and adjust if necessary. Ladle into four ramekins or moulds (which have been brushed with a thin coat of oil) and then refrigerate until fully set.

To make the sauce, mix the yoghurt with the mayonnaise, then add the seasoning and dill. Pour the sauce over four plates. Invert the moulds onto the sauce. Garnish with the reserved cucumber slices and prawns.

SERVING SUGGESTION Pass around slices of Melba toast* or thin slices of buttered brown bread with the crusts removed.

VARIATION For a less expensive mousse, or if you want to make a vegetarian dish, prepare without the prawns.

SNAILS IN MUSHROOMS

THE CLASSIC FRENCH dish, *Escargots à la bourguignonne*, calls for hefty specimens from the vineyards of Burgundy, served sizzling in their shells with great quantities of rich garlic butter and fresh crusty bread.

The following recipe, while less traditional, provides a very good starter: the snails are baked on a large mushroom 'plate', topped with garlic butter and a sprinkling of breadcrumbs.

PREPARATION TIME: 20 MINUTES
COOKING TIME: 25 MINUTES
PREHEAT OVEN TO 200°C (400°F, MARK 6)

INGREDIENTS FOR FOUR
1 tin (125 g/4¼ oz) snails
4 very large mushrooms
130 g (4½ oz) butter
3 cloves garlic, crushed
1 tablespoon chopped parsley
A squeeze of lemon juice
Freshly ground black pepper
1 tablespoon fine breadcrumbs
  (optional)
Chopped parsley for garnish

Drain the snails and put aside. Rinse the mushrooms and dry them thoroughly. Trim the stalks, melt 30 g (1¼ oz) of the butter and brush it all over the mushrooms. Place them stalk-side up in individual ovenproof dishes. They should fit snugly. Cream the rest of the butter with the garlic and parsley, adding the lemon juice and a grinding of black pepper. Smear each mushroom with a little garlic butter and keep the remainder for the snails.

Divide the snails among the mushrooms. Top each snail with a dab of garlic butter and sprinkle lightly with fine breadcrumbs (if used). Bake the mushrooms in the preheated oven for 25 minutes, or until they are just tender. Place the hot dishes on dinner plates and sprinkle their contents with parsley.

SERVING SUGGESTION Serve with fingers of fresh white or brown bread, buttered and with the crusts removed.

VARIATIONS Leave out the snails and instead serve the piping hot mushrooms with chunks of crusty bread. You can, of course, use small black mushrooms, but in this case you should reduce the cooking time.

If you wish to serve snails in garlic butter, push the snails into shells and then pack them generously with the butter. Bake in a very hot oven (230°C, 450°F, mark 8) and cook for about 10 minutes. The traditional way to serve snails is in dimpled plates (called *escargotières*) and with tongs for picking up the hot shells and special forks for twisting the snails out of the shells.

LETTUCE AND CHICKEN LIVER SALAD

THIS SALAD OFFERS interesting contrasts in taste, texture and also temperature. Be sure to prepare the cold ingredients first, because proper timing is essential for successful results. Try to choose a crisp lettuce which has a firm heart and no limp leaves.

PREPARATION TIME: 25 MINUTES
COOKING TIME: 5 MINUTES

INGREDIENTS FOR FOUR
1 large (or 2 small) lettuce
4 spring onions, finely chopped
1 tablespoon chopped parsley
100 ml (3¾ fl oz) sunflower oil
4 tablespoons cream
2 tablespoons white wine vinegar
1 teaspoon French mustard
1 small clove garlic, crushed
Salt and freshly ground black
  pepper
250 g (9 oz) chicken livers, cleaned
  and trimmed
1 tomato, skinned* and cut into
  strips
1 stalk celery, cut into thin
  julienne* strips
1 leek (white part only), thinly
  sliced

Rinse the lettuce leaves and dry well. Place them in a salad bowl with the spring onion and parsley. Beat together 75 ml (5 tablespoons) of the oil with the cream, vinegar, mustard and garlic. Add seasoning to taste.

Quickly sauté the chicken livers in the remaining oil until well browned outside, but still pink inside. Season them lightly and slice thinly. Add the livers to the salad bowl with the dressing, tomato, celery and leek, and toss together. Check the seasoning and serve immediately with fresh wholemeal bread and butter.

CLEANING AND SERVING OYSTERS

When serving oysters raw as an hors d'oeuvre, you should allow six per person. Make sure that the oysters are absolutely fresh; they should be opened just before serving. Alternatively, grill the oysters for 3-4 minutes at a high temperature and top them with a little cream and grated cheese.

To open an oyster, hold it firmly in your left hand with the flat side facing up and wrap a tea towel round your hand and most of the shell, leaving the hinge showing. Hold the shell level to avoid losing juice. Insert the point of a short strong knife (or a special oyster knife) in the crack between the upper and lower shells, near the hinge.

Once the knife has penetrated the crack, ease it about until you feel it cut the muscle attaching the oyster to the flat upper shell. Then twist the knife firmly to prise the shell apart. Keep the flat side uppermost. Remove the flat top half of the shell to reveal the oyster and its juice held in the deeper half.

Make a bed of cracked ice on each plate. Arrange the oysters in their deep shells on top, and serve with lemon quarters and brown bread and butter.

SALMON MOUSSE WITH CUCUMBER SAUCE *A rich dish that benefits from the slightly bitter taste of the cucumber sauce.*

SALMON MOUSSE WITH CUCUMBER SAUCE

A FINE PARTY DISH, this mousse uses a generous amount of tinned salmon for maximum flavour. Tinned salmon comes in several grades, the bright red variety being the best.

The addition of a cucumber sauce to this dish provides an interesting taste and texture. A mousse should be chilled for several hours before serving.

PREPARATION TIME: 40 MINUTES
CHILLING TIME: 4 HOURS
INGREDIENTS FOR SIX
2 tins red salmon (about 225 g/8 oz each)
1 tablespoon gelatine
60 ml (2 fl oz) cold water
¼ green cucumber, peeled and finely diced
1 stalk celery, diced

2 tablespoons lemon juice
4 tablespoons mayonnaise*
¼ teaspoon salt
A few drops of Tabasco
60 ml (2 fl oz) cream

For the sauce:
½ green cucumber, peeled and finely diced
250 ml (9 fl oz) sour cream or natural yoghurt
1 small onion, finely chopped*
A squeeze of lemon juice
Salt and pepper

Drain the salmon. Discard any skin and large bones and flake the fish. Sprinkle the gelatine over the cold water in a small heatproof dish, then dissolve it over a saucepan of simmering water, stirring until the liquid is clear. Mix the salmon, cucumber, celery and lemon juice in a food processor or blender until smooth, making sure that there are no lumps.

Stir in the mayonnaise, salt and Tab-

asco, strain in the dissolved gelatine and mix well together. Whip the cream and fold it in. Spoon the mousse into 6 small moulds, which have been lightly oiled, and refrigerate until set.

Mix the ingredients for the sauce (retain a little cucumber for garnishing) in a food processor or blender until smooth. Check the seasoning, adjust it if necessary, and chill well.

Turn the 6 moulds out onto a serving platter, loosening the edges with a small spatula. Garnish with the chopped cucumber and serve the mousse with the cucumber sauce.

SERVING SUGGESTION Try serving this salmon mousse accompanied by lemon wedges and thin slices of brown bread.

VARIATION Set the mousse in a large mould instead of 6 individual moulds. Turn the mousse out and garnish with thinly sliced rounds of cucumber.

21

SOUPS

SOUPS PROVIDE SUBTLE taste sensations that few other foods can match. They can be consumed hot or cold, thin or thick, and they lend themselves to combination with a huge variety of dishes.

Iced soups are perfect for entertaining on a hot summer's night. Try garnishing a chilled soup with parsley or other chopped herbs and add a swirl of cream.

Thick soups make more substantial dishes, and are often served as meals in themselves. They are generally cooked more slowly than other soups, and are simmered for longer to soften cheaper cuts of meat and blend the flavours of the vegetables – usually root vegetables.

The classic soups such as vichyssoise, Scotch broth or minestrone need not conform exactly to the original recipe. Try varying the ingredients – experiment with cream, lemon juice and extra vegetables, and alter the texture of the soup by using a sieve or blender. For an exotic treat, make a wonton soup, or an ice-cold gazpacho.

AVGOLEMONO

AVGOLEMONO HAS FEATURED in Greek cuisine for centuries, possibly since lemons were brought from Byzantium about a thousand years ago. This dish, named after the Greek words for 'egg' and 'lemon', is eaten not only as a soup, but also as a flavouring for other soups and as a sauce for vegetable dishes.

PREPARATION TIME: 20 MINUTES
COOKING TIME: 25 MINUTES

INGREDIENTS FOR SIX
50 g (2 oz) rice
Juice of 1 lemon
3 eggs, beaten
1.5 litres (52 fl oz) hot chicken
  stock*
50 g (2 oz) cooked chicken meat,
  finely chopped
Salt and white pepper
2 tablespoons finely chopped
  parsley for garnish

Cook the rice in boiling, salted water for 10-15 minutes and drain well.

Meanwhile, add the lemon juice to the beaten egg and mix well. Add 150 ml (¼ pint) of the hot stock, a little at a time, beating well after each addition.

Bring the remaining stock to the boil, remove from the heat and mix in the cooked chicken and rice. Season lightly with salt and pepper. Whisk in the egg mixture and return to a low heat. Stir continuously without boiling for about 5 minutes, or until the soup is heated through and has a rich creamy texture. Season and serve garnished with parsley.

AVGOLEMONO *This traditional Greek soup is flavoured with egg and lemon.*

PEA SOUP WITH MINT

FRESH GARDEN PEAS make an exquisite soup. In hard times, even their pods have been used – they give a thinner, less well-flavoured dish, but still very palatable. This soup is a rich green velvet, thickened with cream and egg yolks and flavoured with fresh mint.

PREPARATION TIME: 20 MINUTES
COOKING TIME: 35 MINUTES

INGREDIENTS FOR SIX
50 g (2 oz) butter
1 small onion, peeled and finely
  chopped*

700 g (1½ lb) shelled fresh peas
1 litre (1¾ pints) vegetable stock*
Salt and white pepper
¼ teaspoon caster sugar
2 sprigs of mint
2 egg yolks
150 ml (¼ pint) cream

For the garnish:
125 g (4¼ oz) shelled and boiled
  young peas
1 tablespoon finely chopped mint

Heat the butter in a heavy-based medium saucepan, put in the onion and cook it over a low heat for 10-15 minutes, or until soft and transparent. Add the peas and continue to cook over a low heat until the butter has been absorbed; take care not to let the peas burn.

Stir in the stock, season with salt and pepper, and add the sugar and sprigs of mint. Bring to the boil, cover and simmer gently for about 10 minutes, or until the peas are tender. Pass the soup through a fine sieve or food mill and return the purée to a clean pan.

Beat the egg yolks with the cream until smooth, and add to the soup. Heat through, stirring all the time until the soup has thickened. Do not let it boil, or the soup will curdle. Check the seasoning. Garnish with the peas and freshly chopped mint. Serve with crusty wholemeal rolls or thinly sliced brown bread.

SCOTCH BROTH

D R SAMUEL JOHNSON, the acerbic 18th-century writer and critic, was introduced to this soup while travelling in Scotland. Asked whether he had tried the dish before, Johnson replied: 'No, sir: but I don't care how soon I eat it again.'

Like all good country soups, this can be made with whatever is in season. A little meat, barley and vegetables are the only essentials.

SOAKING TIME: OVERNIGHT
PREPARATION TIME: 20 MINUTES
COOKING TIME: 3¼-4 HOURS

INGREDIENTS FOR SIX
1 kg (2¼ lb) scrag-end of lamb or mutton, with all excess fat trimmed off
5 litres (9 pints) water
125 g (4¼ oz) pearl barley
125 g (4¼ oz) split peas, soaked in water overnight
Bouquet garni*
Salt and freshly ground black pepper
1 large leek, washed and sliced
1 medium onion, peeled and finely chopped*
1 small turnip, peeled and diced
2 large carrots, peeled and diced
100-125 g (4-4½ oz) cabbage, shredded
1 tablespoon finely chopped parsley for garnish

Place the meat in a large, heavy-based saucepan and add the water, barley, drained soaked peas and bouquet garni. Season with salt and freshly ground black pepper.

Bring the pan slowly to the boil and skim off any white scum which may rise to the surface. Cover and simmer for 2 hours.

Add the leek, onion, turnip and carrots to the soup, and continue to simmer for 1 hour, occasionally skimming off any fat that rises to the surface.

Remove the meat from the soup with a slotted spoon and leave it to stand until it is cool enough to handle. Strip all of the meat from the bones and cut it into small, even pieces.

Return the meat to the soup and add the cabbage. Adjust the seasoning and continue to simmer for another 30 minutes. Garnish each serving with a sprinkling of parsley.

WONTON SOUP

T HIS POPULAR Chinese recipe combines a thin but tasty chicken soup with traditional Chinese wontons that are filled with minced pork and finely chopped spinach.

PREPARATION TIME: 45 MINUTES
STANDING TIME: 30 MINUTES
COOKING TIME: 20 MINUTES

INGREDIENTS FOR FOUR
For the wonton wrappers:
200 g (7 oz) flour
¼ teaspoon salt
1 egg
3 tablespoons water

For the filling:
200 g (7 oz) lean pork, finely minced
175 g (6 oz) cooked, well-drained, finely chopped spinach
A small piece of fresh green ginger, finely chopped
1 teaspoon soy sauce
¼ teaspoon salt

For the soup:
1 litre (1¾ pints) Chinese chicken stock*
1 teaspoon soy sauce
1 teaspoon salt
A pinch of pepper
Watercress or spinach or shallots, finely chopped for garnish

To make the wonton dough, sift the flour and salt into a bowl. Beat the egg with the cold water, then pour the mixture into the centre of the flour and knead well together to form a smooth, stiff dough.

If necessary, add a little more flour or water to get the right consistency. Cover the dough with a damp cloth and leave for 30 minutes.

Prepare the wrappers following the instructions (right) and fill them with a mixture of the minced pork, finely chopped spinach, ginger, soy sauce and salt, all well pounded together.

Drop the prepared wontons into a large saucepan of boiling water. Reduce the heat slightly and cook uncovered for 10 minutes, or until tender. Drain and reheat them in the chicken stock, which has been brought to the boil. Season with the soy sauce, salt and pepper, sprinkle with the leaves, and serve.

Wontons can also be deep fried and served with sweet and sour sauce*.

HOW TO MAKE WONTONS

Divide the dough into four and place on a lightly floured board. Then roll out the pieces, one at a time, into rectangles about 20 cm × 30 cm (9 in × 12 in).

Dust each sheet of dough lightly with flour. Cut the rectangles to make six 10 cm (5 in) square wrappers. Otherwise, use a pasta machine to roll out the dough.

Place 1 teaspoon of the filling in the centre of each individual square of dough. Bring the diagonally opposite corners together, and seal the parcels by pinching the top edges firmly together (moisten the edges if necessary).

Fold the other two corners together and seal. Keep the prepared wontons covered with a dry tea towel.

GAZPACHO *A light, chilled soup, it is the perfect antidote to the heat of summer.*

GAZPACHO

THIS LIGHT VERSION of the famous Andalusian soup, traditionally made in an earthenware pot from ingredients pounded together with pestle and mortar, is in many ways a liquid salad. It is certainly a cool and refreshing antidote to the heat of summer.

PREPARATION TIME: 30 MINUTES
CHILLING TIME: 1 HOUR

INGREDIENTS FOR SIX
700 g (1½ lb) ripe tomatoes
225 g (½ lb) fresh breadcrumbs
5 tablespoons olive oil
1 cucumber, peeled and chopped
2 green peppers, with cores and seeds removed, chopped
2 large cloves garlic, peeled
60 ml (2 fl oz) red wine vinegar
600 ml (21 fl oz) water
1 tablespoon tomato paste
Salt and freshly ground black pepper
12 ice cubes
For the accompaniments:
2 slices white bread, prepared as croûtons*
2 hard-boiled eggs, shelled and chopped
6 spring onions, trimmed and finely sliced
½ small cucumber, peeled and finely diced
1 small red pepper, finely chopped after core and seeds have been removed

Skin the tomatoes*, remove the cores and seeds, and chop the flesh. Place the breadcrumbs in a blender, switch it on and gradually pour in the olive oil. Continue blending for about 1 minute, or until all the oil has been absorbed by the bread. Add the tomatoes and continue liquidising until the mixture is reduced to a smooth paste, then transfer to a bowl.

Place the cucumber, green peppers and garlic in the blender and process for about 1 minute, or until they have been reduced to a smooth purée. Combine with the puréed tomatoes and stir in the vinegar, water and tomato paste. Taste and add salt and pepper if necessary. Cover the bowl and chill the soup in a refrigerator for at least 1 hour. Serve cold in shallow soup bowls, with two ice cubes added to each. Serve the accompaniments in separate bowls.

VARIATION To make a creamy soup, add mayonnaise*.

MEDITERRANEAN FISH SOUP

On a cold winter's evening, this thick soup serves almost as a meal in itself. It can be prepared well in advance and reheated just before serving without losing any of its delicate flavour.

PREPARATION TIME: 20 MINUTES
COOKING TIME: 45 MINUTES

INGREDIENTS FOR SIX TO EIGHT
350 g (¾ lb) each of grey mullet, whiting and plaice
1 large onion
6 tablespoons olive oil
1 clove garlic
400-450 g (14-16 oz) tin tomatoes
2 tablespoons tomato paste
1 tablespoon chopped parsley
850 ml (1½ pints) fish stock* or water
150 ml (¼ pint) dry white wine
1 bay leaf
Large piece lemon peel
Salt and black pepper
150 ml (¼ pint) cream

For the garnish:
Prawns
Tomato slices

Clean, fillet and skin the fish*; use the trimmings and bones as a base for the fish stock. Cut the fish fillets diagonally into 5 cm (2 in) pieces. Peel and finely chop the onion. Heat the oil in a heavy-based pan and cook the onion in this until soft, but not browned. Crush and add the garlic, fry for a minute or two before adding the tinned tomatoes with their juice, tomato paste and chopped parsley. Mix it all together thoroughly and simmer slowly for 15 minutes.

Add the fish, stock, wine, bay leaf and lemon peel, bring back to the simmer, cover with a lid and cook slowly for 20 minutes. Discard the bay leaf and lemon peel. Season with salt and freshly ground pepper and cool the soup slightly.

Remove one piece of fish for each serving and keep warm; liquidise the rest, along with the contents of the pan, until blended to a smooth creamy consistency.

Stir in the cream and reheat the soup without bringing it to the boil. Place one piece of fish in each individual bowl and pour over the soup. Float slices of skinned tomatoes*, garnished with a few peeled prawns, on top of each bowl.

FRENCH ONION SOUP

For many years, porters at the Paris market of Les Halles kept out the early morning cold by drinking large mugs of thick onion soup laced with cheese. It became such an attraction that late-night revellers made Les Halles a fashionable spot to end a wild evening. The market has long since disappeared, but the soup remains as popular as ever.

PREPARATION TIME: 10 MINUTES
COOKING TIME: 45 MINUTES

INGREDIENTS FOR FOUR
4 medium onions
50 g (2 oz) butter
2 tablespoons flour
125 ml (4 fl oz) dry white wine
625 ml (22 fl oz) beef or chicken stock*
Salt and freshly ground black pepper
Butter for spreading
4 slices French bread (1 cm/½ in thick)
150 g (5 oz) Gruyère or Emmenthal cheese, grated

Peel and slice the onions* thinly into rings. Cook them in the 50 g (2 oz) butter over a medium heat until soft and lightly golden, stirring them often. Do not let them burn, or they will impart a bitter taste to the soup. Instead, a gentle caramelising gives the soup its rich appetising colour.

Stir in the flour and cook for 1 minute. Add the wine, stock and seasoning and simmer for 25-30 minutes, until the onions are meltingly soft. Check the seasoning. Meanwhile, butter both sides of each slice of bread and then grill them until golden and crisp. Sprinkle over half the cheese and continue to grill until the cheese has melted. Spoon the remaining cheese into the bottom of four individual soup bowls. Ladle over soup and float the cheese toast on top. Serve the soup at once so that the toast remains crisp and has not had time to become soggy.

SERVING SUGGESTIONS Add a dash of sherry to each bowl of soup. For a really traditional soupe gratinée, float a slice of toasted French bread in each ovenproof bowl. Then sprinkle the slices with cheese and place the bowls in a hot oven or grill them for a few minutes to melt the cheese slightly.

VARIATIONS To make a creamy soup, whisk together 2 egg yolks and 125 ml (4 fl oz) cream. Stir or whisk this mixture into the soup just before serving and reheat it gently.

The soup can be sieved or puréed, but in this case omit the bread and cheese and stir in 125 ml (4 fl oz) cream (with or without egg yolks).

You can make leek soup in the same way, but without the cheese and bread. Sieve or purée half of the soup and combine the two halves with 125 ml (4 fl oz) cream or 4 tablespoons grated hard cheese, such as Cheddar or Gruyère, to make a hearty soup with character and an interesting texture.

SPINACH SOUP

Vitamins and iron are abundant in spinach. Children, who are sometimes unwilling to eat this vegetable on its own, should enjoy this soup, which is both creamy and nutritious.

PREPARATION TIME: 30 MINUTES
COOKING TIME: 20 MINUTES

INGREDIENTS FOR SIX
1.5 kg (3 lb 3 oz) fresh spinach (or 500 g/1 lb 2 oz frozen spinach)
25 g (1 oz) butter
500 ml (17 fl oz) chicken stock*
250 ml (9 fl oz) cream
250 ml (9 fl oz) milk
1 level teaspoon salt and a pinch of coarsely ground pepper
1 teaspoon lemon juice

If using fresh spinach, wash it well under cold running water and pat it dry. (If using frozen spinach, it is not necessary to thaw it before cooking.) Place the spinach in a large saucepan with the butter and simmer gently, stirring from time to time, until it is just tender. Allow to cool slightly, then liquidise or press the spinach through a sieve. Return it to the saucepan, add the chicken stock, cream and milk, and bring it to the boil. Flavour with salt, pepper and lemon juice, and serve hot or well-chilled, if preferred.

SERVING SUGGESTIONS Serve with a drizzle of cream or a sprinkling of Gruyère, accompanied by fingers of hot wholemeal toast.

Croûtons* fried with a little garlic would also complement this soup.

HOW TO SKIN AND SEED TOMATOES

Many recipes require the addition of skinned tomatoes, and sometimes they also need to be seeded. The following method is quick and simple.

Place the tomatoes in a bowl and cover with boiling water, allowing them to stand for 30-60 seconds.

Drain the tomatoes and rinse under cold running water (this saves you from burning your fingers).

Peel off the skin (with some types of tomato, the skin comes off more easily if it is peeled while still hot).

To seed the tomatoes, cut them in half crosswise and squeeze them over a bowl with the palm of your hand.

TOMATO AND CARROT SOUP *A garnish of marigold petals adds to its visual appeal.*

TOMATO AND CARROT SOUP

MANY YEARS AGO, the tomato was known as the love apple – a fruit thought capable of arousing dangerous passions, and therefore to be treated with suspicion.

In this recipe the carrot and apple combine beautifully with the flavour of the tomatoes to create both a subtle and unusual-tasting soup.

PREPARATION TIME: 15 MINUTES
COOKING TIME: 1¼ HOURS

INGREDIENTS FOR FOUR
15 g (½ oz) butter
2 teaspoons sunflower oil
1 onion, peeled and finely chopped*
2 cloves garlic, peeled and finely chopped
2 medium carrots, peeled and finely chopped
500 g (1 lb 2 oz) tomatoes, skinned* and roughly chopped
1 apple, peeled, cored and chopped
Bouquet garni* of thyme, marjoram and 1 bay leaf
1 litre (1¾ pints) vegetable or chicken stock*
Salt and freshly ground black pepper

For the garnish:
4 tablespoons cream
4 tablespoons croûtons*

Heat the butter with the oil in a large, heavy-based saucepan. Put in the onion and garlic, and cook over a low heat for 10-15 minutes until the onion is soft and transparent. Add the carrots and stir over a low heat until all the fat has been absorbed. Add the tomatoes, apple, bouquet garni and stock, season with salt and pepper and bring to the boil. Cover and simmer for 45 minutes.

Remove and discard the bouquet garni and pass the soup through a fine sieve or a blender. Return it to a clean pan, heat through and adjust the seasoning.

Pour the soup into warm bowls and garnish with a spoonful of cream and croûtons. For a really unusual garnish, use a sprinkling of marigold petals.

CHILLED CARROT VICHYSSOISE WITH MINT

THIS SOUP IS A delicious variation on a well-loved theme. It has a lovely colour and a light and delightful flavour, and is perfect for a summer lunch or as a starter before fish or poultry. It improves when it is made ahead of time, and is equally good served hot, garnished with a dollop of sour cream.

PREPARATION TIME: 1 HOUR
CHILLING TIME: 4 HOURS

INGREDIENTS FOR SIX
1 medium onion, chopped*
2-3 leeks, well washed and chopped (include 5 cm/2 in of the green tops)
25 g (1 oz) butter
2 large potatoes, peeled and cut into small dice
4 carrots, scraped and sliced
3 tablespoons chopped fresh mint
1 teaspoon dried oregano
250 ml (9 fl oz) water
250 ml (9 fl oz) milk
250 ml (9 fl oz) chicken stock*
Salt and freshly ground white pepper
125 ml (4 fl oz) sour cream

For the garnish:
2 medium carrots, finely grated
2 tablespoons finely chopped fresh mint leaves

In a large saucepan, sauté the onion and leeks in butter until soft and golden. Add the potatoes, carrots, mint, oregano and water. Bring to the boil, turn down the heat and simmer (covered) for about 45 minutes – until all the vegetables are soft. Add the milk and stock, reheat and season to taste.

Blend the soup to a fine purée in a blender or food processor, then sieve into a bowl. Stir in the sour cream, cover, and chill for at least 4 hours.

Check the seasoning again before serving and give the soup a good stir. Serve in pretty bowls, garnishing with grated carrot and chopped mint.

SERVING SUGGESTION For a light lunch, serve the soup with cheese bourekitas*.

CHILLED CARROT VICHYSSOISE WITH MINT *A variation of an old favourite.*

BEAN SOUP

THIS POPULAR DISH is thought to have originated in northern Germany, from where it spread to Holland and beyond. Because the German and Dutch housewives had to cater for relatively large appetites, they learned to appreciate the value of good, filling soups such as this one, which is based on pulses and shin of beef.

SOAKING TIME: 12 HOURS
PREPARATION TIME: 15 MINUTES
COOKING TIME: 2¼ HOURS

INGREDIENTS FOR EIGHT
150 g (5 oz) dried red kidney or borlotti beans
3 litres (5½ pints) cold water
100 g (3¾ oz) pork fat with rind, or bacon with rind
450 g (1 lb) shin of beef
1 onion, finely sliced*
1 teaspoon salt
¼ teaspoon pepper
125 ml (4 fl oz) chopped parsley
1 blade mace or a little grated nutmeg
1 tablespoon flour
1 tablespoon melted butter
250 ml (9 fl oz) milk
1 tablespoon lemon juice

Soak the beans in water for 12 hours (or overnight), then wash them. Dried kidney beans can cause severe stomach upsets if not thoroughly cooked, so always boil them energetically for 10 minutes before use. Drain the beans and place them in a large saucepan with the 3 litres (5½ pints) of cold water.

Add the pork fat (or bacon) and shin, and cook for an hour. Add the sliced onion, salt, pepper, chopped parsley, mace or nutmeg. Cook for another hour.

Put the soup through a sieve, mash the beans and remove the shin bones. Reheat the soup to boiling point. Meanwhile, combine the flour and melted butter, add the milk as for a white sauce* and stir it over a low heat until it thickens; add the mixture to the soup. Cook and stir for another 10 minutes, adding the lemon juice just before serving.

SERVING SUGGESTION Serve with croûtons or with the traditional German rye bread called pumpernickel. To complete the feast, offer thinly sliced cheese.

MURGH AUR KHADDU HALEEM

INDIAN SOUPS (known as haleems) are substantial and nutritious, and in some cases they are regarded as a main dish. Eastern spices are used for more than just their flavour and aroma, they are also highly valued for their health-giving properties.

Chicken and pumpkin soup makes a heartening dish on cold days. The pumpkin turns the soup into a golden orange colour, which makes it pleasing to the eye and tempting for children.

PREPARATION TIME: 1 HOUR
STANDING TIME: 30 MINUTES

INGREDIENTS FOR EIGHT
1.5 kg (3 lb 3 oz) chicken, cut into pieces

1½ teaspoons salt
3 tablespoons melted butter
2 onions, chopped*
8 cardamom pods
5 cm (2 in) fresh green ginger, scraped and pounded with a little water to a paste
200 g (7 oz) pumpkin, diced
¼ teaspoon turmeric
1 teaspoon pepper
¼ teaspoon chilli powder or paprika
2 tomatoes, chopped
1 litre (1¾ pints) warm water

For the garnish:
2 tablespoons chopped mint or coriander leaves (known as dhania) or parsley

Wash the chicken pieces and pat them dry. Sprinkle salt over the pieces and leave them to stand for 30 minutes. Heat the butter in a deep saucepan, add the onions and sauté for 2 minutes (or until soft). Place the chicken and remaining ingredients (except the garnish) in the saucepan, cover with the lid and simmer gently for an hour or until the chicken is tender. Remove the chicken pieces from the soup, cut the meat from the bones, chop them finely and return to the soup.

VARIATIONS If pumpkins are not readily available, use marrow. Try serving a heap of steaming rice with the soup.

BORSHCH

THOUGH NOW REGARDED as something of a delicacy, this thick beetroot soup was for centuries the staple diet of the pre-Revolution Russian peasantry and the basis of their main daily meal. Borshch without doubt ranks among the best of the world's classic soups.

PREPARATION TIME: 25 MINUTES
COOKING TIME: 1 HOUR .

INGREDIENTS FOR SIX
350 g (¾ lb) whole, uncooked beetroot with leaves intact
2 large carrots, peeled
1 tablespoon sunflower oil
100-125 g (about ¼ lb) streaky bacon, without rinds and cut into small pieces (optional)
1 large onion, peeled and finely chopped*
3 stalks celery, trimmed and cut into matchstick strips
1.5 litres (52 fl oz) chicken stock*
1 tablespoon vinegar
Salt and freshly ground black pepper
250 g (9 oz) tomatoes, skinned*, cored and seeded
125 ml (4 fl oz) sour cream for garnish

Wash the beetroot and leaves well. Break off the leaves and separate them from their stalks and ribs. Cut the leaves into fine shreds and chop the stalks and ribs finely. Peel the beetroot and cut the flesh into thin strips. Slice the carrots thinly lengthways and cut into fine strips.

Heat the oil in a large, heavy-based saucepan and fry the bacon (if used) over a low heat until the fat runs. Add the beetroot flesh, carrots, onion and celery to the pan and stir over a low heat until the fat has been absorbed.

BORSHCH *The sliced beetroot in this soup gives it a rich deep colour.*

Add the stock and vinegar, stir well and season with salt and pepper. Bring to the boil and simmer (covered) for 30 minutes. Pass the tomato flesh through a fine sieve or food mill to make a purée. Add it to the soup with the beetroot leaves and stalks. Continue to simmer for a further 15 minutes, or until the beetroot is tender.

Serve very hot with a swirl of sour cream in each serving.

VARIATIONS The classic borshch is always thick with vegetables, but if you prefer a less robust soup, strain it after cooking and serve it as a clear liquid, either hot or cold, with a spoonful of sour cream added to each bowl.

Try adding cucumber, pickled in dill-flavoured vinegar and chopped finely, to the soup or the sour cream.

VICHYSSOISE

DESPITE ITS FRENCH name, this soup was created by the chef of a New York hotel in 1910 and has since become universally famous.

It can be served hot or well chilled, but the true flavour of the leeks is retained more when the soup is cold.

PREPARATION TIME: 20 MINUTES
COOKING TIME: 25 MINUTES
CHILLING TIME: 4 HOURS

INGREDIENTS FOR EIGHT
3 leeks, finely chopped
1 medium onion, finely chopped*
30 g (1¼ oz) butter
4 medium potatoes, thinly sliced
1 litre (1¾ pints) chicken stock*
250 ml (9 fl oz) cream
Salt and pepper
Chopped chives for garnish

Sauté the leeks and onion in the heated butter in a medium-sized pan until soft, stirring constantly.

Add the potatoes and stock, then simmer (covered) for 15 minutes, or until tender. Push the mixture through a sieve, or liquidise, then add the cream and salt and pepper to taste.

Serve the vichyssoise well chilled, sprinkled with chopped chives.

VARIATIONS In addition to serving the vichyssoise hot, you can also substitute yoghurt for the cream.

CHILLED CUCUMBER SOUP *Chopped walnuts add an interesting dimension.*

CHILLED CUCUMBER SOUP

THIS IS A refreshing soup that is very nutritious owing to the vitamins B and C in the cucumbers.

PREPARATION TIME: 10 MINUTES
STANDING TIME: 30 MINUTES
CHILLING TIME: 2 HOURS

INGREDIENTS FOR SIX
500 g (1 lb 2 oz) green cucumber
Salt and pepper
250 ml (9 fl oz) natural yoghurt
125 ml (4 fl oz) cream
1 clove garlic, crushed
2 tablespoons olive oil
2 tablespoons white wine vinegar
50 g (2 oz) walnuts, chopped

Peel the cucumber and dice into tiny cubes. Put these on a flat dish, sprinkle lightly with salt and leave standing for 30 minutes. Rinse the cucumber cubes in a colander under cold running water and then drain thoroughly.

In a bowl, blend the yoghurt with the cream, the crushed garlic, the oil and the vinegar, and season to taste with the salt and pepper.

Fold in the cucumber and just over half the chopped walnuts; blend thoroughly and then chill in the refrigerator for about 2 hours.

Spoon the chilled soup into individual bowls, sprinkle the remaining chopped walnuts on top, and serve.

SERVING SUGGESTIONS Serve with thin slices of crisp Melba toast* or wedges of pitta bread*. Cucumber soup makes an excellent appetiser for a summer menu. Follow the soup with barbecued chicken peri-peri*.

Pour the oil into a heavy-bottomed pot and heat. Add the salt, garlic and all the vegetables except the cooked beans and tomatoes. Allow the vegetables to cook until they become transparent (do not allow them to brown).

Gradually add the boiling water to the saucepan, then add the cooked beans and tomatoes, basil and pepper. Cover and cook for 45 minutes.

Add the pasta shells to the simmering soup about 20 minutes before serving the minestrone. Check the seasoning and then serve with a sprinkling of freshly grated Parmesan cheese in each bowl.

MINESTRONE, *a hearty Italian soup, has become a worldwide favourite.*

MINESTRONE

T HIS MUCH-LOVED vegetable soup forms the basis for many other Italian soups. Originally it was more like a stew and, for this reason, some versions of this recipe are stews rather than soups.

It is important that the vegetables should not be overcooked, or they will lose the colour that makes this soup especially pleasing to the eye. Minestrone is quite a filling dish and is often served as a meal on its own, especially when accompanied by fresh crusty bread.

PREPARATION TIME: 30 MINUTES
COOKING TIME: 1½ HOURS

INGREDIENTS FOR EIGHT
3 tablespoons sunflower oil
2½ teaspoons salt
3 cloves garlic, crushed
2 large onions, chopped*
2 potatoes, diced
2 fresh young carrots, diced
2 leeks, sliced
2 turnips, diced
4 stalks celery, chopped
2 florets cauliflower, divided into sprigs
100 g (3¾ oz) green beans, sliced
2 litres (3½ pints) boiling water
300 g (11 oz) borlotti beans or haricot beans, cooked
3 medium-sized ripe tomatoes (unskinned), chopped
2 tablespoons chopped fresh basil leaves or 1 tablespoon dried
Salt and freshly ground black pepper
50 g (2 oz) pasta shells
Parmesan cheese

AVOCADO SOUP

A SATINY-SMOOTH SOUP which retains all the rich flavour of the ever-popular avocado pear. It is usually served well-chilled, but a hot version is ideal for cooler nights. Whether served hot or cold, this is a particularly delicious soup.

PREPARATION TIME: 10 MINUTES
COOKING TIME: 25 MINUTES
CHILLING TIME: 2 HOURS

INGREDIENTS FOR SIX
30 g (1¼ oz) butter
1 small onion, finely chopped*
1 green pepper, seeded and finely chopped (optional)
2 tablespoons flour
250 ml (9 fl oz) warm milk
750 ml (26 fl oz) chicken stock*
2 ripe avocado pears, mashed
Salt and freshly ground black pepper
Chopped chives for garnish

Melt the butter in a medium-sized saucepan and gently sauté the onion and green pepper until soft. Remove from the heat, stir in the flour and gradually stir in the milk. Return to heat and bring to the boil. Add the chicken stock, cover and simmer for 20 minutes. Blend a little of the hot soup with the mashed avocado. Stir in the remaining soup and season to taste. Blend and chill, and sprinkle with the chives before serving.

VARIATION Serve hot, garnished with thinly sliced avocado first marinated in lemon juice, and a spoonful of sour cream. Remove from the stove as soon as it is hot enough, as overheating causes the avocado to taste bitter.

OYSTER SOUP

THERE IS A SCENE in the Dickens classic *Pickwick Papers* in which a character named Sam Weller said: 'It's a wery [sic] remarkable circumstance sir, that poverty and oysters always seem to go together.' These days, however, oysters are relatively expensive. Although usually served on the half shell, oysters also make a very tasty soup.

PREPARATION TIME: 20 MINUTES
COOKING TIME: 45 MINUTES

INGREDIENTS FOR SIX
24 fresh oysters
50 g (2 oz) butter
2 tablespoons flour
450 ml (¾ pint) hot milk or veal basic stock*
125 ml (4 fl oz) dry white wine
¾ teaspoon anchovy essence (optional)
½ teaspoon nutmeg, freshly grated
Cayenne pepper
125 ml (4 fl oz) cream
Salt and freshly ground black pepper
1 teaspoon lemon juice
1½ teaspoons chopped parsley for garnish

Open the oysters* and discard the upper shells. Loosen the oysters left in the deep shells, leaving the liquid intact, and spoon both oysters and their juice into a bowl.

Melt the butter in a large saucepan and stir in the flour. Cook gently for 2-3 minutes (without browning) and add the milk or stock gradually, beating it well to make a smooth soup.

Pour in the wine, season with the anchovy essence (if you are including it), and add the nutmeg and cayenne pepper. Stir in the cream and simmer gently for 15-20 minutes.

Just before serving, add the oysters and their liquid to the soup and heat through for 1-2 minutes. Do not overcook; the oysters are ready when they begin to curl at the edges. Correct the seasoning, sharpen the flavour with lemon juice and serve the soup immediately, each serving garnished with ¼ teaspoon parsley.

VARIATIONS For a heartier soup, simmer 250 g (9 oz) chopped white leek stems and 125 g (4¼ oz) diced potato in 750 ml (26 fl oz) fish stock* until tender. Purée, season and reheat it (do not boil) with cream and oysters.

Alternatively, substitute the fresh oysters with two 225 g (8 oz) jars of drained oysters, mussels or clams.

OYSTER SOUP *is a tasty combination of interesting spices, a hint of anchovy and cream with lightly cooked oysters.*

FISH

Fish IS AT ITS BEST fresh from the water when the simplest preparation turns it into a dish fit for royalty. Before the advent of modern freezing techniques and refrigerated transport – which has brought seafood to the dinner tables of those who do not live close to the coast – smoking and drying were common methods of preserving fish. But there is no end to the ways in which fish can be prepared today. Recipes range from the family standby of fish and chips to something more exotic, such as South Indian fish curry.

Fish is popular in many cultures. Try a Spanish paella, which combines a variety of seafoods in a colourful rice dish, Chinese steamed sweet and sour fish, or a Hungarian fish dish with paprika cream sauce.

Fish is the perfect slimmer's food – as long as you choose the simpler methods of cooking such as grilling, poaching or steaming, and steer clear of recipes with rich, cream sauces. But you need not keep it entirely plain: you can often make a dish less fattening by simply substituting yoghurt for cream.

CHINESE STEAMED SWEET AND SOUR FISH

THE CHINESE PREFER to cook fish whole – they feel that a fish without a head and tail is incomplete. For this purpose they use steamer dishes made of bamboo. Chinese bamboo steamers come in many sizes and stack on top of each other so that as many as four to five dishes can be steamed over one wok of boiling water.

PREPARATION TIME: 15 MINUTES
STANDING TIME: 30 MINUTES
COOKING TIME: 20 MINUTES

INGREDIENTS FOR SIX
A 1.5 kg (3 lb 3 oz) whole fish, cleaned
2 teaspoons salt
3 tablespoons sunflower oil
1 chilli, seeded and shredded
6 spring onions, cut in 5 cm (2 in) pieces
6 slices fresh green ginger, shredded
1 red pepper, seeded and sliced
1 tin (230 g/8 oz) bamboo shoots, finely sliced
3 tablespoons soy sauce
3 tablespoons vinegar
5 teaspoons sugar
5 teaspoons tomato paste
3 tablespoons orange juice
2 teaspoons cornflour dissolved in 75 ml (2½ fl oz) chicken stock*

Rub the fish inside and out with the salt and 1 tablespoon of the oil, and allow to stand for 30 minutes. Place the fish in an oval ovenproof dish which can be used at the table. Put the dish in a steamer and steam it over vigorously boiling water for 10 minutes, then turn and steam for a further 10 minutes.

Heat the remaining oil over moderate heat. Add the chilli and stir-fry for a minute. Add the rest of the ingredients, except the cornflour paste, and stir-fry these for half a minute. Add the cornflour paste and stir it until the sauce thickens. Remove the dish of fish from the steamer, pour the sauce over the fish and serve.

SERVING SUGGESTION For a special dinner party, try serving as part of a Chinese meal – with fried rice, beef in oyster sauce* and stir-fried vegetables.

VARIATION Instead of using a whole fish you may use 500 g (1 lb 2 oz) fish fillets.

SOUTH INDIAN FISH CURRY

SOUR TAMARIND AND CURRY leaves are typical flavourings used in the south of India and Southeast Asia. This fresh fish in a thick tomato gravy has a sharp and hot taste, with aniseed, coriander and garlic flavouring. A firm fish is best for this dish.

You can make the fish curry a day ahead, giving it time to absorb the flavours, or you can freeze it for later use.

PREPARATION TIME: 45 MINUTES
MARINATING TIME: 3-4 HOURS
COOKING TIME: 45 MINUTES

INGREDIENTS FOR SIX
1 kg (2¼ lb) fresh fish, sliced
60 ml (2 fl oz) sunflower oil
2 teaspoons salt
1 teaspoon turmeric
1 teaspoon chilli powder
1 teaspoon aniseed, crushed
2 teaspoons coriander seeds, crushed
2 tablespoons flour
30 g (1¼ oz) tamarind pulp
10 curry leaves
1 green chilli, sliced lengthways
6 cloves garlic, finely crushed
1 onion, grated or finely chopped*
6 ripe tomatoes, pulped
2 teaspoons sugar
4 sprigs fresh coriander (dhania) leaves, chopped, for garnish

Wash the fish, pat it dry and put on one side. Make a paste by mixing 1 tablespoon of the oil with the salt, turmeric, chilli powder, aniseed and coriander seeds. Rub the paste well over the fish slices and then leave them to stand for 3-4 hours.

Mix the flour with 2 tablespoons water, then dissolve the flour paste in 190 ml (6½ fl oz) water.

Soak the tamarind in 125 ml (4 fl oz) water for 10 minutes, then remove the pips by straining, and reserve the purée.

Heat the remaining oil in a saucepan, then add the curry leaves, green chilli and garlic. Brown for about 10 seconds, then add the onion and stir-fry for about 30 seconds. Add the tomatoes, flour paste, tamarind purée and sugar. Stir, cover the saucepan, and simmer for 20 minutes.

Add the fish and marinade to the gravy, cover the saucepan and cook for 12-15 minutes, or until the fish is tender. Garnish with the coriander leaves and serve with rice and a crisp salad topped with minted yoghurt dressing*.

FISH MEUNIÈRE

MEUNIÈRE IS A FRENCH TERM meaning 'in the style of the miller's wife.' In cooking parlance it refers to fish coated with flour, cooked in butter, and served with parsley and lemon juice.

PREPARATION TIME: 15 MINUTES
COOKING TIME: 20 MINUTES

INGREDIENTS FOR FOUR
800 g (1¾ lb) fish fillets
30 g (1¼ oz) flour
A pinch of salt
White pepper
Juice of 1 lemon
1 tablespoon chopped parsley
2 teaspoons chopped fresh chives or tarragon
50 g (2 oz) butter
1 tablespoon sunflower oil

Wipe the fillets and pat them dry. Mix the flour with a little salt and pepper and use it to coat the fish: shake off the excess. Combine the lemon juice and herbs with salt and pepper.

In a large frying pan, heat 20 g (¾ oz) of the butter and the oil until it foams. Add a single layer of fish and cook over a medium-high heat for 1-3 minutes, until the fillets turn golden-brown (do not overcook, or they will fall apart). Turn the fish and brown the other side. Transfer the fish to a serving dish and keep it warm while you fry the remaining fillets.

To make the sauce, wipe out the frying pan, put in the remaining butter and heat it until it turns nut-brown. Add the lemon juice mixture, stirring to blend properly, and pour the foaming mixture over the fish. Scatter a handful of finely chopped parsley over the fish and serve at once.

VARIATION Lay the fillets side by side in a buttered ovenproof dish, dot with butter, and bake at 220°C (425°F, mark 7), basting with butter every 5 minutes: they should be cooked in about 18 minutes. Add 2 tablespoons of flaked almonds to the butter in the pan, and brown slightly before adding the lemon juice. Sprinkle over the fish.

FISH AND CHIPS *This crisp and golden favourite is one of the most traditional and popular family recipes.*

FISH AND CHIPS

TRADITIONAL FISH AND CHIPS can be made quite easily at home. The main secret of making crisp, firm chips is to ensure that the cooking oil is hot enough; otherwise they will be unpleasantly limp and soggy.

Peanut (groundnut) oil is very well-suited to deep frying. It will attain a high temperature without burning and does not have an overpowering flavour of its own as, for example, corn oil does.

PREPARATION TIME: 50 MINUTES
STANDING TIME: 30 MINUTES
COOKING TIME: 25 MINUTES
PREHEAT OVEN TO 140°C (275°F, MARK 1)

INGREDIENTS FOR FOUR
*4 fish fillets (with the skin left on,
   if preferred)
3 large potatoes, peeled
575 ml (1 pint) peanut (groundnut)
   oil
Lemon slices for garnish*

For the batter:
*200 g (7 oz) self-raising flour
½ teaspoon baking powder
1 teaspoon salt
Water*

First make the batter. Mix the flour, baking powder and salt in a bowl. Add the water, beating in a very little at a time, until the mixture is of pouring consistency. Leave the batter to stand for about 30 minutes before using it.

Cut the potatoes lengthways into chips about 1 cm (½ in) wide. Pat them dry with paper towels. Do not wash them, as this will make the chips too brittle.

Pour the oil into a deep pan. For a pan about 15 cm (6 in) deep, pour in enough oil to reach the halfway mark and then heat to about 170°C (340°F). It will be at the right temperature when a cube of day-old bread browns in 1¼ minutes.

Fry the chips in small batches so that they can move about in the pan freely. As soon as they start to brown, lift them out of the pan with a slotted spoon and drain on a thick layer of paper towels. A wire chip-basket makes draining easier.

Put the chips into the preheated oven in a dish lined with paper towels while you cook the fish. Heat the oil to 190°C (375°F) – a bread cube should brown in about 1 minute.

Dip the fish in the batter, turning it over so that it is well coated. Lower the fish into the oil, skin side down, in order to stop it curling.

When the fish starts to turn golden (about 4 minutes), turn the pieces over and fry them for the same amount of time on the other side. Serve with the chips, garnished with lemon slices.

VARIATIONS For crisper chips, heat the oil up to 190°C (375°F) – a bread cube dropped into the oil should brown in about 1 minute – and put the chips back in the pan for 1 minute.

You can make a simpler batter by dipping the slices of fish in beaten egg and then in flour. Fry the fish in hot oil over a medium heat until golden on both sides.

FISH BOBOTIE

BOBOTIE IS ONE OF the best-known South African dishes, introduced there by Muslim slaves in the late 17th century. It was traditionally made from leftover meat (the roast leg of mutton from the Sunday meal was served as bobotie on Monday).

It can also, however, be made with fish. Most kinds of white fish are suitable for this tasty dish.

PREPARATION TIME: 45 MINUTES
COOKING TIME: 40 MINUTES
PREHEAT OVEN TO 140°C (275°F, MARK 1)

INGREDIENTS FOR SIX
1 kg (2¼ lb) white fish
Salt and freshly ground black
     pepper
6 teaspoons lemon juice or white
     vinegar
1 tablespoon skim milk powder
1 slice of white bread, 2 cm (¾ in)
     thick (with crust)
1 medium-sized onion, peeled and
     finely chopped*
15 g (½ oz) butter
4 teaspoons curry powder
2 teaspoons sugar
2 large eggs
12 blanched almonds*
Fresh lemon leaves or curry leaves
125 ml (4 fl oz) milk

Poach the fish in a small quantity of seasoned water to which 2 teaspoons of the lemon juice or vinegar has been added. Remove the fish from this stock, cool it and flake it. Enrich 250 ml (9 fl oz) of the stock with the milk powder and soak the bread in it.

Using a covered pan, sauté the onion in the butter until it is just transparent. Add the curry powder, sugar and the remaining lemon juice, and simmer, covered, for 5 minutes. Add this sauce to the pieces of flaked fish.

Remove the bread from the stock, squeeze out the stock (all of which should be kept for the custard), mash and add to the fish and the sauce.

When the fish mixture has cooled, add one lightly whisked egg. Mix well and spoon the mixture into a buttered dish, smoothing it down well.

Stick the almonds at intervals into the surface, leaving the round ends protruding. Cut off the stems of the lemon or curry leaves and twist the leaves into

FISH BOBOTIE *A spicy and decorative fish dish.*

little cones. Insert them into the fish mixture at regular intervals, so that each serving has at least one leaf.

Whisk the remaining egg with the whole milk and the strained residue of liquid in which the bread was soaked. Pour this over a spoon onto the fish mixture so that the lemon or curry leaves and almonds are not disturbed.

Place the baking dish in a pan of boiling water on the lower shelf of the oven. Bake for about 40 minutes, until the custard is set.

SERVING SUGGESTIONS Serve the dish with steamed white rice, and an apple or cucumber sambal*.

VARIATIONS Make a traditional meat bobotie with 1 kg (2 lb) minced mutton or beef in place of the fish. Cook the meat in a little boiling water, flavoured with chopped onion and a bay leaf, for about 15-20 minutes. Follow the above recipe, adding 75 g (3 oz) seedless raisins and 3 tablespoons of chutney to the meat mixture.

Alternatively, you could use leftover meat. Chop finely or mince, but remember that a bobotie made with cooked meat will have a finer texture than one made with raw mince.

TROUT WITH ALMONDS

THIS TRADITIONAL FRENCH DISH has gained popularity throughout the world, and is regarded as a culinary delight wherever trout is eaten. When cleaning the trout, take care not to tear the skin, or you will spoil the effect.

PREPARATION TIME: 12 MINUTES
COOKING TIME: 30 MINUTES
PREHEAT OVEN TO 180°C (350°F, MARK 4)

INGREDIENTS FOR SIX
6 trout, each 180-200 g (6-7 oz)
Salt and freshly ground pepper
100 g (3¾ oz) flaked almonds
Flour for dredging
200 ml (7 fl oz) clarified butter* or
     ghee
60 ml (2 fl oz) sunflower oil
Juice of 1 lemon

Clean the trout through the gills and wash them thoroughly. Sprinkle with salt and pepper and put aside. Spread the almonds on an oven pan and place them in the preheated oven. Roast until golden-brown, turning from time to time (about 25 minutes), and put aside.

Meanwhile dredge the fish with flour and shake off any surplus flour. Melt half the butter in a large frying pan and add half the oil. Fry 3 trout over a medium heat for 6 minutes on each side. Place on a heated serving dish and scatter with the roasted almonds. Keep warm while frying the remaining trout (using the rest of the butter and oil). Scatter these with almonds and sprinkle lemon juice over all 6 trout. Garnish with lemon wedges.

FISH AND NOODLE CASEROLE

THE NOODLES AND CHEESE used in this fish casserole make the dish a very satisfying and filling meal.

PREPARATION TIME: 30 MINUTES
COOKING TIME: 30 MINUTES
PREHEAT OVEN TO 180°C (350°F, MARK 4)

INGREDIENTS FOR FOUR
500 g (1 lb 2 oz) fish, skinned and filleted*
1 large onion, peeled and finely chopped*
50 g (2 oz) butter
2 tablespoons sunflower oil
2 carrots, finely chopped
125 ml (4 fl oz) water
3 tablespoons finely chopped parsley
Salt and pepper
250 g (9 oz) broad noodles, cooked*
1 egg yolk
250 ml (9 fl oz) sour cream
50 g (2 oz) Cheddar cheese, grated

Rinse the fish and pat it quite dry, then cut it into strips. Soften the onion in the hot butter and oil. Add the carrots and cook gently until they soften. Stir in the fish, adding more oil or butter if necessary.

Add the water, 1 tablespoon of the chopped parsley and some seasoning. Simmer gently for 10 minutes or until the fish is just cooked through.

Butter an ovenproof dish and arrange half the cooked noodles in it. Cover with a layer of the fish and then the remaining noodles. Pour over the egg yolk and cream, beaten together until just blended.

Sprinkle the dish with the cheese. Bake for 30 minutes, or until it is lightly browned. Garnish it with the rest of the chopped parsley.

FISH WITH PAPRIKA CREAM SAUCE *A Hungarian dish with a tangy pink sauce.*

FISH WITH PAPRIKA CREAM SAUCE

HUNGARY HAS NO COASTLINE, so freshwater fish, such as carp, tend to figure prominently in its cuisine. In this Hungarian recipe, however, more readily obtainable saltwater fish such as monkfish, bream or snapper may be substituted without really altering the character of the dish.

It is the paprika – a fine, subtle spice with a distinctive red colour – that adds the true Hungarian quality.

PREPARATION TIME: 10 MINUTES
STANDING TIME: 30 MINUTES
COOKING TIME: 30 MINUTES

INGREDIENTS FOR SIX
900 g (2 lb) firm white fish fillets
Salt
50 g (2 oz) butter
2 teaspoons paprika
1 large onion, peeled and finely chopped*
150 ml (¼ pint) sour cream
1 red pepper, seeded and finely chopped
1 tomato, skinned* and finely chopped

Cut the fish into cubes, about 2.5 cm (1 in) square, and sprinkle them with salt. Set aside for 30 minutes.

Melt the butter in a saucepan and fry the onion gently until transparent.

Remove from the heat, sprinkle on the paprika and stir in the sour cream. Return to the heat and add the fish pieces. Turn the fish gently in the pan and then add the chopped pepper and tomato. Cover, and cook over a very low heat for 20-25 minutes.

SERVING SUGGESTIONS Serve with parsley dumplings* or noodles. Toss the noodles in butter and poppy seeds. Follow with a fresh green salad*.

PREPARING CALAMARI

Calamari, or squid, has long been popular with Mediterranean cooks for frying, stewing, or even stuffing (using large calamari). It can be bought cleaned, sliced and cut into rings or whole. If frozen, calamari must be thawed out thoroughly before cooking.

To clean calamari, hold the body in one hand and the head section in the other, and gently pull apart. Skin and remove the fins.

Using a sharp knife, cut the tentacles and arms off just below the eyes. Lift out the silver-grey ink sac: this will come away with the head section. If the calamari is very young, however, the sac may not be present.

Dislodge the small 'beak' with your fingers. Pull the long piece of plastic-like material out of the body, and discard. Thoroughly rinse the inside of the body – it may in fact be possible to turn it inside out for this purpose.

The body can now be sliced into 1 cm (½ in) rings for frying or freezing. The fins, tentacles and arms are ideal for stuffing when chopped.

FRIED CALAMARI

Tender rings of squid, or calamari (as it is known as in Greece), can be crisply coated in breadcrumbs and then deep-fried in oil.

If you are using frozen calamari, make sure it is completely thawed before you slice and fry it.

PREPARATION TIME: 15 MINUTES
STANDING TIME: 45 MINUTES
COOKING TIME: 10 MINUTES

INGREDIENTS FOR SIX
800 g (1¾ lb) calamari (squid)
60 ml (2 fl oz) lemon juice
4 tablespoons flour
4 tablespoons fine breadcrumbs
2 eggs
Sunflower oil for deep-frying
Salt and freshly ground pepper

Clean the calamari and slice into 1 cm (½ in) rings. Cut the tentacles and fins into bite-sized pieces. Marinate the calamari in lemon juice for 30 minutes.

Put the flour and breadcrumbs in a paper bag and shake well. Beat the eggs and 2 tablespoons oil in a wide soup plate. Place the flour mixture in a wide, shallow dish.

Drop the calamari into the egg and oil mixture, a few rings at a time, and then toss in the flour and breadcrumb mixture. Set aside in a single layer on a tray for 15 minutes to settle.

Heat oil for frying to 200°C (400°F, mark 6) in a deep saucepan fitted with a basket. Fill the basket a quarter of the way up with calamari and deep fry for about 16 seconds (if fried for too long, the calamari will toughen).

Drain on paper towels and sprinkle with salt and pepper. Fry the remaining calamari in the same way.

SERVING SUGGESTIONS Serve on a bed of hot rice with tartare sauce*, wedges of lemon and a French salad. If serving as a starter, omit the rice.

VARIATIONS Prepared calamari rings can be treated in a variety of ways. Fry them lightly in a little oil and then simmer until tender in a Napolitana sauce*. Serve with freshly cooked pasta and a green salad*.

Alternatively, try an Oriental approach. Follow the recipe for beef with oyster sauce*, but substitute calamari for the beef.

FISH MAURITIAN

A SPICY, CREOLE-INFLUENCED DISH from the tropical island of Mauritius, this tasty pickled fish makes a good starter for a dinner party, since it can be prepared well in advance.

PREPARATION TIME: 15 MINUTES
COOKING TIME: 30 MINUTES
MARINATING TIME: 3 DAYS

INGREDIENTS FOR SIX
6-8 fillets or steaks of cod (about 200 g/7 oz each)
Salt and freshly ground black pepper
250 ml (9 fl oz) sunflower oil
200 g (7 oz) pickling onions, or 2 medium-sized onions, sliced in rings*
4 cloves garlic, chopped
1 tablespoon chopped fresh green ginger
3 tablespoons turmeric
300 ml (½ pint) red wine vinegar
125 ml (4 fl oz) water

Sprinkle the fish pieces with salt and pepper and fry them in half the oil for 3-4 minutes until half cooked. Remove the fish and arrange the pieces (in a single layer) in a large, shallow dish. Blanch the onions in boiling salted water for 5 minutes. Drain and dry. Fry them in the leftover oil until golden. Add the onions to the fish.

Wipe out the frying pan, add the remaining oil and heat gently. Fry the garlic and ginger until the garlic is soft. Mix the turmeric, vinegar and water and add to the garlic mixture. Boil these ingredients gently for 3 minutes, then pour over the fish. Cover and marinate in the refrigerator for 3 days, or longer. Serve cold.

SERVING SUGGESTION Sprinkle the fish with chopped spring onions and serve with hot, crusty bread.

If serving as a main course, arrange the fish on a bed of lettuce and accompany with a potato salad*.

PAELLA

THIS IS ARGUABLY the best-known Spanish dish outside Spain. It is prepared all over Spain with slight variations, but it is at its best along the Valencian coast. Paella is a combination of many different ingredients, resulting in a wonderful taste sensation.

PREPARATION TIME: 45 MINUTES
COOKING TIME: 1 HOUR

INGREDIENTS FOR EIGHT

250 g (9 oz) spicy small salami, cut into big slices.
3 tablespoons olive oil
8 portions chicken (legs and thighs)
250 g (9 oz) chicken livers
3 cloves garlic, crushed
1 large onion, peeled and chopped*
1 green pepper, cut into strips
300 g (11 oz) rice
750 ml (26 fl oz) chicken stock*
½ teaspoon cayenne pepper
A good pinch of saffron
4 ripe tomatoes, skinned, seeded* and thinly sliced
6 large prawns or 2 small (cooked) crayfish or lobster, cut into pieces
12 mussels (preferably fresh)
1 small tin red pimiento, cut into strips
White wine for moistening
100 g (3¾ oz) green peas (frozen or fresh), cooked
For the garnish:
12 black olives
Lemon wedges

Heat a paella dish over moderate heat (or use an electric frying pan set on high). Fry the salami until brown on both sides. Remove and put aside. Add oil to the pan and fry the chicken pieces until golden in colour; then remove from the heat.

Add the chicken livers and two cloves of crushed garlic, and lightly brown; then set aside. Add the onion and green pepper, and fry until golden. Stir in the rice and cook until pale gold in colour. Pour in half of the chicken stock, add the cayenne pepper, saffron, tomatoes and the remaining garlic. Return the salami, chicken and liver to the pan, then the prawns or crayfish, mussels and pimiento.

Cook carefully, stirring frequently. Add the remaining stock and, if necessary, some wine. Cook for about 30 minutes (or until the rice is tender). Stir in the green peas, taste and correct the seasoning. Garnish with the olives and lemon wedges.

SERVING SUGGESTION Paella is ideal for a buffet party. Prepare up to a day in advance, and heat through in an oven-proof dish before serving. Serve with a courgette (zucchini) salad*.

PAELLA is a delicious marriage of a wide assortment of seafoods, meats, spices and vegetables.

FISH AND POTATOES WITH CHEESE TOPPING *is both fluffy and filling.*

FISH AND POTATOES WITH CHEESE TOPPING

Bite into a fluffy cheese soufflé to discover the flavour of fish and potato underneath. The dish can be prepared (up to the point before the topping is made) ahead of time, refrigerated until needed, then topped and baked.

PREPARATION TIME: 40 MINUTES
COOKING TIME: 25 MINUTES
PREHEAT OVEN TO 200°C (400°F, MARK 6)

INGREDIENTS FOR FOUR
600 g (1 lb 5 oz) white fish, filleted
   and skinned*
5 medium-sized potatoes, peeled
   and sliced
1 teaspoon salt
1 tablespoon flour
1 teaspoon brown sugar
A pinch of pepper
3 tablespoons melted butter

For the cheese topping:
3 tablespoons thick mayonnaise*

45 g (1¾ oz) mature Cheddar
   cheese, grated
¾ teaspoon dry mustard
A pinch of cayenne pepper
1 egg, separated

Divide the fish into suitable portions and put to one side. Steam the sliced potatoes or cook in a little salted boiling water until tender. Line a medium-sized oven-proof dish with the cooked potatoes.

Mix the salt, flour, sugar and pepper on a chopping board. Dip the fish portions into the seasoned flour, and then into the melted butter. Place the fish on the bed of potatoes and bake for 10 minutes while you prepare the topping.

Mix together the mayonnaise, grated cheese, mustard, cayenne pepper and egg yolk. Beat the egg white until fluffy and fold it into the mixture with a metal spoon. Remove the dish from the oven and spread the cheese topping evenly over the fish portions to cover them completely. Bake for a further 15 minutes until the soufflé is puffed up and golden-brown. Serve immediately.

COQUILLES EN BROCHETTE

Fresh scallops are often served in a cream sauce, but in this French recipe they are skewered and grilled with bacon and peppers. Allow three or four scallops per skewer, and two skewers per person for a main course. For a first course, serve one skewer per person.

PREPARATION TIME: 25 MINUTES
COOKING TIME: 15-20 MINUTES

INGREDIENTS FOR TWO TO FOUR
12 scallops
2 shallots
150 ml (¼ pint) dry white wine
1 parsley sprig
Salt and black pepper
1 egg
2 tablespoons fresh white
   breadcrumbs
225 g (½ lb) thin rashers green
   streaky bacon
2 green peppers
16 mushroom caps
2 tablespoons oil

For the garnish:
Fresh bay leaves

Slide the scallops from the flat shells and remove the gills and black threads. Peel the shallots and cut them in half. Put the scallops in a saucepan with the shallots and parsley, a little salt and freshly ground pepper; add sufficient wine to cover. Poach the scallops over gentle heat for about 7 minutes or until tender.

Lift out the scallops, cut out the orange-coloured roes and coat them in the lightly beaten egg and the bread-crumbs. Set aside. Cut each white scallop part in half horizontally. Remove the rind from the bacon, stretch the rashers with the blade of a knife and cut each into three. Wrap a piece of bacon around each white scallop portion.

Remove the stalk ends and seeds from the peppers, wash and dry them, then cut them into 2 cm (¾ in) wedges. Wash or trim the mushrooms, leaving them whole. Thread the scallops (the coated roes and the bacon-wrapped white pieces) onto skewers, alternating with the pepper squares and the mushrooms.

Brush the skewers with oil and put them under a hot, preheated grill. Cook for 8-10 minutes, turning the skewers several times to grill evenly.

SERVING SUGGESTION Arrange the skewers on a bed of plain or saffron-coloured rice garnished with fresh bay leaves. A bowl of tartare sauce would go well with the scallops.

VARIATION Scallops can be expensive, so for a more economical dish, substitute firm-fleshed white fish for some of the scallops. Cut the fish into 2.5 cm (1 in) cubes and cook as for the scallops, but reduce the poaching time to 3 minutes (fish will cook faster than scallops).

CLEANING AND OPENING MUSSELS

Discard all mussels with slightly open or gaping shells, or any that do not close when lightly tapped.

With a stiff brush, thoroughly scrub and clean the shells under the cold tap. Scrape away the black weed, or beard, from the outside of the shells.

Shells open during cooking. Follow the recipe, or place in a heavy-based pan with 1.5 cm (½ in) of water or white wine and chopped parsley and onions. Cook with the lid on for about 5 minutes over a low heat (until the shells open). Discard any mussels that remain closed.

MOULES MARINIÈRE

THIS WONDERFUL COMBINATION of shellfish, herbs and wine has the fresh taste of the sea. Mussels should be eaten very fresh but when these are not available, or if you are short of time, you can use tinned or frozen mussels.

PREPARATION TIME: 2 HOURS
COOKING TIME: 20 MINUTES

INGREDIENTS FOR FOUR
48-60 mussels, or 2 tins (900 g / 2 lb each) mussels in shells
70 g (2½ oz) butter
1 large onion, peeled and finely chopped*
300 ml (½ pint) dry white wine
60 ml (2 fl oz) red wine
1 teaspoon dried thyme
2 tablespoons chopped parsley
1 bay leaf
1 teaspoon salt
Freshly ground black pepper
2 teaspoons flour (optional)

Clean the mussels well (following the instructions on the left).

Melt 60 g (2 oz) of the butter and fry the onion until soft. Add the wine, thyme, 1½ tablespoons of the parsley, the bay leaf, salt and a good twist of black pepper. Cover and simmer for 8 minutes, then strain the liquid. Drain the mussels, add them to the liquid in the saucepan, and cook gently until the shells open (5-10 minutes). Remove the mussels with a slotted spoon, cover, and keep warm.

Cook the liquid until slightly reduced. Melt the remaining butter in a pan, remove from the heat and stir in the flour if used. Return to the heat and gradually stir in the reduced liquid. When this soup thickens, pour over the mussels and sprinkle with leftover parsley.

SERVING SUGGESTION Serve with warm crusty French bread, or garlic bread. To make this, slice a French loaf at 5 cm (2 in) intervals and spread the slices with garlic butter*. Wrap the loaf in foil and heat through in a moderate oven (180°C/350°F/mark 4) for 20-30 minutes. The butter will melt into the bread.

VARIATION If there are mussels left over, remove them from their shells, place them in a glass jar or bowl and marinate in a vinaigrette*. They will keep (if well chilled) for about 2 weeks.

FISH IN CURRY SAUCE

THIS TASTY DISH can be prepared quickly and easily, using ingredients that most cooks will usually have to hand. The strength of the curry sauce can be altered simply by adding more or less chilli powder, according to one's taste.

PREPARATION TIME: 45 MINUTES
COOKING TIME: 1 HOUR

INGREDIENTS FOR FOUR TO SIX
1 kg (2¼ lb) firm, white fish fillets, skinned*
75 ml (2½ fl oz) sunflower oil
1 tablespoon crushed coriander seeds
½ teaspoon turmeric
1 teaspoon ground cumin
1 teaspoon chilli powder
2 cloves garlic, crushed
1 large onion, peeled and finely chopped*
Salt
1 tin tomatoes (400 g / 14 oz) chopped
1 tablespoon desiccated coconut (optional)
175 ml (6 fl oz) fish stock* or water
A pinch of sugar
125 ml (4 fl oz) cream or sour cream

Dry the fish thoroughly and cut into 3 cm (1¼ in) pieces. Heat 60 ml (2 fl oz) of the oil and gently fry the fish until lightly browned, being careful not to overcook. Drain and set aside.

Mix the spices with the garlic and a little water to make a stiff paste. Fry the onion in the remaining oil until lightly browned. Add the spice paste and cook for 1-2 minutes, stirring in another 1 tablespoon of water if necessary.

Add all the remaining ingredients (except the cream or sour cream) and simmer gently until the sauce is thick – about 15 minutes. Gently immerse the fried fish in the sauce and cook for 4-5 minutes until it is tender and has fully absorbed the flavour. Check the seasoning and stir in the cream.

SERVING SUGGESTION Sprinkle the fish with freshly chopped parsley and eat it with boiled rice, fresh chutney and a selection of sambals*.

VARIATION Adapt this recipe by using chicken breasts instead of the fish.

WHOLE BAKED FISH

AN INCREASINGLY POPULAR WAY of serving large fish such as salmon is to bake them whole. These deliciously flavoured fish can be served both hot or cold, and are ideal party fare.

PREPARATION TIME: 10 MINUTES
COOKING TIME: 30-40 MINUTES
PREHEAT OVEN TO 180°C (350°F, MARK 4)

INGREDIENTS FOR SIX
A 1.5 kg (3 lb 3 oz) whole fish, cleaned and prepared (with head and tail intact)
Salt and pepper
Juice of 1½ lemons
60 ml (2 fl oz) clarified butter* or ghee

Clean the fish* and season the body cavity with salt and pepper. Sprinkle with lemon juice and brush with butter, then butter a dish large enough to hold the fish, or wrap it loosely in buttered aluminium foil.

Place the fish in the oven and cook for 30-40 minutes (basting frequently if not wrapped in foil). Test to see if the fish is cooked by inserting a thin sharp knife into the flesh near the bone. If it comes away easily, and the juice runs clear, then the fish is cooked.

SERVING SUGGESTIONS Serve the fish with a Napolitana* or caper* sauce, accompanied by boiled new potatoes (with parsley) and peas.

VARIATIONS Sprinkle the body cavity and skin with any herbs of your choice. Use olive oil instead of butter, and serve with Napolitana sauce.

If serving the fish cold, decorate it with slices of cucumber, overlapping them to achieve the effect of fish scales. Place stuffed olives in the eye cavities and arrange bunches of asparagus tips along the sides. Serve with herb mayonnaise* and a salad.

For cold salmon, serve the classic accompaniment of paper-thin slices of cucumber marinated in tarragon vinegar.

WHOLE BAKED FISH *A recipe suitable for a number of different types of fish.*

GEFILTE FISH

IF ONE WERE ASKED to name a traditional Jewish dish, almost certainly the first to come to mind would be gefilte fish. This dish was originally enjoyed in eastern Europe, where Jewish cooks made use of freshwater lake fish such as carp and bream.

The fish was chopped very finely and seasoned before being stuffed into the skin of a carp and poached in a jellied fish stock.

These days, however, cooks generally use ready minced fish, avoiding the arduous process of stuffing the skin. If possible, use at least three different types of fish – and preferably more – for the best results.

PREPARATION TIME: 35-45 MINUTES
COOKING TIME: 35-40 MINUTES
COOLING TIME: 2 HOURS

INGREDIENTS FOR SIX
1 kg (2¼ lb) fish, skinned and filleted*
2 medium-sized carrots
1 medium-sized onion, peeled and chopped*
2 tablespoons matzo meal, or a 10 cm (4 in) slice of white bread, crusts removed and soaked in water
2 eggs
1½ teaspoons salt
¼ teaspoon white pepper
1 tablespoon sugar
60-125 ml (2-4 fl oz) water
500 ml (17 fl oz) fish stock*

Mince together the fish, 1 carrot (grated), the onion, matzo meal or soaked bread, eggs, salt and pepper, sugar and water. With wet hands, form the mixture into balls about the size of small apples.

Place the balls and the remaining carrot (sliced) into the boiling fish stock, and cook gently for 35-40 minutes.

Arrange the balls in a large deep serving dish, place a slice of the carrot on top of each ball and pour the stock over. Allow to cool and place in the refrigerator until you are ready to serve them.

SERVING SUGGESTION Serve a potato salad dressed with vinaigrette*.

VARIATIONS Use one kind of fish only for a simple, everyday version.

The onion can be fried in 1 tablespoon oil before being added to the fish.

TUNA BAKED WITH ANCHOVIES AND GARLIC

THIS UNUSUAL TUNA DISH was originally devised in France during the 19th century. Although the recipe has subsequently been adapted, it has lost none of its original appeal. Use either fresh or frozen tuna.

PREPARATION TIME: 45 MINUTES
COOKING TIME: 1 HOUR
PREHEAT OVEN TO 180°C (350°F, MARK 4)

INGREDIENTS FOR FOUR
1 kg (2¼ lb) tuna steaks
1 tin (55 g/2 oz) flat anchovy fillets, soaked in cold water for 30 minutes
1 teaspoon basil
A little olive oil
2 bunches young spinach, well washed and trimmed
150 g (5 oz) tomatoes, skinned,* seeded and sliced
6 cloves garlic, crushed
2 onions, peeled and finely sliced*
1 large lemon, rind removed, and sliced
Salt and coarsely ground black pepper
250 ml (9 fl oz) dry white wine

Blanch the tuna by pouring boiling water over it, then pat dry with paper towels. 'Lard' the fish by making incisions in the flesh at 3 cm (1¼ in) intervals and filling them with the anchovy fillets (on only one side of the steak). Sprinkle both sides of the fish with dried basil.

Pour a little olive oil into the base of a casserole that is just large enough to accommodate the fish.

Line the bottom with half the spinach leaves, then layers of tomatoes (sprinkled with garlic), onions and lemon slices. Season and arrange the fish on top. Add a layer of shredded spinach and moisten with a little more olive oil. Cover with another layer of tomatoes (again sprinkled with garlic), onions, lemon and shredded spinach.

Pour over the wine, sprinkle with oil, and cover with aluminium foil or a lid. Cook at 180°C (350°F, mark 4) for about 1 hour. Remove the top layer of spinach and serve the contents hot from the dish.

SERVING SUGGESTION Serve the tuna with buttered new potatoes, sprinkled with freshly chopped parsley.

PRAWN CURRY

SEAFOODS ARE POPULAR along India's coastal areas, where prawns are flavoured with garlic and cooked in many ways. In this recipe, prawns are simmered gently in a thick tomato gravy and flavoured with aniseed. The prawn curry can be frozen for a month or more without losing its flavour.

PREPARATION TIME: 20 MINUTES
COOKING TIME: 35 MINUTES

INGREDIENTS FOR FOUR
800 g (1¾ lb) prawns, shelled*
1 teaspoon salt
4 cloves garlic
A 2 cm (¾ in) piece of fresh green ginger
60 ml (2 fl oz) sunflower oil
6 curry leaves
2 green chillies, sliced lengthways
2 medium-sized onions, peeled and chopped*
½ teaspoon chilli powder
¼ teaspoon turmeric
1 teaspoon aniseed, crushed
½ teaspoon coriander seeds, crushed
5 ripe tomatoes, skinned*
4 sprigs fresh coriander (dhania) leaves, chopped, for garnish

De-vein* and wash the prawns, patting them dry with paper towels. Sprinkle them with salt and then leave aside for 15 minutes. Meanwhile, peel and crush the garlic and ginger.

Heat the oil in a saucepan, add the curry leaves and green chillies, and allow to brown for 10 seconds. Add the onions and fry until translucent, then stir in the garlic and ginger.

Place the chilli powder, turmeric, aniseed and crushed coriander seeds in the saucepan and fry for 2 minutes.

Cut the tomatoes in half and add to the saucepan. Cover and simmer for 15 minutes on a medium heat. Place the prawns in the saucepan, stir and simmer gently for a further 15 minutes.

Garnish with the fresh coriander leaves and serve.

SERVING SUGGESTION Prawn curry is excellent with saffron rice or chapatis*.

For a complete Indian meal, add another dish such as Kesar Masala Murgh* and serve a selection of Indian accompaniments.

DE-VEINING AND SHELLING PRAWNS

Prawns are one of the world's great delicacies. Although once considered a luxury item, they are now more widely available for use in everyday cooking. Like all shellfish, they are low in kilojoules (calories). If using frozen prawns, thaw them completely before de-veining.

If the head is attached, use a sharp knife to slit the prawn from head to tail. If the head is not attached, use a pair of scissors.

Lift the vein with a cocktail stick and pull it out with your fingers.

To shell the prawn, pull off the tail shell, twist off the head, then peel off the body shell. It should come off in one piece.

SOLE VÉRONIQUE *A delicately flavoured and sophisticated dish – ideal for summertime entertainment.*

SOLE VÉRONIQUE

THIS IS A SUMMER CLASSIC that never fails to please. Delicately poached sole fillets are topped with a rich, creamy sauce containing pale green grapes which impart a subtle, fruity flavour to the sauce and provide a particularly interesting contrast in textures.

PREPARATION TIME: 1½ HOURS
(INCLUDING PEELING THE GRAPES)
COOKING TIME: 30 MINUTES

INGREDIENTS FOR FOUR TO SIX
10-12 fillets of sole
*1 small onion, peeled and finely chopped**
50 g (2 oz) butter
125 ml (4 fl oz) white wine
*200 ml (7 fl oz) fish stock**
1 teaspoon dried tarragon
Salt and freshly ground white pepper
1 egg yolk
*125 ml (4 fl oz) thick béchamel sauce**
60 ml (2 fl oz) cream
225 g (8 oz) green grapes
Boiling water

Peel the green grapes and extract the seeds using the looped end of a hair grip or a bent pin.

Sauté the onion in the butter (in a large pan) until soft and golden. Add the wine, stock and tarragon, simmer for 10 minutes, then strain. Meanwhile, season the fillets of sole lightly with salt and pepper, roll them up and fasten with a cocktail stick. Butter the cleaned pan lightly and arrange the fish rolls in it.

Pour over the strained stock, cover and poach the fish gently for 12-15 minutes, basting from time to time. Remove the cocktail sticks and arrange the soles carefully on a heated platter. Spoon a little of the stock over the fish. Cover with a lid or aluminium foil and keep warm.

Now reduce the fish stock to about a quarter, remove it from the heat, and strain. Beat the egg yolk into the béchamel sauce with the cream and add the reduced stock. Return to the heat to warm through (but not boil) and correct the seasoning if necessary

While the sauce is heating, warm the grapes in a little boiling water, drain and distribute around the fish. Pour over the cream sauce.

SERVING SUGGESTIONS Serve garnished with small clusters of grapes. The sauce can make this dish look a little bland and uninteresting, so a pretty floral or pale green platter provides a pleasant foil to the lemon-coloured sauce. Fresh tarragon makes an attractive garnish if you have some.

Rosti* would make a delicious accompaniment, but plain rice also complements the creamy sauce. It is best not to serve a great variety of vegetables with this dish, because the flavour is lost with too many distractions. A simple salad to follow is quite adequate.

VARIATIONS Although it is not strictly 'Véronique', a sliced crayfish or lobster tail or some prawns added to the sauce while warming is delicious.

Tinned grapes can be used when grapes are not in season, and these need no peeling. They are considerably sweeter than fresh grapes.

You could make a more substantial meal by using a large type of fish, cut into steaks. Allow one per person, and adjust the poaching time according to the size of the steaks.

SEAFOOD STEW

THIS DELICIOUS STEW has a distinctly Mediterranean flavour. The garlic and anchovy paste adds tremendous flavour to this rich and filling dish. Do not be tempted to omit any ingredients – each adds its own distinctive flavour to the overall taste.

PREPARATION TIME: 45 MINUTES
COOKING TIME: 35 MINUTES

INGREDIENTS FOR FOUR TO SIX
3 tablespoons sunflower oil
1 large onion, peeled and finely
    chopped*
1 clove garlic, crushed
250 ml (9 fl oz) dry white wine
1 large tin tomatoes (about
    800 g/28 oz)
1 small tin tomato paste
A pinch of sugar
1 bay leaf
2 teaspoons dried oregano
Salt and freshly ground black
    pepper
500 g (1 lb 2 oz) filleted firm white
    fish, cubed
500 g (1 lb 2 oz) shrimps or prawns,
    shelled*
1 crayfish tail, cut into 6 pieces
18 fresh mussels, cleaned* (or a
    small tin of mussels with shells)
500 g (1 lb 2 oz) cleaned calamari*
    (squid), sliced

For the anchovy and garlic paste:
4 tablespoons finely chopped
    parsley
4 cloves garlic, finely chopped
4 anchovy fillets, finely chopped
Finely grated rind of 1 lemon

For the garnish:
Parmesan cheese, grated
A few unshelled prawns

Heat the oil in a heavy casserole. Add the chopped onion and cook gently until softened. Stir in the clove of crushed garlic, then the wine, and reduce over a high heat. Add the tomatoes finely chopped, plus the juice from the tin, the tomato paste, sugar, bay leaf and 1 teaspoon of the oregano and seasoning.

Reduce the heat and simmer, half-covered, for 10 minutes. Add the white fish and cook for 5 minutes. Stir in the shrimps or prawns, crayfish and mussels, and cook (covered) for about 5 minutes (discarding any mussels that have not opened). Uncover the casserole and add the calamari. Cook for a minute or two until the calamari is opaque and tender. Add the remaining teaspoon of oregano and check the seasoning.

To make the anchovy and garlic paste, mix together the chopped parsley, garlic, anchovy fillets and lemon rind to form a paste. Serve the paste in a separate bowl.

SERVING SUGGESTION Serve with freshly cooked spaghettini – 500 g (1 lb 2 oz) should be enough. Toss the well-drained hot pasta in 4 tablespoons heated olive oil and a clove of crushed garlic. Turn onto a heated plate and pile the seafood stew on top. Pass around a bowl of Parmesan cheese with the anchovy and garlic paste.

SEAFOOD SALAD WITH MELON AND LEMON CREAM SAUCE

THIS WHITE, GREEN and pink salad looks most appetising and attractive with its pale, lemon-coloured sauce.

PREPARATION TIME: 1 HOUR
COOKING TIME: 45 MINUTES
COOLING TIME: 2 HOURS

INGREDIENTS FOR SIX TO EIGHT
500 g (1 lb 2 oz) monkfish, bream
    or snapper, filleted, skinned*
    and cut into 1 cm × 3 cm (about
    ½ in × 1¼ in) slices
500 ml (17 fl oz) well-flavoured fish
    stock*
250 g (9 oz) calamari (squid),
    cleaned* and cut into slices
    about 6 mm (¼ in) wide
100 ml (3½ fl oz) semi-sweet white
    wine
2 tablespoons lemon juice
30 g (1¼ oz) beurre manié*
Salt and freshly ground pepper
125 ml (4 fl oz) cream
1 teaspoon grated lemon rind
Watercress or shredded lettuce for
    garnish
1 tin (about 350-400 g/12-14 oz)
    prawns in brine (drained)
250 g (9 oz) green honeydew melon
    balls, chilled, or 250 g (9 oz) kiwi
    fruit, sliced and chilled
75 g (3 oz) pecan nuts or walnuts,
    coarsely chopped
75 g (3 oz) bean sprouts*, washed
    and picked over

Place the fish slices in a large saucepan and cover with the hot stock. Simmer over a gentle heat for 10 minutes (they must be done but not overcooked). Use a slotted spoon to transfer them to a dish, and leave to cool.

Cook the calamari rings in the same stock for about 3-5 minutes (until they turn opaque). Do not overcook, or they will toughen. Remove the calamari from the stock with a slotted spoon and leave to cool.

Now pour the wine into the stock, add the lemon juice, and reduce by half.

Thicken the boiling stock very slightly by gently adding the beurre manié.

Remove the sauce from the heat, strain it through muslin, and chill. When chilled thoroughly, season to taste. Whip the cream lightly and stir it into the sauce with the lemon rind. Correct the seasoning if necessary. Cover and chill while you arrange your salad platter.

Make a bed of well-washed fresh watercress or shredded lettuce on a large, preferably fish-shaped, dish (white and green are suitable colours). Arrange the fish, calamari, prawns, melon balls or kiwi fruit, nuts and bean sprouts on the greens, cover with plastic wrap, and chill. Serve cold but not icy (cellar temperature describes it well) with the lemon sauce.

If you are serving at the table, ladle some of the sauce onto a plate and serve the salad on top of the sauce, garnished with watercress.

Alternatively, make up servings ahead of time with the salad arranged attractively on individual platters, and serve the rest of the sauce in a sauceboat.

SERVING SUGGESTIONS This salad is very good as a separate fish course after a light soup, as a starter, or as a light lunch dish served with fresh French bread.

VARIATIONS Almost any well-flavoured, fairly firm-textured fish (crayfish or bream) can be used as a substitute for monkfish.

The dark green of the watercress contrasts beautifully with the lemon sauce and melon balls, but if you are using lettuce, enhance the colour with a few parsley sprigs.

Cherry tomatoes or sliced celery can replace the melon balls – but in this case the colour scheme will be different, and not quite as appealing. Watermelon is too sweet, and the flavour of cantaloup melon is not suitable for the dish.

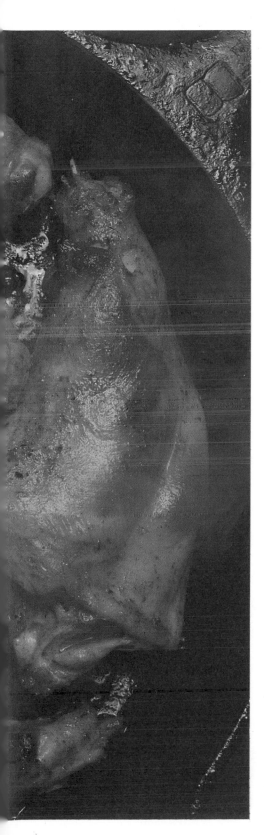

MEAT

M EAT IS LIKELY TO BE the most expensive item on your grocery list and is often the centrepiece of the meal. As such, it is important to ensure that it is not ruined by overcooking or by using the incorrect cooking method for a particular cut. Recipes taken from the culinary traditions of many countries will help you to make the best of whatever meat you buy – from the most expensive fillet steak down to oxtail for an economical stew.

One of the greatest pleasures of cooking with meat is that it lends itself so well to innovation. For a delicious change from traditional family favourites such as roast beef and Yorkshire pudding, try some of the more exotic recipes – vitello tonnato (an Italian veal dish with tuna sauce), stir-fried beef with oyster sauce or a mutton biriani served with a selection of Malay accompaniments.

ROAST BEEF AND YORKSHIRE PUDDING

THIS MOST FAMOUS of English dishes has become popular in many parts of the world. In Yorkshire it was (and in some places still is) the custom to serve the pudding with gravy as a first course to help blunt hearty appetites. Other cooks serve it with the meat.

PREPARATION TIME: 20 MINUTES
COOKING TIME: 1¼-2¼ HOURS
PREHEAT OVEN TO 220°C (425°F, MARK 7)

INGREDIENTS FOR SIX
1.5-2 kg (3-4½ lb) joint of roasting beef
2 tablespoons dripping or lard

For the Yorkshire pudding:
125 g (4¼ oz) flour
¼ teaspoon salt
2 large eggs
200 ml (7 fl oz) milk
2 tablespoons cold water

For the gravy:
1 tablespoon flour
300 ml (½ pint) beef basic stock*

Wipe the joint and put it in a baking dish with the dripping or lard. Roast for 15 minutes, then reduce the oven temperature to 190°C (375°F, mark 5). Continue roasting the meat for a further 15 minutes per 500 g (1 lb 2 oz) for rare beef, and 20 minutes per 500 g (1 lb 2 oz) for medium-rare beef.

To make the Yorkshire pudding, sieve the flour and salt into a large basin and make a well in the centre. Break the eggs into the well and add a little of the milk. With a wooden spoon gradually draw in the flour, and mix the ingredients together, adding milk a little at a time until you have a thick batter. Beat with the wooden spoon until the batter is smooth, then stir in the remaining milk. Leave the mixture to stand for about 1 hour, or until the meat is cooked. Remove the joint from the oven and keep it hot.

Increase the oven temperature to 230°C (450°F, mark 8). Cover the bottom of a baking dish with a thin layer of fat from the roast, and put it in the oven until the fat is smoking hot. Quickly stir the batter, mix in the cold water and pour it into the dish. Bake on the top shelf of the oven for 25 minutes, until the batter has

risen and is crisp and golden-brown.

While the Yorkshire pudding is cooking, make the gravy in the baking dish. Pour off almost all the fat, but retain the brown juices. Mix the flour into the juices until smooth, then gradually add the stock, stirring continuously to loosen any meaty residue. Place the dish over a gentle heat and continue stirring until the gravy thickens and comes to the boil.

As soon as the Yorkshire pudding is cooked, cut it into squares and arrange them around the joint.

SERVING SUGGESTION Roast potatoes and a green vegetable are excellent accompaniments to roast beef.

VARIATIONS If you like, you can make small puddings in a bun (muffin) tray instead of one large pudding. Put 1 teaspoon fat from the baking dish into each section and put the tray in the top of the oven until the fat is smoking hot. Put 2 tablespoons batter into each section and bake for 15 minutes.

For a thinner gravy, omit the flour and strengthen the gravy by reducing over a high heat. Substitute red wine for half the stock to enrich the flavour.

ROAST BEEF AND YORKSHIRE PUDDING *A traditional English recipe that is enjoyed worldwide.*

BEEF STROGANOFF

THIS IS ONE of the best-known Russian recipes, created during the 19th century. The dish is made from slender strips of beef fillet, cut across the grain. They are sautéed very quickly in butter and oil so that they are brown on the outside but still rare inside. The meat strips are then mixed into a delicious sour cream and mushroom sauce.

PREPARATION TIME: 45 MINUTES
COOKING TIME: 20 MINUTES

INGREDIENTS FOR FOUR
750 g (1 lb 10 oz) fillet of beef
2-3 onions, peeled and thinly sliced*
30 g (1¼ oz) butter
200 g (7 oz) mushrooms, sliced
Salt and freshly ground pepper
250 ml (9 fl oz) sour cream, or fresh cream soured with juice of ½ lemon

Cut the fillet into strips across the grain (they should be about the size of your little finger).

Slowly fry the onion in butter until golden-brown, then remove and keep warm. Fry the mushrooms in the same pan and add to the onion.

Increase the heat and quickly fry half of the beef in the very hot frying pan (3-4 minutes on each side) so that the juices are firmly sealed in and the meat is lightly browned outside and rare inside.

Lift the first batch of meat out and set it aside while frying the second batch in the really hot pan. Return all the meat to the pan, season well with salt and freshly ground pepper, add the onion and mushrooms, and stir together for 1 or 2 minutes.

Pour in the cream, bring quickly to the boil, and serve immediately.

SERVING SUGGESTION Spoon over boiled rice or buttered noodles.

VARIATIONS Add 1 tablespoon brandy and 1 tablespoon tomato paste to the cream sauce.

For a slightly different dish, sauté 1 cm (½ in) thick slices of beef fillet in butter to seal, and add 2 tablespoons brandy, sour cream, seasoning and lemon juice. Serve with buttered baby potatoes and green beans or mushrooms.

Strips of pork fillet can be treated in the same way.

FILLET STEAK CARAMEL

THE PREPARATION AND GRILLING of fillet steak have started many arguments, some people claiming it should be seared for a matter of seconds and served immediately, and others maintaining that it should be 'properly' cooked to enjoy the true flavour. Whatever your choice, avoid overcooking the meat.

PREPARATION TIME: 30 MINUTES
COOKING TIME: 5-10 MINUTES
PREHEAT OVEN TO 110°C (225°F, MARK ¼)

INGREDIENTS FOR SIX
6 pieces of fillet steak, cut 4 cm (1½ in) thick
Freshly ground black pepper
2 tablespoons sugar
30 g (1¼ oz) butter
Coarse salt

Preheat a plate in the oven. Gently pound the steaks with a wooden mallet, reducing their thickness by a third. Grind pepper over both sides and allow to stand while you prepare the caramel.

Heat a heavy frying pan until it is extremely hot. Test the heat by dropping a few grains of sugar onto the pan: if the grains go up in smoke, the pan is ready.

Scatter 1 tablespoon of the sugar in the pan. When it blackens (after a few seconds), drop half the butter into the pan: it will caramelise immediately. Place 3 of the steaks in the pan and allow them to sizzle for a minute, then turn and sizzle for another minute.

If you prefer your steaks rare, remove them from the pan at this stage, transfer to the preheated plate in the oven and leave to stand for 5 minutes. Reheat the pan, and repeat the process for the other 3 steaks. While this is being done, sprinkle a little salt over the steaks in the oven: they will 'relax' and release a small amount of delicious gravy.

For those who prefer their steak well done, double the cooking time (turning the meat frequently).

BRAISED BEEFBURGERS WITH VEGETABLES

THIS COMBINATION of beefburgers and fresh vegetables takes a while to prepare, but it makes a nourishing meal with an interesting variety of flavours to tempt the palate.

PREPARATION TIME: 45 MINUTES
COOKING TIME: 1 HOUR

INGREDIENTS FOR FOUR
1 kg (2¼ lb) lean beef mince
1 egg, beaten
2 large handfuls finely chopped celery leaves
1 onion, peeled* and grated
1 teaspoon Worcestershire sauce
1 tablespoon tomato sauce
1 tablespoon chutney
1 teaspoon dried thyme
1 teaspoon salt
Freshly ground black pepper
1 thick slice wholemeal bread, crumbled
125 ml (4 fl oz) water
2 tablespoons sunflower oil
1 onion, peeled and thinly sliced*
6 medium-sized carrots, scraped and sliced
3 or 4 turnips, peeled and diced
4 parsnips, peeled and diced
4 potatoes, peeled and quartered
250 ml (9 fl oz) beef basic stock*
Beurre manié*
Finely chopped parsley for garnish

Mix the beef mince with the egg, celery, grated onion, sauces, chutney, thyme, salt and pepper. Soak the crumbled bread in the water and add to the meat mixture.

Form the mixture into 12-16 patties and fry in a casserole or heavy saucepan in the hot oil (6-8 at a time) until they are lightly browned on both sides. Return all the patties to the casserole or saucepan and add the remaining vegetables with a little more seasoning.

Pour in the beef stock. Cover tightly and simmer for about 40 minutes, adding a little more stock only if necessary. Once everything is tender, thicken the sauce with beurre manié, then check the seasoning. Sprinkle generously with chopped parsley and serve.

SERVING SUGGESTION Pasta shells, tossed in butter and black pepper, would go well with the beefburgers. For a family meal, serve mashed potato.

STIR-FRIED BEEF IN OYSTER SAUCE *Beef cooked in the oriental way.*

STIR-FRIED BEEF WITH OYSTER SAUCE

THE TASTE OF RICH, dark brown oyster sauce predominates in this dish. The sauce is used in stir-fried dishes in place of soy sauce, or to complement it. In Chinese recipes, beef is generally cut into very fine slices. Put the meat in the freezer for 30 minutes beforehand to make slicing easier.

PREPARATION TIME: 30 MINUTES
COOKING TIME: 15 MINUTES

INGREDIENTS FOR SIX
750 g (1 lb 10 oz) boneless lean beef
3 spring onions, thinly sliced
3 tablespoons soy sauce
3 tablespoons water
5 teaspoons cornflour
5 teaspoons dry sherry
½ teaspoon salt
3 tablespoons sunflower oil
3 tablespoons oyster sauce
1¼ teaspoons sugar

Cut the meat (with the grain) into 4 cm (1½ in) strips. Cut each strip across the grain into slices 5 mm (¼ in) thick. Combine the spring onions, soy sauce, water, cornflour, sherry and salt with the beef, mixing to coat it well. Allow to marinate for 15 minutes.

Place a wok or heavy frying pan over a high heat and add half the oil. When the oil is hot enough to ripple as the wok or pan is tilted from side to side, add half the meat mixture and stir-fry until browned. Remove from the wok or pan. Repeat the process using the remaining oil and the other half of the meat mixture.

Return all the cooked meat to the wok or frying pan, add the oyster sauce and sugar, and stir-fry for 1 minute. Serve on a heated dish. Accompany with fried rice.

VARIATION Substitute boned, skinned, sliced chicken breasts for the beef. Stir-fry until just cooked through.

For a more economical dish, replace some of the beef with strips of green pepper or thin slices of carrot.

CORNISH PASTIES

ONE OF THE MANY SAYINGS told in Devon is that if the Devil crossed the Tamar – the river dividing Devon from Cornwall – the Cornish would make him into a pasty. Perhaps this is a reference to the 'horns' of the Cornish pasty.

The pastry for a pasty used to be cut over a dinner plate, so it was quite a hefty size. It was the custom to mark one corner with an initial so that the half-eaten pasty could be claimed later.

PREPARATION TIME: 30 MINUTES
COOKING TIME: 40 MINUTES
PREHEAT OVEN TO 220°C (425°F, MARK 7)

INGREDIENTS FOR 4 PASTIES
350 g (¾ lb) chuck steak, diced
Shortcrust pastry* using 450 g (1 lb) flour
4 medium-sized potatoes, peeled
1 medium-sized onion, peeled* and diced
125 g (4¼ oz) swede, peeled and diced
Parsley, roughly chopped (optional)
50 g (2 oz) butter
Salt and pepper
1 egg, beaten, for glazing

Roll out the pastry to about 5 mm (¼ in) thick and cut out four 15 cm (6 in) rounds.

Cut the potatoes into very fine wafers. Put a few pieces of potato in the centre of each pastry round.

Cover the potato with some diced onion and diced swede, and then some of the diced meat. If using parsley, add it now. Dot with the butter. Season well and cover with more potato slices to prevent it from drying.

Dampen the edges of the pastry and fold each round over to make a half-moon shape. Turn the edges round a little to make 'horns'.

Pinch and crimp the pastry edges into ridges to give a rope-like effect. Glaze with beaten egg and put the pasties on a greased baking tray.

Bake in the preheated oven for 10 minutes. Lower the heat to 180°C (350°F, mark 4), and then continue to cook for 30 minutes until golden.

The pasties are delicious hot or cold. They will stay warm for an hour or two if you wrap them up in a tea towel, and make an ideal basis for a picnic.

VITELLO TONNATO *is a veal-based Italian speciality that makes a perfect dish for a summer's day.*

VITELLO TONNATO

ITALIANS CONSIDER vitello tonnato to be something of a luxury dish, and it is certainly a culinary delight – a classic cold dish that is especially suitable for an elegant buffet. It combines veal with a delicious tuna sauce.

PREPARATION TIME: 25 MINUTES
COOKING TIME: 1½-2 HOURS
INGREDIENTS FOR EIGHT
1.5 kg (3 lb 3 oz) veal (fillet end of leg)
1 tin (55 g/2 oz) flat anchovy fillets, drained
1 large clove garlic
2 carrots, peeled and chopped
3 stalks celery, chopped
2 onions, peeled and chopped*
1.25 litres (2¼ pints) water
2 chicken stock cubes

375 ml (13 fl oz) dry white wine
6 sprigs parsley

For the tuna sauce:
4 teaspoons capers
180 ml (6 fl oz) sunflower oil
1 egg yolk
1 tin (200 g/7 oz) tuna in oil
2 tablespoons lemon juice
Salt and pepper

For the garnish:
Salad greens
Black olives, stoned
Lemon slices or wedges

Using the tip of a sharp knife, make small cuts along the length of the veal. Cut 4 anchovy fillets into 1 cm (½ in) pieces, then insert these into the veal with garlic slivers.

Place the veal in a saucepan, cover with cold water, bring to the boil and boil (uncovered) for 1 minute. Pour off the water and rinse the veal thoroughly under cold water.

Place the carrots, celery and onions in a saucepan with the veal, water, crumbled stock cubes, wine and parsley. Bring to the boil, reduce the heat and simmer (partly covered) for 1½-2 hours, or until the veal is tender. Remove the veal from the stock and leave it to cool. You only need to reserve about 60 ml (2 fl oz) stock for the sauce.

To make the sauce, allow the reserved stock to cool, then purée in a blender or food processor together with the sauce ingredients until it is all well mixed.

Cut the cooled veal into thin slices. Dip the slices in the sauce and arrange in overlapping slices around a platter. Spoon on extra sauce. Before serving, garnish the centre of the platter with salad greens, and arrange black olives and lemon slices around the edge.

53

Osso Buco

THIS DISH IS A WELL-LOVED speciality of Milan in Italy – the name means 'hollow bone'. Veal, the prime ingredient, is easily Italy's favourite meat. Ask your butcher to cut the meat into pieces for you to make the preparation easier.

PREPARATION TIME: 20 MINUTES
COOKING TIME: 1½-2 HOURS
PREHEAT OVEN TO 180°C (350°F, MARK 4)

INGREDIENTS FOR SIX

2 kg (4½ lb) veal shanks or knuckles (cut into 6 cm/2½ in pieces by your butcher)
Flour for dusting
Salt and freshly ground black pepper
90 g (3½ oz) butter
2 carrots, peeled and coarsely chopped
3 stalks celery, sliced
*2 large onions, peeled and coarsely chopped**
4 cloves garlic, crushed
60 ml (2½ fl oz) sunflower oil
2 tins (each 425 g/15 oz) tomatoes
*500 ml (17 fl oz) beef basic stock**
125 ml (4 fl oz) dry white wine
1 teaspoon basil
1 teaspoon thyme
1 bay leaf
A 2.5 cm (1 in) strip of lemon rind

For the garnish:
1 teaspoon grated lemon rind
3 tablespoons freshly chopped parsley
4 cloves garlic, chopped

Dust the meat with flour and season with salt and black pepper.

Heat 30 g (1¼ oz) of the butter in a pan. Add the carrots, celery, onions and garlic, and cook gently until the onions turn golden. Transfer to a large ovenproof casserole with a lid.

Heat the remaining butter and oil in a large frying pan, add the veal and lightly brown it on all sides. Carefully pack the veal on top of the vegetables in the ovenproof dish (stand shanks upright to retain the marrow in the bones).

Pour away all the fat from the pan in which the meat was cooked. Pour in the tinned tomatoes (and their juice). Add the stock, wine, basil, thyme, bay leaf and lemon rind. Season, bring to the boil and simmer for a few moments.

Pour the sauce over the veal and vegetables, cover the casserole and bake in the preheated oven (stirring occasionally) for 1½ hours – or until the veal is very tender.

Before serving, mix together the garnish ingredients, which constitute 'gremolata', the classic Italian seasoning, and sprinkle over the dish.

SERVING SUGGESTION Arrange the osso buco on a bed of boiled pasta or rice, before garnishing.

Saltimbocca alla Romana

THIS POPULAR AND TASTY Italian dish can be prepared using either thin veal escalopes or beef steaks. If you have a friendly butcher, ask him to pound them as thinly as possible for you.

PREPARATION TIME: 15 MINUTES
COOKING TIME: 10 MINUTES

INGREDIENTS FOR SIX

8 veal escalopes or beef steaks, pounded thinly
90 g (3½ oz) butter
150 g (5 oz) mushrooms, sliced
8 thin slices ham
4 slices mozzarella cheese, halved
4 tablespoons grated Parmesan or Cheddar cheese
Salt and freshly ground black pepper
2 large cloves garlic, crushed
½ teaspoon dried sage
60 ml (2 fl oz) sunflower oil

Pat the escalopes or steaks dry with paper towels. Melt 30 g (1¼ oz) of the butter in a saucepan and add the mushrooms. Cook gently until tender, then drain and discard the pan juices from the mushrooms.

Place a slice of ham and mozzarella on each escalope or steak. Divide the cooked mushrooms into 8 portions and arrange on top of the mozzarella.

Sprinkle Parmesan or Cheddar, salt, black pepper, crushed garlic and dried sage on each escalope, then roll them up and secure with toothpicks or metal skewers.

Heat the oil and remaining butter and fry (on a medium heat) for 4 minutes. Serve immediately

SERVING SUGGESTIONS Serve with pasta or rice steamed with wine, chicken stock and herbs, and whole spinach leaves stir-fried with a little olive oil and garlic.

Blanquette de Veau

BLANQUETTE IS THE TRADITIONAL name for stews which are made from white meats and coated with a smooth white sauce. This recipe is for veal with a creamy mushroom sauce.

PREPARATION TIME: 30 MINUTES
COOKING TIME: 1½ HOURS

INGREDIENTS FOR FOUR

1 kg (2¼ lb) boneless veal, cut into 2 cm (¾ in) strips
200 g (7 oz) button mushrooms, washed
1-2 tablespoons lemon juice
60 ml (2 fl oz) water
45 g (1¾ oz) butter
Salt and freshly ground black pepper
3 medium-sized carrots, scraped and cut into 2 cm (¾ in) lengths
*2 medium-sized onions, peeled**
4 cloves
A pinch of mixed herbs
*1 bouquet garni**
1 bay leaf
1 tablespoon flour
80 ml (2½ fl oz) cream
2 egg yolks
Freshly grated nutmeg
Chopped parsley

Cut the meat into 2 cm (¾ in) strips and set aside. Mix the mushrooms with most of the lemon juice, the water, 15 g (½ oz) of the butter and seasoning in a small saucepan. Cover and boil for 1 minute.

Arrange the meat in a heavy-based saucepan and strain the mushroom liquid over it with enough cold water to cover the meat by 2 cm (¾ in). Add salt and bring to the boil. Skim the top 2 or 3 times, taking off any foam and adding a little extra water if necessary.

Add the carrots, the onions studded with the cloves, the mixed herbs, bouquet garni and bay leaf, making sure all are completely under water.

Simmer very gently for about 1 hour, or until the meat is tender. Strain the liquid through a sieve and reserve. Pick out the onions, cloves, bouquet garni and carrots. Put the carrots on one side.

Melt the remaining butter in a clean saucepan, stir in the flour and cook for 1 minute without browning.

Slowly add the meat liquid and bring to the boil, stirring continuously to make a smooth sauce. Simmer for 10 minutes or until the sauce is thick enough to lightly coat the meat.

Meanwhile, mix together the cream and egg yolks with pepper and nutmeg, and carefully stir in 2 tablespoons of the sauce. Remove the sauce from the heat and whisk the egg mixture into it. Reheat it gently, check the seasoning, add the meat and mushrooms (and chopped carrots if liked) and stir well. Sprinkle with parsley and serve.

SERVING SUGGESTION This dish is best served with something simple such as rice or buttered noodles with a sprinkling of poppy seeds. Add colour to a blanquette meal by serving small bunches of green beans which have been bound together with a thin strip of bacon and lightly boiled until just tender.

VARIATION Give leftover roast chicken the blanquette treatment by coating with the same sauce, but using chicken stock instead of the meat liquid. Serve sprinkled with grated Parmesan cheese and finely chopped parsley.

BEEF OR VEAL OLIVES

BEEF OR VEAL OLIVES made their earliest appearances in the Middle Ages, alongside such delicacies as pudding of porpoise and morsels of whale. The 'olives' consist of meat slices wrapped around herb stuffing and baked.

PREPARATION TIME: 30 MINUTES
COOKING TIME: 40 MINUTES
PREHEAT OVEN TO 170°C (340°F, MARK 3½)

INGREDIENTS FOR FOUR
6 thin frying beef steaks, or 6 large
    veal escalopes
600 ml (21 fl oz) brown stock*
25 g (1 oz) butter
25 g (1 oz) flour
3 tablespoons sherry

For the stuffing:
125 g (4¼ oz) fine white
    breadcrumbs
2 anchovy fillets, mashed and
    pounded in a mortar or with a
    wooden spoon in a small bowl
1 teaspoon dried thyme
½ teaspoon dried sage
1 small onion, peeled and very
    finely chopped*
1 egg, well beaten
Salt and pepper

VEAL OLIVES 'Parcels' of herb stuffing wrapped in veal.

First make the stuffing by mixing all the ingredients in a bowl. Form the mixture into 12 small balls.

Pound the steaks or escalopes with the back of a heavy knife to flatten them. Trim off any fat and cut each piece in two lengthways. You should have 12 pieces, each about 6 cm × 12 cm (2¼ in × 5 in).

Place a ball of stuffing on each, and roll the meat tightly around it. Tie each olive round the middle with fine string.

Lightly grease a shallow ovenproof dish and lay the olives in it so that they touch each other (this helps them to stay in shape). Pour the stock over the olives, cover the dish closely with foil, and cook in the preheated oven for 40 minutes.

Lift the olives very carefully onto a warm serving dish, reserving the stock. Snip the strings with scissors and pull them away. Keep the olives warm and covered while you prepare the gravy.

Make a roux* with the butter and flour, stir in the stock and bring to the boil. Add the sherry and check the seasoning. Pour the gravy over the olives and serve immediately.

SERVING SUGGESTION Serve the olives with pommes gratin dauphinois* and buttered leeks.

VARIATION Change the character of the olives by using a rasher of finely minced bacon in the place of the anchovies. Replace the thyme and sage with basil and marjoram in the herb stuffing.

WIENER SCHNITZEL

THESE QUICK AND EASY veal treats – and their equally delicious variations – have long been popular items on restaurant menus throughout the world. The secret to making successful schnitzels lies in chilling them to ensure that the crumbs adhere well.

PREPARATION TIME: 15 MINUTES
CHILLING TIME: 1 HOUR
COOKING TIME: 10 MINUTES

INGREDIENTS FOR FOUR
8 thin slices leg of veal
Salt and freshly ground pepper
Flour for coating
2 eggs, beaten
Fine dried breadcrumbs for
    coating
Sunflower oil, clarified butter* or
    ghee
8 lemon wedges or slices

First prepare the schnitzels for frying. Place the veal slices between sheets of greaseproof paper and pound with a rolling pin to flatten them evenly. Season with salt and pepper. Dip in the flour and shake off the surplus, then dip in the egg followed by the breadcrumbs. Dip again into egg and breadcrumbs to ensure an all-over coating. Chill in the refrigerator for at least an hour so that the crumb coating will adhere during frying.

Fry in hot oil, clarified butter or ghee over a medium heat until golden-brown on both sides.

As you finish frying each schnitzel, place them onto bunched-up paper towels to drain off the excess fat. Keep them warm, and when they are all cooked, arrange on a large oval dish and garnish with the lemon wedges or slices.

SERVING SUGGESTIONS Sautéed potatoes, buttered green beans or young peas make good accompaniments.

VARIATIONS Use skinned and filleted chicken breast instead of the veal.

To make veal cordon bleu, sandwich a slice of baked ham and Gruyère cheese between 2 pounded veal escalopes, then dip in the prepared coating.

Cover each fried escalope with a slice of ham and a slice of mozzarella cheese. Place in a hot oven at 220°C (425°F, mark 7) for a few minutes until the cheese has melted. Serve immediately.

HONEYED LAMB

THE MARRIAGE OF LAMB and honey is a particularly successful one, especially when a few fresh herbs are added to heighten the subtle flavour of the dish.

PREPARATION TIME: 10 MINUTES
COOKING TIME: 1¼ HOURS
PREHEAT OVEN TO 230°C (450°F, MARK 8)

INGREDIENTS FOR SIX
1.5-2 kg (3-4½ lb) shoulder of lamb
1 clove garlic
Salt and freshly ground black
    pepper
4 tablespoons honey
500 ml (17 fl oz) cider
1 teaspoon chopped fresh mint
1¼ teaspoons chopped fresh thyme
1 tablespoon flour
1 teaspoon lemon juice

Line a baking dish with a piece of aluminium foil large enough to wrap over the top of the joint. Rub the meat all over with the clove of garlic. Place the joint in the dish and season well with salt and freshly ground pepper.

Mix the honey with 300 ml (½ pint) of the cider, and pour the mixture over the joint. Sprinkle the top with the chopped mint and thyme. Fold the foil loosely over the joint and cook in the preheated oven for 30 minutes. Open the foil and baste with the remaining cider.

Close up the foil again, reduce the oven temperature to 180°C (350°F, mark 4) and cook for a further hour, folding back the foil to brown the meat after 30 minutes. Remove the meat from the oven, place in a serving dish, and keep it hot, back in the oven again.

To make the gravy, pour the juices from the baking dish into a small saucepan, leave to stand for 5 minutes, then skim off the fat from the surface. Blend the flour in a basin with 60 ml (2 fl oz) of the juices, then stir the gravy back into the saucepan.

Bring to the boil, stirring constantly until smooth and thickened. Season with salt and pepper, and stir in the lemon juice. Serve the gravy piping hot in a sauceboat with the joint, so that people can help themselves.

SERVING SUGGESTION Baked onions* and boiled new potatoes sprinkled with mint, together with creamed cabbage* or carrots, are excellent with honeyed lamb.

MUTTON BIRIANI

BIRIANI IS A TRADITIONAL Indian rice dish. Made here with mutton or lamb, it will appeal to those with an adventurous palate and a penchant for spicy food.

PREPARATION TIME: 1 HOUR
COOKING TIME: 2½ HOURS

INGREDIENTS FOR SIX
1.5 kg (3 lb 3 oz) mutton or lamb
4 medium-sized onions, peeled and
    sliced*
125 ml (4 fl oz) sunflower oil
A 2.5 cm (1 in) piece of fresh green
    ginger
3 cloves garlic
6 cinnamon sticks
4 cardamom seeds
6 cloves
6 allspice berries
3 chillies, seeded and sliced
2 teaspoons ground coriander
2 teaspoons garam masala
5 medium-sized potatoes, peeled
    and sliced
250 g (9 oz) rice
Salt
100 g (3¾ oz) brown lentils
6 eggs, hard-boiled*
125 g (4¼ oz) butter
1 teaspoon saffron

Wash the mutton or lamb and cut into cubes. Sauté the onions in half the oil, together with pounded ginger and garlic, cinnamon, cardamom, cloves, allspice and chillies. Cook until the onions are golden. Add the meat, coriander and garam masala.

Fry the potato slices in the remaining oil. Boil the rice in salted water (uncovered) until nearly soft, then strain and steam the rice in a colander. If preferred, you can add the rice to the meat at this stage and mix them together.

Boil the lentils until soft, and slice the eggs. Spoon a layer of rice into a large saucepan and then, in sequence, the potatoes, meat mixture, eggs and lentils. Repeat, ending with a layer of rice mixed with the butter and saffron.

Cover with a tight-fitting lid and place over a very low heat. Allow the biriani to steam or simmer very slowly for 1 hour. Do not remove the lid until the moment that you are ready to serve so that the food remains piping hot. Offer chapati* and sambals* as accompaniments.

CROWN ROAST OF LAMB

THE ELEGANT CROWN ROAST of lamb was particularly fashionable at small country-house dinners in Edwardian times. A crown needs special preparation, so you may find you have to order it from your butcher in advance.

PREPARATION TIME: 30 MINUTES
COOKING TIME: 1½ HOURS
PREHEAT OVEN TO 200°C (400°F, MARK 6)

INGREDIENTS FOR FOUR
Crown of 12 best-end-of-neck lamb cutlets
75 g (3 oz) butter

For the sauce:
300 ml (½ pint) gravy
2 teaspoons redcurrant jelly
2 tablespoons sherry

For the filling:
500 g (1 lb 2 oz) stuffing of your choice, or 500 g (1 lb 2 oz) hot mixed vegetables simmered together in salted water until tender. Choose a wide selection of vegetables such as green peas, diced carrots, diced turnips, sliced celery, sliced courgettes (zucchini), tiny new potatoes, tiny onions and florets of cauliflower

Place the butter in small pieces in a baking dish large enough to hold the roast and stand the crown upright. If you are using stuffing for the filling, spoon the mixture into the centre of the crown before roasting. If using vegetables, cook the meat without the filling.

Place the roast in the preheated oven for 15 minutes. Reduce the heat to 180°C (350°C, mark 4) and roast for another 1¼ hours. While the crown is cooking, baste the top of the stuffing repeatedly with the dripping from the dish, or prepare the alternative filling.

To make the sauce, heat the gravy thoroughly in a small pan and stir in the redcurrant jelly and sherry.

Lift the cooked crown carefully onto a hot serving dish and, if not filled with stuffing, spoon the very hot mixed-vegetable filling into the centre.

If the crown is filled with stuffing, you can put small heaps of vegetables (as suggested for the filling) around it. Serve the sauce separately.

SERVING SUGGESTION For a dinner party, top each rib bone with a paper frill.

VARIATION Omit the gravy and serve the crown roast with Hollandaise sauce*.

CROWN ROAST OF LAMB *This elegant-looking dish is one of the most delicious ways of eating lamb cutlets.*

GREEK LAMB WITH YOGHURT *This is an ideal dish for those with a palate for herbs and garlic-flavoured meat.*

GREEK LAMB WITH YOGHURT

EVERY COOK'S REPERTOIRE should include this recipe. Its preparation is
easy: a strongly garlic-flavoured joint of
lamb is smeared with herb butter before
baking and served with rich gravy.

Yoghurt is used frequently in Greek
cookery and has long been recognised as
an aid to the digestion. Here, it serves to
counteract the richness of the roast lamb
as a refreshing sauce.

PREPARATION TIME: 20 MINUTES
COOKING TIME: 1 HOUR 40 MINUTES
PREHEAT OVEN TO 180°C (350°F, MARK 4)

INGREDIENTS FOR SIX TO EIGHT
*1.5-2 kg (3-4½ lb) leg of lamb
3-4 cloves garlic
50 g (2 oz) butter, softened
1 tablespoon chopped rosemary
1 tablespoon chopped thyme
Salt and freshly ground black
  pepper
Juice of 1 lemon*

For the gravy:
*2 teaspoons flour
250 ml (9 fl oz) vegetable or basic
  stock*, or wine
Salt and freshly ground black
  pepper*

For the sauce:
*200 ml (7 fl oz) natural yoghurt
2 cloves garlic, crushed
2 teaspoons chopped chives
2 teaspoons chopped mint
Salt and freshly ground black
  pepper*

Make little knife slits all over the outer
skin of the lamb and press in the garlic,
cut into slivers. Beat the softened butter
with rosemary, thyme and seasoning,
and spread it all over the meat. Pour over
the lemon juice.

Roast the meat on a rack over a baking
dish allowing 20-25 minutes for each
500 g (1 lb 2 oz), basting from time to
time. Transfer the meat to a serving dish
and leave to 'set' in a warm oven for
15-20 minutes.

To make the gravy, pour off any excess

fat from the baking dish and stir in the
flour to mop up the remaining fat.

Cook for 1 minute, then add the stock
or wine, and season with salt and freshly
ground black pepper.

Bring to the boil, strain and keep hot.
To make the sauce, mix all the ingredients together and season well. Serve
slices of meat topped with a spoonful of
gravy and a dollop of yoghurt sauce.

SERVING SUGGESTIONS This dish is perfect with rice or baked potatoes, green
beans or broccoli, or a Greek salad*.

VARIATION Spread the lamb with fresh
white breadcrumbs (from 2 slices of
bread) mixed with 1 teaspoon mixed
herbs, grated rind of 1 lemon, 50 g (2 oz)
butter, 8 chopped olives, ¾ teaspoon salt
and a dash of pepper. Roast without
basting the joint so that the breadcrumbs
form a crisp, golden crust.

The yogurt sauce is a delicious foil to
all kinds of roast and barbecued meats.
Serve it with lamb chops that have been
smeared with herb butter and grilled over
charcoal, or with grilled steaks.

GIEMA CURRY

GIEMA CURRY is a Malay dish made of minced meat. As any convert to spicy foods will tell you, Malay curry made at home – with fresh ingredients – has a rich flavour all its own.

PREPARATION TIME: 30 MINUTES
COOKING TIME: 1¼ HOURS

INGREDIENTS FOR SIX

1 kg (2¼ lb) minced mutton or beef
2 large onions, peeled and chopped*
2 tablespoons sunflower oil
2 cloves garlic
A 2 cm (1 in) piece of fresh green ginger
A few cinnamon sticks
A few cardamom seeds
A few cloves
A few allspice berries
2 teaspoons turmeric
1 tablespoon paprika
1 teaspoon ground fennel
1 teaspoon ground cumin seeds
1 teaspoon ground coriander
2 large tomatoes, skinned* and mashed
2 chillies, chopped
3 large potatoes, peeled and sliced
Salt
450 g (1 lb) peas, fresh or frozen (optional)

Cook the onions in a saucepan with the oil and pounded garlic and ginger, and add the cinnamon, cardamom, cloves and allspice. Allow the mixture to brown.

Add the meat to the onion mixture, stir and cook (uncovered) for 30 minutes, or until tender. Mix the rest of the spices with the tomato pulp and chillies, then add to the meat, together with the potatoes. Simmer slowly for about 25 minutes until the potatoes are soft, and season with salt.

Add the peas (if used) at this stage and continue simmering the dish until done (5-10 minutes).

ACCOMPANIMENTS TO MALAY DISHES

A Southeast Asian culinary tradition is to grate vegetables such as carrots and cucumbers, or fruit such as apples and quinces, then season them with salt, vinegar and chillies to make a relish known as a sambal. These are then served with curries or with meat or fish dishes. The following four sambal recipes are particularly popular. As a general rule, people help themselves to 1-2 spoonfuls of each sambal so, when catering, allow 1-2 tablespoons of each sambal per person.

APPLE SAMBAL

PREPARATION TIME: 20 MINUTES
STANDING TIME: AT LEAST 30 MINUTES

INGREDIENTS TO YIELD 500 ML (17 FL OZ)
3 firm green apples (not floury in texture), coarsely grated
1 teaspoon salt
2 cloves garlic, crushed
2 green chillies, seeded and sliced

Sprinkle the grated apples with the salt and leave the fruit to stand for at least 30 minutes to draw out some of the water, then drain thoroughly. (Sometimes, if the apples are particularly sour, a little boiling water is added to the apples after salting.) Add the garlic and chillies.

SERVING SUGGESTIONS Use as an accompaniment to meat dishes or curry.

CARROT SAMBAL

PREPARATION TIME: 15 MINUTES
STANDING TIME: AT LEAST 30 MINUTES

INGREDIENTS TO YIELD 375 ML (13 FL OZ)
3 medium-sized carrots, coarsely grated
1 teaspoon salt
1 small onion, peeled* and grated
1 clove garlic, crushed
1 green chilli, seeded and chopped
1 teaspoon sugar
5 teaspoons vinegar or lemon juice

Sprinkle the grated carrots with the salt and allow to stand for at least 30 minutes to draw out some of the water, then drain in a sieve.

Add the onion, garlic and chopped chilli. Then add the lightly mixed sugar and vinegar or lemon juice. It is important that the sambal is not too mushy.

SERVING SUGGESTIONS Serve with meat or curry dishes.

Carrot sambal makes as good an accompaniment for plain roast meats as it does for curries and spicy casseroles. The sweetness of the carrots particularly complements the flavour of lamb, so try serving with barbecued or grilled lamb dishes.

ONION SAMBAL

PREPARATION TIME: 10 MINUTES
STANDING TIME: 5 MINUTES

INGREDIENTS TO YIELD 125 ML (4 FL OZ)
3 medium-sized onions, peeled* and coarsely grated
¾ teaspoon salt
Boiling water
5 teaspoons vinegar
1 teaspoon sugar
3 chillies, seeded and chopped

Sprinkle the grated onions with salt, pour boiling water over and leave for 5 minutes. Drain and rinse the onions under cold water in a sieve or colander. Press out all the surplus water.

Arrange the dried onion in a salad bowl. Add the mixed vinegar and sugar, and the chillies, and then mix these ingredients together.

SERVING SUGGESTIONS This sambal is usually served with a variety of curried dishes or fried fish.

CUCUMBER SAMBAL

PREPARATION TIME: 15 MINUTES
STANDING TIME: AT LEAST 30 MINUTES

INGREDIENTS TO YIELD 500 ML (17 FL OZ)
2 fresh cucumbers, peeled and coarsely grated
2 teaspoons salt
2 green chillies, seeded and sliced
1 clove garlic, crushed
1 teaspoon sugar
4 teaspoons vinegar

Sprinkle the grated cucumber with salt and allow to stand for at least 30 minutes to draw out the water.

Squeeze out all the water. Add the chillies, garlic and the mixed sugar and vinegar.

SERVING SUGGESTIONS Serve with meat dishes or curry.

Cucumber also goes well with fish dishes, so if you are planning a menu which includes a fish curry, serve this sambal as one of your accompaniments.

PARSI DHANSAK

DHANSAK IS THE FAVOURITE Sunday food of many Parsees, the religious community which settled in India after fleeing Persia more than a thousand years ago. In time, they created a distinct Parsee cuisine, combining something of both lands.

The dish is a rich mutton curry with a thick, golden-brown gravy. Dhansak can be frozen for up to two months.

PREPARATION TIME: 30 MINUTES
COOKING TIME: 1½-2 HOURS

INGREDIENTS FOR FOUR TO SIX

1 kg (2¼ lb) mutton
250 g (9 oz) red lentils
1.5 litres (52 fl oz) warm water
100 g (3¾ oz) pumpkin or marrow, peeled and cubed
100 g (3¾ oz) aubergines (eggplants), peeled and cubed
3 tablespoons finely chopped parsley
1 teaspoon turmeric
2 teaspoons salt
60 ml (2 fl oz) sunflower oil
2 medium-sized onions, peeled and sliced*
A 4 cm (1½ in) piece of fresh green ginger, peeled and pounded to a paste with a little water
10 cloves garlic, peeled and crushed to a paste
1 tablespoon chilli powder
1 whole green chilli, sliced lengthways
1 tablespoon cumin seeds, roasted in a dry saucepan for 2 minutes, then coarsely crushed
1 tablespoon crushed coriander seeds (roasted as above)
2 tomatoes, chopped
2 tablespoons finely chopped coriander (dhania) leaves

Cut the mutton into convenient-sized pieces and wash. Wash the lentils and set aside. Pour the warm water into a large saucepan. Add the mutton, lentils, pumpkin or marrow, aubergines (egg-plants), parsley, turmeric and salt.

Cover the saucepan and cook on a medium heat for an hour, or until the mutton pieces are soft (stir occasionally). Extra water may be added to keep the gravy to a pouring consistency. Remove from the heat and stir well. The vegetables and lentils should blend into a smooth, thick gravy.

Heat the oil in a smaller saucepan. Add the sliced onions and allow to cook to a golden colour. Add the ginger and garlic to the onions and fry for 1 minute, then add the chilli powder, green chilli, cumin, coriander seeds and tomatoes.

Fry on a medium heat until soft and well blended with the spices. Pour the tomato and onion gravy onto the cooked meat, stir well together and simmer on a medium heat for 15 minutes.

Garnish with the chopped coriander leaves, and serve.

SERVING SUGGESTION Serve with piping hot rice, lemon wedges and cucumber raita* or an apple sambal*.

PARSI DHANSAK A rich mutton dish with a spicy flavour.

LAMB CHOPS IN FILO

WRAPPED IN CRISP layers of pastry, these chops are delicious served with a tomato and onion sauce, buttered green beans and steamed new potatoes, garnished with mint or parsley.

PREPARATION TIME: 20 MINUTES
COOKING TIME: 20 MINUTES
PREHEAT OVEN TO 200°C (400°F, MARK 6)

INGREDIENTS FOR SIX

6 thick loin lamb chops
2 tablespoons sunflower oil
Salt and freshly ground black pepper
6 squares of feta cheese (about 100 g/3¾ oz)
1 teaspoon dried oregano
6 sheets filo pastry* or puff pastry*
4 tablespoons melted butter

Trim all the fat from the chops. Brown the chops on both sides in the hot oil and season. Slit each chop across and push in a square of feta cheese. Sprinkle with oregano.

Brush each pastry sheet with melted butter and wrap around a chop. Brush with more butter and bake for 15-20 minutes, or until crisp and golden.

MOUSSAKA

MOUSSAKA WAS AN ARAB dish which was introduced to Europe by Turkish invaders. But Greece has made the dish especially its own.

PREPARATION TIME: 45 MINUTES
SOAKING TIME: 30 MINUTES
COOKING TIME: 1 HOUR
PREHEAT OVEN TO 150°C (300°F, MARK 2)
INGREDIENTS FOR SIX

750 g (1 lb 10 oz) lean raw lamb or
  beef, minced
900 g (2 lb) aubergines (eggplants)
60 ml (2 fl oz) olive oil
25 g (1 oz) butter
1 large onion, peeled and finely
  chopped*
2 cloves garlic, crushed
7-8 medium-sized tomatoes,
  skinned* and quartered
1 teaspoon dried thyme
1 teaspoon dried rosemary
Salt and pepper
450 ml (¾ pint) cheese sauce*
2 egg yolks, well beaten
50 g (2 oz) Parmesan cheese, grated

Slice the unpeeled aubergines (eggplants) thinly and soak them in salted water for 30 minutes. Drain well and pat dry.

Heat half the oil in a large frying pan, and put in a layer of aubergine (eggplant) slices. Fry gently for 1 minute, then fry the other side for 2 minutes. Turn again and fry the first side for another minute. Transfer to a plate and fry the rest of the slices, adding more oil if needed. Set the slices aside.

Heat the butter in a large saucepan and fry the onion. After 3-4 minutes, add the garlic and minced meat. Fry, stirring all the time, for about 3 minutes, to brown the mince a little. Stir in the tomatoes, thyme and rosemary, and season well. Simmer for 15-20 minutes, stirring occasionally. Meanwhile, make the cheese sauce. Cool for 5 minutes and stir in the beaten egg yolks.

Butter a deep, oblong, ovenproof dish or a bread tin and place a layer of aubergine (eggplant) slices in the bottom. Cover with a layer of mince about 2 cm (¾ in) deep. Put in another layer of aubergines (eggplants) and another layer of mince, and finish with a layer of aubergines (eggplants). Cover with the cheese sauce and sprinkle with the Parmesan. Bake for 1 hour, or until the top is crisp.

KHEEMA KEBABS

KEBABS ARE AMONG India's classic meat preparations. The combination of spices in these kheema kebabs is perfectly balanced to give the beef or lamb meatballs an outstanding flavour.

Kheema kebabs can also be placed on skewers and baked in the traditional tandoor clay oven. The kebabs may be frozen (after cooking) for up to 4 weeks. Defrost thoroughly before reheating.

PREPARATION TIME: 20 MINUTES
COOKING TIME: 30 MINUTES

INGREDIENTS FOR FOUR

500 g (1 lb 2 oz) beef or lamb mince
1 medium-sized onion, finely
  chopped*
1 teaspoon salt
1 teaspoon turmeric
1½ teaspoons ground ginger
4 small cloves garlic, crushed
1 teaspoon crushed cumin seeds
1 teaspoon crushed coriander seeds
2 green chillies, chopped
2 tablespoons chopped coriander
  (dhania) leaves
3 tablespoons clarified butter* or
  ghee
2 tomatoes, roughly chopped

Place the mince in a large mixing bowl and break it up with your fingers. Squeeze the juice from the onion, then add the flesh with the salt, turmeric, ginger, garlic, cumin, coriander seeds, chillies and coriander leaves to the meat. Mix well and form into balls which are about the size of walnuts.

Heat the butter in a saucepan. Place the mince balls in the saucepan and fry them gently for 10 minutes.

Add the chopped tomato, cover the saucepan and simmer for a further 20 minutes over a low heat.

SERVING SUGGESTIONS Serve with dhania phoodini chatni*, wedges of lemon and fresh chapatis*.

After frying the meatballs, add them to saffron rice*. Arrange the rice and meatballs on a large dish and serve with minted yoghurt sauce*.

KHEEMA KEBABS *Spicy meatballs prepared in the classic Indian way.*

LAMB CASSEROLE WITH ORANGE

THIS IS A MAGNIFICENT RECIPE to try when navel oranges are at their sweetest and best. It is not a spur-of-the-moment dish – take your time in preparing and cooking it, and the results will exceed your highest expectations.

PREPARATION TIME: 45 MINUTES
COOKING TIME: 3 HOURS

INGREDIENTS FOR SIX

2.5 kg (5½ lb) lamb shoulder, boned
 and cut into 3 cm (1¼ in) cubes
5 teaspoons flour
60 ml (2 fl oz) olive or sunflower oil
3 carrots, scraped and cut into
 2 cm (¾ in) pieces
3 leeks, well washed, trimmed and
 coarsely chopped
3 stalks celery, washed, trimmed
 and coarsely chopped
3 cloves garlic, peeled and crushed
375 ml (13 fl oz) dry white wine
375 ml (13 fl oz) orange juice
4 sprigs parsley
2 bay leaves
Rind of ½ orange, cut into
 julienne* strips
2 tablespoons white sugar
Salt and freshly ground pepper
3 large navel oranges, peeled and
 segmented, with pith and
 membrane removed

Dredge the meat with the flour, shaking off the excess, and put it on one side. Heat the oil in a large ovenproof casserole and gently sauté the carrots, leeks, celery and garlic until soft and golden. With a slotted spoon, transfer the vegetables to a dish, then turn up the heat.

Sear the lamb cubes in batches in the casserole, adding a little more oil if necessary, for about 2 minutes (until they are well browned).

Return all the meat cubes to the casserole, adding the wine and the orange juice. Bring the liquid slowly to the boil before adding the gently sautéed vegetables to the lamb.

Tie the parsley, bay leaves and julienne strips of orange rind in a piece of clean muslin and add to the casserole. Turn the heat to very low and simmer the dish (covered) for 1 hour.

Next, heat the sugar in a small saucepan until it melts and caramelises, and carefully add 125 ml (4 fl oz) of the stew juices to the caramel. Stir it until smooth, add to the casserole, and season with salt and pepper. Cook for another hour, or until the lamb is tender.

Using a slotted spoon, transfer the lamb to a dish. Cover the lamb and keep it warm in a very low oven, 110°C (225°F, mark ¼), while you make the sauce and prepare the garnish.

Discard the muslin bag and strain the cooking liquid into a saucepan, pressing the vegetables through a sieve.

You could also liquidise the soft vegetables in a blender or food processor, but this will result in a much thicker sauce.

Boil the cooking liquid for 10 minutes to reduce it and skim off as much of the fat as you can.

Return the meat and sauce to the casserole and add the orange segments. Bring to the boil, correct the seasoning if necessary, and serve.

SERVING SUGGESTIONS Garnish with any of the following: 2 tablespoons finely chopped parsley; 1 tablespoon grated orange rind; or 2 cloves of garlic, peeled and finely chopped. Try serving the casserole with crusty bread and a salad of spinach with bacon, sprouts* and orange segments with pith and skin removed.

VARIATION For a summer version, leave out the orange juice, rind and orange segments and substitute chicken stock* mixed in equal proportions with apple juice. Add baby beans (cooked until still firm) and fresh lychees, peeled and stoned, towards the end of cooking. Garnish with coarsely chopped celery and decorate with celery leaves.

Serve with peeled new potatoes (in lemon butter*) and carrots garnished with chopped, fresh basil. Alternatively, serve with sliced courgettes (zucchini).

LAMB CASSEROLE WITH ORANGE *effectively marries a variety of flavours.*

HARICOT OF MUTTON

THE WORD HARICOT at first meant a stew of mutton and turnips. The beans were included later, possibly as a result of confusion over their name, which is derived from the old Norman word *halicot* meaning 'chopped up'.

PREPARATION TIME: 30 MINUTES
SOAKING TIME: OVERNIGHT
COOKING TIME: 2 HOURS
PREHEAT OVEN TO 180°C (350°F, MARK 4)

INGREDIENTS FOR FOUR

500 g (1 lb 2 oz) lean lamb from the
 leg, cut into 2.5 cm (1 in) cubes
175 g (6 oz) dried haricot beans
25 g (1 oz) seasoned flour
75 g (3 oz) butter
2 medium-sized onions, peeled and
 sliced*
4-5 medium-sized carrots, scraped
 and sliced
1 turnip, peeled and cut into 2 cm
 (¾ in) cubes
1 leek, cleaned and cut into 2.5 cm
 (1 in) lengths
1 teaspoon dried thyme
1 clove garlic, crushed
Salt and pepper
850 ml (1½ pints) vegetable* or
 basic stock*
1 tablespoon finely chopped
 parsley

Wash and drain the beans. Pour cold water over them and soak overnight.

Dip the pieces of lamb in the seasoned flour. Melt 50 g (2 oz) of the butter in a large frying pan and lightly fry the lamb. Turn two or three times to brown evenly. Lift the meat onto a plate, and keep it warm while you prepare the vegetables.

In the same pan, fry the onions, carrots, turnip and leek until they begin to brown. Turn the vegetables into a deep casserole and place the meat on top. Add the thyme, garlic, salt and pepper. Pour in the stock and add the drained beans, which should be covered by the stock.

Cook the casserole, uncovered, for 2 hours. As the beans soften they will form a crust over the meat and vegetables. After 1 hour, remove the casserole from the oven, dot the beans with the remaining butter and return to the oven. When the dish is ready to serve, sprinkle the top with the parsley. The casserole needs little accompaniment, so simply serve a green salad* afterwards.

IRISH STEW

THE ORIGINAL IRISH STEW was made with the meat of a young male goat. It was cooked, suspended over a peat fire, in a bastable oven – an all-purpose iron pot used for boiling, roasting and even for baking bread.

PREPARATION TIME: 20 MINUTES
COOKING TIME: 2 HOURS

INGREDIENTS FOR FOUR TO SIX

1 kg (2¼ lb) lamb cutlets, trimmed
 of skin and fat
Salt and freshly ground black
 pepper
4 large onions, peeled* and
 quartered
10 large potatoes, peeled and
 thickly sliced
850 ml (1½ pints) cold water

Lay half the cutlets in the bottom of a large ovenproof casserole and season them with a little salt and pepper.

Cover the meat with half of the onions, season, cover with half the potatoes and season again. Repeat the layers, ending with a layer of potatoes.

Pour in the water and bring slowly to the boil. Remove any white scum, then lower the heat, cover and simmer very gently for 2 hours. Just before serving, remove the lid and either grill or place the pan in a hot oven to brown the top layer of potato slices.

Serve the stew with glazed carrots*.

ROAST SADDLE OF LAMB

BUY A SHORT SADDLE of lamb, which comprises the loins – with flaps of meat attached, called aprons – and strips of fillet underneath the backbone.

PREPARATION TIME: 15 MINUTES
COOKING TIME: 1 HOUR
PREHEAT OVEN TO 200°C (400°F, MARK 6)

INGREDIENTS FOR FOUR

1.5 kg (3 lb 3 oz) short saddle of
 lamb
1 tablespoon sunflower oil
1 teaspoon dry mustard
Salt
Coarsely crushed black
 peppercorns
1 or 2 sprigs fresh rosemary
125 ml (4 fl oz) red wine

Trim the outer layer of fat from the meat and any other excess fat. Rub the meat with the oil, mustard, salt and pepper. Place in a baking dish just large enough to accommodate it. Tuck the rosemary underneath and roll the aprons under the lamb so that they touch.

Roast for 45 minutes, then allow the roast to stand in a warm oven for 15 minutes (this makes for easier carving). Skim the fat from the juice in the baking dish by patting with paper towels. Pour in the wine and reduce on top of the stove over a high heat. Check the seasoning.

To carve, slice each section separately, sharing the slices equally. Slice the eye of the loin lengthways into long strips. Carve each fillet and each apron across.

LANCASHIRE HOTPOT

LANCASHIRE HOTPOT was traditionally cooked in the farmhouse bread oven at the end of a busy baking day.

PREPARATION TIME: 30 MINUTES
COOKING TIME: 3 HOURS
PREHEAT OVEN TO 180°C (350°F, MARK 4)

INGREDIENTS FOR SIX

1.5 kg (3 lb 3 oz) best end of the
 neck of lamb, divided into chops
Salt and pepper
4 large onions, peeled and sliced*
900 ml (31 fl oz) basic stock*
225 g (½ lb) mushrooms
9 medium-sized potatoes, peeled
 and thickly sliced
25 g (1 oz) butter, in small pieces

Place a layer of lamb chops, lying head to tail, in a large casserole with a lid, or in a large, deep pie dish. Sprinkle the meat with salt and pepper.

Cover this first layer of chops with a layer of onions and season again. Repeat with the rest of the chops, covering each layer with sliced onions and seasoning with salt and pepper. Pour in the stock until it almost covers the meat.

Place the mushrooms over the chops and onions, and cover thickly with overlapping potato slices. Dot with half the butter pieces, cover tightly and then cook in the preheated oven for 2 hours. Remove the cover, dot with the remaining butter and cook for a further hour in order to brown the potatoes. Serve with a green vegetable or glazed carrots*.

COOKING WITH WINE

Do experiment with wine in cooking. Wine adds relish to the simplest recipe and, when properly used, can turn a meal into a feast. It need not be an expensive wine either.

All the alcohol evaporates from the wine during the cooking process, leaving a delicate flavour that will enhance a large variety of dishes. Never drown a dish in wine.

When cooking fish, veal, chicken, sweetbreads and similar delicate foods, use a medium dry white wine, such as a riesling.

Red meats, such as lamb, beef and game, are prepared with red wines. However, certain classic poultry dishes, such as coq au vin, should also be prepared with red wine.

Apart from adding flavour to food, wine can be used to make it moist and tender. Fish marinated in white wine and meat steeped in red wine are enhanced in both texture and taste. Fish need not be marinated for more than an hour; but dry meats, such as venison or beef, may be left for up to four days. A useful marinade consists of 1 part olive oil to 3 parts red or dry white wine (depending on the use), to which a bouquet garni*, grated onion and garlic are added.

Wine left over after a meal can be kept for use in cooking or as a marinade. Pour the wine into a small bottle, cork it to keep out the air and store in the refrigerator. You can, if you wish, seal the leftover wine with a film of oil; or alternatively freeze the wine in ice trays – then take out as many iced wine cubes as needed. Boxed (cask) wine is useful for cooking since small quantities can be used at a time without exposing the wine to the air.

Fortified and dessert wines, such as Marsala, port, sherry and vermouth, can be used to enhance simple dishes. Marsala is an ingredient of the Italian dessert zabaglione, and sherry is added to trifles.

Wine is not the only alcoholic drink that improves a dish. Beer and cider can also be used in cooking, although they do not have as many uses as wine.

Spirits, such as brandy, whisky or gin, can be used to flame shellfish, steaks, veal escalopes, and other dishes which do not require long cooking. Before flaming a dish, warm the spirit slightly in a ladle. Then set it alight with a match and pour it over the hot food.

DEVILLED LAMB KIDNEYS

THIS RECIPE FOR DEVILLED kidneys can be served as a supper or lunch dish, but is equally suitable for a hearty breakfast for those with an appetite.

PREPARATION TIME: 10 MINUTES
COOKING TIME: 5 MINUTES

INGREDIENTS FOR SIX
12 lamb kidneys, trimmed
50 ml (2 fl oz) beef basic stock*
75 ml (2½ fl oz) red wine
4 tablespoons cornflour
Salt and freshly ground black pepper
60 g (2 oz) butter
2 teaspoons sunflower oil
1 clove garlic, crushed
2 red chillies, seeded and finely chopped, or a pinch of cayenne pepper

Remove the surrounding fat from the kidneys before peeling the skin off with your fingers. Slice the kidneys almost through so that the two halves can be opened out flat, and remove the white core. Wash the kidneys well in salted cold water, dry and set aside.

Mix the stock and wine, and slake the cornflour with a little of the mixture. Add the remaining mixture until smooth, and season with salt and pepper.

Heat the butter and oil, and quickly fry the kidneys (3-5 minutes). Transfer with a slotted spoon to a warm dish. Season with salt and pepper.

Add the garlic and chillies or cayenne pepper, and stir-fry quickly. Add the cornflour mixture and cook over high heat until clear. Adjust the seasoning, add the kidneys and transfer immediately to a warmed serving dish.

SERVING SUGGESTION If serving as a supper or lunch dish accompany with buttered noodles sprinkled with parsley or mashed potatoes, and a green vegetable such as broccoli.

VARIATIONS Add one or two seeded and finely chopped sweet peppers when frying the chillies.

Chopped onion* can also be added, and a good sprinkling of chopped parsley added afterwards gives a pleasant colour to the dish.

For a more robust supper dish, fry or grill small sausages and add to the kidneys just before serving.

POT-ROAST CUSHION OF PORK WITH APPLE AND PRUNE STUFFING

THIS IS A RICHLY FLAVOURED dish which combines pork, apples and prunes with such success that the individual flavours are easily identified yet complement each other to produce a memorable taste sensation.

PREPARATION TIME: 45 MINUTES
SOAKING TIME FOR PRUNES: OVERNIGHT
COOKING TIME: 2 HOURS

INGREDIENTS FOR SIX
2 kg (4½ lb) boned loin of pork
Salt and freshly ground black pepper
4 fresh sage leaves or 1 teaspoon dried sage
A little grated fresh ginger
2 tablespoons sunflower oil
30 g (1¼ oz) butter
250 ml (9 fl oz) apple juice
60 ml (2 fl oz) cider vinegar

For the filling:
6 prunes, soaked overnight in 60 ml (2 fl oz) gin
2 tablespoons sugar
3 apples, peeled, cored and sliced
60 g (2 oz) butter

For the sauce:
Grated rind and juice of 1 orange
125 ml (4 fl oz) dry white wine

Season the meat inside and out with salt and pepper, sage and ginger.

To make the filling, stone the prunes, then sprinkle the sugar over the apples. Heat the butter and fry the apples until golden-brown. Add the prunes and gin, and cook until all the liquid has evaporated. Leave to cool, then fill the meat. Roll up and tie with string.

Next, heat the oil and butter, and brown the meat all the way around. Heat the apple juice and vinegar, and add it to the meat. Cover and simmer for 1½-2 hours, until the meat is tender. Remove the meat and let it stand for 10-15 minutes. Slice and arrange the slices of meat on a serving platter. Cover and keep warm in the oven.

Add the orange rind, juice and white wine to the pan juices, and heat to boiling point. Taste and adjust the seasoning if necessary. Reduce by half and spoon over the meat. Serve with new potatoes.

FRIED YOUNG RABBIT *A tasty treat to delight family or friends.*

FRIED YOUNG RABBIT

HISTORICALLY, THE TERM 'young rabbit' is something of a misnomer. Until the 18th century at least, the word 'rabbit' meant the animal up to a year old; after that age it was called a 'coney'.

The following recipe makes a tasty family supper or can be served at a small informal dinner party.

PREPARATION TIME: 1¼ HOURS
(INCLUDING MAKING THE STOCK)
COOKING TIME: 30 MINUTES

INGREDIENTS FOR FOUR
2 young rabbits, jointed
50-75 g (2-3 oz) butter
2 tablespoons sunflower oil
250 g (9 oz) spinach, washed and drained, or young cabbage leaves, finely chopped
Salt and pepper

For the stock:
Trimmings from the rabbits
1 carrot, roughly cut
1 turnip, roughly cut
1 onion, peeled and roughly chopped*
Salt and pepper

Ask the butcher to joint the rabbits. Use only the back and thighs for the dish.

To make the stock, place the rabbit trimmings in a saucepan with the carrot, turnip, onion and seasoning. Add just enough water to cover, then simmer, covered, for 1 hour. Strain and set aside the stock while you fry the rabbit pieces.

Heat 25 g (1 oz) of the butter and the oil together in a large frying pan with a well-fitting lid, and fry the rabbit pieces on both sides over a medium heat for 5 minutes, turning occasionally. Remove the back pieces and keep them warm in a covered dish, leaving the thighs to continue cooking for a further 5 minutes.

Return the back pieces to the pan, with the spinach or cabbage, 150 ml (¼ pint) of the stock, and salt and pepper. Cover with the lid, and simmer for 10 minutes.

Remove the spinach or cabbage from the pan and put it on a hot serving dish. Arrange the rabbit pieces over the vegetable and keep warm.

Quickly make a sauce by breaking the rest of the butter in small pieces, then stirring them into the remaining liquid in the frying pan. Season to taste with salt and pepper, pour the sauce over the rabbit and vegetable, and serve.

SERVING SUGGESTION Boiled new potatoes sprinkled with chopped mint would be a good accompaniment. Alternatively, boil rice with a pinch of dried thyme and add a knob of butter before serving. If using rice, arrange the rabbit on top.

CHOP SUEY

ALTHOUGH MOST Westerners consider chop suey to be typically Chinese, it actually originated in America, and is unknown in China. There are many variations in the preparation of chop suey, and you can substitute or add to the ingredients depending on whatever you have available.

PREPARATION TIME: 25 MINUTES
COOKING TIME: 30 MINUTES

INGREDIENTS FOR SIX
2 boned, skinned chicken breasts
1 large carrot
1 tin (about 230 g/½ lb) bamboo shoots
250 ml (9 fl oz) water
2 teaspoons cornflour
1 chicken stock cube
1 tablespoon soy sauce
2 tablespoons sunflower oil
250 g (9 oz) pork, minced
½ Chinese or ordinary cabbage, shredded
125 g (4¼ oz) green beans, sliced diagonally
4 spring onions, sliced
3 stalks celery, sliced diagonally
250 g (9 oz) prawns, shelled and de-veined*

Steam the chicken breasts until tender, then cool and cut into cubes. Clean the carrot and cut it into julienne* strips, then drain and rinse the bamboo shoots and slice them into strips.

Combine the water, cornflour, crumbled stock cube and soy sauce and set aside.

Heat the oil in a wok or a heavy frying pan and add the minced pork. Stir-fry until well browned before adding the cabbage, beans, carrots, spring onions and celery. Combine well and stir-fry over a high heat for 2 minutes.

Make a well in the centre of the wok, add the cornflour mixture and stir until the sauce boils and thickens. Add the chicken, prawns and bamboo shoots and cook the mixture for a further 3 minutes (or until the prawns are done).

SERVING SUGGESTIONS Serve in a heated shallow bowl surrounded by crisp Chinese prawn crackers. As an accompaniment, serve fried rice*.

VARIATIONS Use lamb instead of pork or use only seafood and chicken.

LOIN CHOPS WITH MUSTARD SAUCE

PORK LOIN CHOPS can be rather dry and tough if not cooked carefully. Simmered with wine and rosemary, they become superbly succulent, and the sauce made with the pan juices is the perfect accompaniment.

PREPARATION TIME: 15 MINUTES
COOKING TIME: 3 HOURS

INGREDIENTS FOR SIX
6-8 pork loin chops, about 1 cm
    (½ in) thick
50 g (2 oz) dripping
2 onions, peeled and sliced*
1-2 teaspoons dried rosemary
1 clove garlic, peeled and crushed
Pepper
250 ml (9 fl oz) white wine
250 ml (9 fl oz) water

For the sauce:
2 tablespoons flour
125 ml (4 fl oz) white wine
125 ml (4 fl oz) water
125 ml (4 fl oz) milk
1 tablespoon dry mustard
2 teaspoons brown sugar
¾ teaspoon rosemary
Salt and freshly ground black
    pepper

Melt the dripping in a large frying pan or electric frying pan and sauté the onion until soft. Remove the onion from the pan with a slotted spoon, and set aside. Brown the chops lightly on either side, doing two or three chops at a time.

Pour the fat out of the pan and return the chops, with the onion, rosemary and garlic. Season them lightly with pepper and pour over the wine. Cover the pan and simmer, turning the chops from time to time, until all the liquid has been absorbed (about 1½ hours).

Now add the water, a little at a time, and braise until the chops are tender – adding water as it is needed. When they are done, use a slotted spoon to transfer the chops to a heated platter. Cover them with foil and keep warm: you should now have a nice brown pan with a little bit of pan juice. To make the sauce, stir in the flour to make a smooth paste, add the 125 ml (4 fl oz) wine and 125 ml (4 fl oz) water (stirring until the mixture thickens), and then the milk. Stir to make a smooth, glossy sauce.

Mix the mustard and sugar together with a little wine and stir it into the sauce. Add the rosemary and correct the seasoning. Spoon some of the sauce over the chops and serve the remaining sauce in a heated sauceboat.

SERVING SUGGESTIONS This dish is good with rice or baked potatoes* and green vegetables such as broccoli or courgettes (zucchini) cooked until they are just tender – never serve them overcooked.

CHILLI CON CARNE

THE MEXICAN NATIONAL dish of beef and bean stew is strongly flavoured with chilli powder, and for an even spicier dish, a few cumin seeds may be added. Serve straight from the dish, with crusty bread and a tossed green salad*.

PREPARATION TIME: 30 MINUTES
COOKING TIME: 2-2½ HOURS
PREHEAT OVEN TO 150°C (300°F, MARK 2)

INGREDIENTS FOR SIX
450 g (1 lb) lean minced beef
350 g (¾ lb) dried or 2 large tins red
    kidney beans
2 onions
2 tablespoons olive oil
400-450 g (14-16 oz) tin of
    tomatoes
2 level teaspoons chilli powder or
    1 finely chopped chilli pepper
Salt
Cumin seeds (optional)

Soak the beans in cold water overnight. Drain them and put in a pan with plenty of fresh water (no salt). Bring to the boil and keep boiling for 10 minutes. Lower the heat, cover the pan with a lid and simmer for 1 hour. Peel and thinly slice the onions.

Heat the oil in a flameproof dish over low heat and fry the onions until soft. Stir in the meat and continue to fry, stirring occasionally, until the meat has browned. Blend in the drained kidney beans, add the tomatoes with their juice, and season to taste with chilli, salt and crushed cumin seeds.

Cover the pan with a lid and cook in the centre of a preheated oven, at 150°C (300°F, mark 2) for 1-1½ hours. Alternatively, cook on top of the stove. Add a little water to the juices if the stew dries out during cooking.

OX TONGUE

TONGUE CAN BE DELICIOUS, whether served hot or cold. Mustard sauce is the traditional accompaniment, but this recipe gives some equally appetising alternatives.

PREPARATION TIME: 20 MINUTES
SOAKING TIME: 1-2 HOURS
COOKING TIME: 3¼ HOURS

INGREDIENTS FOR EIGHT TO TEN
1 ox tongue (about 1.5-2 kg/
    3-4½ lb)
2 medium-sized carrots, scraped
2 medium-sized onions, peeled*
    and quartered
1 medium-sized turnip, peeled and
    quartered
12 peppercorns
Bouquet garni*

Wash the tongue thoroughly and soak it in cold water for 1-2 hours. Drain, place in a very large saucepan and cover with water heated until tepid. Bring slowly to the boil and remove the scum.

Add the carrots, onions, turnip, peppercorns and the bouquet garni to the saucepan. Cover and boil gently for about 3 hours.

Lift the tongue onto a board and very carefully remove the skin and any small bones. Discard the stock, which tends to be greasy and tasteless. If the tongue is to be served hot, place it in its natural shape on a large serving dish.

SERVING SUGGESTIONS Serve with a homemade parsley sauce*, Napolitana sauce* or caper sauce*. Pour a little of the sauce over the meat and serve the rest separately in a sauceboat.

VARIATION If the tongue is to be served cold, curl the boned and skinned tongue in a large, round cake tin or soufflé dish. Dissolve 15 g (½ oz) gelatine in 570 ml (1 pint) beef basic* or chicken stock*, and pour into the tin or dish until it is just level with the top of the tongue. Cover with aluminium foil and place a heavy weight on the meat. Leave in the refrigerator overnight. The next day, turn out the pressed tongue and carve it horizontally in thin, round slices.

Serve the cold ox tongue with a variety of salads. A mushroom salad* would go particularly well with the tongue or try a leek vinaigrette*. Sliced tomatoes and a potato salad* are also delicious.

OXTAIL STEW *Mouthwatering in appearance, this filling dish is a good choice for hungry friends.*

OXTAIL STEW

O XTAIL IS A RELATIVELY inexpensive, nourishing but fatty meat. It requires a great deal of cooking, but the end result is well worth it. It is quite a rich dish, best served with rice or mashed potato, and a green vegetable.

PREPARATION TIME: 25 MINUTES
COOKING TIME: 3-4 HOURS
PREHEAT OVEN TO 150°C (300°F, MARK 2)

INGREDIENTS FOR FOUR
1 kg (2¼ lb) oxtail, jointed
2 tablespoons sunflower oil
2 medium-sized onions, peeled and finely sliced*
2 leeks, trimmed and sliced
8-10 medium-sized carrots, cut in rounds
2 stalks celery, sliced

2 tablespoons seasoned flour*
2 bay leaves
¼ teaspoon thyme
6 cloves
12 peppercorns
1 clove garlic, crushed
1 litre (1¾ pints) boiling water, or half water and half red wine
2-3 medium-sized tomatoes, skinned* and quartered
1 tablespoon cornflour (optional)
1 tablespoon finely chopped parsley for garnish

Heat the oil in a heavy-based frying pan and fry the oxtail for 5 minutes, turning frequently. Lift the pieces onto a dish.

Fry the onions, leeks, carrots and celery in the fat until they begin to brown, then place them in a large, deep casserole. Rub the cooled oxtail pieces with the seasoned flour and put them in the casserole. Add the bay leaves, thyme, cloves, peppercorns and garlic, and cover with the water, or the wine mixture.

Cover the casserole tightly and place it in the preheated oven for 2½-3½ hours, or until the meat is tender. Add the quartered tomatoes and cook the dish for a further 30 minutes.

Check the seasoning. If the gravy seems too thin, thicken it by mixing the cornflour with a little water and pour a cup of the hot gravy onto it, stirring all the time. Stir the mixture back into the casserole and place in the oven for a further 5 minutes. Garnish with parsley.

VARIATION Arrange thick slices of potato (parboiled) over the stew after you have added the tomatoes. Dot with butter. At the end of the cooking time, turn the oven up to 200°C (400°F, mark 6) and cook for a further 20 minutes to cook the potato slices through and brown them.

67

STEAK AND KIDNEY PIE *is a popular dish among young and old alike.*

STEAK AND KIDNEY PIE

THIS MUST RANK as one of the most popular pie dishes. This recipe calls for a lid of light, rich puff pastry. If the filling is cooked the day before and the pastry is ready to roll out, you can complete the pie in very little time.

PREPARATION TIME: 50 MINUTES
STANDING TIME: (FOR PASTRY) 1 HOUR
COOKING TIME: 2 HOURS 5 MINUTES
COOLING TIME: SEVERAL HOURS
PREHEAT OVEN TO 150°C (300°F, MARK 2)

INGREDIENTS FOR FOUR
500 g (1 lb 2 oz) stewing steak, cut in 2 cm ($\frac{3}{4}$ in) cubes
350 g ($\frac{3}{4}$ lb) ox kidney
Puff pastry* using 350 g ($\frac{3}{4}$ lb) flour
50 g (2 oz) butter
1 large onion, peeled and sliced*
2 tablespoons seasoned flour
250 g (9 oz) mushrooms, sliced
Salt and pepper
1 tablespoon flour
About 300 ml ($\frac{1}{2}$ pint) brown stock*
2 hard-boiled eggs (optional)
1 egg, beaten

Prepare the puff pastry and allow to stand for an hour before folding it over the pie. Heat the butter in a frying pan and cook the onion in it until soft. Use a slotted spoon to transfer the onion to a warmed plate.

Remove any fat from the cubes of steak and dip them in the seasoned flour. Then brown the cubes in the pan in which the onion was cooked, adding a little more butter if necessary. Remove from the pan.

Chop the kidney thinly, remove all skin and fat, and dip the kidney in the seasoned flour. Lightly brown it in the same pan.

Arrange the steak, kidney, sliced mushrooms and onion in layers in a large pie dish, lightly seasoning each layer.

Use a wooden spoon to stir the flour into the pan in which the meat and onion were browned, and add the stock. Cook together for a few minutes, stirring all the time, until the stock has slightly thickened.

Pour enough stock into the dish to almost cover the meat. Cover the dish tightly with aluminium foil and cook in the preheated oven for 1½ hours, adding more stock during cooking if the meat

becomes dry. Remove from the oven and allow to cool completely (this part of the recipe may be done the day before you want to eat the pie, if you prefer).

Increase the oven temperature to 230°C (450°F, mark 8). When the meat is cold, cut the hard-boiled eggs into quarters, if you are using them, and add them to the pie dish.

Roll out the pastry to make a lid for the pie. Lay it over the filling, decorate the top with pastry scraps, and glaze with the beaten egg. Bake in the preheated oven for 10 minutes. Reduce the heat to 180°C (350°F, mark 4) and cook for a further 25 minutes, or until the pastry is crisp and golden-brown.

SERVING SUGGESTION Serve with mashed potatoes and glazed carrots*.

CALF LIVER WITH ONIONS

WHEN PROPERLY PREPARED, liver makes a succulent dish. To achieve the tastiest results, always choose calf rather than ox liver. The Italians combine liver with sage for an excellent marriage of flavours. Use fresh sage, if possible, and be sparing when using the dried variety.

PREPARATION TIME: 15 MINUTES
COOKING TIME: 25 MINUTES

INGREDIENTS FOR SIX
750 g (1 lb 10 oz) calf liver or lamb's fry, thinly sliced
Salt and freshly ground black pepper
Flour for coating
60 ml (2 fl oz) sunflower oil
60 g (2 oz) butter
3 medium-sized onions, peeled and thinly sliced*
Juice of 1 lemon
60 ml (2 fl oz) dry white wine
1 tablespoon chopped fresh sage leaves, or $\frac{1}{2}$ teaspoon dried sage
Finely chopped parsley for garnish

Pat the liver slices quite dry with paper towels. Season and coat them lightly with flour. Heat half the oil and half the butter in a frying pan and add the onions. Cook very gently for 15-20 minutes, or until soft and pale golden in colour, then season lightly and keep warm in a separate dish.

Heat the rest of the oil and butter in the

same pan. Add the liver and sauté quickly until brown outside but still pink inside. Place on top of the onions. Add the lemon juice and wine to the pan. Stir in the sage and bring to the boil, stirring all the time. Pour over the hot liver and onions, sprinkle with parsley and serve immediately.

SERVING SUGGESTION Serve with golden sautéed potatoes and buttered spinach.

VARIATIONS After frying the onions, add 1 tablespoon butter to the pan and cook 250 g (9 oz) sliced mushrooms. Remove from the pan, and keep warm while cooking the liver.

Add a thinly sliced small avocado when heating up the lemon juice and wine sauce (be careful not to overheat the avocado, because it will become bitter).

BEEF STEW WITH PARSLEY DUMPLINGS

PARSLEY DUMPLINGS MAKE excellent companions to set off this cider-flavoured stew. The green of the chopped parsley contrasts attractively with the white of the basic dumpling.

PREPARATION TIME: 20 MINUTES
COOKING TIME: 2½ HOURS

INGREDIENTS FOR FOUR TO SIX
For the stew:
900 g (2 lb) beef shin
40 g (1½ oz) well-seasoned flour
50 g (2 oz) beef dripping or butter
2 large onions, peeled and sliced*
600 ml (21 fl oz) brown stock*
300 ml (½ pint) cider
Salt and freshly ground black pepper
3 carrots, peeled and diced
3 turnips, peeled and diced
2 stalks celery, cleaned and diced

For the dumplings:
3 tablespoons self-raising flour
30 g (1¼ oz) fresh breadcrumbs
2 tablespoons shredded suet
1 tablespoon finely chopped parsley
2 teaspoons finely grated lemon rind
Salt and freshly ground pepper
1 egg, beaten

Cut the meat into 2.5 cm (1 in) cubes and toss them in the seasoned flour. Heat the

BEEF STEW WITH PARSLEY DUMPLINGS *Visually appealing and delicious.*

dripping in a heavy-based pan or oven-proof casserole and cook the onions in it gently until transparent. Add the meat and fry until brown.

Stir in the stock and cider, scraping up any bits sticking to the pan, and season with salt and pepper. Bring the contents to the boil, and remove any white scum from the surface.

Add the carrots, turnips and celery. Reduce the heat, cover the pan with a lid, and simmer the stew for about 2½ hours, or until the meat is tender.

To make the dumplings, put the flour, breadcrumbs, suet, parsley and grated lemon rind in a large bowl. Mix together well with a fork or wooden spoon. Season with salt and pepper, and blend in the beaten egg.

Use lightly floured hands to shape the mixture into balls the size of large walnuts. Place them on top of the stew for the last 15-20 minutes of cooking.

If you want to cook the dumplings on their own, poach them in a large sauce-

pan of boiling, salted water. They will rise to the surface when they are cooked (after about 15 minutes).

SERVING SUGGESTION Ladle the stew and vegetables into a deep dish and surround with the dumplings. Serve immediately with hunks of crusty bread.

VARIATION Instead of using parsley in the dumplings, try adding a tablespoon of a different chopped herb to the basic dumpling mixture. Thyme would go particularly well.

If fresh herbs are not readily available, you can use a teaspoon of the dried herb of your choice.

Give a Hungarian feel to your beef stew by adding paprika and a tablespoon of tomato purée before the stock goes in. Make up the liquid quantities by substituting chopped tomatoes and extra stock for the cider, and change the dumpling mixture, putting in lightly crushed caraway seeds (omit the lemon rind and parsley).

POULTRY

S AY 'POULTRY' and most people think immediately of chicken, but the category of poultry covers a wide range of edible birds, including duck, turkey, guinea fowl, goose, and pigeon.

Poultry has traditionally been a festive dish – particularly in the form of roast turkey at Christmas. In fact, roasting is probably the most popular way to cook all poultry – whether boned and stuffed, or simply flavoured and accompanied by crisp roast potatoes.

Many other cooking methods are suitable for poultry – it is superb curried, casseroled with vegetables and herbs, or pot-roasted. Poultry also lends itself well to being cooked in wine, or with liqueurs, as in the recipe for roast duck with orange and Grand Marnier.

Almost as rich in body-building proteins as red meat, poultry was expensive until fairly recently, when battery rearing turned chicken into a popular budget food.

For hot summer days you can exploit the full value of chicken and turkey in light salads, or enrich your daily diet with Eastern-inspired dishes – such as chicken biriani, kesar masala murghi or Chinese chicken with cashew nuts.

CHICKEN FRICASSEE WITH SHERRY

FRICASSEE IS AN OLD French word for a stew served with white sauce. The secret of a good fricassee is to cook the chicken slowly at a low temperature, to produce a succulent and tender dish. The ideal bird to use in this recipe would be an older boiling fowl.

PREPARATION TIME: 30 MINUTES
COOKING TIME: 1½ HOURS

INGREDIENTS FOR SIX
1 whole chicken (2 kg/4½ lb)
750 ml (26 fl oz) water
250 ml (9 fl oz) white wine (or water)
1 carrot, scraped and sliced
1 onion, peeled* and studded with 4 cloves
1 bay leaf
Salt and freshly ground pepper

For the sauce:
3 tablespoons butter
2 tablespoons flour
¼ teaspoon cayenne pepper
1 teaspoon sugar
125 ml (4 fl oz) medium sherry
250 g (9 oz) cooked peas
5 medium-sized carrots, scraped, sliced and cooked
4 stalks celery, sliced and cooked

Place the chicken in a large pot or pressure cooker, add the water, wine, carrot, onion, bay leaf and salt and pepper. Bring to the boil, then turn down the heat and simmer gently (covered) until the meat is tender.

Remove the chicken from the stock and cut it into serving-sized pieces, removing the skin, breastbone and backbone and wing tips. Arrange the chicken pieces in a large, fairly deep, heated casserole dish and moisten it lightly with a few spoonfuls of stock. Cover it tightly and keep warm.

Return the skin and bones to the stockpot and reduce the stock down to about half the original quantity.

Melt the butter in a saucepan and stir in the flour to make a smooth paste. Strain the stock and add it slowly (stirring constantly) to form a thickish sauce, leaving the sauce to bubble gently for a minute or so. Add the cayenne pepper, sugar, sherry and cooked vegetables and heat through. Pour the sauce over the chicken pieces and serve immediately.

SERVING SUGGESTION Buttered brown rice and a good green salad* make ideal companions for this simple, hearty dish.

VARIATION Try adding cream (about 5 tablespoons) to the sauce, and instead of butter and flour, use 2 egg yolks to thicken the sauce.

CHICKEN PERI-PERI

A SPICY DISH of Portuguese origin, this is probably among the best-known of the 'hot' chicken dishes. For those with sensitive tastebuds, simply reduce the chilli content.

PREPARATION TIME: 20 MINUTES
MARINATING TIME: 2 HOURS
COOKING TIME: 15 MINUTES

INGREDIENTS FOR FOUR
8 small portions chicken, or 1 chicken cut into 8 small portions
2 tablespoons coarsely crumbled dried hot chillies
3 large cloves garlic, crushed
1 teaspoon salt
250 ml (9 fl oz) sunflower oil

For the sauce:
70 g (2½ oz) butter
60 ml (2 fl oz) lemon juice

Wipe the chicken portions and set aside. Combine the chillies, garlic, salt and 125 ml (4 fl oz) of the oil in a blender and process thoroughly. Pour the mixture into a deep bowl and stir in the remaining oil (if you wish to make the sauce by hand, pound the chillies and garlic to a paste in a small bowl and stir in the oil and salt).

Add the chicken pieces to the chilli mixture and coat them evenly. Marinate at room temperature for about 2 hours, then place the chicken on a baking tray, and grill about 5 cm (2 in) from the heat for about 7-8 minutes on each side (until cooked through). Keep the chicken warm while making the sauce. Melt the butter gently, stir in the lemon juice, and pour the sauce over the chicken.

SERVING SUGGESTION A spicy dish such as this is best served with plain rice.

VARIATION Prawns or fish can be marinated in the same mixture and grilled for 2-3 minutes as a substitute for chicken.

ROAST POUSSINS WITH RICE AND RAISIN STUFFING

THIS RECIPE is for really small chickens, serving one person each. Cooking in stock makes the flesh delightfully moist and succulent (even when cooking a tiny bird).

The skin is crisped only during the last minutes of cooking. The aromatic herbed rice stuffing makes a delicious accompaniment, the raisins adding a slight sweetness which blends well with the tarragon.

PREPARATION TIME: 1 HOUR
COOKING TIME: 1 HOUR
PREHEAT OVEN TO 180°C (350°F, MARK 4)

INGREDIENTS FOR SIX
6 poussins (spatchcocks), about 250-300 g/9-11 oz each
Salt and freshly ground black pepper
250 ml (9 fl oz) chicken stock*
100 ml (3½ fl oz) white wine
2 tablespoons lemon juice
2 teaspoons dried tarragon
3 tablespoons butter

For the stuffing:
3 tablespoons butter
1 onion, finely chopped*
125 g (4½ oz) rice
500 ml (17 fl oz) chicken stock*
3 tablespoons seedless raisins
2 tablespoons finely chopped parsley
1 teaspoon dried tarragon
2 tablespoons lemon juice
2 tablespoons melted butter

For the gravy:
5 teaspoons flour
500 ml (17 fl oz) chicken or vegetable stock* or water

Remove the giblets (retain for use in the stock) and wipe the poussins inside and out with a damp cloth. Season the insides lightly with salt and pepper.

To make the stuffing, melt the butter in a saucepan and sauté the onion on a low heat until soft. Add the rice and stir with the butter until it turns golden, then add the stock. Cook until the rice is done (but still firm in the centre). Drain if necessary and mix the rice with the raisins, parsley, tarragon and lemon juice. Season to taste and add the melted butter.

Stuff the poussins lightly and truss*

ROAST POUSSINS WITH RICE AND RAISIN STUFFING *Topped with lemon and parsley, this makes an attractive dish.*

them. Place in a baking dish which is large enough to contain the poussins neatly, but not too close together. Pour over the stock, wine and lemon juice, add a sprinkle of tarragon and dot the poussins with butter. Cover loosely with wax paper, tucking it in at the sides to contain the moisture.

Roast the poussins, basting frequently, for 30-45 minutes – until the juice from the thigh runs clear (the birds will have browned lightly through the paper). Now remove the paper and turn the heat up to 220°C (425°F, mark 7). Quickly complete browning the poussins, basting with the juices, which should have reduced considerably.

When they are nicely browned, transfer the poussins carefully to a heated serving plate. To make the gravy, stir the flour into the juices in the dish to make a smooth paste. Stir in the hot stock or water, seasoning to taste. Serve the gravy separately in a heated sauceboat.

SERVING SUGGESTIONS Arrange the poussins on a large platter and garnish with lemon and fresh parsley. Green beans, cooked whole and then mixed with sautéed mushrooms, spring onions and round game chips make a good accompaniment to this dish.

Any excess stuffing can be used as a bed on which to serve the poussins.

VARIATIONS Sprinkle the insides with seasoning and tarragon, adding a nut of butter and a quarter of lemon. Roast in the way described in the original recipe and serve with a spoonful of the reduced pan juices poured over the poussins just before serving. Serve with baked potatoes* and a sour cream dressing, and a substantial salad containing mushrooms, lettuce, tomatoes and cucumbers doused with garlic-flavoured vinaigrette*.

Alter the stuffing by using burghul (cracked wheat) or millet instead of the rice, and flavour it with crushed coriander seeds. In this case, omit the dried tarragon from the mixture so that it does not clash with the coriander.

73

BONING A CHICKEN

To bone a chicken effectively, you need a short, flexible knife. Keep it as close to the bone as possible, scraping and easing the flesh away rather than cutting. If you intend to roast the boned chicken, leave the wings intact to give shape to the bird. For a chicken roll or galantine, however, cut off the wing tips and middle section, and remove the largest wing bone.

Hold the bird breast side down and slit through the skin along the backbone, scraping and easing the flesh away on either side and exposing the rib cage.

When you get to the wings and legs, cut through the tendons close to the carcass at the joints, leaving the wings and legs attached to the skin (not the carcass).

Work round the bird, taking care not to puncture the skin – especially at the breastbone, which is close to the surface.

To bone the legs work from the thicker end of the joint and ease out the bones, scraping off the flesh as you pull carefully.

Spread the boned chicken on the work surface, skin side down, and lay stuffing down the middle.

Sew up the chicken along the back so as to enclose the stuffing completely. The final step is to truss* the bird.

STUFFED BONED CHICKEN

MANY BONED DISHES have a long history, some dating from the days when help in the kitchen was cheap and cooks had more time to spend on complicated preparation.

Stuffed boned chicken is worth mastering. It not only gives a neatly shaped piece of meat that cooks evenly and is more moist than usual, but is also easier to carve and a wonderful way of impressing your guests.

PREPARATION TIME: 30 MINUTES
COOKING TIME: 1½ HOURS
PREHEAT OVEN TO 190°C (375°F, MARK 5)
INGREDIENTS FOR SIX
1 chicken (1.5-2 kg/3-4½ lb), boned
Sunflower oil
1 teaspoon butter
1 small onion, peeled and finely
  chopped*
1 carrot, finely chopped
1 bay leaf
400 ml (14 fl oz) chicken stock*,
  made from the bones
Salt and pepper

For the stuffing:
1 tablespoon butter
1 small onion, peeled and finely
  chopped*
250 g (9 oz) pork sausage meat
2 tablespoons fresh white
  breadcrumbs
1 small apple, peeled and chopped
1 teaspoon fresh sage, chopped
1 large egg
Salt and freshly ground black
  pepper

To make the stuffing, melt the butter and fry the onion in it until soft. Mix with the remaining stuffing ingredients and season well. Spread the boned chicken onto a work surface (skin side down) and lay the stuffing down the middle.

Bring up the sides to enclose it and sew or tie them together with string to make a neat parcel. Heat a little oil in a large casserole, and add butter: when it begins to foam, put in the chicken and brown it. Remove the bird and reduce the heat.

Add the onion and carrot, return the chicken to the casserole and add the bay leaf, stock and seasoning. Cover and bake at 190°C (375°F, mark 5) for 1½ hours. Transfer the chicken to a serving plate to keep warm, and then remove all the string, so it is ready to carve.

To make the sauce, skim the fat from the cooking juices and blend or sieve the vegetables and remaining liquid. Return to a clean saucepan and boil rapidly until the mixture thickens. Carve the chicken and serve the sauce separately.

SERVING SUGGESTION Garnish the dish with watercress. Try serving the chicken cold, carved into slices, and with a tossed green salad*.

VARIATIONS For a thinner, more delicate sauce, strain the cooking juices into a clean saucepan and discard the vegetables. Reduce the sauce to a syrup and enrich it with cream.

Beef sausage meat could be used as an alternative to pork.

Wholemeal breadcrumbs are a tasty variation to white breadcrumbs.

CHICKEN KIEV

THIS IS A CLASSIC Ukrainian speciality of boned chicken breasts rolled around a finger of butter, coated with crumbs and fried just long enough to cook the chicken without losing the butter inside until they are cut. Traditionally, chicken suprêmes (the whole of the white breast meat, including the wing bone) should be used, but boned breasts are just as successful.

PREPARATION TIME: 45 MINUTES
CHILLING TIME: AT LEAST 3 HOURS
COOKING TIME: 30 MINUTES

INGREDIENTS FOR FOUR
4 large boned chicken breasts
Sunflower oil for deep-frying

For the herb butter:
100 g (3¾ oz) butter
Grated rind and juice of 1 lemon
1 tablespoon freshly chopped
  parsley
1 teaspoon chopped tarragon
1 teaspoon chopped chives
2 cloves garlic, very finely chopped
  (optional)
Salt and freshly ground black
  pepper

For the coating:
50 g (2 oz) flour, seasoned with salt
  and pepper
1 extra-large egg, beaten with
  1 teaspoon sunflower oil and
  1 teaspoon water
75 g (3 oz) dry white breadcrumbs

CHICKEN KIEV A deep-fried and delicious way of preparing poultry.

Trim any skin or gristle from the chicken breasts and place them about 4 cm (1½ in) apart between two large sheets of greaseproof paper. Beat them with a meat pounder or wooden rolling pin until flat and large enough to hold a stick of butter about the diameter of your little finger (do not puncture the chicken meat).

To make the herb butter, blend the butter, lemon rind, juice, herbs and garlic (if used) with plenty of seasoning. Shape into a cake 6 cm (2 in) square on a sheet of greaseproof paper. Cover and chill or freeze until very firm, then cut into 4 long sticks of equal width.

Place one stick in the centre of each piece of flattened chicken (the inner surface) and roll the chicken up around it, tucking in the ends to make a neat, sausage-shaped package that completely seals in the butter. Roll the chicken packages in seasoned flour, brush or dip them in the beaten egg mixture, and roll them in crumbs – pressing them firmly onto the chicken.

Chill the packages (uncovered) for at least 3 hours or overnight. You could also freeze them, but in this case you should allow them to thaw for about 6-7 hours in the refrigerator before cooking.

Heat the oil in a deep-fryer to 180°C (350°F) – a cube of day-old bread should turn golden-brown in 1-1¼ minutes – and fry the chicken breasts, two at a time, until golden-brown (about 5 minutes). Drain on paper towels and keep hot in an oven (with the door ajar) for 5-10 minutes while frying the remaining chicken. Arrange the pieces side by side on a serving dish, and serve immediately.

CHICKEN WITH CASHEW NUTS *is a quick and easy dish to prepare and can be eaten either hot or cold.*

CHICKEN WITH CASHEW NUTS

SLICED CHICKEN BREASTS, pineapple pieces and other ingredients are cooked quickly in a wok and served immediately to provide a very tasty meal. This Oriental dish tastes good even when cold and it reheats very successfully.

PREPARATION TIME: 10 MINUTES
FREEZING TIME: 30 MINUTES–1 HOUR
COOKING TIME: 10 MINUTES

INGREDIENTS FOR SIX
6 chicken breasts
1½ teaspoons salt
Pepper
1½ tablespoons cornflour
1 tin (425 g/15 oz) pineapple pieces
1 tablespoon sugar
1 tablespoon light soy sauce
1 tablespoon vinegar
2 tablespoons dry sherry
1 tablespoon Hoisin (or plum) sauce
4 tablespoons sunflower oil
100 g (3¾ oz) unsalted cashew nuts, split into halves
1 clove garlic, crushed
1 teaspoon grated fresh green ginger

Freeze the chicken breasts until they are firm enough to slice thinly. Combine the salt, a sprinkling of pepper and 1 tablespoon of the cornflour and then dredge the sliced chicken in the mixture. Drain the tinned pineapple, reserving the juice.

Mix the remaining cornflour with the pineapple juice, sugar, soy sauce, vinegar, sherry and Hoisin (or plum) sauce.

Heat half the sunflower oil in a wok or pan, then add the cashew nuts and stir-fry them until golden. Turn out into paper towels and reserve.

Heat the remaining oil in the same pan, add the garlic and ginger and stir-fry for half a minute. Add the chicken and stir-fry for 2 minutes. Remove the chicken from the wok and add the tinned pineapple.

Turn the pineapple pieces over in the pan, add the sauce and cook until it thickens, then add the chicken and cashew nuts and stir-fry for 1 minute.

If you do not intend to serve immediately, do not stir-fry after adding the chicken and nuts. Allow to cool and then refrigerate. To reheat, stir-fry very quickly in 1 tablespoon hot oil (just until it is heated through).

SERVING SUGGESTIONS Spoon the mixture onto a warm oval platter and surround with deep-fried Chinese vermicelli or deep-fried egg noodles, or alternatively serve with steamed rice.

VARIATION Substitute fried almonds for the cashew nuts. Thinly sliced pork fillet or other white meat can be used in place of chicken. A handful of bean sprouts* would add extra crunch.

STIR-FRIED CHICKEN AND VEGETABLES

Freshness is a most important quality for vegetables in all Chinese cooking. Several vegetables (with varying textures) are usually combined – those with the firmest textures being placed in the pan first. Factors such as the way a vegetable is cut, its freshness, the size of the pan and the degree of heat all affect the cooking time. Small quantities of meat and poultry can be stretched by cooking with this method.

PREPARATION TIME: 45 MINUTES
COOKING TIME: 10 MINUTES

INGREDIENTS FOR FOUR
375 g (13 oz) chicken meat, cubed
3 tablespoons sunflower oil
2 teaspoons grated fresh green ginger
1 clove garlic, crushed
2 onions, peeled* and cut into wedges, then separated
2 stalks celery, sliced diagonally into 1 cm (½ in) lengths
250 g (9 oz) broccoli, stems sliced diagonally, heads separated into small florets
4-5 dried Chinese mushrooms, soaked in boiling water for 30 minutes, then squeezed dry and sliced, or 50 g (2 oz) button mushrooms
125 g (4¼ oz) young green beans, trimmed
6 spring onions, sliced diagonally into 1 cm (½ in) lengths
4 teaspoons cornflour
250 ml (9 fl oz) water
40 ml (1½ fl oz) dry sherry
4 teaspoons soy sauce
2 teaspoons chicken stock powder
1 small tin baby corn, drained

Heat the oil to a high heat in a wok or pan, add the ginger and garlic, then the cubed chicken, and stir-fry for 1 minute. Add the onions, celery and broccoli stalks, stir-fry for 1 minute, then add the mushrooms, beans and spring onions and stir-fry for about 1 minute before adding the broccoli florets.

Mix the cornflour with a few drops of the water, then add the rest of the water, sherry, soy sauce and chicken stock powder. Pour the mixture into the pan and bring to the boil. Add the baby corn, simmer for 4 minutes and serve.

DEVILLED CHICKEN

Dr Kitchiner, in his *Cook's Oracle* (1817), introduces Devil Sauces with fine Regency aplomb: 'Every man must have experienced that when he has got deep into his third bottle ... his stomach is seized with a certain craving which seems to demand a stimulant. The provocatives used on such an occasion an ungrateful world has combined to term devils.'

Throughout the 19th century, devilling – flavouring to give a hot, sharp taste – was a popular and lively means of returning the remains of the previous day's joint or fowl to the table.

PREPARATION TIME: 20 MINUTES
COOKING TIME: 10-15 MINUTES

INGREDIENTS FOR FOUR
6-8 meaty poultry joints, such as chicken or turkey, cooked or freshly part-cooked

For the sauce:
100 g (3¾ oz) butter
1 tablespoon dry mustard
2 tablespoons stale breadcrumbs
1 tablespoon Worcestershire sauce
1 tablespoon mango or fruit chutney
Salt and cayenne pepper

Place the chicken joints on a sheet of aluminium foil, lightly greased with butter or sunflower oil, ready to be grilled.

To make the sauce, put the butter, mustard, breadcrumbs, Worcestershire sauce and chutney in a bowl and blend together with a fork or the back of a spoon. Break up any pieces of fruit or vegetable in the chutney and then season with salt and cayenne pepper.

Spread the sauce over the chicken joints and grill gently so that the meat heats through, and cooks as the sauce browns. Serve on warmed plates.

SERVING SUGGESTIONS Serve the chicken with a variety of salads such as coleslaw* or potato salad*.

Add any sauce left to a little gibler or game basic stock*. Heat thoroughly and pour it around the devilled joints.

VARIATION You do not have to confine yourself to devilled poultry. Any cooked meat – left over from a Sunday roast, perhaps – would be suitable, particularly mutton or lamb.

DEVILLED CHICKEN *for those with a hankering for spicy foods.*

GREEK CHICKEN *offers a delectable combination of appetising flavours.*

SPANISH CHICKEN WITH RICE

THIS IS A VERSION of the traditional Spanish dish known as *arroz con pollo*. It makes use of ingredients such as onions, tomatoes, sweet red peppers and saffron. The rice is cooked in the same pot as the chicken, making it a simple meal-in-one dish that is easy to prepare.

PREPARATION TIME: 20 MINUTES
COOKING TIME: 1 HOUR

INGREDIENTS FOR FOUR TO SIX
8 *chicken pieces*
3 *tablespoons olive or sunflower oil*
1 *large onion, peeled and thinly sliced**
1 *large clove garlic, crushed*
1 *large sweet red pepper, thinly sliced*
4 *ripe red tomatoes, skinned, seeded* and roughly chopped*
A good pinch of saffron
Salt and freshly ground black pepper
400 g (14 oz) *rice*
500 ml (17 fl oz) *hot chicken stock**
12 *black olives, stoned*
1 *tablespoon capers (optional)*
125 g (4¼ oz) *frozen peas*

Choose a heavy-based or non-stick pan (with a tight-fitting lid) and fry the cleaned and well-dried chicken pieces in the oil until lightly browned on both sides. Remove from the pan and set aside.

Add the onion to the pan and fry gently for 5-10 minutes (or until soft). Add the garlic and sliced red pepper and cook gently for another 5-10 minutes.

Stir in the chopped tomatoes and saffron, and cook for another 10 minutes, then add the chicken pieces. Season and cook (tightly covered) for 15 minutes.

Stir in the rice and half the chicken stock and simmer for 15 minutes. Stir in the rest of the stock, adding the olives, capers (if used) and peas, and cook for another 15 minutes (or until the rice is tender and the liquid has been absorbed). Stir the pot now and again. If necessary, add a little extra stock to complete cooking the rice. Check the seasoning and serve with a green salad.

VARIATION Stir in 4 tinned or bottled artichoke hearts (cut into quarters) along with the peas for a more exotic result.

GREEK CHICKEN

THIS DISH CONSISTS essentially of chicken flavoured with cinnamon and baked with black olives. Its taste is piquant and, to the converted, quite irresistible.

PREPARATION TIME: 15 MINUTES
COOKING TIME: 1 HOUR
PREHEAT OVEN TO 190°C (375°F, MARK 5)

INGREDIENTS FOR SIX
6 *large portions of chicken*
2 *cloves garlic, crushed*
Salt and freshly ground black pepper
2 *tablespoons olive oil*
6 *cinnamon sticks*
4 *tomatoes, skinned* and sliced*
150 g (5 oz) *black olives, stoned and halved*
6 *slices lemon*
125 ml (4 fl oz) *dry white wine*
60 ml (2 fl oz) *orange juice*

Arrange the chicken pieces side by side in a shallow ovenproof dish. Smear them all over with crushed garlic and then sprinkle with the salt, pepper and olive oil. Place the cinnamon sticks under and around the chicken.

Arrange slices of tomato and halved olives around the chicken pieces, with slices of lemon on top. Pour over the wine and orange juice, and cover with aluminium foil.

Put in the oven and bake at 190°C (375°F, mark 5) for about 1 hour, remove the cinnamon sticks, and serve.

SERVING SUGGESTION This chicken dish tastes very good served with either buttered noodles or rice and a simple traditional Greek salad consisting of lettuce, cucumber and feta cheese.

VARIATIONS Add chopped or crushed fresh ginger or a mixture of both in the place of cinnamon. You could also substitute thinly sliced fennel for the cinnamon, giving an aniseed flavour.

CHICKEN STEW WITH ORANGE AND TOMATO

THE COMBINATION OF ORANGE and tomato, though it may sound illogical, is actually quite delicious. Sweet basil and caraway seeds add a very compatible piquancy to a dish which, although inexpensive, is stylish enough for a dinner party.

PREPARATION TIME: 20 MINUTES
COOKING TIME: 2 HOURS

INGREDIENTS FOR SIX
2 kg (4½ lb) chicken thighs or
    1 large chicken, cut into serving-
    sized portions
2 onions, peeled and sliced*
50 ml (2 fl oz) sunflower oil
3 cloves garlic, crushed
2 teaspoons basil
1 tin (400 g/14 oz) skinned
    tomatoes or 500 g (1 lb 2 oz)
    fresh tomatoes, skinned*
2 tablespoons tomato paste
250 ml (9 fl oz) orange juice
Rind of 1 orange, grated
100 ml (3½ fl oz) white wine
Salt and freshly ground black
    pepper
¼ teaspoon caraway seeds
2 tablespoons cornflour mixed to a
    paste with water

For the garnish:
Chopped parsley
Parmesan cheese

Wipe the chicken pieces and set aside. In a heavy-based saucepan, brown the sliced onion in oil, remove with a slotted spoon, and brown the chicken pieces. Pour off the fat and return the chicken to the pot.

Add the onion, garlic, basil, tomatoes, tomato paste, orange juice, orange rind and wine. Cover and simmer on a low heat until tender (1½-2 hours). Season to taste and add the caraway seeds. Thicken the sauce with the cornflour paste, and bring to the boil once again. If making in advance, thicken when reheating.

SERVING SUGGESTIONS Serve on a large, heated plate, surrounded by scraped new potatoes rolled in parsley butter* or herb butter*. Garnish with chopped parsley and Parmesan cheese.

This dish is also excellent served with fettucine or vermicelli, in which case it is best to bone* the chicken pieces (before or after cooking).

Fresh greens, crisply and simply cooked, are also good with this rich, tasty dish. Similarly, courgettes (zucchini), green beans, spinach or cabbage are all compatible.

VARIATION Fennel seed used instead of the caraway will give a slightly different, but equally delicious, flavour.

ROAST STUFFED CHICKEN

ROAST CHICKEN has long met with universal approval, especially since any leftovers can be eaten cold during the following few days or used in a hot pie or even a fricassee flavoured with sherry.

PREPARATION TIME: 30-40 MINUTES
COOKING TIME: 1½ HOURS
PREHEAT OVEN TO 200°C (400°F, MARK 6)

INGREDIENTS FOR SIX
1 large roasting chicken (1.5-2 kg/
    3-4½ lb)
2 tablespoons butter or chicken
    dripping

For the stuffing:
4 slices stale bread with crusts
    removed, or 100-125 g (3¾-4¼ oz)
    fresh breadcrumbs
150 ml (¼ pint) milk or chicken
    stock*
Chicken liver
1 tablespoon fresh parsley, thyme
    and chives, mixed and chopped,
    or 1½ teaspoons dried mixed
    herbs
Grated rind and juice of 1 lemon
1 small onion, chopped*
1 tablespoon shredded chicken fat,
    or 30 g (1¼ oz) butter
1 tablespoon ground almonds
Salt and pepper

For the gravy:
300 ml (½ pint) chicken stock* or
    cider
2 teaspoons cornflour (optional)

Wipe the chicken, remove the giblets and set aside the liver. To make the stuffing,

CHICKEN STEW WITH ORANGE AND TOMATO *A piquant and unusual dish.*

soak the bread in the milk. If you are using breadcrumbs, add the milk or stock gradually (do not oversaturate). Leave for 20 minutes or until all the moisture has been fully absorbed.

Add the chopped chicken liver, herbs, lemon rind and juice, onion, chicken fat or butter and ground almonds. Mix together well and then season with salt and pepper to taste.

Spoon the stuffing into the neck cavity of the chicken until the breast is plump, but be careful not to pack it too tightly; the stuffing will swell a little during the cooking. Secure with a skewer or with a trussing needle and string.

Use the remainder of the stuffing to fill the body of the bird from the tail end, or shape into small stuffing-balls (to be added to the pan juices for the last 30 minutes of cooking).

Lightly grease a baking dish. Rub the breast and legs of the chicken with the butter or dripping and sprinkle with salt and pepper. Put the chicken in the dish and cover loosely with greaseproof paper or aluminium foil.

Roast in the centre of the preheated oven for 1 hour. Then reduce the oven temperature to 180°C (350°F, mark 4), remove the greaseproof paper or foil, baste well and cook for a further 30 minutes (or until golden-brown on top). Keep the chicken warm.

To make the gravy, pour off the fat from the baking dish. Add the strained chicken stock or cider. Stir well and boil rapidly on top of the stove for a few minutes. Season to taste. To make a thicker gravy, add the cornflour to the cold stock and stir all the time as you bring it gradually to the boil.

VARIATIONS The ways to vary roast stuffed chicken are practically limitless. All you have to do is adjust the stuffing recipe to suit your taste.

To the basic ingredients of breadcrumbs, onion and stock, you can add chopped herbs or spices. Try a combination of crushed coriander seeds and grated orange rind. Chopped nuts or small quantities of chopped, cooked vegetables will also enhance the stuffing.

BRAISED CHICKEN WITH SWEET POTATO AND PUMPKIN

THE DISTINCTIVE FLAVOURS of sweet potato and pumpkin are retained in this quick family meal. For the best results, serve as soon as the chicken and vegetables are cooked.

PREPARATION TIME: 30 MINUTES
COOKING TIME: 1 HOUR

INGREDIENTS FOR FOUR TO SIX
8 chicken portions
1 tablespoon sunflower oil
1 large onion, peeled and thinly sliced*
2 sticks cinnamon
Salt and freshly ground black pepper
1 clove garlic, crushed
500 g (1 lb 2 oz) sweet potato, peeled and cubed
500 g (1 lb 2 oz) pumpkin, peeled and cubed
250 ml (9 fl oz) chicken stock*
125 g (4¼ oz) prunes

Pat the chicken quite dry, then brown in the hot oil. Add the onion, cinnamon and season. Cook gently until golden taking care not to let the onion burn.

Add the garlic, sweet potato and pumpkin and a little more seasoning, then pour in the stock and bring to the boil. Cover and reduce the heat, cooking gently for 40 minutes (or until everything is quite tender).

Add the prunes and allow them to heat through until they are plump and soft.

If there appears to be too much liquid, remove the chicken and vegetables with a slotted spoon and keep warm on a suitable dish while you reduce the stock over a brisk heat (uncovered). Check the seasoning and pour the stock over the hot chicken and vegetables.

VARIATION If pumpkin is hard to find, replace it with marrow. You can also use ordinary potatoes, but this will change the texture of the dish.

BRAISED CHICKEN WITH SWEET POTATO AND PUMPKIN *Filling and nutritious.*

ROAST GOOSE WITH RUM-SOAKED APPLES

IN THE LATE 18TH CENTURY, onion, sage and apples were considered the ideal stuffing for roast goose. The ingredients and the goose complement one another, while the apple also does much to counteract any greasiness.

PREPARATION TIME: 30 MINUTES
SOAKING TIME: 4 HOURS
COOKING TIME: 4 HOURS
PREHEAT OVEN TO 180°C (350°F, MARK 4)

INGREDIENTS FOR SIX
1 goose (about 4.5 kg/10 lb)
Salt and freshly ground black pepper
3 tablespoons sunflower oil or dripping
850 ml (1½ pints) poultry stock*
100-125 ml (3¼-4 fl oz) dark rum

For the stuffing:
6 large eating apples, peeled, cored, chopped and soaked in rum for 4 hours
1 large onion, peeled and chopped* and softened with 2 tablespoons butter in a frying pan
3 finely chopped sage leaves or ¼ teaspoon dried sage
¼ teaspoon ground mace or nutmeg
350 g (¾ lb) freshly made breadcrumbs

Remove the giblets and wipe the goose clean, inside and out.

Mix the stuffing ingredients together and spoon into the body of the bird. If there is any left, put it into the neck cavity under the flap of skin.

Rub salt and pepper into the skin and then prick it all over. Place the goose on a rack in a baking dish and smear the legs and wings with the oil or dripping. Cover the breast with a large piece of aluminium foil or greaseproof paper. Place in the centre of the preheated oven.

Roast for 30 minutes, then spoon off any excess fat and baste well with the warm poultry stock: do this every 30 minutes. After 2½ hours, remove the foil or greaseproof paper so that the breast can crisp and brown for the last 1½ hours.

Place the goose on a warmed serving dish and keep warm. Strain off excess fat from the juices in the baking dish and boil rapidly to reduce and make gravy.

Heat the rum in a ladle or small pan and pour over the bird, then set it alight.

SERVING SUGGESTIONS Serve immediately with mashed celeriac and potatoes or a purée of turnips, parsnips or Jerusalem artichokes, and a salad. Or serve with carrots, and broccoli when in season.

CHICKEN SALAD

THIS FRESH, RICH SALAD goes well with virtually anything, and is also a meal in itself. For the best results make sure all the greens are crisp and crunchy.

PREPARATION TIME: 15 MINUTES

INGREDIENTS FOR FOUR TO SIX
1 cooked chicken, skinned and cut into cubes
4 stalks celery, sliced
6 spring onions, finely sliced
1 green apple, core removed and thinly sliced
1 green pepper, thinly sliced or chopped
125 ml (4 fl oz) mayonnaise*
4 tablespoons cream
Salt and freshly ground black pepper
Large lettuce leaves
1 ripe avocado, sliced and brushed with lemon juice

For the garnish:
2 teaspoons chopped fresh tarragon or parsley

Combine the chicken, celery, spring onions, apple, green pepper, mayonnaise, cream, salt and pepper. Toss the ingredients together and taste to correct the seasoning.

Arrange the lettuce leaves on a flat serving platter, place the avocado on the lettuce leaves and spoon over the chicken mixture. Garnish the salad with the chopped tarragon or parsley.

SERVING SUGGESTION Try serving with home-baked brown bread and butter and a bottle of well-chilled white wine.

VARIATIONS Add 1 teaspoon curry powder to the cream and mayonnaise to make a curried chicken salad.

Instead of the mayonnaise and cream, mix together 30 g (1¼ oz) Roquefort cheese, 3 tablespoons wine vinegar and 90 ml (3 fl oz) sunflower oil, and blend with the other ingredients as directed.

KESAR MASALA MURGHI

THIS POPULAR DISH, chicken in saffron gravy, improves on standing, and can be prepared well ahead of the serving time – in fact it tastes better if you do so. Spiced chicken pieces are browned, braised with onions, then cooked slowly until done. The cooked chicken can be frozen for up to 2 months.

PREPARATION TIME: 20 MINUTES
COOKING TIME: 1 HOUR

INGREDIENTS FOR SIX
1 chicken (1.5 kg/3 lb 3 oz), cut into small pieces
2 teaspoons chilli powder
1 teaspoon turmeric
About 10 cloves garlic, peeled and crushed finely
30 g (1¼ oz) fresh green ginger, scraped and pounded to a paste with a little water
1½ teaspoons salt
½ teaspoon saffron
250 ml (9 fl oz) milk
60 ml (2 fl oz) sunflower oil
2 cinnamon sticks
6 cloves
6 cardamom pods
1 onion, peeled and sliced*
125 ml (4 fl oz) natural yoghurt
250 ml (9 fl oz) hot water
2 tomatoes, cut in half and roughly chopped
1 tablespoon chopped coriander leaves

Wash the chicken pieces and drain. In a bowl, mix the chilli powder, turmeric, garlic, ginger and salt and rub over the chicken pieces. Place the saffron in the milk and set aside.

Using a large saucepan, heat the oil, then add the cinnamon, cloves and cardamom and brown for 10 seconds. Add the sliced onion and brown lightly. Add the chicken pieces to the pot and braise with the onion for 10 minutes. Pour the yoghurt, saffron milk and hot water over the chicken, then add the chopped tomatoes. Stir, cover the saucepan and cook on a medium heat for 45 minutes. Garnish with chopped coriander.

SERVING SUGGESTIONS Prepare 500 g (1 lb 2 oz) white or basmati rice to serve with the saffron gravy.

Alternatively, serve with chapati* and cauliflower, cooked until just tender and lightly fried with garlic.

81

ACCOMPANIMENTS TO INDIAN DISHES

One of the most enjoyable aspects of eating Indian food is the wide assortment of accompaniments that are traditionally used. Some are hot and spicy, while others serve to cool the palate.

CHAPATI

PREPARATION TIME: 10 MINUTES
STANDING TIME: 30 MINUTES
COOKING TIME: 30 MINUTES

INGREDIENTS FOR 12 CHAPATI
250 g (9 oz) wholemeal flour
¼ teaspoon salt
100 ml (3½ fl oz) water

Mix the flour and salt in a bowl, then add the water to make a dough. Knead thoroughly until smooth and place in a bowl. Cover with a damp cloth and leave the dough for 30 minutes.

Meanwhile, heat a large, heavy frying pan over a medium heat. Cut the dough into 12 pieces, shape them into balls, and roll each one out very thinly, using plenty of flour. Put the chapati into the frying pan 2 or 3 at a time and cook them until the edges start to curl, then turn and cook the other side. Wrap in a napkin and serve.

POPPADOMS

Buy the wafer-thin pancakes and fry in oil until crisp and golden (be careful not to burn them; the process takes only a few seconds). Drain and serve with curry.

KHAJOOR NI CHATNI

PREPARATION TIME: 20 MINUTES

INGREDIENTS TO YIELD 250 ML (9 FL OZ)
40 g (1½ oz) tamarind (available at specialist grocers)
80 ml (2½ fl oz) water
12 dates, pitted
A 2.5 cm (1 in) piece of fresh green ginger, scraped
1 small onion, peeled*
1 teaspoon ground cumin
1 teaspoon ground coriander
¾ teaspoon salt
¾ teaspoon chilli powder

Soak the tamarind in 80 ml (2½ fl oz) water for 10 minutes. Remove the bits and strain, retaining the water. Purée the remaining ingredients in a blender with the tamarind water to a smooth pulp.

This chatni not only goes well with Indian meals, but would also be delicious served with a pilaff of lamb and apricots*.

DHANIA PHOODINI CHATNI

PREPARATION TIME: 20 MINUTES

INGREDIENTS TO YIELD 250 ML (9 FL OZ)
1 bunch (about 115 g/4 oz) fresh coriander
Small handful fresh mint leaves
½ ripe tomato
2 teaspoons cumin seeds
1½ teaspoons salt
1-2 green chillies, cut into 2.5 cm (1 in) pieces
4 cloves garlic, peeled
2 tablespoons lemon juice
1 tablespoon malt vinegar

Remove the coriander roots and wash several times. Wash the mint and drain, then cut the tomato into wedges. Place all the ingredients in a blender and reduce to a thick, smooth pulp. Transfer the chutney to a small bowl and serve.

CUCUMBER RAITA

PREPARATION TIME: 5-10 MINUTES
STANDING TIME: 1 HOUR
CHILLING TIME: 30 MINUTES

INGREDIENTS FOR FOUR TO SIX
1 green cucumber
1 tablespoon salt
1 clove garlic, peeled and crushed
150 ml (¼ pint) natural yoghurt
2 tablespoons freshly chopped mint
2 tablespoons lemon juice
A pinch of cayenne pepper

Peel the cucumber and slice it thinly. Arrange the slices on a flat dish and sprinkle them with salt, leaving them to stand for 1 hour to extract the moisture. Drain the cucumber and pat dry with a paper towel.

Stir the crushed garlic into the yoghurt with the mint, lemon juice and a pinch of cayenne pepper. Pour the mixture over the cucumber, mix together well and chill for about 30 minutes.

Cucumber raita is an excellent accompaniment to all kinds of dishes. It cools the palate after a hot curry, or can counteract the richness of roast meats. For a vegetarian meal, serve with Inda Nu Sakh* and lentils garnished with onion.

CHICKEN BIRIANI

BIRIANI IS A SAVOURY DISH of meat or fish, rice, usually lentils and eggs. Indian people regard it as food fit for a king, and it is an established favourite.

PREPARATION TIME: 30 MINUTES
COOKING TIME: 2 HOURS

INGREDIENTS FOR SIX
1 chicken (1.5 kg/3 lb 3 oz)
Salt
90 ml (3 fl oz) sunflower oil, clarified butter* or ghee
1 large onion, chopped or sliced into rings*
2.5 cm (1 in) piece fresh green ginger
2 cloves garlic
½ teaspoon cumin seeds
1 teaspoon coriander
¼ teaspoon cayenne pepper
A few fresh coriander or bay leaves
1 large tomato, skinned* and grated
80 ml (2¼ fl oz) sour milk
4 small potatoes, cut into quarters
250 g (9 oz) rice
A few cardamom seeds
2 cloves
A pinch of saffron
250 ml (9 fl oz) boiling water

Cut the chicken into small pieces, salt and put aside. Heat 60 ml (2 fl oz) of the oil, clarified butter or ghee and sauté the onion in it until golden. Pound the ginger, garlic, cumin seeds, coriander, cayenne pepper and leaves in a mortar, add to the onions and cook for 4 minutes over a very low heat.

Add the chicken and cook for another 7 minutes. Next, add the tomato and sour milk, and let the chicken simmer slowly for 30 minutes. Heat the remaining sunflower oil, fry the potatoes in it and add them to the chicken mixture. In the meantime, cook the rice with salt, cardamom and cloves until almost done; then strain.

Spoon a layer of rice into a large, heavy-bottomed saucepan, followed by a layer of the chicken mixture. Repeat, ending with a layer of rice.

Dissolve the saffron in the boiling water and pour over the rice. Cover the saucepan with a tight-fitting lid and cook over a very low heat. Do not remove the lid until you are ready to serve.

ROAST DUCK WITH ORANGE AND GRAND MARNIER

THIS RECIPE DESCRIBES a wonderfully rich dish which is well worth the time and trouble spent in preparing it. The duck and its accompaniments make up a substantial menu.

PREPARATION TIME: 30-45 MINUTES
COOKING TIME: 2 HOURS
PREHEAT OVEN TO 210°C (425°F, MARK 7)

INGREDIENTS FOR FOUR
1 duck (about 2 kg/4½ lb), cleaned
    and patted dry
1 teaspoon salt
1 clove garlic, crushed
4 black peppercorns
2 oranges, quartered (unpeeled)
2 stalks celery, sliced
1 onion, peeled* and quartered
4 tablespoons Grand Marnier
4 tablespoons orange marmalade

For the orange sauce:
2 oranges
3 tablespoons butter
Duck liver
3 tablespoons brandy
1 clove garlic, crushed
2 tablespoons flour
2 teaspoons tomato paste
1½ teaspoons beef extract
A dash of white pepper
250 ml (9 fl oz) chicken stock*
4 tablespoons Grand Marnier
4 tablespoons orange marmalade

For the garnish:
2 oranges, peeled and divided into
    segments
Fresh watercress

Sprinkle the inside of the duck with salt and rub with the crushed garlic. Stuff the duck with the peppercorns, oranges, celery and onion, and pour in the Grand Marnier. Place the duck breast side up on the rack of the grilling pan and roast at 210°C (425°F, mark 7) for 30 minutes, pricking the flesh from time to time to release the fat. Discard the fat in the pan and place the duck on a rack in a baking dish filled with 125 ml (4 fl oz) water. Reduce the oven temperature to 180°C (350°F, mark 4). Spread the duck with the marmalade and roast for 1½ hours.

While the duck is roasting, make the orange sauce. Peel the rind of one orange and cut it into fine slivers. Squeeze the juice from both oranges and put on one side. Melt 2 tablespoons of butter and gently fry the duck liver until brown on both sides and pink inside. Remove from the heat.

In a small saucepan, heat the brandy and ignite. Pour the flaming brandy over the liver: when the flame subsides, remove the liver and add the remaining tablespoon of butter, orange peel and garlic. Cook for 3 minutes, then remove from the heat and stir in the flour, tomato paste, beef extract and pepper until they are well mixed.

Gradually stir in the chicken stock, Grand Marnier, marmalade and orange juice. Bring to the boil, then reduce the heat and simmer for 15 minutes. Chop the liver and add to the sauce. Pour the hot orange sauce into a gravy boat.

SERVING SUGGESTION Place the duck on a heated serving dish and decorate with orange segments and watercress. Serve the roast duck with crisp roast potatoes and minted peas.

VARIATION This recipe can be used equally for roast goose. Experiment with other liqueurs, either orange-based, such as Cointreau, or try Van der Hum which is based on tangerines.

ROAST DUCK WITH ORANGE AND GRAND MARNIER *Rich, delicious and attractive.*

83

PEKING DUCK

THE ESSENCE OF PEKING DUCK is its crisp skin, which is stripped off the cooked duck and served separately. To obtain this, the skin of the uncooked duck should be thoroughly dried.

PREPARATION TIME: 2 HOURS
HANGING TIME: 3-4 HOURS,
OR OVERNIGHT
COOKING TIME: 1¼ HOURS
PREHEAT OVEN TO 200°C (400°F, MARK 6)

INGREDIENTS FOR SIX
1 large duck (about 2.5 kg/5½ lb)
2 tablespoons brandy, vodka or
    gin (optional)
18 spring onions

For the pancakes:
450 g (1 lb) flour
600 ml (21 fl oz) boiling water
2 tablespoons sesame oil

For the table sauce:
125 ml (4 fl oz) Hoisin (or plum)
    sauce
4 teaspoons sugar
4 teaspoons sesame oil
4 teaspoons cold water

For the basting sauce:
3 tablespoons soy sauce
4 teaspoons caster sugar
150 ml (¼ pint) cold water

Wipe and dry the duck and pass a length of string under the wings so that it can be suspended from a rod or broom handle placed across the seats of two chairs. Set a plate under the duck to catch any drips.

Rubbing the skin with the brandy, gin or vodka aids the drying process. Direct a blast of cold air onto the duck from an electric fan and leave it for at least 3-4 hours. Alternatively, hang the duck overnight in a draughty place.

Remove any bits of roots and blemished leaves from the spring onions – trimming the onions to a length of about 10 cm (4 in). Wash them thoroughly. Use a sharp knife to make two vertical cuts, 1-2 cm (½-1 in) long, at the bulb end of each onion, then make two similar cuts at right angles to the first cuts. Put the onions in a large bowl of iced water and leave in the refrigerator until required. The cut end will fan out to resemble a small brush.

To make the pancakes, sift the flour into a bowl and, mixing all the time, add about 600 ml (21 fl oz) boiling water to make a soft dough that leaves the sides of the bowl clean. Knead the dough for 10 minutes on a lightly floured surface until it becomes rubbery. Cover with a cloth and leave for 20 minutes.

Roll the dough out, 5 mm (¼ in) thick, and cut it into rounds with a plain 5 cm (2 in) scone cutter.

Brush the top of half the rounds with sesame seed oil and place an unbrushed round on top. Roll out each pair of pancakes as thinly as possible, to a diameter of about 15 cm (6 in).

Heat an ungreased heavy frying pan for 30 seconds, then lower the heat. Put in the first pancake, turning it when bubbles appear on the surface and the underside is flecked with brown and looks floury.

Cook all the pancakes in this way (they may puff up into balloons), and allow them to cool. Wrap the cooked pancakes in aluminium foil parcels and store them in the refrigerator until needed.

Mix the table sauce ingredients together in a small pan, and bring the sauce to the boil; stir over a low heat for 2-3 minutes. Pour the sauce into a serving bowl and leave to cool.

Mix the ingredients for the basting sauce, and brush the sauce all over the duck. Place the duck, breast upwards, on a wire rack in a baking dish. Pour in enough boiling water to reach 6 mm (¼ in) up the sides of the dish. Roast the duck in the lower part of the preheated oven for 1¼ hours. Brush with the basting sauce every 15 or 20 minutes. After 45 minutes, turn up the heat to 230°C (450°F, mark 8). Put the parcels of prepared pancakes into the oven to reheat.

To assemble the final dish, cut the duck skin with scissors or a sharp knife in 5 cm (2 in) squares; place on a serving dish and keep warm. Carve the meat into long, thin slivers and arrange on another dish to keep warm. Pile the pancakes on a hot dish and cover with a napkin or folded cloth to keep them warm. Put the onion brushes in a bowl or dish and arrange all these dishes, with the sauce, on the table.

To eat Peking duck, carefully pull the two halves of a pancake apart, starting where the join can be seen quite clearly. Dip an onion brush in the sauce and brush it liberally onto the soft moist side of the open pancake. Top with pieces of duck skin and slivers of meat; fold or roll up the pancake.

BRAISED GUINEA FOWL

THIS RECIPE IS FOR GUINEA FOWL cooked in a rich sauce. When choosing your birds, try to obtain them well matured. Otherwise hang them in a cool place for 5-7 days – depending on the climate – to achieve the best results.

PREPARATION TIME: 15 MINUTES
COOKING TIME: 1¼ HOURS

INGREDIENTS FOR SIX TO EIGHT
2 guinea fowl
2 tablespoons melted butter
2 tablespoons sunflower oil
Salt and freshly ground black
    pepper
300 g (11 oz) pickling onions,
    peeled*
2 tablespoons flour
500 ml (17 fl oz) chicken stock*
Grated rind and juice of 1 large
    orange
1 tablespoon apple jelly
1 tablespoon cider vinegar

Brown the guinea fowl in the butter and oil (using a deep frying pan). Remove from the frying pan and place in an ovenproof dish. Season with salt and black pepper, then brown the onions in the frying pan. Remove the onions and set aside.

Add the flour to the pan juices, stir and cook for 2 minutes. Slowly add the stock, whisk until the sauce is smooth and add it to the guinea fowl. Mix the orange rind, orange juice, jelly and vinegar, and pour over the guinea fowl. Cover and simmer for one hour.

Remove the lid, add the browned onions, and simmer until the sauce has been reduced and the meat is soft. Taste, adjust the seasoning if necessary, and serve at once.

SERVING SUGGESTION Boiled rice or boiled potatoes make suitable accompaniments to this dish, or instead, serve parsnips (which have been boiled and glazed with butter and a little sugar) and stir-fried cabbage greens to add colour to the meal.

VARIATIONS Replace the stock with dry white wine and whisk 125 ml (4 fl oz) sour cream into the sauce just before adding the onions.

If you prefer, the pickling onions can be replaced with leeks, which should be cut into 2.5 cm (1 in) lengths.

TURKEY SALAD WITH CHEESE AND SESAME SEEDS *is a perfect way of using leftover meat to make a light, tasty dish.*

TURKEY SALAD WITH CHEESE AND SESAME SEEDS

Turkey leftovers lend themselves to the creation of many interesting salad dishes. Water chestnuts and diced celery give this particular salad a nice crunchy texture, contrasting well with the Gruyère. The dressing serves to flavour the meat, keeping it moist.

PREPARATION TIME: 45 MINUTES
COOKING TIME: 5-10 MINUTES
CHILLING TIME: 3 HOURS

INGREDIENTS FOR FOUR
425-450 g ($\frac{3}{4}$-1 lb) diced cooked turkey meat or smoked breast of turkey
4 stalks celery, sliced
1 tin (230 g/8 oz) water chestnuts, diced
4 thinly sliced spring onions
75 g (3 oz) thinly sliced strips of Gruyère cheese

For the dressing:
1 tablespoon sesame seeds
125 ml (4 fl oz) olive oil or sesame oil
60 ml (2 fl oz) white vinegar
60 ml (2 fl oz) lemon juice
1 teaspoon French mustard
Salt and freshly ground black pepper

Combine all the salad ingredients in a bowl. Sauté the sesame seeds in the olive oil or sesame oil until lightly browned, then remove from the heat and leave until they are cool.

When the sautéed sesame seeds have cooled, mix together the vinegar, lemon juice and mustard and then pour on the oil, with the sesame seeds, in a thin stream. Whisk the mixture as you pour in order to amalgamate thoroughly so that the dressing is very well blended.

Season to taste and pour over the turkey salad. Toss the salad to coat it well with the dressing, cover, and refrigerate for 3 hours.

SERVING SUGGESTIONS Serve the turkey salad on a bed of shredded lettuce garnished with egg and tomato wedges, and serve with crispy rolls or French bread.

This turkey salad makes an ideal light supper dish or lunch dish and is particularly recommended as a summer meal or even as an hors d'oeuvre.

VARIATIONS Julienned* strips of thinly sliced Emmenthal cheese make a good substitute for the Gruyère.

Slices of fresh or tinned pineapple are delicious in place of the egg and tomato garnish. Instead of using sesame seeds in the dressing, try adding very finely chopped walnuts.

85

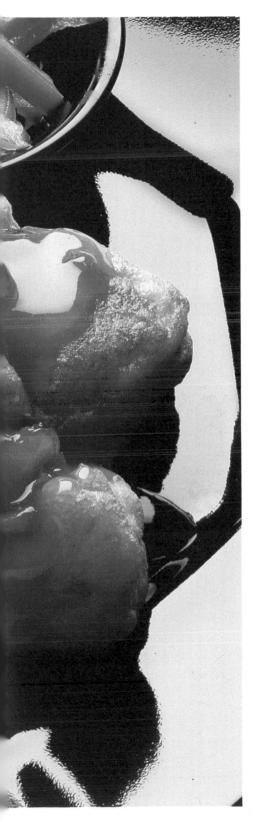

SAUCES

IT IS QUITE FITTING that the English word 'sauce' should have its origin in an old French word, since the chefs of France have probably perfected the art of making sauces. The French, in turn, derived the word from the Latin for 'salted', and many people regard salt as the ultimate flavour-enhancer.

The choice of sauce can do much to transform even the most everyday dish into something quite special and sauces are often an integral part of dishes, as in avocado vinaigrette, eggs Benedict and steak chasseur. Others have become such a part of culinary tradition that some people would not think of serving, say, roast pork without apple sauce or Christmas turkey without bread sauce.

The richer, more flavourful sauces are useful in perking up otherwise bland foods such as poached fish or often-used budget foods such as chicken. But at the other end of the scale, you can complement a tender, top-grade cut of meat, such as a juicy fillet steak, with a classic béarnaise sauce.

MAYONNAISE

THE SECRET of making perfect mayonnaise lies in the 'unremitting beating of the olive oil into the egg yolks'. That was the pronouncement of Antonin Carême, the master chef regarded as the founder of classic French cookery.

It does not take a great deal of skill and patience to make this classic sauce, which is a rich and subtle complement to many cold dishes and salads. You can even whisk it in a blender or food processor. Make sure all the ingredients are at room temperature before you start.

PREPARATION TIME: 20 MINUTES

INGREDIENTS TO YIELD ABOUT 275 ML
(9½ FL OZ)
2 egg yolks
1 tablespoon lemon juice or wine
 vinegar
¼ teaspoon salt
¼ teaspoon dry mustard
300 ml (½ pint) olive or sunflower
 oil, or a mixture of both
1 tablespoon boiling water
¼ teaspoon freshly ground black
 pepper

Put the egg yolks in a mixing bowl (do not use a metal one) and whisk well for 1 minute. Add the lemon juice or vinegar, the salt and mustard, and beat the mixture for 1 minute more.

Add the oil, drop by drop, whisking continuously. After about a quarter of the oil has been added, the mayonnaise takes on the consistency of thin cream. The rest of the oil can be added more rapidly; beat well after each addition.

When all the oil is absorbed, whisk in the boiling water. This helps to ensure that the mayonnaise does not curdle (it will also keep better). If it does curdle, beat another egg yolk in a clean bowl, then beat the curdled mixture into it, drop by drop.

Taste, add a little more lemon juice and salt if necessary, and stir in the pepper. Store in a sealed glass jar in the refrigerator.

VARIATION If you are making the mayonnaise in a food processor or blender, place all the ingredients except the oil and water in the container and blend for 4 seconds. Add the oil in a steady stream until the sauce is thick and creamy, then blend in the boiling water.

SAUCES BASED ON MAYONNAISE

Curry Mayonnaise To 250 ml (9 fl oz) mayonnaise add 2 teaspoons mild curry powder, ¼ teaspoon ground ginger, 1 teaspoon honey, 1 tablespoon chutney, 1 teaspoon lemon juice and 1 tablespoon slivered almonds. This mayonnaise makes a good accompaniment to chicken or fish salads.

Herb Mayonnaise To 250 ml (9 fl oz) mayonnaise add 2 tablespoons chopped marjoram, 2 tablespoons chopped parsley, 2 tablespoons chopped chives (or fennel, watercress, tarragon or chervil – or combine as you wish) and 1 teaspoon dried mixed herbs (optional). Serve the herb mayonnaise with chicken, egg or seafood dishes.

Seafood Mayonnaise To 250 ml (9 fl oz) mayonnaise add 2 tablespoons tomato purée, 2 teaspoons onion juice, 1 finely chopped anchovy fillet, 1 clove crushed garlic, 1 tablespoon chopped chives, 1 tablespoon lemon juice and a little sugar and Tabasco to taste.

Tartare Sauce To 300 ml (½ pint) mayonnaise add 3 small gherkins, chopped, 2 spring onions, trimmed and chopped, 1 hard-boiled egg, finely chopped, 1 tablespoon capers, chopped, 1 teaspoon dried tarragon, ¾ teaspoon dry mustard, 1 teaspoon lemon juice, 1 teaspoon sugar, 1 tablespoon chopped chervil or parsley and seasoning. Serve with fried fish or chicken or mix with 150 ml (¼ pint) yoghurt to make a dip,

Thousand Island Dressing To 250 ml (9 fl oz) mayonnaise add a dash of Tabasco, 2 tablespoons chopped green pepper, 2 teaspoons minced pimiento, 1 teaspoon chopped chives, 1 tablespoon tomato sauce, 1 tablespoon vinegar and ½ teaspoon paprika. Cover and chill before using with salads and fish.

Horseradish Mayonnaise To 250 ml (9 fl oz) mayonnaise add 4 tablespoons freshly grated horseradish (or bottled horseradish, well drained), 2 teaspoons grated lemon rind and 60 ml (2 fl oz) sour cream. Serve this mayonnaise with smoked mackerel, smoked salmon or any smoked meat or fish.

Slimmers' Mayonnaise Mix 150 ml (¼ pint) low-fat yoghurt with 150 ml (¼ pint) mayonnaise and then add flavourings, such as dill or chives.

CHASSEUR SAUCE

THIS TASTY tomato and mushroom sauce is easy to prepare. It is useful to make a fairly large quantity of basic brown sauce and keep it in the freezer so that it is handy for recipes such as this.

PREPARATION TIME: 15 MINUTES

INGREDIENTS TO YIELD ABOUT 750 ML
(26 FL OZ)
125 g (4¼ oz) mushrooms, sliced
30 g (1¼ oz) butter
250 ml (9 fl oz) basic brown sauce*
125 ml (4 fl oz) white wine
2 tablespoons brandy
5 tablespoons tomato paste
Salt and freshly ground black
 pepper

Sauté the mushrooms in the butter, then add the rest of the ingredients and simmer for 5 minutes. Season the sauce to taste with salt and pepper.

SERVING SUGGESTION This popular steak sauce is also good with lamb chops.

VARIATIONS Crushed garlic can be added to taste, and a little sage combines well with the other flavours.

The success of the sauce depends on the quality of the brown sauce, but a very acceptable alternative can be made using gravy made with pan juices as a base.

BREAD SAUCE

THIS MILK-BASED SAUCE, first recorded in Scotland, is sometimes maligned because of the unfortunate practice of boiling the breadcrumbs for too long. To avoid this, serve the sauce immediately and do not re-boil.

PREPARATION TIME: 15 MINUTES
STANDING TIME: 30 MINUTES

INGREDIENTS TO YIELD 500 ML (17 FL OZ)
1 medium-sized onion, peeled*
4 cloves
¼ teaspoon ground mace or nutmeg
4 peppercorns
500 ml (17 fl oz) milk
70 g (2½ oz) fresh white
 breadcrumbs
Salt and pepper
1½ teaspoons butter
2 tablespoons cream

Stud the onion with the cloves and put it in a pan with the mace, peppercorns and milk. Bring to the boil, then remove the pan from the heat immediately and leave it to infuse (covered with a lid) for about 30 minutes.

Strain the milk into another pan and stir in the breadcrumbs. Return to the heat, stirring continuously until the mixture boils and becomes quite thick.

Season to taste and stir in the butter and cream. Serve warm, but make sure that the sauce does not re-boil.

SERVING SUGGESTION Serve the sauce with roast chicken, turkey or game.

HORSERADISH SAUCE

FOR CENTURIES the main uses of horseradish were medicinal, and it is possible that the essentially English practice of serving grated horseradish with roast beef was introduced to aid digestion. Today, many people consider horseradish essential with beef.

PREPARATION TIME: 30 MINUTES

INGREDIENTS TO YIELD 250 ML (9 FL OZ)
*1 large horseradish root, to give
    4 tablespoons when grated, or
    use 4 tablespoons bottled
    horseradish
1 tablespoon caster sugar
½ teaspoon dry mustard
2 tablespoons white wine vinegar
150 ml (¼ pint) cream, lightly
    whipped*

Wash and peel the horseradish root, then grate it finely into a bowl. If you are using bottled horseradish, drain it very well. Stir in the sugar, mustard and vinegar, add the cream and chill.

SERVING SUGGESTIONS Serve with roast beef, smoked fish or salads.

VARIATIONS Horseradish gives out pungent fumes, so a more comfortable method of preparing the clean, peeled root is to chop it roughly and shred or mince it in a food processor with a little water. Drain, then add the other ingredients.

To make hot horseradish sauce, grate about 3 tablespoons of the root into 275–300 ml (about ½ pint) white sauce*. Simmer, stirring from time to time, for about 10 minutes.

NAPOLITANA SAUCE *One of Italy's most popular pasta sauces.*

NAPOLITANA SAUCE

IT IS DIFFICULT to imagine Italian cookery without fresh tomato sauce. Certainly Italy was the first European country to adopt the *pomodoro* or 'golden apple' without reservations.

This is one of the most widely used sauces – with fish, poultry, meat, vegetables, rice, pasta or eggs, or as a base for other sauces or composite dishes.

PREPARATION TIME: 15 MINUTES
COOKING TIME: 35-45 MINUTES

INGREDIENTS TO YIELD 500 ML (17 FL OZ)
*40 g (1½ oz) butter, or 1 tablespoon
    olive oil
1 small onion, peeled and finely
    chopped*
1 kg (2¼ lb) ripe tomatoes, skinned*
    and quartered, or a large tin
    (about 800 g/1¾ lb) of tomatoes
1 bay leaf
1 sprig thyme
2 tablespoons red wine (optional)
1 clove garlic, peeled and crushed
    or finely chopped
¼ teaspoon salt
¼ teaspoon sugar
¼ teaspoon freshly ground black
    pepper
2 teaspoons lemon juice or vinegar
½ teaspoon each finely chopped
    fresh basil and marjoram, or
    ¼ teaspoon each dried basil and
    marjoram*

Heat the butter or oil in a large heavy-based pan. Add the onion and cook gently, stirring occasionally, until it is soft but not brown.

Put the tomatoes in the pan with the bay leaf, thyme, wine (if used), garlic and salt. Stir, cover and simmer until tender.

Rub through a sieve and return to the cleaned pan. Bring to the boil and cook for about 20 minutes until reduced to a thick, smooth purée.

Season the sauce with the sugar, pepper, lemon juice or vinegar and remaining herbs. Taste and adjust the seasoning.

SERVING SUGGESTION There are few more simple and satisfying summer dishes than this sauce served over a plate of pasta with a little grated cheese.

89

MUSHROOM SAUCE

MUSHROOM SAUCE can have either a white or brown sauce base, the white sauce being more suitable for chicken or fish dishes.

PREPARATION TIME: 20 MINUTES
COOKING TIME: 30 MINUTES

INGREDIENTS TO YIELD 1 LITRE (1¾ PINTS)
125 g (4¼ oz) fresh button
  mushrooms, sliced
60 g (2 oz) butter
2 tablespoons flour
500 ml (17 fl oz) fish* or chicken
  stock*, or half cream and half
  stock
1 tablespoon grated onion,
  blanched* for 1-2 minutes
Salt and freshly ground white
  pepper
2 tablespoons medium cream
  sherry

Sauté the mushroom slices in the butter and remove them from the saucepan.

Stir the flour into the pan juices to make a smooth paste and then stir in the stock gradually. Bring to the boil, lower the heat and simmer for about 5 minutes. Add the mushroom slices and onion to the sauce and simmer for a further 10 minutes. Season and add the sherry.

MUSTARD SAUCE

THE ROMANS THOUGHT that many things tasted better with mustard, and so took the seeds with them to the outermost parts of their empire. Hot mustard sauce is delicious with boiled tongue or roast meats.

PREPARATION TIME: 5 MINUTES
COOKING TIME: 15 MINUTES

INGREDIENTS TO YIELD 600 ML (21 FL OZ)
600 ml (21 fl oz) milk
40 g (1½ oz) butter
25 g (1 oz) flour
1 tablespoon dry mustard
1 tablespoon vinegar
1 teaspoon sugar
Salt

Put the milk in a pan over a gentle heat. Remove when warm, put the lid on the pan and set aside.

Melt the butter over the same gentle heat in another pan. Mix in the flour with a wooden spoon until smooth, and continue to cook gently for 2-3 minutes, stirring all the time to avoid lumps.

Remove from the heat and add the warm milk, stirring continuously. Return to the heat and bring the sauce to the boil, stirring. Simmer for 5 minutes, stirring from time to time.

When the sauce is smooth and creamy, remove it from the heat and stir in the mustard, vinegar, sugar and salt.

EGG AND LEMON SAUCE

ORIGINATING IN GREECE, this sauce is especially suited to the subtle flavours of poached chicken or fish, but it is also enjoyable with roast chicken or even roast lamb.

PREPARATION TIME: 5 MINUTES
COOKING TIME: 45 MINUTES

INGREDIENTS TO YIELD 375 ML (13 FL OZ)
30 g (1¼ oz) butter
2 tablespoons flour
250 ml (9 fl oz) hot chicken stock*
3-4 egg yolks, or 2 eggs
Juice of 2 lemons, strained
2 tablespoons cold water
Salt and freshly ground white
  pepper

Melt the butter and stir in the flour to make a smooth paste. Do not allow the butter and flour to brown.

Add the hot stock slowly, stirring all the while, until the mixture is smooth and thick and starts to bubble. Turn down the heat and simmer the sauce, stirring all the time, for 5 minutes.

When cooked, keep the sauce hot while you beat the egg yolks or whole eggs until they are light and frothy. Add the lemon juice and cold water to the eggs, and stir together. Now remove the sauce from the heat and add one-quarter of the sauce to the egg mixture, 1 tablespoon at a time, beating as you go.

Then add the rest of the egg mixture slowly to the sauce, stirring well all the time. Correct the seasoning if necessary and reheat the sauce, being careful not to bring the mixture to the boil or the eggs in the sauce will curdle.

SERVING SUGGESTIONS This sauce is very good with poached fish* or chicken dishes and is also served with roast lamb, chicken or vegetables. Do not freeze it.

PERI-PERI SAUCE

THIS IS AN IDEAL basting sauce for chicken or prawns 'peri-peri'. The strength of the peri-peri flavour is determined by the number of times you anoint the food while grilling or barbecuing it. The sauce may also be used with pork sausages or fish.

PREPARATION TIME: 5 MINUTES
COOKING TIME: 5 MINUTES

INGREDIENTS TO YIELD 625 ML (22 FL OZ)
250 g (9 oz) butter
125 ml (4 fl oz) olive or sunflower
  oil
125 ml (4 fl oz) lemon juice
2 teaspoons paprika
2 teaspoons chilli powder
4 cloves garlic, peeled and crushed
  or finely chopped
2 teaspoons salt

Combine the ingredients in a saucepan and stir together vigorously over medium heat until the butter has melted and all the ingredients are well mixed (if necessary, use an electric beater or balloon whisk to blend the ingredients).

SERVING SUGGESTIONS Brush the mixture onto chicken pieces, fish or prawns before grilling. Serve on a bed of rice, accompanied by a green salad*.

To ensure that thick chicken pieces (such as thighs) are cooked to the bone, simmer in a little wine or chicken stock* before basting and grilling.

Pork sausages are delicious with a light brushing of peri-peri sauce; serve with simple accompaniments such as boiled new potatoes (with a sour cream dressing*) and a fresh green salad*.

Leftover peri-peri sauce can be stored in a glass jar in the refrigerator for about 2 weeks, or it may be frozen for up to a month. (The sauce will eat through plastic or aluminium foil.) Shake the jar well before using.

VARIATIONS If you require less sauce, simply halve the ingredients.

Try adding herbs such as basil, rosemary or oregano, or for an even hotter sauce, seed 1 or 2 red chillies, chop them finely and add to the ingredients.

Use the sauce on barbecued steak. Brush a large, thick steak with the sauce, and grill over hot coals. To serve, slice the cooked steak into thin strips.

CAPER SAUCE

THIS PIQUANT AND UNUSUAL sauce will provide a tasty contrast if you serve it with mutton and other meats.

PREPARATION TIME: 10 MINUTES

INGREDIENTS TO YIELD 500 ML (17 FL OZ)
25 g (1 oz) butter
25 g (1 oz) flour
500 ml (17 fl oz) hot vegetable or
    basic stock*
1 tablespoon capers
2 teaspoons finely chopped parsley
2 teaspoons lemon juice
Salt and pepper
1 tablespoon cream

Melt the butter in a pan over a gentle heat. Mix in the flour, and cook for 2-3 minutes, stirring continuously. Remove the pan from the heat and gradually add the hot stock, stirring with a wooden spoon until smooth and creamy.

Put the pan back on the heat and bring to the boil, stirring continuously, then simmer for a further 5 minutes, stirring from time to time. Add the capers, the chopped parsley and lemon juice. Season to taste and stir in the cream.

SERVING SUGGESTION Serve with boiled mutton or lamb.

HOLLANDAISE SAUCE

AUGUSTE ESCOFFIER, the renowned French chef, listed Hollandaise sauce as one of five basic sauces which no cook should be without. This classic French sauce is, as its name suggests, of Dutch origin, and was originally made with the best butter on Dutch farms.

There are two basic methods of preparing the sauce: by whisking the ingredients or by using a food processor or blender. Both methods are given.

PREPARATION TIME: 5 MINUTES
COOKING TIME: 10-15 MINUTES

INGREDIENTS TO YIELD 375 ML (13 FL OZ)
225 g (½ lb) butter
3 egg yolks
1 tablespoon water
1 tablespoon lemon juice
Salt and pepper

Whisking method Cut the butter into pieces and place all but about 25 g (1 oz) in a small, heavy-based pan. Put the pan on a very gentle heat and remove as soon as the butter has melted.

Half-fill a large pan with water. Bring to the boil, then remove from the heat. Put the egg yolks with the tablespoon of water in a bowl over the pan of hot water (do not use a metal bowl, or the eggs will discolour when you beat them), and whisk for 1-2 minutes.

Put the pan back over a low heat and add half the reserved cold butter to the bowl. Whisk again for 1 minute.

Whisk in the other half of the reserved butter, remove from the heat, but keep the bowl over the hot water. The mixture should look smooth and creamy.

Gradually add the melted butter, whisking it in until the sauce is thick. Then beat in the lemon juice and season with salt and pepper to taste.

If the sauce curdles during the cooking, remove it from the heat immediately. Put another egg yolk in a bowl and gradually beat the sauce into it. Then resume the cooking. If the sauce is too thick, add 1-2 teaspoons hot water.

Processor/blender method It is easier to make Hollandaise sauce using a food processor or blender. For this method, the ingredients are the same but the way they are combined varies slightly.

Melt the butter in a saucepan until it starts to bubble. Meanwhile, blend the egg yolks with the lemon juice, salt and pepper in a blender or food processor for 1 second – just long enough to mix but not froth them. When the butter is hot, switch the blender on to high and gradually pour in the butter in a thin stream.

When all the butter has been incorporated, turn the machine off immediately. Pour this sauce into a small plastic or glass bowl and put it over hot (not boiling) water until it is required. If you find that your sauce is too thin after beating in the butter, this 'rest' on top of a bowl of warm water will often be enough to thicken it.

If you need to reheat the sauce, beat it over hot water until it is warmed through and fluffy.

SERVING SUGGESTIONS Hollandaise sauce can be served warm with fish, asparagus, broccoli, artichokes, or courgettes (zucchini).

Try Hollandaise or béarnaise with crown roast of lamb.

VARIATIONS TO HOLLANDAISE SAUCE

Béarnaise Sauce can be made in much the same way as Hollandaise. Combine 2 tablespoons chopped spring onion, 2 tablespoons chopped fresh tarragon (or 2 teaspoons dried) with 60 ml (2 fl oz) tarragon vinegar. Reduce in a pan to 1 tablespoon and then add 1 tablespoon cold water and 3 egg yolks. Continue as for Hollandaise, using 225 g (½ lb) melted butter. Just before serving, add chopped parsley or make a green peppercorn sauce by adding 2 tablespoons tinned green peppercorns, well-drained.

Caper Sauce can be made by adding 2-3 tablespoons capers to 250 ml (9 fl oz) Hollandaise sauce.

Cucumber Hollandaise is made with the addition of half a peeled and grated cucumber (well squeezed in a dry cloth to remove excess moisture) and a pinch of cayenne pepper to 250 ml (9 fl oz) Hollandaise sauce. This is delicious with any poached* or grilled fish.

Horseradish Hollandaise is good with rare roast beef. Add 4 tablespoons fresh grated horseradish (or use bottled horseradish, well drained) and 125 ml (4 fl oz) whipped cream to 500 ml (17 fl oz) Hollandaise sauce. If the sauce is too hot, add more whipped cream; if it is too mild, add more horseradish.

Maltaise Sauce is a classic accompaniment to asparagus and is also good with broccoli, courgettes (zucchini), artichokes, fish or chicken. Add 3 tablespoons orange juice and 1 teaspoon grated orange rind to 250 ml (9 fl oz) Hollandaise sauce.

Mousseline Sauce is another classic based on Hollandaise. Add 4 tablespoons whipped cream to 250 ml (9 fl oz) Hollandaise sauce and serve with poached eggs, fish or vegetables.

Try spreading a fairly thick layer of mousseline sauce over fresh asparagus or cooked chicken, and grilling it swiftly just before serving.

Mustard Hollandaise can be made by adding 4 teaspoons French mustard to 250 ml (9 fl oz) Hollandaise sauce.

Sauce Toulouse is made by adding 6 medium-sized mushrooms, sautéed and minced or very finely chopped, to 250 ml (9 fl oz) Hollandaise sauce that has been made with a white wine base.

AÏOLI *A generous addition of garlic is the mainstay of this popular sauce.*

AÏOLI

ORIGINALLY FROM PROVENCE, this rich garlic sauce provides the flavouring for various delicious speciality dishes in that district and has been adopted and adapted widely in many lands.

PREPARATION TIME: 30 MINUTES

INGREDIENTS TO YIELD 300 ML (½ PINT)
1 slice fresh white bread, about 1.5 cm (½ in) thick with crusts removed
3 tablespoons milk
3 cloves garlic, peeled and crushed
2 large egg yolks, lightly whisked
250 ml (9 fl oz) olive oil
2 tablespoons lemon juice
Salt and freshly ground white pepper

Soak the bread in the milk for 10 minutes, then crumble and squeeze out the excess milk. Put the bread into a blender with the garlic and process at high speed, adding the egg yolks fairly slowly.

Add the olive oil, still processing at speed, first drop by drop and then in a thin stream, processing until the mixture thickens. Add the lemon juice and season the mixture to taste. Thin the sauce, if necessary, with cream or water.

SERVING SUGGESTIONS Serve aïoli as a dip for crudités* or fondues, with poached fish or asparagus, over hard-boiled eggs or as a sauce with baked jacket potatoes. It is also very good with boiled beef or mutton. Serve with fish soup or stew, or with a seafood salad of tender squid rings*, prawns and cubes of cooked potato (use a waxy variety), arranged on a bed of crisp, sliced lettuce.

To make green beans Provençale, serve aïoli over topped and tailed, boiled green beans (hot or cold).

VARIATION If you add 4 tablespoons ground almonds, 4 tablespoons extra fresh white breadcrumbs, 2 tablespoons chopped parsley and a little more lemon juice this makes a *skordalia* sauce. Serve it in the same way as aïoli.

CHEESE SAUCE

CHEESE SAUCES are often made with Cheddar, which gives a sharp tang to the sauce.

Experiment with other strong cheeses, if you like: you will find a variety of local and imported cheeses in your local supermarket or delicatessen. The character of the sauce will change, sometimes subtly, sometimes dramatically.

PREPARATION TIME: 15 MINUTES
COOKING TIME: 15 MINUTES

INGREDIENTS TO YIELD 700 ML (24 FL OZ)
600 ml (21 fl oz) milk
40 g (1½ oz) butter
40 g (1½ oz) flour
1 teaspoon dry mustard
125 g (4¼ oz) Cheddar cheese, grated
A pinch of cayenne pepper, or ¼ teaspoon ground nutmeg

Heat the milk through gently in a saucepan. Remove when warm, cover with the lid and set aside.

Melt the butter over the same gentle heat in another pan. Mix in the flour, using a wooden spoon, and continue to cook gently for 2-3 minutes, stirring all the time. Add the mustard.

Remove from the heat and add the warm milk, stirring continuously. Return the pan to the heat and bring the sauce up to the boil, still stirring, then simmer for about 5 minutes, stirring from time to time.

When the sauce is creamy, add the cheese, a little at a time, stirring. Season with the cayenne pepper or nutmeg.

SERVING SUGGESTIONS This sauce is an excellent accompaniment to fish, eggs, vegetables, pasta or pancakes and it will enhance otherwise bland ingredients.

CELERY SAUCE

THIS THICK, CREAMY celery sauce is particularly suitable as an accompaniment to poultry, ham or veal.

PREPARATION TIME: 20 MINUTES
COOKING TIME: 45 MINUTES

INGREDIENTS TO YIELD 1 LITRE (1¾ PINTS)
1 large head of celery, washed, drained and finely chopped

575 ml (1 pint) water, or chicken
  stock*
Salt and pepper
¼ teaspoon ground nutmeg
40 g (1½ oz) butter
40 g (1½ oz) flour
500 ml (17 fl oz) milk
2 tablespoons cream (optional)

Put the chopped celery in a pan with the water or stock. Bring it to the boil, then simmer (covered) until tender – about 20 minutes. Drain, reserving the cooking liquid, and rub the celery through a sieve or purée in a blender. Season with salt, pepper and nutmeg.

Melt half of the butter and stir in half of the flour. Cook the sauce gently for about 2-3 minutes, stirring continuously with a wooden spoon.

Add the milk and 100 ml (3½ fl oz) of the celery stock, stirring well to avoid lumps. Bring to the boil, then simmer for about 5 minutes. Stir in the puréed celery.

Blend the remaining butter with the remaining flour, and add to the sauce in small pieces, stirring well until the sauce is smooth and thick. Add the cream, if used. Serve hot.

MINTED YOGHURT SAUCE

THIS SAUCE has Middle Eastern origins and is very good with many Greek, Lebanese or Turkish dishes. It can also be used as a dip.

PREPARATION TIME: 15 MINUTES
STANDING TIME: 2 HOURS
CHILLING TIME: 2 HOURS OR OVERNIGHT

INGREDIENTS TO YIELD 750 ML (26 FL OZ)
500 ml (17 fl oz) natural yoghurt
2 teaspoons cumin seeds (optional)
250 ml (9 fl oz) sour cream
1 clove garlic, peeled and crushed
  (optional)
4 tablespoons chopped fresh mint
1 teaspoon salt

Line a sieve with a single layer of damp paper towel and set it over a bowl. Pour the yoghurt into the sieve and leave it to drain for 2 hours.

Meanwhile, if you are using the cumin, heat a heavy-based pan and toast the seeds, shaking the pan continuously, for 1½ minutes, or until they are brown and begin to pop. Then pulverise the seeds with a pestle and mortar, or use the

SAVOURY BUTTERS

Savoury butters are used to garnish meat, fish or vegetable dishes, or are added to sauces. Softened butter is flavoured with varying ingredients according to the dish it is to garnish. Allow 25 g (1 oz) butter for each person.

Soften the butter in a bowl before blending in the flavouring ingredient. Herbs and vegetables must be finely chopped, pounded or thoroughly crushed. A mortar and pestle are ideal for this purpose.

When all the ingredients are combined, roll the savoury butter flat between two sheets of damp greaseproof paper. Chill thoroughly in the refrigerator before cutting the butter into small fancy shapes.

Anchovy Butter Rinse 6 anchovy fillets in cold water to remove the salt and oil. Dry, rub through a sieve and blend with 100 g (3¾ oz) butter. Serve with grilled meat or fish. Alternatively, add to a white sauce*.

Lemon Butter Blend the grated rind of half a lemon with 100 g (3¾ oz) butter. Season to taste with salt and black pepper.

Tomato Butter Blend 2 tablespoons tomato paste with 100 g (3¾ oz) butter. Serve with grilled meat or fish, or add to sauces and thick soups.

Chive Butter Blanch* and drain 50 g (2 oz) chives, then chop finely and pound to a paste. Blend into 100 g (3¾ oz) butter. Serve with grilled meat or fish.

Maître d'Hôtel Butter Blend 1 tablespoon finely chopped parsley with 100 g (3¾ oz) butter and season to taste with salt, freshly ground black pepper and a few drops of lemon juice. Serve with grilled meat.

Tarragon Butter Blanch* 50 g (2 oz) fresh tarragon leaves in scalding hot water, then drain and dry. Pound to a paste and blend with 100 g (3¾ oz) butter.

Nut Butter Crush 50 g (2 oz) blanched* almonds, walnuts or pistachio nuts to a fine paste, adding a few drops of water to prevent it from becoming oily. Blend the paste with 100 g (3¾ oz) butter. Add to sauces and soups.

Sesame and Almond Butter Blend 50 g (2 oz) ground almonds, 4 tablespoons toasted sesame seeds and 2 tablespoons chopped fresh parsley with 100 g (3¾ oz) butter. Serve with plain rice or pasta.

Garlic Butter Peel and crush 4 cloves of garlic and blend with 100 g (3¾ oz) butter. Serve with grilled steaks or fish.

Green Butter Blanch* 115 g (¼ lb) spinach, then drain and press out as much of the moisture as possible. Pound until smooth, then blend with 100 g (3¾ oz) butter. Add to white sauces.

Horseradish Butter Pound 4 tablespoons grated horseradish (or bottled, well-drained horseradish) in a mortar together with 100 g (3¾ oz) butter. Add to white sauces or serve with grilled steak.

Mushroom Butter Chop 115 g (¼ lb) button mushrooms finely, then cook them lightly in 25 g (1 oz) butter, and season to taste with salt and black pepper. Pound until smooth, then blend with 100 g (3¾ oz) butter. Add to white sauces.

Mustard Butter Blend 1 tablespoon dry mustard thoroughly with 100 g (3¾ oz) butter. Serve with grilled meat or fish.

Butter for Snails Chop 1 tablespoon onion* and 1 teaspoon parsley. Peel and crush 2 fat cloves garlic, add to the chopped onion and parsley, and blend with 100 g (3¾ oz) butter, seasoning to taste with salt and black pepper. Serve stuffed into snail shells.

handle of a knife and a small, strong dish.

Blend the yoghurt with the sour cream, garlic (if used), mint, salt and half the cumin seeds until the mixture is smooth and pale green. Pour into a serving bowl, cover and chill for at least 2 hours or overnight. When the sauce is ready to serve, sprinkle on the remaining crushed cumin seeds (if used).

SERVING SUGGESTIONS Serve the sauce with crudités*, stir-fried mixed vegetables*, fish croquettes, chicken kebabs or lamb meatballs, or as a dressing for

cucumber salad. It may also be served as an accompaniment to roast lamb.

VARIATIONS Omit the mint and add grated cucumber to make a delicious sambal to serve with curry.

If you are short of time, the yoghurt need not be drained, but the sauce in this case will be thinner.

In place of the cumin seeds and chopped mint, use celery seeds and finely chopped fresh celery to flavour the yoghurt. Marinate chicken pieces in the sauce for 2-3 hours before grilling.

SWEET AND SOUR SAUCE *This Chinese speciality adds a pleasant piquancy to a variety of meats.*

SWEET AND SOUR SAUCE

SWEET AND SOUR SAUCE is good with the traditional Chinese dish of pork, fish or chicken cubes fried in crispy batter. It also makes a delicious marinade or dipping sauce for fondue.

Here the recipe is for quite a large quantity of sauce, as it freezes well and may be kept for use when required.

PREPARATION TIME: 20 MINUTES
COOKING TIME: 30 MINUTES

INGREDIENTS TO YIELD 1 LITRE (1¾ PINTS)
100 g (3¾ oz) butter
4 onions, peeled and finely sliced*
2 green peppers, wiped, seeded and cut into strips
250 ml (9 fl oz) chicken stock*
250 ml (9 fl oz) pineapple juice
1 425 g (15 oz) tin pineapple pieces (drained)
60 ml (2 fl oz) orange juice
125 ml (4 fl oz) vinegar
125 g (4¼ oz) sugar
60 ml (2 fl oz) soy sauce
1 teaspoon ground ginger
Salt and freshly ground pepper
1 tablespoon cornflour mixed to a smooth paste with 2 tablespoons soy sauce

Heat the butter in a large saucepan and soften the onion slices and green pepper strips in it.

Add the stock, pineapple juice and pieces, orange juice, vinegar, sugar, soy sauce, ginger and seasoning, and simmer for 20 minutes or so.

Thicken the sauce with the cornflour and soy sauce mixture and continue cooking for a further 1-2 minutes.

SERVING SUGGESTIONS Prepare a batter by blending together 3 tablespoons self-raising flour, a pinch of salt, 2 teaspoons sherry and a beaten egg. Coat cubes of meat or fish and deep-fry until golden. Serve with the sauce.

Use as a basting sauce for poussins (spatchcocks) or chicken pieces. If using the sauce after freezing, be sure to thicken on reheating.

VARIATIONS You may wish to liquidise the pineapple pieces in a blender or food processor before you add them to the sweet and sour mixture.

This sauce is also very good with pork sausages or pork loin chops. You should dispense with the soy sauce if the sausages or chops are very salty.

Pork or lamb spare ribs can also be marinated in the sauce before grilling.

CURRY SAUCE

THIS RECIPE is for quite a large quantity of curry sauce as it freezes very well and is useful to have on hand. It can be varied considerably by several delicious additions just before serving.

PREPARATION TIME: 15 MINUTES
COOKING TIME: 1 HOUR

INGREDIENTS TO YIELD 1.5 LITRES
(52 FL OZ)
50 ml (2 fl oz) sunflower oil
4 onions, peeled and finely sliced*
4 cloves garlic, crushed
4 apples, peeled and grated
5 tablespoons curry powder
Juice of 1 lemon
1 litre (1¾ pints) chicken stock*
5 tablespoons chutney
3 tablespoons apricot jam
1 tablespoon salt
2 tablespoons cornflour, mixed to
  a paste with water (optional)

Heat the oil in a large saucepan and sauté the onion, garlic and apple lightly. Add the curry powder, and cook this mixture for 3 minutes. Add the rest of the ingredients, except the cornflour, and simmer, uncovered, for 45 minutes, stirring from time to time. Thicken the sauce slightly with the cornflour if you wish, bringing it to the boil after adding the paste.

SERVING SUGGESTIONS This sauce has many uses. It can dress up poached fish*, halved hard-boiled eggs or leftover chicken pieces.
    To make a delicious pancake filling, combine curry sauce with diced leftover lamb or minced beef, cooked rice and toasted almonds. Place the filled pancakes in an ovenproof dish, brush over plenty of melted butter and bake them until crisp and golden.

VARIATIONS Natural yoghurt or cream, added just before serving, will provide a richer curry sauce.
    Or try 125 ml (4 fl oz) milk in which 2 tablespoons coconut have been infused.
    Raisins, sultanas, almonds, cashew nuts, walnuts or peanuts all make interesting additions.
    This curry sauce freezes very well. Cream, natural yoghurt or milk should be added to it on reheating, and the sauce should also be thickened on reheating.
    Reduce the quantity of cornflour in proportion to meet these variations.

PARSLEY SAUCE

PARSLEY SAUCE, recommended by the famous Mrs Beeton in the 19th century, is the classic complement to broad beans and carrots. It is also good with fish, poultry or ham.

PREPARATION TIME: 10 MINUTES
COOKING TIME: 15-20 MINUTES

INGREDIENTS TO YIELD 600 ML (21 FL OZ)
600 ml (21 fl oz) milk
40 g (1½ oz) butter
40 g (1½ oz) flour
4 tablespoons finely chopped
  parsley
Salt and white pepper

Heat the milk gently in a pan, remove from the heat, cover and set aside.
    Melt the butter gently in a small saucepan. Add the flour, mixing with a wooden spoon, and cook for 2-3 minutes, stirring all the time.
    Remove from the heat and add the warm milk, stirring continuously. Return the pan to the heat and bring to the boil, still stirring, then simmer for about 5 minutes more, stirring occasionally.
    When the sauce is smooth and creamy, add the finely chopped parsley and season to taste. Do not cook further because the taste of the fresh parsley may otherwise be lost.

SAUCE VINAIGRETTE

THIS SAUCE is the classic French dressing for a salad, and is also excellent with hot cooked vegetables.

PREPARATION TIME: 5-10 MINUTES

INGREDIENTS TO YIELD 250 ML (9 FL OZ)
1 teaspoon dry mustard
1 teaspoon sugar (optional)
¼ teaspoon salt
180 ml (6 fl oz) olive oil or good
  vegetable oil
80 ml (2¼ fl oz) wine or cider
  vinegar, or a mixture of both, or
  mixed vinegar and lemon juice
Freshly ground black pepper

Blend together the mustard, sugar (if used) and salt. Whisk in the oil, stir in the vinegar (or vinegar mixture) and add the freshly ground black pepper. Taste and adjust the seasoning.

DRESSINGS BASED ON VINAIGRETTE

One of the easiest ways to vary the taste of vinaigrette is to use herb-flavoured oils as a base.

Avocado Dressing Put a peeled and chopped ripe avocado into a blender or food processor and process it until smooth. Slowly add 250 ml (9 fl oz) vinaigrette and blend until the mixture is smooth, then check for seasoning. This dressing is delicious with poached fish or on sliced, peeled and chilled tomatoes.

Garlic Vinaigrette Add a crushed clove of fresh garlic to the 250 ml (9 fl oz) of basic vinaigrette.

Herbed Vinaigrette Add 1 tablespoon chopped fresh herbs (such as parsley, chives or tarragon) to 250 ml (9 fl oz) vinaigrette (made with lemon juice and wine vinegar).

Horseradish Vinaigrette Add 2-3 teaspoons grated horseradish to 250 ml (9 fl oz) vinaigrette.

Roquefort or Blue Cheese Dressing To 125 ml (4 fl oz) vinaigrette add 3 tablespoons crumbled Roquefort or other blue cheese and 3 tablespoons cream. Beat these ingredients well together. Serve the dressing over a mixed salad.

Ravigote Sauce To 250 ml (9 fl oz) vinaigrette add 70 g (2¼ oz) finely chopped spring onion, 1 tablespoon finely chopped capers, 2 teaspoons finely chopped parsley and ¾ teaspoon finely chopped fresh tarragon (or a pinch of dried tarragon). Beat them well together and serve the sauce on a green salad* or with white meat or fish.

Sesame Dressing Before adding the oil in the basic vinaigrette, lightly brown 1 tablespoon sesame seeds in it. (You may use sesame oil if you prefer.) Allow the oil to cool before adding it with the seeds to the dressing.

Hot Vinaigrette with Egg Bring 250 ml (9 fl oz) vinaigrette to the boil in a saucepan, then add 2 hard-boiled eggs, finely chopped, 1 tablespoon finely chopped parsley, 1 tablespoon finely chopped celery, 1 tablespoon finely chopped chives, ¾ teaspoon dry mustard and ¾ teaspoon Worcestershire sauce. Beat them well together. Serve this sauce with hot asparagus, over hot potato salad or with boiled beef.

VEGETABLES

THE NUTRIENTS in vegetables are essential to health and survival, and few people today need to be reminded how rich in healthy minerals and vitamins they are. In fact many people subsist on a purely vegetarian diet and claim enormous health benefits from so doing.

Needless to say, most vegetables are ideal fare for anyone watching their weight – particularly those vegetables that are high in fibre, such as leaf varieties.

Vegetables are equally useful as starters, main dishes or accompaniments. They can be steamed or boiled, or cooked in a variety of other ways: stuffed and baked, casseroled, curried or *au gratin* (with breadcrumbs and/or melted cheese).

Whether you are serving a hearty meal with creamed spinach and Swiss rösti, or a leek vinaigrette as a meal-in-one salad for a slimmer, few meals are complete without vegetables.

STUFFED AUBERGINES

AUBERGINES (EGGPLANTS) are rich and nutritious vegetables which are high in potassium. They are also very versatile, and can be eaten hot or cold, with or without accompaniments. This relatively simple recipe will produce the most delicious results.

PREPARATION TIME: 1 HOUR
COOKING TIME: 30 MINUTES
PREHEAT OVEN TO 180°C (350°F, MARK 4)

INGREDIENTS FOR SIX
6 small aubergines (eggplants)
    about 12 cm (5 in) long
1 medium-sized onion, peeled and
    finely chopped*
2 cloves garlic, crushed
2 tablespoons sunflower oil
1 medium-sized tomato, skinned*
    and cubed
1 small green pepper, seeded and
    chopped
2 teaspoons chopped fresh basil
75 g (3 oz) cooked rice or 75 g
    (3 oz) fresh breadcrumbs
3 tablespoons chopped parsley
Salt and freshly ground black
    pepper
75-100 g (3-3¾ oz) grated Cheddar
    or sliced mozzarella cheese
250 ml (9 fl oz) chicken* or
    vegetable stock*

Wash and trim the bud ends of the aubergines (eggplants) and boil them in unsalted water for about 10 minutes, or until they begin to soften.

Halve the aubergines (eggplants) lengthways and, when they are cool, remove the pulp – leaving just enough to make the shells into 'boats' that will hold the stuffing without collapsing. Chop the flesh. Sauté the onion and garlic in a little oil, add the tomato, green pepper, basil, rice or breadcrumbs, parsley and chopped pulp, and season.

Fill the skins with this mixture and arrange them close together in an oiled ovenproof dish.

Top with grated cheese, and carefully pour about 2 cm (¾ in) of chicken or vegetable stock into the dish. Bake, un-covered, for 30 minutes.

SERVING SUGGESTIONS Serve on a bed of rice to which some slivered almonds or pine nuts (kernels) and currants have been added. Accompany the stuffed vege-tables with a tossed green salad*.

VARIATIONS Substitute 60 g (2 oz) chopped mushrooms for the green pepper. If basil is not available, use thyme or replace the herb with 1 tea-spoon of ground cinnamon. Use brown rice for a nuttier texture.

AUBERGINES À LA GRECQUE

THIS VEGETABLE is usually cooked in oil to be served as an accom-panying vegetable, or stuffed with a variety of fillings and baked.

Aubergines (eggplants) will keep fresh for longer than most other vegetables, especially if stored in the salad basket of a refrigerator. The following recipe makes an unusual and appetising first course or light lunch.

PREPARATION TIME: 10 MINUTES
COOKING TIME: 30 MINUTES
CHILLING TIME: 2 HOURS

INGREDIENTS FOR FOUR TO SIX
2 medium-sized aubergines
    (eggplants), about 15 cm (6 in)
    long
300 ml (½ pint) white wine
300 ml (½ pint) water
3 tablespoons sugar
3 tablespoons olive oil
6 coriander seeds
Juice of ½ lemon
1 small bay leaf
2 tablespoons tomato paste
1 bouquet garni*
Salt and freshly ground black
    pepper
Chopped basil for garnish

Peel the aubergines (eggplants) and dice them into 3 cm (about 1 in) cubes. Put all the remaining ingredients (except the basil) into a saucepan, seasoning with the salt and freshly ground black pepper. Stir well, then bring this sauce to the boil, add the diced aubergines (eggplants) and bring back to the boil.

Simmer the aubergines (eggplants) for 15 minutes, or until they are tender but still intact. Lift them into a dish with a slotted spoon, and boil the sauce rapidly until it has reduced by a quarter.

Strain the sauce over the vegetables, allow to cool, then chill in the refriger-ator for 2 hours. Sprinkle with basil before serving.

SERVING SUGGESTIONS Spoon the auber-gines (eggplants) and the sauce into deep plates and serve as a first course with crusty bread that can be used to mop up the dressing. For a light lunch, add a green salad*.

VARIATION Instead of aubergines (egg-plants) use button mushrooms. Simmer them, whole, in the sauce, for not more than 10 minutes, when they will be tender but not overcooked.

GLAZED CARROTS

THE SWEET TASTE of the carrot caused it to be referred to in early Celtic literature as 'honey underground'. Throughout the centuries, when sugar has been scarce or expensive, carrots have helped to replace it in puddings, pies and preserves.

In this simple recipe, however, sugar is added. It is used to give the carrots an appetising glaze.

PREPARATION TIME: 10 MINUTES
COOKING TIME: 20-30 MINUTES

INGREDIENTS FOR FOUR TO SIX
10 medium-sized carrots, peeled
    and sliced into 2.5 cm (1 in)
    rounds
450 ml (¾ pint) chicken* or
    vegetable stock*
2 tablespoons brown sugar
75 g (3 oz) butter, cut into small
    pieces
Freshly ground black pepper
Salt
2 tablespoons chopped parsley

Put the carrots in a saucepan with the stock, sugar and butter. Season the mix-ture with pepper. Cover the pan, bring it to the boil, and simmer for about 20 minutes until the carrots are tender and the liquid has reduced to a glaze.

If the liquid does not seem to be reducing fast enough, uncover it towards the end of the cooking time and increase the heat under the pan.

Place the glazed carrots on a warmed serving dish. Add salt to taste and sprinkle the top with parsley.

SERVING SUGGESTION Carrots will bring a splash of colour to a dish. Serve with roast beef, lamb, chicken, pork or game and with any type of fish.

CARROT SALAD *The colourful mixture is packed with vitamins.*

CARROT SALAD

ALTHOUGH CARROTS are known for their high vitamin A content, few people realise that they also contain other important vitamins. They are a boon to slimmers and popular among cooks because they can be prepared in a variety of ways to make delicious dishes.

PREPARATION TIME: 45 MINUTES

INGREDIENTS FOR FOUR TO SIX
5 medium-sized carrots, grated
1 medium-sized green pepper,
*   seeded and finely chopped*
1 stalk celery, finely sliced
3 tablespoons finely chopped
*   parsley*
115 g (4 oz) seedless raisins
Juice of 1 large orange
Juice of 1 lemon
2 tablespoons sunflower oil

Mix the carrots, green pepper, celery, parsley and raisins together and dress with the orange and lemon juices. Sprinkle the sunflower oil over the mixture and serve.

SERVING SUGGESTION Serve the carrot salad on a bed of lettuce with either cottage cheese or Ricotta cheese.
    It would also make a refreshing accompaniment to a spicy Indian meal.

VARIATIONS Omit the celery and peppers and add 175 g (6 oz) sunflower seeds.
    Alternatively, add 175 g (6 oz) fresh chopped pineapple, grapefruit or green melon, and dress with natural yoghurt. Sprinkle the salad with chopped parsley or with alfalfa sprouts.

PREPARING AND SERVING ASPARAGUS

One of the most important criteria for selecting good fresh asparagus is the condition of the tip. The bud cluster should be tightly closed and not show any sign of wilting. Avoid packed asparagus that has gone mouldy in the wrapping, or asparagus with woody-looking root ends.
    The best in locally grown asparagus will range in thickness from about 5 mm ($\frac{1}{4}$ in) to 1.5 cm ($\frac{1}{2}$ in). Choose asparagus of equal thickness so that it cooks evenly.
    Two kinds are available, the slender, green spears grown above ground, or the soft, white spears grown underground to prevent chlorophyll development.

Preparing Wash the spears in cold water, then bunch them together on a chopping board levelling all the heads. Cut off the dry part of the root end and at the same time size them uniformly.
    If you are using young, tender stalks, do not scrape or peel them because you will lose flavour, texture and nutrition. Older stalks can be cleaned with a potato peeler exactly like scraping a carrot – but do not damage the tender tips.

Cooking Steaming is the best way to cook fresh asparagus. Lay the spears neatly in a vegetable steamer basket, and cook in the steam from rapidly boiling water until tender.
    Alternatively, tie the spears together in a bunch with the tips pointing upwards, and cook in a small pot of water. The pot should be small enough to ensure that the bunch does not fall on its side, and the water level should be about halfway up the stems. Cooking time can vary from 8–15 minutes, depending on thickness. The green variety of asparagus should be a bright green colour. Take out one of the spears and bite to test it. The spear should still be slightly resistant. Limp, mushy asparagus is overcooked.

Serving suggestions Melted butter or a Hollandaise sauce* make good accompaniments to hot asparagus. The cooked spears can also be served coated with a strong cheese sauce* made with Cheddar.
    Cold asparagus may be served either with vinaigrette* or a smooth, lemon-flavoured mayonnaise*.
    Asparagus spears can make a wonderfully luxurious addition to a cold buffet. Try wrapping paper-thin slices of cold roast beef around one or two spears.

STUFFED PEPPERS

PEPPERS GO WELL with a great variety of fillings. In this recipe, they are stuffed with a ham, walnut and cottage cheese mixture, and then baked.

PREPARATION TIME: 45 MINUTES
COOKING TIME: 1 HOUR
PREHEAT OVEN TO 180°C (350°F, MARK 4)

INGREDIENTS FOR SIX
6 large, even-sized sweet green, red or yellow peppers
1 large onion, peeled and chopped*
4 tablespoons sunflower oil
1 tin (425 g/15 oz) tomatoes
1 teaspoon dried basil
2 cloves garlic, crushed
125 ml (4 fl oz) red wine
Salt and black pepper
100 g (3¾ oz) ham, chopped
2 tablespoons walnuts, chopped
250 g (9 oz) cottage cheese
4 tablespoons dry breadcrumbs
60 ml (2 fl oz) water
30 g (1¼ oz) Parmesan cheese, grated

For the sauce:
125 ml (4 fl oz) cream or sour cream
1 teaspoon French mustard
1 egg yolk
Chicken* or vegetable stock* or white wine

Cut a lid from the top of each pepper and carefully remove the stem, seeds and membranes.

Fry the chopped onions in the sunflower oil until soft. Add the tomatoes, basil, garlic and wine, season with the salt and pepper, and simmer until the mixture is fairly thick (10-15 minutes).

Stir in the ham, walnuts, cottage cheese and half the breadcrumbs. Check the seasoning, then fill the peppers with the mixture.

Arrange the peppers side by side in a shallow ovenproof dish and pour the water around them. Sprinkle the tops with the rest of the breadcrumbs mixed with the Parmesan cheese. Bake for about 1 hour (or until tender).

To make the sauce, mix together the cream (or sour cream), French mustard and egg yolk, and heat gently, stirring all the time, until the sauce thickens. Do not boil. Stir in a little stock or white wine if the mixture seems too thick, season, and spoon the sauce over the peppers.

BROCCOLI ALLA PARMIGIANA

BROCCOLI IS A NATIVE of Southern Europe and it was first introduced to the cuisines of France and Britain at the start of the 18th century. In Italian the word broccoli means cabbage sprouts or flowers; but broccoletti, meaning little branches, is the name by which the vegetable is sold on the colourful market stalls of Italy.

'Alla Parmigiana' means that the dish contains Parmesan cheese. It also uses mozzarella cheese, and a tomato sauce that is fragrant with basil.

PREPARATION TIME: 45 MINUTES
COOKING TIME: 20 MINUTES
PREHEAT OVEN TO 200°C (400°F, MARK 6)

INGREDIENTS FOR FOUR
1 large head of broccoli
2 tablespoons olive oil
1 medium-sized onion, peeled and finely chopped*
1 clove garlic, chopped
4 tomatoes, skinned*
1 tablespoon chopped fresh basil or 2 teaspoons dried basil
Salt and freshly ground black pepper
100-125 g (3¾-4¼ oz) mozzarella cheese, finely sliced
2 tablespoons grated Parmesan
1 tablespoon dry breadcrumbs

Wash the broccoli head and break it into even-sized spears.

Put all the spears into a steamer (or a colander), and place the steamer in a pan above boiling water. Cover the pan with a tightly fitting lid and steam for about 20 minutes until the broccoli is just tender.

Heat the oil in a heavy frying pan, add the onion and garlic, and fry gently for 5 minutes until soft. Add the tomatoes and basil and cook, stirring, until the mixture forms a thick sauce, moistening with a little water if necessary. Season with salt and freshly ground black pepper.

Arrange the steamed broccoli in an ovenproof dish and pour the tomato sauce over it. Arrange slices of mozzarella cheese on top. Sprinkle the dish with the grated Parmesan cheese, and then top with a sprinkling of breadcrumbs.

Bake the mixture, uncovered, in the preheated oven for about 20 minutes until browned and bubbling. Serve hot in the same dish.

GROWING SPROUTS

There is a simple technique for turning a dormant seed into a living plant packed with life-giving nutrients (especially rich in vitamin C), using only a jar, a piece of cloth and a rubber band.

Bean sprouts were traditionally used in Chinese dishes and more recently they have been used in salads. But you can also allow all the pulses which you would normally use in soups, stews and curries (such as dried peas, beans and lentils) to germinate before use.

Prepare the sprouts by filling a large glass jar one-quarter full with dried peas, beans or lentils.

Cover the mouth of the jar with a clean piece of thin cloth, and fix the fabric in place with a rubber band.

Hold the jar under a tap and cover the seeds with cold water, then drain the water off immediately by turning the jar upside down.

Store the jar, with the damp seeds, on a shelf in a dark cupboard. Rinse the seeds once or twice a day.

Use them in stews, soups and curries when they first start to germinate after about 1½-2 days, or keep them for salads and Chinese dishes when more mature (after 4-5 days). If left to grow longer, however, they may become bitter.

LEEKS VINAIGRETTE

TOO OFTEN RELEGATED to soups and stews, leeks, when fresh and young, make an unusual starter with a delicate flavour. This dish is sometimes referred to as 'the poor man's asparagus'.

PREPARATION TIME: 30 MINUTES
COOKING TIME: 20 MINUTES
CHILLING TIME: 4 HOURS

INGREDIENTS FOR FOUR
500 ml (17 fl oz) water
½ teaspoon salt
1 bay leaf
3 sprigs fresh rosemary
16 leeks, washed and trimmed
Sliced black olives

For the dressing:
4 tablespoons sunflower or olive oil
2 tablespoons tarragon vinegar
¼ clove garlic, crushed
¼ teaspoon salt

CAESAR SALAD *is a delectable combination of crisp lettuce, anchovies, egg and croûtons.*

¼ teaspoon dry mustard
1 teaspoon sugar
1 teaspoon capers, chopped

For the garnish:
Chopped, hard-boiled egg* and/or chopped parsley

Mix the ingredients for the dressing and set it aside for the flavours to blend.

In a wide-based saucepan bring the water, salt, bay leaf and rosemary to the boil and simmer for 10 minutes. Add the leeks, laying them flat, then cover them and cook gently until they are tender (about 10 minutes). Drain the leeks, refresh them quickly under cold water, pat them dry on paper towels, and arrange them on a dish in a single layer.

Pour over as much of the dressing as is necessary to moisten the leeks thoroughly. Add the olives, then cover the dish and chill it. Garnish before serving.

CAESAR SALAD

THIS IS AN UNUSUAL combination of crisp lettuce leaves mixed with anchovies and croûtons, and dressed with an oil and egg mixture. The recipe originated in California.

PREPARATION TIME: 20 MINUTES

INGREDIENTS FOR SIX TO EIGHT
Salt
1 clove garlic, peeled
1 teaspoon dry mustard
1 tablespoon lemon juice
1 teaspoon Worcestershire sauce
3 tablespoons fine olive oil
2 medium-sized lettuces, washed and dried
1 tablespoon finely grated Parmesan cheese
Coarsely ground black pepper

½ tin anchovies, drained and finely chopped
1 egg, coddled* for 1 minute
50 g (2 oz) croûtons* (made with white bread)

Use a wooden salad bowl for the best results. Sprinkle the bowl with a little salt, then rub well with the garlic.

Add the dry mustard, lemon juice and Worcestershire sauce and stir the mixture with a wooden spoon until the salt has dissolved completely.

Gradually stir in the olive oil until all the ingredients are well blended. Tear the lettuce leaves into bite-sized pieces and add them to the salad bowl. Scatter with the grated Parmesan cheese and the black pepper, then add the anchovies, coddled egg and croûtons.

Gently toss so that all the lettuce pieces are well coated with the dressing. Serve the salad immediately.

101

CHINESE STIR-FRIED VEGETABLES

Because of the unique shape of the wok, it is the perfect utensil to use for stir-frying. The oil and juices will constantly run back to the centre of the wok, basting and moistening the ingredients while they are stirred around during the quick frying process. Most of the everyday vegetables, such as cabbage, green beans, broccoli and spinach, lend themselves to being cooked in this way.

How to prepare the vegetables

Cabbage Cut the cabbage head into even-sized wedges. Remove the hard stalk. Place the wedges, flat edge down, on a chopping board and shred very finely with a sharp knife (or use a food processor to facilitate shredding).

Green beans Top and tail the beans. Slice them diagonally into pieces 1-2 cm ($\frac{1}{2}$-$\frac{3}{4}$ in) long.

Broccoli Slice the stems diagonally into neat slivers; cut the flowering heads into miniature florets.

Spinach Wash the spinach very well in cold water. Remove the white stalks. Pile 5 or 6 leaves on top of each other and roll them into a tight roll. With a sharp knife, slice this across into fine shreds.

Spring onions or leeks Remove the root ends and any damaged tips of the green leaves, then slice the onions or leeks into diagonal slices.

Celery Use the thick, milder flavoured table celery. Remove any green leaves and slice the stalks into fine diagonal slices.

How to cook

Place 2-3 tablespoons sunflower oil with 1 or 2 peeled cloves of garlic in the wok. Heat until a blue haze appears, then remove the garlic. Start adding the vegetables in order of how long they will take to cook, that is, start with the beans, then the leeks, then the celery, then the broccoli, cabbage and lastly the spinach.

Lift and turn the vegetables with a flat spatula all the time during the cooking process. Shake the wok from time to time. Do not overcook the vegetables – they must be bright in colour and crisp in texture when served.

Sauce Mix 1 tablespoon cornflour in 125 ml (4 fl oz) water. Add a crumbled chicken or vegetable stock cube and 2 tablespoons soy sauce. Stir this into the vegetable mixture. Allow to cook and glaze before removing from the heat. Stir-fried vegetables must be served promptly after cooking for best results.

Alternative vegetables

Turnips or carrots may be used, cut into julienne* strips.

Green cucumber should be sliced lengthways, seeded and sliced across in fine discs.

Red and green peppers Remove the inner membranes and seeds, cut in half lengthways and shred into fine strips.

Fresh green ginger may also be added to a dish. Peel the ginger root and slice it into fine discs or shred it coarsely.

BUBBLE AND SQUEAK

WHAT MOST PEOPLE think of as bubble and squeak derives from a 19th-century dish of warmed leftovers. The title is a poetic interpretation of the noise the potato, cabbage and onion make while frying.

This recipe is an older and grander version which incorporates pieces of cold roast beef; these may be laid on top, or layered between slabs of the vegetables.

PREPARATION TIME: 10 MINUTES
COOKING TIME: 20 MINUTES

INGREDIENTS FOR FOUR

350 g ($\frac{3}{4}$ lb) cold roast beef
75 g (3 oz) beef dripping or butter
2 medium-sized onions, peeled and chopped*
Salt and freshly ground black pepper
6 medium-sized potatoes, cooked and mashed
175 g (6 oz) cooked green cabbage, well drained and chopped

Cut the roast beef into slices about 5 cm by 2.5 cm (2 in by 1 in). Heat 25 g (1 oz) of the dripping or butter in a large, heavy-based frying pan and fry the onions in it over a gentle heat until they are a light golden-brown. Remove these from the pan and keep them hot.

In the same fat, fry the pieces of beef for 4-5 minutes, stirring or turning them over so that they brown on all sides. Sprinkle with salt and pepper, remove from the pan, cover and keep hot.

Melt half the remaining dripping or butter in the pan and put in the mashed potatoes. Mix in the cabbage, season the mixture with salt and pepper, and spread it out over the base of the pan to make a cake about 2.5 cm (1 in) thick.

Cook this for 4 minutes, or until it is golden-brown underneath, shaking the pan to prevent the mixture from sticking. Put a large plate over the pan and turn the pan upside-down, so that the bubble and squeak is on the plate.

Heat the remaining dripping or butter in the frying pan and slide the cake back into the pan so that the underside will brown. Cook the cake for another 4 minutes. Turn it onto a plate as before, and slide it onto a warmed serving dish. Arrange the onions and beef on half of the cake and fold the other half over it. Serve very hot with a good gravy.

STUFFED MARROW

THE CREAMY TEXTURE and delicate flavour of young marrow make it a good vegetable to cook on its own and serve with a white sauce. When it is older it can be baked with this tasty meat, tomato and herb stuffing.

PREPARATION TIME: 25 MINUTES
COOKING TIME: 1 HOUR
PREHEAT OVEN TO 180°C (350°F, MARK 4)

INGREDIENTS FOR FOUR
1 medium-sized marrow
50 g (2 oz) butter
1 medium-sized onion, peeled and finely chopped*
1 clove garlic, chopped
250 g (9 oz) minced beef
1 medium-sized tomatoes, skinned*, chopped and seeded
2 tablespoons fresh breadcrumbs
1 tablespoon chopped fresh basil or 1½ teaspoons dried basil
2 tablespoons chopped parsley
1 egg, beaten
Salt and freshly ground black pepper

Cut off the end of the marrow and scoop out the seeds with a spoon.

Melt half the butter in a frying pan, add the chopped onion and garlic, and fry gently for 5 minutes until it is soft. Add the minced beef and brown the meat for a few minutes, stirring occasionally to prevent it burning.

Put the onion, garlic and meat in a mixing bowl. Add the chopped tomato flesh, breadcrumbs, basil, parsley and egg. Season with salt and pepper and mix all the ingredients well together.

Stuff the marrow with this mixture and replace the end. Place the marrow in a greased, ovenproof dish and dot it with pieces of the remaining butter. Arrange a layer of aluminium foil loosely over the top, and bake the dish in the oven for 1 hour or until it is tender.

SERVING SUGGESTIONS Marrow stuffed with minced beef and herbs can be served with rice or potatoes as a main course.

For a delicious summertime meal, add a crisp, green salad* as well.

PREPARING AND SERVING GLOBE ARTICHOKES

These thistle-like plants are hardy perennials, with silvery-grey leaves. The bushes grow to about a metre (3 ft) tall and require a minimum of water and attention.

Pick the artichokes when they are fist-sized and well formed, but the overlapping leaves must still hug each other closely. Once the leaves start opening, the artichokes are past their best.

Do not expect to get a large serving from each artichoke; the only edible parts are the bottom – which is known as the heart or fond – and the small fleshy segments at the base of the individual leaves.

How to prepare Artichokes may be served whole with the tips of the leaves trimmed. Or you can serve only the artichoke bottoms, fully trimmed of all the leaves.

Trimming whole artichokes With a sharp, strong knife cut off the top quarter of the artichoke head.

To remove the hairy core, open the middle leaves, reach into the centre and scoop it out (a teaspoon works well).

Trim the base flat by cutting it level, removing the stem at the same time. Then snip the sharp points of the remaining leaves with kitchen scissors so that the artichoke looks more attractive.

To prevent excessive discoloration, keep the prepared artichokes in water to which lemon juice has been added.

Trimming artichoke bottoms With a sharp, strong knife, cut off two-thirds of the artichoke top.

Trim the base flat by cutting it level, removing the stem at the same time.

Peel off the outer leaves, using a sharp vegetable knife, starting at the base and turning the vegetable in your hand as if you were peeling an orange.

Remove the hairy core with a spoon and keep the artichoke bottoms in lemon water until ready to cook.

How to cook Avoid using iron or aluminium cookware as this will cause severe discoloration.

Wash the artichoke and neatly trim it. Then allow it to simmer, submerged in water to which you have added lemon juice (to prevent discoloration), olive oil (to give richness, gloss and flavour), salt, pepper and garlic.

Cook for about 30 minutes. To test whether the artichoke is sufficiently cooked, pierce the base with a fork to check that it is tender.

Serving suggestion Serve one artichoke per guest as a starter, accompanied by melted butter or Hollandaise sauce.

Variations If you are serving just the artichoke bottoms, serve them filled with a seafood or cheese stuffing, hot or cold.

Alternatively, coat the artichoke bottoms with a thick, well-seasoned, white sauce*, bake in the oven, and serve as an extra vegetable or a starter. The bottoms may also be served cold with garlic mayonnaise (aïoli*) or vinaigrette*, or served as part of a salad or vegetable platter.

FENNEL, TOMATO AND MUSHROOM SALAD

FENNEL SALAD is often served at the end of a meal in Italy. The taste of fennel, reminiscent of liquorice, complements the less powerful flavours of tomatoes and mushrooms. Fennel is a nutritious vegetable, too: the Romans believed that it prolonged life.

PREPARATION TIME: 30 MINUTES
CHILLING TIME: 30 MINUTES

INGREDIENTS FOR SIX
2 medium to large heads of fennel
3 large, ripe and firm tomatoes
100 g (3¾ oz) button mushrooms, trimmed and wiped
125 ml (4 fl oz) vinaigrette*, flavoured with a pinch of basil

First, skin* the tomatoes and set aside. Trim the base of the fennel and remove the stalks and leaves. Peel the outer layer from the stalks and bulbs, and slice thinly, then place in iced water for 30 minutes to crisp.

Next, slice the tomatoes and mushrooms. Arrange slices of fennel (drained and dried), tomato and mushroom on a platter and pour over the vinaigrette.

SERVING SUGGESTION This salad goes well with chicken or fish dishes, or serve with another Italian dish, such as pizza or cannelloni.

VARIATIONS Substitute thin slices of peeled orange for the tomato, and add pitted olives to the salad.

Arrange the salad on a bed of watercress and serve with slices of ham rolled into trumpet shapes.

POTATO SALAD

THIS WELL-FLAVOURED potato salad should be made on the day you plan to eat it and served at room temperature, rather than chilled from the refrigerator.

PREPARATION TIME: 15 MINUTES
COOKING TIME: 25 MINUTES

INGREDIENTS FOR SIX TO EIGHT
1 kg (2¼ lb) potatoes (use either large potatoes or tiny new ones)
4 tablespoons apple cider vinegar
1 medium-sized onion, peeled and finely chopped*
125 ml (4 fl oz) homemade mayonnaise*
125 ml (4 fl oz) sour cream
Salt and freshly ground black pepper
Chopped parsley or paprika for garnish

Boil the potatoes in their jackets until tender. If you are using large potatoes, peel them as soon as they are cool enough to handle and slice. Leave baby new potatoes whole and unskinned.

Place the prepared potatoes in a salad bowl and moisten with the vinegar. Mix in the onion, then the mayonnaise and sour cream.

Using two spatulas, mix these ingredients together until the potatoes are well coated with the dressing.

Season and sprinkle the salad with paprika or a little finely chopped parsley.

SERVING SUGGESTIONS Serve with cold meats, or at a barbecue.

VARIATIONS Use natural yoghurt instead of the sour cream.

Use a bunch of chopped spring onions instead of the whole onion.

Garnish with some chopped pickled cucumber and 2 hard-boiled eggs*, finely chopped.

For a more substantial salad, add thin slices of salami.

THE VERSATILE BAKED POTATO

Crisp-skinned potatoes, with meltingly soft insides, offer a tasty and substantial side dish. With imaginative variations, they become meals in themselves.

Choose large, main crop potatoes (the following suggestions for fillings are for 4 potatoes). Scrub them well and use the point of a sharp knife to remove any eyes or blemishes.

Prick the skin several times with a fork, sprinkle with salt (optional), and bake at 200°C (400°F, mark 6) for 1-1½ hours, or until the potatoes are crisp on the outside and soft inside. (Or first parboil them for 7-10 minutes, then bake until soft – about 40 minutes.)

Sour Cream and Chives Bake the potatoes, slash the tops in a crisscross fashion and squeeze the potatoes gently to force them open. Fill with butter, sprinkle with salt and pepper and top each potato with 2 tablespoons sour cream mixed with 1 tablespoon freshly chopped chives.

Soufflé Bake the potatoes, cut a thin lid from the top of each and scoop out the centres into a bowl, taking care not to break the skins. Mash the filling with a fork, beat in 50 g (2 oz) butter, 125 ml (4 fl oz) cream and 3 large egg yolks. Season, and fold in 3 stiffly whisked egg whites. Spoon into the potato shells and bake at 200°C (400°F, mark 6) for about 15-20 minutes.

Garlic Bake the potatoes, then cut a thin lid off the top and scrape the insides into a bowl. Add 125 g (4¼ oz) cream cheese mixed with herbs, 1 clove crushed garlic, 50 g (2 oz) butter, salt and pepper. Beat until smooth, press the mixture back into the shells, sprinkle with grated Cheddar and grill until the cheese melts.

Bacon and Leek Bake the potatoes, cut a lid off the top, scoop out the centres and reserve. Fry 8 rashers of chopped streaky bacon until just crisp. Remove from the pan and fry 3 sliced leeks, adding 50 g (2 oz) butter if necessary. Reduce the heat and simmer until tender. Add the bacon and leeks to the potato filling, with 50 g (2 oz) butter, 100 ml (3½ fl oz) cream and seasoning. Mix well, pile into the potato shells, sprinkle with grated cheese and grill until the cheese melts.

Egg Bake the potatoes, halve and scoop out the centres. Add butter and seasoning and mash until smooth. Pile the mixture back into the shells and make a hollow in the centre of each. Break an egg into each hollow and bake until the whites have set but the yolks are still soft.

Smoked Fish Flake 100 g (3¾ oz) smoked, cooked fish with a pinch of cayenne pepper. Add this to the scooped-out baked potato, together with 1 tablespoon finely chopped parsley (and a little cream if it is too stiff). Spoon the mixture back into the potatoes, dot with butter and reheat.

Mushroom and Ham Sauté 1 finely chopped onion in butter. Add 150 g (5 oz) sliced mushrooms and 100 g (3¾ oz) diced ham. Stir into the mashed potato filling and pile back into the shells. Dot with butter and bake in a hot oven.

Caviar Bake the potatoes, split, and serve topped with sour cream, chopped chives and lumpfish roe (Danish caviar).

POMMES GRATIN DAUPHINOIS

IN THIS CLASSIC DISH, named after the mountainous Dauphine area of France that borders on Switzerland, butter and cream are the rich local ingredients that combine with potatoes.

When cooked, the potatoes are brown on top and the sauce has thickened and tastes of cheese, even though in fact there is no cheese in the recipe.

PREPARATION TIME: 15 MINUTES
COOKING TIME: 1 HOUR
PREHEAT OVEN TO 180°C (350°F, MARK 4)

INGREDIENTS FOR FOUR
1 clove garlic
450 g (1 lb) potatoes, peeled and sliced very thinly
Salt and freshly ground black pepper
285 ml (½ pint) cream
40 g (1½ oz) butter, cut into pieces

Grease an ovenproof dish with a little butter, and rub it well with the clove of garlic. Arrange a layer of potato slices in the dish and season them with salt and pepper. Add another layer, season it and continue in this way until all the potato slices have been used up.

Pour over the cream until it comes to within 2 cm (¾ in) of the top of the potatoes. Dot the potatoes with butter.

Place the dish in the preheated oven and bake for 1 hour until the top is nicely browned. If necessary, turn up the heat for the last 10 minutes to allow the top to brown completely.

Serve the potatoes hot with grilled meat, roast beef, pork, lamb or chicken, and cold meats.

ROSTI *The golden potato crust hides a tender interior.*

ROSTI

THIS SWISS POTATO CAKE is crisp and deliciously golden on the outside but soft and tender inside. Rosti can be prepared and cooked in less than an hour – a boon to the busy cook.

PREPARATION TIME: 30 MINUTES
COOKING TIME: 25 MINUTES

INGREDIENTS FOR SIX
10 medium-sized potatoes
75 g (3 oz) butter
Salt and freshly ground black pepper

Scrub the potatoes and place them in a saucepan of cold water. Cover and boil for 10-15 minutes, or until they are barely tender. Drain and leave to cool, then peel the potatoes and grate on a fairly coarse blade of the grater.

Melt the butter in a large, heavy-based frying pan. Add the grated potatoes and sprinkle with salt and pepper. Pat into a cake and fry over a medium heat for about 10 minutes until lightly browned. Then put a plate over the pan and invert the cake onto the plate.

Add more butter to the pan if necessary, and slide the rosti back into the pan to cook on the other side for about 10 minutes until lightly brown.

Loosen with a spatula and invert the potato cake onto a large, round serving plate. Serve immediately.

SERVING SUGGESTIONS Rosti makes a pleasant accompaniment to grilled sausages, chops or bacon.

If you like, serve each portion of rosti topped with a fried egg.

VARIATIONS Finely sliced*, cooked onion, chopped ham or sausage can be added to the grated potato mixture before it is patted into a cake and fried.

For a vegetarian meal, sprinkle 125 g (4¼ oz) grated Gruyère or Emmenthal cheese (and a little grated nutmeg) onto the cake after frying. Grill until the cheese bubbles and serve immediately with a watercress salad.

VEGETABLE CASSEROLE

THIS CASSEROLE is particularly suitable for a cold winter's evening. It is equally tasty with pastry, baked into a hot and nutritious pie.

PREPARATION TIME: 30 MINUTES
COOKING TIME: 1 HOUR
PREHEAT OVEN TO 180°C (350°F, MARK 4)

INGREDIENTS FOR SIX
225 g (½ lb) green beans, trimmed, washed and cut into 2.5 cm (1 in) pieces
2 medium-sized carrots, thinly sliced
2 stalks celery, sliced
½ medium-sized cauliflower, separated into florets
½ green or red pepper, cut into thin strips
2 courgettes (zucchini), thinly sliced
225 g (½ lb) shelled peas or 250 g (9 oz) frozen peas
*1 medium-sized onion, peeled and sliced**
2 medium-sized tomatoes, skinned and cut into wedges*
*150 ml (¼ pint) vegetable stock**
2 tablespoons olive oil
2 cloves garlic, crushed
1 teaspoon salt
1 bay leaf
1 teaspoon basil
4 tablespoons grated Parmesan cheese
1 tablespoon finely chopped parsley

Layer all the vegetables in an ovenproof dish. Heat the stock with the olive oil, garlic, salt, bay leaf and basil. When the liquid boils, pour it over the vegetables. Cover the dish and bake for 1 hour. Sprinkle over the Parmesan cheese and the finely chopped parsley, and then serve the casserole immediately.

SERVING SUGGESTION Accompany with fresh pasta or a risotto Milanese*.

VARIATION Make the recipe into a vegetable pie by cooking the vegetables as above but using Cheddar cheese instead of Parmesan and covering with puff pastry*. Cut a slit in the pastry to allow the steam to escape and brush with a little beaten egg or milk. Bake at 200°C (400°F, mark 8) for about 15 minutes, or until the pastry is puffed and golden.

STEWED RED CABBAGE *A truly appetising line-up of ingredients.*

CREAMED CABBAGE

OVER THE YEARS, cabbage has become an everyday vegetable, often overcooked and served with insufficient seasoning. This recipe transforms it in flavour and appearance, making it an ideal accompaniment to grilled meat.

PREPARATION TIME: 10 MINUTES
COOKING TIME: 15 MINUTES

INGREDIENTS FOR FOUR
50 g (2 oz) butter
450 g (1 lb) cabbage, coarsely
   chopped
1 clove garlic, finely chopped
   (optional)
Salt and freshly ground black
   pepper
¼ teaspoon freshly grated nutmeg
80 ml (2½ fl oz) cream

Melt the butter in a heavy frying pan. Add the cabbage and the garlic (if used). Fry gently, stirring frequently, for about 10 minutes, until the cabbage has just softened, but is still crunchy. Season with salt, pepper and nutmeg, and stir in the cream. Cook for 3-5 minutes, stirring. Remove from the heat and serve at once.

STEWED RED CABBAGE

APPLES, ONIONS AND SPICES, along with port and wine vinegar, are the traditional ingredients to cook with red cabbage. The long, slow cooking allows the flavours to be absorbed, and gives the spicy, sweet and sour taste for which this dish is renowned.

The addition of the port helps both colour and flavour, and prevents the cabbage from turning blue.

PREPARATION TIME: 20-25 MINUTES
COOKING TIME: 2½-3 HOURS
PREHEAT OVEN TO 150°C (300°F, MARK 2)

INGREDIENTS FOR SIX
25 g (1 oz) butter
2 medium-sized onions, peeled and
   chopped*
3 carrots, peeled and chopped
4 rashers bacon, rinds removed,
   chopped
4 cooking apples, peeled, cored
   and chopped
1 kg (2¼ lb) red cabbage, finely
   chopped
1 clove garlic, finely chopped

Salt and freshly ground black
   pepper
½ teaspoon freshly grated nutmeg
1 bay leaf
2 cloves
2 tablespoons port
2 tablespoons red wine vinegar

Melt the butter in an ovenproof dish. Add the onions, carrots and bacon, and cook for 5 minutes until they are soft.

Remove them from the heat and add the chopped apples, cabbage and garlic. Season with salt, black pepper and nutmeg, and add the bay leaf and cloves. Mix all these ingredients well together, then stir in the port and the vinegar.

Cover the dish and bake in the preheated oven for 2½ to 3 hours. Serve it hot or cold, as you wish.

SERVING SUGGESTIONS Red cabbage goes well with duck, goose, venison and pork, and is also good with ham and sausages. It can be served cold or reheated with a little cooked bacon added to it.

VARIATION You could also make this recipe using white cabbage, sherry and white wine vinegar, if you prefer.

COURGETTES IN CHEESE SAUCE

THIS IS A VERY USEFUL vegetarian dish that can be made ahead of time, then baked before serving.

PREPARATION TIME: 30 MINUTES
COOKING TIME: 35 MINUTES
PREHEAT OVEN TO 180°C (350°F, MARK 4)

INGREDIENTS FOR SIX
12 medium-sized courgettes
   (zucchini) (about 700 g/1½ lb)
30 g (1¼ oz) butter
2 tablespoons flour
250 ml (9 fl oz) milk
100 g (3¾ oz) feta or Cheddar
   cheese, grated
2 egg yolks
2 tablespoons cream
Salt and freshly ground black
   pepper
1 tablespoon finely grated
   Parmesan cheese for sprinkling

Cut the courgettes (zucchini) in half lengthways. Drop them into a large saucepan of boiling, salted water. When the water has returned to the boil (about 5 minutes) remove the vegetables and drain well.

Make a thick white sauce by melting the butter, stirring in the flour until smooth, then gradually adding the milk, stirring all the time, until the sauce is thick and smooth.

Stir in the feta or Cheddar cheese. Beat the egg yolks with the cream and add the sauce gradually to this mixture. Add a grinding of pepper to the sauce, but add salt only if it is needed.

Place the courgettes (zucchini) in an oiled, ovenproof dish, and pour over the cheese sauce. Sprinkle the surface lightly with the Parmesan, and bake for 30-35 minutes until golden.

COURGETTE SALAD

THESE VEGETABLES are much enjoyed for their delicate flavour when cooked. However, the full nutritional benefit is derived only when they are eaten raw, because their high sodium content is dissipated once they have been cooked, especially if they are boiled.

PREPARATION TIME: 15 MINUTES
COOKING TIME: 5 MINUTES
MARINATING TIME: OVERNIGHT

INGREDIENTS FOR FOUR TO SIX
6 medium-sized courgettes (zucchini) (about 350 g/¾ lb), sliced into 2 cm (¾ in) rounds
Salt and freshly ground black pepper
1 teaspoon chopped fresh basil
1 teaspoon chopped fresh oregano
1 tablespoon chopped parsley
150 ml (¼ pint) garlic dressing*
1 medium-sized tomato

Cook the courgettes (zucchini) in a minimum of water for 3 minutes, or steam them. Drain, then add the seasoning and basil, oregano and parsley. Add the garlic dressing and marinate overnight. Chop the tomato and use as garnish.

SERVING SUGGESTION Serve individual portions on a bed of lettuce or watercress accompanied by a baked potato*.

VARIATION Instead of the garlic dressing, dress with natural yoghurt and scatter chopped mint over the top.

RATATOUILLE

COLOURFUL AND RICHLY flavoured, ratatouille is a blend of vegetables and herbs that has in it the authentic taste of the South of France. Onions, peppers aubergines (eggplants), courgettes (zucchini) and tomatoes all intermingle their flavours as they stew slowly in olive oil.

Two rules must be observed when making ratatouille – always use olive oil and never add water.

PREPARATION TIME: 40 MINUTES
STANDING TIME: 40 MINUTES
COOKING TIME: 1 HOUR

INGREDIENTS FOR SIX
2 large aubergines (eggplants), cut into 2 cm (¾ in) slices
8 courgettes (zucchini), cut into 2 cm (¾ in) slices
Salt
2 tablespoons olive oil
2 large onions, peeled and sliced*
3 green peppers, seeded and sliced
2 cloves garlic, finely chopped
4-5 medium-sized tomatoes, skinned* and sliced
1 tablespoon crushed coriander seeds
Freshly ground black pepper

For the garnish:
1 tablespoon chopped basil
1 tablespoon chopped parsley

Put the sliced aubergines (eggplants) and courgettes (zucchini) into a colander and sprinkle them with salt. Leave them for 40 minutes so that the salt has time to draw out some of the excess moisture, and then dry the slices thoroughly with paper towels.

Heat the olive oil in a large frying pan. Add the sliced onions and green peppers, and cook these for 5 minutes until the onions are soft and transparent. Add the aubergines (eggplants), courgettes (zucchini) and garlic. Cover the frying pan and simmer this mixture over medium heat for 10 minutes.

Add the tomatoes and coriander seeds. Season with salt and pepper. Cover again and cook for 45 minutes over a gentle heat, checking occasionally to make sure the vegetables are not sticking to the bottom of the pan.

Check and if necessary adjust the seasoning, sprinkle the dish with the chopped basil and parsley, and serve.

SERVING SUGGESTIONS Serve the ratatouille hot or cold with freshly baked bread as a first course and, if liked, top each portion with a fried egg.

Or serve it as an accompaniment to roast or grilled meat or chicken.

SPICED CAULIFLOWER

CAULIFLOWER is a popular vegetable with a delicate flavour that can, however, all too easily be lost in the cooking. For a change, try this spicy version to complement grilled fish, chicken or lamb chops.

PREPARATION TIME: 15 MINUTES
COOKING TIME: 25 MINUTES

INGREDIENTS FOR SIX
1 large cauliflower
4-6 tablespoons sunflower oil
2 medium-sized onions, peeled and finely chopped*
¼ teaspoon mustard seeds
1 teaspoon ground ginger
1 teaspoon salt
1¼ teaspoons turmeric
2 large tomatoes, skinned* and finely chopped
½ teaspoon cumin (optional)
2 tablespoons finely chopped parsley
1 teaspoon sugar

Trim the leaves and stalk from the cauliflower, divide into florets and wash thoroughly in water.

Heat the sunflower oil in a heavy-based pan, and cook the onions for a few minutes on medium heat until they are soft and transparent. Add the mustard seeds, ground ginger, salt and turmeric. Cook this mixture, stirring all the time to blend, for about 5 minutes.

Add the cauliflower florets to the pan, turning them until they are thoroughly coated with the spice mixture.

Stir the finely chopped tomatoes into the cauliflower mixture with the cumin, if used, and the chopped parsley. Add sugar to taste.

Cover the pan with a lid and continue cooking over a gentle heat for 10-15 minutes. Stir the mixture occasionally to prevent it from burning. Do not overcook or allow the mixture to become a mush. Each floret should still retain a trace of crispness in the stalk.

PEELING, SLICING AND CHOPPING ONIONS

The onion must surely be the cornerstone of aromatic cooking the world over. Originally a native of Asia, it has been cultivated since earliest times. Onions are readily available the whole year round.

Buy firm, well-shaped onions that feel heavy for their size. The protective dry papery skins should be smooth and shiny, never soft, dark spotted, stained or blotchy. The onions should have small tight necks. A sprouting, opened neck is a sign of over-maturity or incorrect storage.

Some people find onions indigestible, in which case leeks make a satisfactory and tasty substitute.

Peeling One way to simplify the peeling of a large number of onions is to blanch them in boiling water first for 5-10 minutes. The skin will then slip off more easily and your eyes will not suffer so much from the onion vapours.

Chopping onions Cut the onions in half lengthways from root end to neck end. Cut off a thin slice at both ends and slip off the skin. Place the onion, flat side down, on a chopping board. Grip the rounded sides with your four fingers on one side and your thumb on the other side. Slice thinly, starting on the side with four fingers and ending near your thumb. Your second series of cuts will be at right angles to the first one. Turn the onion through 90 degrees and slice in exactly the same way, but across the bulb this time. The closer the cuts the finer will be the chopped onion pieces.

Slicing onions Cut off a thin slice at both the root and neck ends. Make a shallow cut through the papery skin from the root to the neck and slip off the skin. Slice a very thin disc off one side to provide the onion with a flat surface on which to stand it. Grip the sides of the onion between your four fingers on one side and thumb on the other side and, starting at either the root or neck end, slice across in slices. The slices can then easily be broken apart to form onion rings, if required.

Minimising tears The various methods of counteracting onion vapours are usually more trouble than they are worth. Use a sharp knife, cut with quick clean movements and work near an open window or door.

BAKED ONIONS *are a tasty accompaniment to meat or fish.*

BAKED ONIONS

ALTHOUGH ONIONS' health-giving properties may have been slightly exaggerated in the past, they are undoubtedly beneficial and they are frequently the basic flavouring ingredient in traditional recipes.

PREPARATION TIME: 5 MINUTES
COOKING TIME: 2-3 HOURS
PREHEAT OVEN TO 160°C (325°F, MARK 3)
INGREDIENTS FOR FOUR
8 medium-sized onions
Salt and freshly ground black pepper
50 g (2 oz) butter
2 tablespoons chopped parsley for garnish

Wash the onions in their skins, removing as much grit as possible. Dry them well.

Line a baking dish with aluminium foil to prevent the onions from sticking to the dish. Put in the onions and place the dish in the preheated oven. Bake for 2-3 hours until the onions are tender when pierced with a skewer.

Sprinkle them with salt and pepper and put a knob of butter on each.

Garnish the onions with the chopped parsley, and serve.

SERVING SUGGESTIONS Serve baked onions with grills, roast beef, lamb or chicken, or as an accompaniment to fish.

VARIATION If you like, you can flavour the butter with cinnamon and a good pinch of cayenne pepper.

CREAMED ONIONS

LITTLE ONIONS have a light, delicate flavour: when they are brought to the table, bathed in their creamy sauce, it is not difficult to believe that the word 'onion' comes from the Latin *unio* – meaning 'a large pearl'. Creamed onions go well with a variety of meat dishes.

PREPARATION TIME: 30 MINUTES
COOKING TIME: 40 MINUTES

INGREDIENTS FOR SIX
1 kg (2¼ lb) pickling onions
150 ml (¼ pint) chicken stock* or dry white wine
50 g (2 oz) butter, softened
2 tablespoons flour
450 ml (¾ pint) milk
150 ml (¼ pint) cream
1 bay leaf
Salt and freshly ground black pepper
¼ teaspoon freshly grated nutmeg
1 tablespoon chopped parsley

Bring a large pan of water to the boil and drop in the onions. Boil them for a few minutes. Drain and, while still hot, slip off their skins.

Put the onions back in the clean saucepan and add the chicken stock or white wine. Cover and simmer on a low heat for about 30 minutes.

Meanwhile, melt 25 g (1 oz) of the butter in a small saucepan and add the flour. Cook over a low heat for 2 minutes, stirring all the time, but do not allow to brown. Add the milk and cream, and bring to the boil, still stirring. Add the bay leaf. Season with salt and pepper and simmer, stirring continuously, until the sauce has thickened.

Drain the onions, return them to the pan and pour the sauce over them. Place over a gentle heat and mix in the rest of the butter in small pieces.

Transfer to a warmed serving dish, sprinkle with nutmeg and parsley, and serve while still very hot.

SERVING SUGGESTIONS Serve as a rich accompaniment to plain roast chicken or turkey, grilled chops, steak, or liver and bacon casserole.

VARIATION Add 2 tablespoons sherry to the onions and arrange over slices of cooked ham. Top with mashed potato and bake until the potato is golden-brown and the sauce is bubbling.

STUFFED MUSHROOMS

IN ANCIENT EGYPT, only the Pharaohs were allowed to eat mushrooms, ordinary mortals being considered unworthy of this exotic food. In ancient Rome, too, they were reserved solely for the Caesar and the aristocracy.

Commercial production today enables mushrooms to be enjoyed by all, and they are available throughout the year.

PREPARATION TIME: 25 MINUTES
COOKING TIME: 20 MINUTES
PREHEAT OVEN TO 180°C (350°F, MARK 4)

INGREDIENTS FOR SIX
8-12 large mushrooms (about 450 g/1lb)
2 tablespoons sunflower oil
30 g (1¼ oz) butter
1 small onion, peeled and finely chopped*
1 clove garlic, crushed
1 teaspoon fresh rosemary, finely chopped
4 tablespoons fine, dry, brown breadcrumbs
1 tablespoon soy sauce
A pinch of sugar
60 g (2 oz) mozzarella cheese, coarsely grated
Salt and freshly ground black pepper

For the topping:
Flaked almonds
Paprika

Wipe the mushrooms with a damp cloth, cut off the stems of the mushrooms and, using a grapefruit knife, carefully enlarge the hollows of the caps. Chop the stems and other mushroom parings finely.

Heat the oil and butter in a frying pan, add the onion, garlic, rosemary and mushroom parings, and sauté until soft. Bind with the crumbs.

Remove from the heat and season the mixture with the soy sauce. Add the pinch of sugar and the coarsely grated mozzarella, and mix well.

Arrange the mushroom caps in a liberally buttered ovenproof dish. Sprinkle them lightly with salt and black pepper and divide the stuffing equally between the caps, mounding them slightly.

Top each mushroom with flaked almonds, allowing about 1 teaspoon per cap. Sprinkle with paprika and bake (uncovered) in the preheated oven for 20 minutes until tender.

SERVING SUGGESTIONS Serve the mushrooms with buttered wholemeal bread.

This dish can be prepared and assembled beforehand, then covered and refrigerated, but in this case you should allow it to return to room temperature before baking it in the oven.

VARIATION Vary the flavour with different herbs (such as oregano, parsley, chives or thyme) and different cheeses (a mild Cheddar or Gruyère).

SWEET CORN FRITTERS

THIS IS A CLASSIC accompaniment to fried chicken – crisp, golden fritters popping with tender whole-kernel sweet corn.

PREPARATION TIME: 10 MINUTES
COOKING TIME: 20 MINUTES

INGREDIENTS FOR SIX
2 extra-large eggs, separated
Salt and freshly ground black pepper
A pinch of sugar
1 tin (425 g/15 oz) whole-kernel sweet corn (not creamed)
1 teaspoon baking powder
50 g (2 oz) fresh breadcrumbs
Sunflower oil for frying

Beat the egg yolks with salt and pepper, then add the sugar and the sweet corn drained of all its liquid. Whisk the egg whites until stiff and fold into the yolk mixture, together with the baking powder and crumbs.

Pour oil into a frying pan to a depth of about 5 mm (¼ in) and drop tablespoons of the mixture into the pan. Fry until golden-brown, then turn and fry the other side. Drain well and serve hot.

SERVING SUGGESTIONS Serve as a quick lunch, snack or 'brunch' dish, with fresh tomato and onion sauce* or mushroom sauce*, or with grilled bacon, sausages or cooked sliced ham.

VARIATIONS To make the fritters more substantial, add finely chopped onion*, diced ham or sliced cooked sausage to the basic mixture.

The fritters can also be made with flour batter, but this version will be lighter and tastier.

Substitute diced, blanched carrot – or another vegetable – for the sweetcorn.

A SIMPLE GREEN SALAD

Lettuce leaves tossed in a good dressing, fragrant with fresh herbs, make an excellent, simple salad. Chopped fresh parsley, chives, thyme, mint, chervil and dill are all good. To make the salad more interesting, use a mixture of lettuce leaves, when more than one variety is available, or add shredded cabbage.

For extra texture, make use of any greenstuffs in season. Try leaves of chicory, the curly endive leaves, very young spinach leaves and watercress. Fresh sprouts* are nice to add as well.

For a more substantial salad, add spring onions, chunks of celery, thin slices of cucumber, avocado and green pepper. Sprinkle with croûtons.

Salad dressing Mix the following ingredients: 8 tablespoons sunflower oil; 4 tablespoons lemon juice. Use olive oil (or half olive and half sunflower oil) for a robust Mediterranean type dressing, with a crushed, fat clove of garlic and 1 teaspoon dried oregano.

Add 1 teaspoon mustard – the hot powder or a more gentle seed mustard. If the dressing seems too sharp, soften it with honey, or a pinch of sugar. Add 4 tablespoons natural yoghurt for variety. Season with salt and freshly ground black pepper. Pour the dressing over just before serving. Do not drown the salad, add only enough dressing to ensure that the greens glisten.

SALADE NIÇOISE

THE SIMPLE INGREDIENTS that go into this delightful salad make it an ideal lunch dish for a hot day. Follow tradition by serving it with a light, dry, white wine and crusty French bread.

PREPARATION TIME: 30 MINUTES

INGREDIENTS FOR SIX

500 g (1 lb 2 oz) green beans, trimmed, washed and dried
1 lettuce, washed and patted dry
*1 medium-sized onion, peeled and finely sliced**
3 ripe medium-sized tomatoes, cut into wedges
125 g (4¼ oz) black olives
1 tin (55 g/2 oz) anchovy fillets, drained
2 tins (200 g/7 oz each) tuna, drained and broken into chunks
2 hard-boiled eggs, sliced*
2 teaspoons chopped parsley

For the salad dressing:
125 ml (4 fl oz) olive oil
4 tablespoons sunflower oil
4 tablespoons red wine vinegar
1 clove garlic (optional)
Salt and freshly ground black pepper

Blanch* the beans for 4 minutes in a pan of rapidly boiling water and then immediately cool under cold running water. Drain and reserve.

Arrange the lettuce leaves on a large, round platter. Overlap them with the beans, onion rings, tomato wedges, olives, anchovies, tuna and hard-boiled eggs. Sprinkle with the chopped parsley.

To make the salad dressing, process the oils, vinegar, garlic (if used), salt and pepper in a blender (or beat thoroughly) and pour over the salad. Alternatively, serve the salad with aïoli*.

BHAJI MASOOR NI DHAL

THIS TASTY INDIAN RECIPE consists primarily of red lentils cooked with spinach and onions. The lentils thicken into a gravy to make a versatile dish which can be served with bread or rice, or on its own as a nourishing soup.

PREPARATION TIME: 15 MINUTES
COOKING TIME: 30 MINUTES

INGREDIENTS FOR SIX

400 g (14 oz) red lentils
750 ml (26 fl oz) water
*1 medium-sized onion, peeled and chopped**
3 cloves garlic, sliced
8 curry leaves
2 green chillies, sliced lengthways
¼ teaspoon turmeric
1 teaspoon salt
100 g (3¾ oz) spinach, shredded
3 tablespoons sunflower oil
1 teaspoon mustard seeds

Wash and drain the lentils. Bring the water to the boil in a saucepan, add the lentils, onion, garlic, curry leaves, chillies, turmeric, salt, spinach and 1 tablespoon of the oil. Cover the saucepan and cook for 15 minutes.

Heat the remaining oil in a small saucepan, add the mustard seeds and allow them to brown. Pour over the lentil curry, stir, and gently simmer for a further 10 minutes.

GREEK SALAD

AN OLD FAVOURITE on many restaurant menus, a traditional Greek salad offers a fresh and tasty combination of ingredients dominated by the sharp taste of feta cheese and olives.

PREPARATION TIME: 20 MINUTES

INGREDIENTS FOR SIX

1 lettuce
2-3 medium-sized tomatoes, cut into wedges
½ cucumber, sliced
*1 large onion, peeled and thinly sliced**
1 green pepper, sliced
6 radishes, sliced
1 tin (400 g/14 oz) artichoke hearts, drained and quartered (optional)
125 g (4¼ oz) ripe black olives
100 g (3¾ oz) feta cheese, cubed
½ teaspoon oregano
*125 ml (4 fl oz) garlic dressing**

Place the rinsed, well-drained lettuce leaves in a salad bowl. Add the remaining prepared vegetables. Top with the cheese and sprinkle with the oregano. Toss in the dressing at the table, or at the very last minute just before serving.

COLESLAW

WIDELY POPULAR as a salad, coleslaw combines the crisp freshness of cabbage with a variety of other appetising flavours.

PREPARATION TIME: 15 MINUTES

INGREDIENTS FOR SIX TO EIGHT

1 small cabbage
1 medium-sized green pepper, seeded and chopped
1 large carrot, coarsely grated
*1 medium-sized onion, peeled and chopped**
*200 ml (7 fl oz) mayonnaise**
4 tablespoons sour cream
Salt and pepper

Shred the cabbage and crisp it in a bowl of iced water. Drain it well and then mix with all the remaining ingredients, seasoning to taste with salt and pepper.

Present the coleslaw in a salad bowl, or arrange it on lettuce on side plates and decorate with walnuts.

CHICORY AND ORANGE SALAD

AN UNUSUAL COMBINATION of ingredients helps to make this a memorable salad. The chicory leaves have a slightly bitter, though pleasant, flavour.

PREPARATION TIME: 30 MINUTES

INGREDIENTS FOR SIX

6 heads of chicory
3 medium-sized oranges, peeled and segmented (remove all the pith and membrane)
3 medium-sized carrots, scraped and shredded into fine julienne* strips
125 ml (4 fl oz) vinaigrette* flavoured with ¾ teaspoon grated orange rind and ¾ teaspoon basil

Trim the root end of each head of chicory, discard the outside leaves and remove the conical core formed by the inside leaves at the base. Wash well and wipe dry.

Slice into thick (about 2.5 cm/1 in) diagonal pieces and divide the pieces into rings. Mix with the prepared orange segments and shredded carrot and moisten with the flavoured vinaigrette.

SERVING SUGGESTION Serve with cold roast lamb or chicken.

VARIATION Substitute cooked and chilled cubes of beetroot for the carrot, and add thinly sliced circles of Spanish onion.

BUTTER BEANS WITH TOMATO

THIS MAKES a very good vegetarian dish, perhaps topped with squares of feta. It is also an ideal accompaniment to roast lamb.

PREPARATION TIME: 20 MINUTES
SOAKING TIME: OVERNIGHT
COOKING TIME: 2 HOURS

INGREDIENTS FOR SIX

350 g (¾ lb) dried butter beans
2 medium-sized onions, peeled and thinly sliced*
1 medium-sized carrot, sliced
2 fat cloves garlic, crushed
1 bay leaf
1 sprig rosemary
4 tablespoons sunflower oil
4 medium-sized tomatoes, skinned* and chopped
Salt and freshly ground pepper
Chopped fresh basil or parsley

Soak the beans overnight in cold water – or cover with water, boil, take from the stove and leave covered for an hour.

Place the soaked beans plus the soaking liquid in a heavy saucepan (ensure that there is enough water to cover the beans) and bring to the boil with 1 sliced onion, the sliced carrot, 1 clove crushed garlic, the bay leaf and the rosemary. Reduce the heat and simmer for about an hour. Add half the oil and simmer until the beans are tender. Drain the beans (reserve the stock).

Gently heat the rest of the oil in a large frying pan. Add the remaining slices of onion and cook very gently until softened. Stir in the remaining clove of garlic and the tomatoes. Cook for 5-10 minutes, then add the drained beans and heat through, adding a little of the stock if necessary. Season, and serve sprinkled with basil or parsley.

BUTTER BEANS WITH TOMATO *The beans are slowly simmered, and garlic adds tang.*

PASTA, RICE AND CEREALS

T HE ROMAN GODDESS of agriculture, Ceres, gave her name to cereal, the edible grains that form the staple food of most of the world. But domestic use of cereal pre-dates the Romans by a few millenia – people have been eating grains for at least eight thousand years.

The staple cereal of more than half the world's population is rice, of which there are several varieties. Although rice, like pasta, forms the basis of many hearty meal-in-one family dishes, it is often served as a side dish. Rice and pasta, both rich in carbohydrates, make tasty, substantial salads too.

Noodles, made from flour and water (sometimes with eggs added), have probably been around in most cultures for as long as people have been making flour from grains. Marco Polo returned to Italy from his expedition to China at the beginning of the 14th century with tales of the various noodle dishes he had eaten there. By that time, pasta in many shapes was already the staple food in his home country, and today the wide variety of Italian pasta types with their delicious sauces and stuffings have become firmly ensconced in international cuisine.

CANNELLONI

SHEETS OF PASTA (or pancakes) are filled with a meat and spinach mixture, then baked with a tomato and béchamel sauce until hot and bubbly.

PREPARATION TIME: 3 HOURS
COOKING TIME: 20-30 MINUTES
PREHEAT OVEN TO 190°C (375°F, MARK 5)

INGREDIENTS FOR SIX
1 small onion, peeled and finely
  chopped*
2 tablespoons sunflower oil
2 large cloves garlic, crushed
250 g (9 oz) frozen spinach,
  chopped
300 g (11 oz) lean beef, finely
  minced
Salt and freshly ground pepper
4 tablespoons freshly grated
  Parmesan cheese
2 tablespoons cream (optional)
2 eggs, lightly beaten
1 teaspoon dried oregano
12 cooked homemade cannelloni
  cases* (using 200 g/7 oz basic
  pasta) or bought cannelloni or
  12 pancakes (lightly cooked on
  one side only)
375 ml (13 fl oz) Napolitana sauce*
375 ml (13 fl oz) béchamel sauce*
15 g (½ oz) butter

Gently fry the onion in half the oil until softened, but not browned. Stir in the garlic and spinach over a high heat until all the moisture has evaporated, then remove the contents from the saucepan.

Add the rest of the oil to the pan and stir in the minced beef. While cooking, stir all the time to prevent lumps forming. Once the mince is lightly browned, stir in the spinach mixture and allow to cool slightly. Season to taste, then mix with half the Parmesan, the cream (if used) and eggs. Add the oregano and check the seasoning.

Divide this filling between the cannelloni cases or pancakes (placing it on the cooked sides of the pancakes), then roll them up to form tubes. Pour a little of the strained Napolitana sauce over the bottom of an oblong ovenproof dish. Place the rolled-up pasta or pancakes on top. Cover with the béchamel sauce, then with the rest of the Napolitana sauce. Sprinkle with the rest of the Parmesan and dot with the butter. Bake for 20-30 minutes.

SPAGHETTI WITH BOLOGNESE SAUCE

THIS IS AN EXCELLENT recipe for one of the most popular spaghetti sauces. A vital step is the slow simmering of the sauce, which helps to bring out the full flavour of all the ingredients.

PREPARATION TIME: 20 MINUTES
COOKING TIME: 1 HOUR

INGREDIENTS FOR SIX
OR TO YIELD 1.25 LITRES (2¼ PINTS)
125 g (4¼ oz) smoked ham, chopped
  (optional)
1 large onion, peeled and
  chopped*
1 medium-sized carrot, scraped
  and chopped
2 stalks celery, chopped
3 tablespoons sunflower or
  olive oil
500 g (1 lb 2 oz) lean beef mince
125 ml (4 fl oz) dry white wine
375 ml (13 fl oz) beef stock*
2 tablespoons tomato paste
1 clove garlic, crushed
125 ml (4 fl oz) cream (optional)
250 g (9 oz) chicken livers
  (optional), sautéed in 15 g (½ oz)
  butter and roughly chopped
Freshly grated nutmeg
Salt and freshly ground black
  pepper
500 g (1 lb 2 oz) spaghetti
Chopped parsley for garnish
Grated Parmesan cheese for
  sprinkling

To make the sauce, chop the ham (if used) and vegetables together very finely. Fry gently in a heavy saucepan in half the oil until they are softened, and slightly tinged with brown.

Remove the mixture, add the rest of the oil, then the minced beef, and cook over a medium heat, stirring all the time to prevent lumps.

Add the wine and then increase the heat. Allow to boil, and keep on stirring until the liquid has almost evaporated.

Mix in the softened vegetables, stock, tomato paste and garlic. Bring to the boil, then reduce the heat and simmer, half covered, for 45 minutes – stirring from time to time.

If you are using cream, add it while the dish is simmering. You can also add the chicken livers (if used) at the simmering stage. Add nutmeg and season to taste.

Towards the end of the cooking time for the sauce, cook the spaghetti. Drain well and sprinkle with the parsley.

Serve the sauce over the spaghetti and pass around grated Parmesan cheese for sprinkling over individual servings.

RAVIOLI

SQUARES OF HOMEMADE pasta are filled with a meat, cheese and spinach mixture, cooked until tender and then served with Napolitana sauce.

PREPARATION TIME: 2¼ HOURS
STANDING TIME: 30 MINUTES FOR THE
  PASTA
COOKING TIME: 10 MINUTES

INGREDIENTS FOR SIX
15 g (½ oz) butter
1 small onion, peeled and finely
  chopped*
250 g (9 oz) veal, finely minced
250 g (9 oz) frozen spinach,
  chopped
2 eggs, lightly beaten
4 tablespoons freshly grated
  Parmesan cheese
Freshly grated nutmeg
Salt and freshly ground pepper
400 g (14 oz) homemade pasta*,
  rolled into sheets
750 ml (26 fl oz) Napolitana sauce*
Parmesan cheese for sprinkling

Heat the butter and add the onion. Cook gently until softened but not browned. Stir in the veal until it changes colour.

Cook the spinach separately over a high heat, stirring continuously until all the moisture evaporates.

Mix the meat mixture with the spinach, eggs and the 4 tablespoons Parmesan cheese. Add the nutmeg and season to taste with salt and pepper.

Make and fill the ravioli*. Drop the ravioli squares into a large saucepan of boiling, salted water and cook for about 10 minutes until tender. Drain well, and serve with the Napolitana sauce and a sprinkling of Parmesan.

VARIATION Instead of the veal, mix in 300 g (11 oz) ricotta or cream cheese. You can serve this ravioli with Napolitana sauce or heat 60 g (2 oz) butter with 180 ml (6 fl oz) cream and 1 teaspoon dried sage.

PASTITSIO *Easy to prepare, this traditional Greek dish comprises layers of noodles, meat and a rich cheese sauce.*

PASTITSIO

THIS GREEK NOODLE dish is guaranteed to become a firm family favourite. It also makes an excellent party dish. Be generous with freshly grated Parmesan cheese in the cheese sauce, and serve simply with a salad.

PREPARATION TIME: 1 HOUR
COOKING TIME: 1 HOUR
PREHEAT OVEN TO 190°C (375°F, MARK 5)

INGREDIENTS FOR SIX TO EIGHT
*1 large onion, peeled and chopped**
2 tablespoons sunflower oil
1 clove garlic, crushed
750 g (1 lb 10 oz) lean beef mince
*60 ml (2 fl oz) beef stock**
1 tin (425 g/15 oz) tomatoes
125 ml (4 fl oz) red wine
1 cinnamon stick
1 bay leaf
1 tablespoon chopped parsley
1 teaspoon dried oregano
Salt and freshly ground black pepper
500 g (1 lb 2 oz) macaroni, halved and cooked
750 ml (26 fl oz) cheese sauce, using all Parmesan cheese or half Parmesan and half Cheddar cheese*
3 tablespoons grated Parmesan cheese

Gently fry the onion in the heated oil. Stir in the garlic, then add the beef mince, stirring all the time, until the meat has changed colour.

Add the stock, the chopped tomatoes, the juice from the tin and the wine. Stir this mixture until it comes to the boil. Then reduce the heat and simmer it very gently with the spices, herbs and seasoning. Allow the mixture to cook for about 45 minutes, or until it is very tender. Check the seasoning.

To assemble, mix the drained, cooked macaroni with the meat sauce. Turn into a large, oiled ovenproof dish.

Cover the mixture with the prepared cheese sauce and sprinkle over the grated Parmesan cheese.

Bake for 45 minutes, or until the surface is golden. After removing from the oven, allow the dish to stand for about 5-10 minutes before cutting into squares for serving.

Accompany with a Greek salad* or a green salad*, garnished with chives.

VARIATION Use 750 g (1 lb 10 oz) aubergines (eggplants) cubed, instead of the lean beef mince. Add more sunflower oil, if necessary, to sauté the aubergines (eggplants). Cook gently until tender.

You could also make the pastitsio with meat left over from a joint of roast beef or lamb. In this case, dice the cooked meat finely and reduce the cooking time for the sauce by about 20 minutes.

115

SPAGHETTI ALLE VONGOLE

VONGOLE IN ROME, *capperozzoli* in Venice, *arselle* in Genoa and *telline* in Florence: all mean exactly the same thing – the small clams that are used throughout Italy to make soup or sauce for a variety of pasta dishes.

Ensure that the clams are not preserved in vinegar nor smoked and preserved in oil; this can ruin the fine flavour of the sauce.

PREPARATION TIME: 10 MINUTES
COOKING TIME: 40 MINUTES

INGREDIENTS FOR FOUR
75 g (3 oz) butter
1 large onion, peeled and chopped*
2 cloves garlic, crushed
700 g (1½ lb) tomatoes, skinned and seeded*, or 1 tin (about 425 g/15 oz) tomatoes
¼ teaspoon each dried basil and thyme
A good pinch of dried chilli pepper or cayenne pepper, or a few drops of Tabasco
450 g (1 lb) spaghetti
1 tin (290 g/10 oz) clams
Salt (optional)

Melt 50 g (2 oz) of the butter in a large saucepan and fry the onion until soft (about 15 minutes). Lower the heat, stir in the garlic and cook for 2 minutes.

Add the tomatoes with any juice, and the herbs. Cook for a further 10-15 minutes, then stir in the pepper or Tabasco. Keep the sauce on a low heat, stirring occasionally, while you cook the spaghetti in boiling water.

When the spaghetti is almost ready, add the drained clams to the tomato sauce and heat it through gently.

To serve, drain the spaghetti in a colander and pile it into a serving bowl. Add the remaining butter and toss the spaghetti in it.

Taste the sauce, add salt if necessary, and serve separately.

SERVING SUGGESTION Serve a green salad* before or after this dish.

VARIATION Use mussels tinned in brine instead of clams.

The clams in tomato sauce would be just as good served with rice. To keep the Italian theme, try a risotto Milanese*.

SPAGHETTI WITH PESTO SAUCE

WHEN BASIL is in season, this fragrant, unforgettable sauce is an absolute must to accompany pasta.

PREPARATION TIME: 20 MINUTES
COOKING TIME: 15 MINUTES

INGREDIENTS FOR FOUR TO SIX
500 g (1 lb 2 oz) spaghetti, cooked*
70 g (2½ oz) fresh basil leaves
2 cloves garlic
60 ml (2 fl oz) olive oil
125 ml (4 fl oz) sunflower oil
2-4 tablespoons pine nuts (kernels)
100 g (3¾ oz) freshly grated Parmesan cheese
Salt and freshly ground pepper

While cooking the spaghetti, purée the other ingredients in a food processor. If the sauce seems too thick, thin it down with more oil. The sauce should be thin enough to run off a spoon.

You can also thin down the pesto by adding 1 tablespoon of the hot spaghetti water before tossing the sauce with the well-drained, pasta. Serve immediately, with a carrot salad*.

VARIATION You can use walnuts instead of pine nuts (kernels).

SPAGHETTI ALLA CARBONARA

A QUICKLY PREPARED, delicious pasta dish flavoured with eggs, bacon and cream makes for a very filling lunch or supper. Serve it with a green salad.

PREPARATION TIME: 25 MINUTES
COOKING TIME: 10 MINUTES

INGREDIENTS FOR FOUR TO SIX
1 tablespoon olive oil
15 g (½ oz) butter
250 g (9 oz) rindless streaky bacon, diced
6 egg yolks
125 ml (4 fl oz) cream
500 g (1 lb 2 oz) spaghetti, cooked*
150 g (5 oz) freshly grated Parmesan cheese
Salt and freshly ground pepper

Heat the oil and butter in a frying pan, and add the diced streaky bacon. Cook

gently for about 5 minutes. Beat the egg yolks and cream together.

Drain the cooked spaghetti well, then mix it with the hot, cooked bacon, together with the fat from the pan. Mix in the egg and cream mixture, and add the grated Parmesan. Season the mixture and then serve immediately.

VARIATION Mix the sauce with other types of pasta such as tagliatelle, fettucine or pasta shells.

LASAGNE

LASAGNE MAKES a useful family meal as it can be assembled well in advance and baked just before serving. It is a dish that is often mediocre but if properly prepared it can be delicious. Use homemade or fresh pasta if available.

PREPARATION TIME: 2 HOURS
COOKING TIME: 40 MINUTES
PREHEAT OVEN TO 180°C (350°F, MARK 4)

INGREDIENTS FOR SIX TO EIGHT
250 g (9 oz) lasagne sheets*, cooked
500 ml (17 fl oz) Bolognese sauce*
500 ml (17 fl oz) cheese sauce*
4 tablespoons freshly grated Parmesan cheese

Arrange one-third of the lasagne sheets in the bottom of a lightly oiled, oblong ovenproof dish. Spread with one-third of the Bolognese sauce and cover with one-third of the cheese sauce. Repeat this process twice more, ending with the cheese sauce.

Sprinkle over the grated Parmesan and bake for 30-40 minutes, or until golden. Leave the lasagne to stand at room temperature for 5-10 minutes before cutting into squares.

SERVING SUGGESTION Being a rich dish, lasagne needs only a green salad* as an accompaniment.

VARIATIONS Instead of the meat sauce, layer it with 750 ml (26 fl oz) Napolitana sauce* and then add a layer of sautéed sliced mushrooms, or drained flaked tuna, or cooked fish.

Prepare a stack of pancakes and layer them in a deep, round dish or cake tin with the meat and cheese sauce. Bake for 20-30 minutes and slice into wedges.

and sugar, and continue to stir-fry for another minute.

Remove the meat and mushrooms from the wok or pan (leaving the gravy behind) and set aside. Add the remaining 2 tablespoons oil to the gravy in the wok or pan, then add the drained noodles and stir-fry for 1½ minutes. When the noodles are heated through and browned all over by the gravy and oil, add half the meat and half the cooked vegetables. Stir-fry for 1 minute, then remove.

Place the remaining meat and vegetables in the wok or pan, warm through and combine with the noodle mixture. Transfer the noodle mixture to a heated shallow bowl. Garnish with the chopped spring onion.

VARIATIONS Instead of beef, use boned chicken breasts, pork or shelled and deveined prawns*. Substitute carrot for the tinned bamboo shoots.

TAGLIATELLE WITH CREAM AND PARMESAN CHEESE

THIS SUBTLY FLAVOURED noodle dish is ideal for a lunch or supper that needs to be prepared at short notice. Rich and delicious, it is best complemented with a simple green salad.

PREPARATION TIME: 10 MINUTES
COOKING TIME: 15 MINUTES

INGREDIENTS FOR FOUR TO SIX
500 g (1 lb 2 oz) tagliatelle, cooked*
500 ml (17 fl oz) cream
75 g (3 oz) freshly grated Parmesan cheese
3 tablespoons chopped parsley
Freshly grated nutmeg
Salt and freshly ground black pepper

While cooking the tagliatelle, heat the cream, allowing it to reduce slightly. Mix the cream with the hot noodles, stir in the cheese, parsley and nutmeg, and then season to taste.

SERVING SUGGESTIONS If you like, pass around more Parmesan at the table.

VARIATION When simmering the cream, add 300 g (11 oz) button mushrooms, washed and thinly sliced. Alternatively, use another strongly flavoured cheese, such as Cheddar or Gruyère.

BEEF CHOW MEIN *Stir-frying produces crisp vegetables and tender meat.*

BEEF CHOW MEIN

CHOW MEIN IS SURELY one of the best known of Chinese dishes. 'Chow' is the Chinese description for any stir-fried dish, while 'mein' means noodles. This recipe offers a delicious combination of tender beef, noodles and crisp vegetables, creating an interesting contrast in textures.

If you have time, put the beef in the freezer for about 30 minutes beforehand to make slicing easier.

PREPARATION TIME: 30 MINUTES
COOKING TIME: 15 MINUTES

INGREDIENTS FOR SIX
90 ml (3 fl oz) sunflower oil
500 g (1 lb 2 oz) Chinese noodles (or egg noodles or spaghetti), cooked*
1 clove garlic, crushed
¼ teaspoon grated fresh green ginger
100 g (3¾ oz) Chinese or ordinary cabbage, shredded, or celery, sliced

3 spring onions, cut into 1 cm (½ in) lengths
4 pieces tinned bamboo shoots, drained and cut into matchstick strips
500 g (1 lb 2 oz) lean beef, shredded into matchstick strips and tossed with 1 tablespoon cornflour
75 g (3 oz) tinned mushrooms, finely sliced
40 ml (1¼ fl oz) light soy sauce
2 tablespoons dry sherry
1 teaspoon sugar
Chopped spring onion for garnish

Stir 1 tablespoon of the oil into the cooked noodles and set aside.

Place a wok or heavy-based frying pan over a high heat and add 1 tablespoon of the oil. When the oil is hot, add the garlic, ginger, cabbage or celery, spring onions and bamboo shoots. Stir-fry the mixture for 2 minutes over a high heat, remove the mixture from the wok or pan and put on one side.

Heat 2 tablespoons of the oil in the same wok or pan. When the oil is very hot, add the meat and mushrooms. Stir-fry for 1 minute, add the soy sauce, sherry

PLANNING A *RIJSTAFEL*

The *rijstafel* (Dutch for 'rice table') is a blend of Muslim, Hindu and Buddhist cuisine from the spice islands of Indonesia. The unique character of the *rijstafel* stems not only from the variety of dishes offered but also from the clever and abundant use of spices. A *rijstafel* normally consists of one or more dishes of meat, fish, chicken or egg, one or two vegetable dishes, assorted sauces and pickles, and a bowl of fresh fruit. As a general rule, for four people allow 400 g (14 oz) rice, one chicken, one meat, and one vegetable dish with sauces. For each additional extra couple, add a further 200 g (7 oz) rice and an extra dish.

The following menu would provide a *rijstafel* for eight people: Nasi Goreng (Indonesian-style fried rice); Udang Goreng Asam Manis (sweet and sour prawns); Ayam Kuning (yellow chicken); Satay Sapi Pedes (hot beef satay); Saus Kacang Tidak Pedes (peanut sauce); Sambal Goreng Terung (peppery aubergine/eggplant).

To save time, make the following preparations the day before you plan to serve the meal. Cook the rice and measure and prepare the other ingredients. Make the sweet and sour sauce. Cook the yellow chicken, cover and refrigerate (this allows the flavours to develop). Place the beef in the marinade, cover and refrigerate. Last of all, prepare the peanut sauce.

Knives are not needed for a *rijstafel* so either use spoons and forks, or bowls and chopsticks if preferred. A revolving tray (lazy Susan) simplifies the serving of the food. Place the rice at the centre and surround with the other dishes.

To eat from the *rijstafel*, place a mound of rice in the middle of your plate and spoon small helpings from the dishes of your choice around the rice.

NASI GORENG

PREPARATION TIME: 20 MINUTES
COOKING TIME: 30 MINUTES

800 g (1¾ lb) long-grain rice
2 litres (3½ pints) water
4 teaspoons salt
2 chicken breasts, diced
50 ml (2 fl oz) sunflower oil
4 large onions, peeled and sliced*
4 cloves garlic, chopped
1 teaspoon ground coriander
1 teaspoon ground ginger
2 teaspoons anchovy paste (or pounded tinned anchovies or prawns)
1-2 dried red chillies, crushed
50 ml (2 fl oz) soy sauce
200 g (7 oz) cooked shrimps or prawns
8 fried eggs or strips of omelette

Boil the rice in the water with the salt, and then allow to cool. Stir-fry the diced chicken breasts in the oil, add the onions and continue cooking over high heat until the onions brown.

Lower the heat and add the garlic, coriander, ginger, anchovy or prawn paste and chillies. Sauté for 1 minute to develop the flavour in the spices. Add the soy sauce, shrimps (or prawns) and cooked rice.

Warm through while stirring all the time to prevent the rice from burning. Top the dish with fried eggs or strips of omelette, or chopped, toasted peanuts.

UDANG GORENG ASAM MANIS

PREPARATION TIME: 40 MINUTES
COOKING TIME: 20 MINUTES

1 egg
2 tablespoons flour
12 medium-sized prawns, shelled, de-veined* and lightly salted
Sunflower oil for deep-frying

For the sweet and sour sauce:
2 teaspoons soy sauce
1 tablespoon cornflour mixed with 50 ml (2 fl oz) water
1 tablespoon tomato sauce
50 ml (2 fl oz) vinegar
125 ml (4 fl oz) strong chicken stock*
40 g (1½ oz) sugar
¾ teaspoon ground ginger
Salt and pepper

For the garnish:
Julienne* strips of carrot
Pieces of pineapple
Green pepper strips

Mix the egg with the flour and dip the prawns in this batter. Deep-fry in the hot oil and then drain on a paper towel.

To make the sweet and sour sauce, bring all the ingredients except the salt and pepper to a gentle boil, stirring continuously. Taste and season with salt and pepper. Add the vegetables for garnish and pour the hot sauce over the prawns just before serving.

AYAM KUNING

PREPARATION TIME: 20 MINUTES
COOKING TIME: 1 HOUR

1 teaspoon ground coriander
¾ teaspoon ground ginger
2 teaspoons salt
1.5 kg (3 lb 3 oz) chicken pieces
50 ml (2 fl oz) sunflower oil
2 teaspoons turmeric
1 medium-sized onion, peeled and sliced*
2 cloves garlic, chopped
1 teaspoon grated lemon rind
500 ml (17 fl oz) coconut milk
1 tablespoon lemon juice

Make a mixture of the coriander, ginger and salt. Rub it into the chicken pieces. Brown the chicken in the oil and then put it on one side.

Add the turmeric, onion, garlic and lemon rind to the remaining oil in the pan. Sauté for 1 minute. Add the coconut milk and lemon juice, and stir to make a sauce.

Place the browned chicken portions in this sauce and simmer over a very gentle heat for 45 minutes, then serve.

VARIATION If fresh coconut milk is not available, pour boiling water over 80 g (3 oz) desiccated coconut, allow to draw and squeeze out the liquid. You could also use coconut cream – a commercial preparation, available at speciality grocers.

SATAY SAPI PEDES

PREPARATION TIME: 15 MINUTES
MARINATING TIME: AT LEAST 1 HOUR
COOKING TIME: 5-10 MINUTES

500 g (1 lb 2 oz) boneless sirloin
1 small onion, peeled and chopped*
50 ml (2 fl oz) sunflower oil
1 teaspoon chilli sauce
2 tablespoons smooth peanut butter
1 teaspoon ground coriander
A pinch of ground ginger
2 tablespoons lemon juice

Cut the meat into small pieces (about 2 cm/¾ in square). Sauté the onion in the oil until golden-brown then set aside to cool. Mix the chilli sauce, peanut butter, coriander, ginger and lemon juice with the onions. Place the cubed meat in this mixture and marinate for at least 1 hour or overnight if you have time.

Thread the cubes of meat on fine bamboo skewers and grill quickly until done.

If you prefer, use skinned breast of chicken or pork fillet instead of the beef.

SAUS KACANG TIDAK PEDES

PREPARATION TIME: 10 MINUTES
COOKING TIME: 10 MINUTES

3 tablespoons smooth peanut butter
125 ml (4 fl oz) water or plain drinking
    yoghurt
1 clove garlic, finely chopped
1 teaspoon anchovy paste
    (or pounded anchovies or prawns)
1 teaspoon brown sugar
1 tablespoon dark soy sauce
1 tablespoon lemon juice
1 teaspoon salt

Blend the peanut butter with the water or yoghurt over a medium heat until the mixture boils. Turn off the heat and add the rest of the ingredients. Serve lukewarm. This sauce is especially good with skewered meat (satay).

Satay sticks and peanut sauce are often served as a starter with chunks of unpeeled cucumber and cubes of compressed rice. Boil short-grain rice until cooked, turn it into a greased, shallow dish and press a plate onto it until it is cold and set. Then cut the rice into cubes.

SAMBAL GORENG TERUNG

PREPARATION TIME: 15 MINUTES
COOKING TIME: 15 MINUTES

2 medium-sized aubergines (eggplants)
1 teaspoon salt
1 tablespoon lemon juice
1 small onion, peeled and sliced*
2 tablespoons sunflower oil
1 teaspoon ground coriander
1 teaspoon brown sugar
1 dried red chilli, crushed
2 teaspoons anchovy paste

Slice the aubergines (eggplants) (with the skin) into 1 cm (½ in) thick slices. Sprinkle with the salt and lemon juice.

Sauté the onion in the oil. Add the coriander, brown sugar, chilli and anchovy paste. Place the slices in this mixture, turn to coat and sauté for about 10 minutes in an open pan until cooked. A little water may be added to speed up the cooking and prevent burning. Be careful not to reduce the vegetables to a pulp.

VARIATIONS Serve more than one sambal with your rijstafel. Sambals generally consist of grated vegetables or fruits which are then seasoned with salt, vinegar and fresh or dried chillies. Try a carrot*, apple*, onion* or cucumber* sambal, or experiment with your own combinations.

RISOTTO MILANESE *is a rich, delicious way of preparing rice.*

RISOTTO MILANESE

R ISOTTO IS THE ITALIAN way of preparing rich and creamy rice dishes. They can be as simple as the traditional *risotto Milanese* recipe offered here, or as elaborate as you choose to make them.

PREPARATION TIME: 5 MINUTES
COOKING TIME: 45 MINUTES

INGREDIENTS FOR SIX

50 g (2 oz) butter
1 medium-sized onion, peeled and
    finely chopped*
400 g (14 oz) rice
125 ml (4 fl oz) dry white wine
1 litre (1¾ pints) hot chicken stock*
A pinch of saffron
30 g (1¼ oz) soft butter
100 g (3¾ oz) freshly grated
    Parmesan cheese
Salt and freshly ground black
    pepper

Melt the 50 g (2 oz) butter in a heavy-bottomed saucepan. Stir in the onion and cook very gently, stirring often, until softened but not browned. Stir in the rice and cook for 1-2 minutes, stirring all the time so that the rice does not stick.

Pour in the wine and allow it to boil rapidly until it is almost all absorbed. Pour in half the hot stock and cook, uncovered, until this, too, is almost absorbed into the rice.

Stir the saffron into the remaining hot stock and add to the rice. Once again, cook until the stock is almost absorbed. If the rice is not yet tender, add a little more stock and cook until the rice is soft. If necessary, keep adding a bit more stock until the rice is tender. Stir in the 30 g (1¼ oz) soft butter and the Parmesan, and season to taste. Serve immediately.

VARIATION Stir-fry 400 g (14 oz) shelled prawns* in the hot butter. Remove and set aside. You can add more butter if necessary when softening the onion. Try using a fish stock* instead of the chicken stock (add the prawn shells when making the fish stock to give it a prawn flavour). Return the prawns to the rice just before it is cooked so that they can heat through.

PILAFF WITH LAMB AND APRICOTS

THIS PILAFF lends itself well to variations, and makes a good vehicle for leftovers, allowing you to use virtually any cooked and cubed meat or fish.

PREPARATION TIME: 30 MINUTES
COOKING TIME: 1½ HOURS

INGREDIENTS FOR SIX
1 tablespoon sunflower oil
2 large onions, peeled and sliced*
100 g (3¾ oz) butter
750 g (1 lb 10 oz) lamb shoulder (or thick chump chops), boned and cut into 1 cm (½ in) cubes
125 g (4¼ oz) dried apricots, coarsely chopped
400 ml (14 fl oz) beef or chicken stock*
Salt and freshly ground black pepper
1 green pepper, seeded and coarsely chopped
2 cloves garlic, crushed
1-2 tomatoes, skinned*, seeded and chopped
4 tablespoons seedless raisins
100 g (3¾ oz) flaked almonds, lightly toasted*
400 g (14 oz) rice
1 litre (1¾ pints) water

Heat the oil in a large saucepan and sauté the sliced onions until golden. Transfer to a large bowl with a slotted spoon and add half the butter to the saucepan. Brown the lamb cubes over a fairly high heat in batches, transferring the meat to the bowl with a slotted spoon as it is browned. Do not overcook.

When all the meat is sufficiently browned, return it to the saucepan together with the onions, apricots and stock, and simmer (covered) for 1 hour, or until the meat is very tender. Season to taste with salt and pepper.

While the lamb is cooking, sauté the green pepper, garlic and tomatoes in the remaining butter for 4-5 minutes, and then stir in the raisins, almonds and rice.

Stir-fry for 2 minutes, or until the rice is slightly translucent, and add the water. Simmer for 10 minutes or so, until the water is absorbed. Season the rice to taste with salt and pepper.

Spread one-third of the rice mixture in an even layer in a large, ovenproof casserole and top with one-third of the

lamb. Add another layer of rice and lamb, and continue until you have used up all the ingredients, ending with a layer of lamb (the rice layers should be fairly thick compared to the lamb layers).

Cover and cook over a low heat until the rice is tender (about 20 minutes) and the dish is heated through.

SERVING SUGGESTION Serve this lamb pilaff in the casserole in which it was cooked, accompanied only by a large bowl of natural yoghurt and a cucumber salad with a mint dressing.

SAFFRON RICE

SAFFRON IS A HIGHLY PRIZED (and expensive) spice that imparts a brilliant yellow colour and delicate flavour to a variety of dishes. This recipe is for a subtly flavoured rice dish which is sprinkled with cashew nuts fried in clarified butter.

PREPARATION TIME: 15 MINUTES
COOKING TIME: 45 MINUTES

INGREDIENTS FOR SIX
400 g (14 oz) rice (preferably basmati rice)
125 ml (4 fl oz) melted clarified butter* or ghee
2 tablespoons cashew nuts, halved
2 cinnamon sticks, about 5 cm (2 in) each
3 medium-sized onions, peeled and sliced*
1½ teaspoons salt
2 medium-sized carrots, scraped and grated
¼ teaspoon saffron strands, soaked for 15 minutes in 125 ml (4 fl oz) warm milk
500 ml (17 fl oz) hot water

Sort and wash the rice several times, then allow to drain. Heat the butter or ghee in a heavy-based saucepan and fry the cashew nuts in it until golden-brown. Remove the cashew nuts and put them on one side.

Add the cinnamon to the butter or ghee and brown for a few seconds, then place the onions in the pan and stir-fry for 5 minutes. Place the rice, salt, carrots and saffron (with milk) in the saucepan, and stir well. Add the hot water and cover the saucepan with a well-fitting lid.

Simmer on a low heat for 20-30

minutes, or until the rice is tender. Stir with a fork, garnish with the nuts and serve warm.

FRIED RICE

RICE IS AN ESSENTIAL accompaniment to most Oriental meals. This fried rice dish – cooked quickly in the Chinese manner – may also be served with many Western-style dishes.

PREPARATION TIME: 30 MINUTES
COOKING TIME: 10 MINUTES

INGREDIENTS FOR SIX
2 tablespoons sunflower oil
2 eggs, well beaten
200 g (7 oz) rice, cooked*
60 g (2 oz) frozen peas
25 g (1 oz) mung bean sprouts*
2 spring onions, sliced
1 tablespoon light soy sauce

Heat 1 tablespoon of the oil in a wok or heavy-based frying pan, add the beaten eggs and swirl them around in the pan until they are firm. Turn onto a board and, when slightly cooled, slice into thin strips and keep warm.

Heat the remaining oil in the pan, add the rice and fry gently. Add the peas, bean sprouts, spring onions and soy sauce, stir-fry briefly, then remove from the heat.

Pile the rice into a heated serving bowl and sprinkle the egg strips over the top.

VARIATION The egg yolks and whites may be cooked separately for a colourful mixed garnish of yellow and white.

RICE SALAD

RICE, COOKED in a well-flavoured stock, is the basis of this tasty salad. Vinaigrette makes a tangy change from the more usual mayonnaise dressing.

PREPARATION TIME: 25 MINUTES

INGREDIENTS FOR FOUR
150 g (5 oz) rice, cooked in 375 ml (13 fl oz) chicken* or vegetable stock*
75 g (3 oz) stuffed olives, finely sliced
2 hard-boiled eggs*, diced

1½ stalks celery, finely sliced
1 dill pickle, chopped
¼ small green pepper, chopped
1 small onion, peeled and finely
  chopped*
80 ml (2½ fl oz) vinaigrette*

Put the rice in a medium-sized bowl and mix in the olives, eggs, celery, dill pickle, green pepper and onion. Pour over the dressing while the rice is still hot. Toss and set aside to cool.

SERVING SUGGESTIONS Serve on a bed of lettuce leaves surrounded with slices or wedges of tomato and cucumber. If you serve the salad with tuna fish or prawns, it makes a meal in itself.

PIZZA

THE PIZZA is a popular and inexpensive dish that is both tasty and filling. It lends itself to a multitude of variations. This is a traditional Italian recipe for pizza.

PREPARATION TIME: 40 MINUTES
RISING TIME: 20 MINUTES
COOKING TIME: 20 MINUTES
PREHEAT OVEN TO 240°C (475°F, MARK 9)

INGREDIENTS FOR FOUR TO SIX
For the dough:
1 tablespoon dried yeast, or 25 g
  (1 oz) fresh yeast
¼ teaspoon sugar
125 ml (4 fl oz) warm water
200 g (7 oz) flour
¼ teaspoon salt
1 tablespoon sunflower oil

For the topping:
250 ml (9 fl oz) Napolitana sauce*,
  or 4 tomatoes, skinned* and
  chopped
150 g (5 oz) mozzarella cheese,
  grated
100 g (3¾ oz) Parmesan cheese,
  grated
6 anchovy fillets, or 10 slices
  salami
12 black olives
6 fresh button mushrooms, sliced
3 slices Parma ham (prosciutto),
  cut in strips
1 small sweet red, green or yellow
  pepper (if available), sliced
2 cloves garlic, crushed
1 teaspoon dried oregano
1 tablespoon sunflower oil

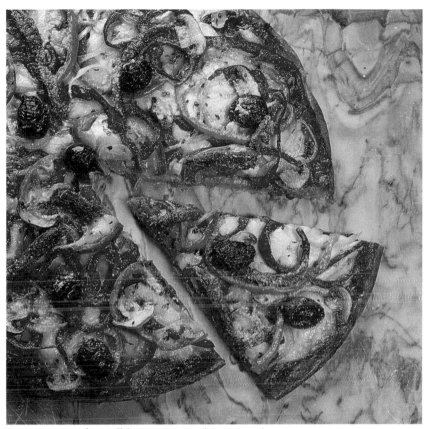

PIZZA *A recipe that will have everyone clamouring for more.*

Mix the yeast and sugar with the warm water in a large bowl. Allow to stand for 10 minutes, or until frothy.

Sieve half the flour into the bowl, add the salt, then stir until smooth. Gradually mix in enough of the remaining flour to form a stiff dough. Add the oil and knead well until the dough is smooth and feels elastic.

Leave for about 20 minutes before rolling out to fit a large, well-oiled 23 cm (9 in) pizza pan.

To make the topping, spread the dough with the Napolitana sauce or the tomatoes. Sprinkle with the grated mozzarella and Parmesan cheese. Top with anchovy fillets (or slices of salami), black olives, sliced mushrooms, strips of ham and strips of sweet pepper (if they are being included).

Add the crushed garlic and oregano. Drizzle with the oil and bake on the lowest shelf of the preheated oven for about 20 minutes, or until the crust is lightly browned and crisp, and the topping is piping hot.

VARIATIONS You can fold the round of pizza dough over to enclose the filling and bake for about 30 minutes, or until golden. In this case prepare a mixture of 1 egg, 3 tablespoons grated Parmesan cheese and 250 g (9 oz) ricotta – or use cream cheese mixed with 2 tablespoons cream and rubbed through a sieve – and smear this mixture on half the dough. Cover with a layer of thinly sliced salami and a sprinkling of tiny cubes of mozzarella cheese before folding and baking.

To make a deep pan pizza, brush a 23 cm (9 in) layer cake tin with oil and sprinkle with cornflour. Press the dough in to fit, pushing it firmly up the sides. Mix 250 g (9 oz) grated mozzarella cheese with 100 g (3¾ oz) grated Parmesan. Set aside 125 g (4¼ oz) of this to sprinkle on top. Add 250-375 ml (9-13 fl oz) Napolitana sauce to the remaining cheese and use to fill the pizza. Add any of the ingredients suggested for the flat pizza before sprinkling the reserved cheese on top. Bake the deep pan pizza at 230°C (450°F, mark 8) for 25 minutes.

121

MACARONI CHEESE

THE SECRET OF SUCCESS with macaroni cheese – always a good standby meal – is simply to be lavish with the strongly flavoured cheese sauce.

This dish is quick and easy to prepare and makes a popular and filling meal for the family.

PREPARATION TIME: 30-35 MINUTES
COOKING TIME: 20 MINUTES
PREHEAT OVEN TO 190°C (375°F, MARK 5)

INGREDIENTS FOR FOUR
350 g (¾ lb) macaroni
25 g (1 oz) fine homemade
   breadcrumbs
15 g (½ oz) butter, cut into pieces

For the sauce:
25 g (1 oz) butter
25 g (1 oz) flour
500 ml (17 fl oz) milk
Salt and freshly ground pepper
¼ teaspoon freshly grated nutmeg
115-125 g (4-4¼ oz) Cheddar cheese,
   grated

Bring a large pan of well-salted water to the boil, and put in the macaroni. Cook it for 15-20 minutes, or until just tender. Do not overcook, or it will not absorb the sauce. Drain well.

To make the cheese sauce, melt the 25 g (1 oz) butter in a medium-sized saucepan. Stir in the flour and let it cook for 2-3 minutes over a gentle heat. Gradually add the milk, stirring all the time with a wooden spoon to obtain a smooth, velvety sauce. Season, then add the nutmeg.

Let the sauce cook gently for 10-15 minutes, stirring from time to time, then add the cheese. When the cheese has melted, stir in the cooked, drained macaroni. Check the seasoning, and pour the mixture into a pie dish.

Sprinkle the top with the breadcrumbs, dot all over with the cut butter, and bake in the preheated oven for 20 minutes (or until golden-brown).

SERVING SUGGESTION Serve with baked tomatoes and a green vegetable or salad.

VARIATIONS Add a layer of sautéed tomatoes and onions in the middle.

Mix in 50 g (2 oz) chopped ham as an extra ingredient.

To make an even more substantial meal, pour the mixture over leftover fish.

TABBOULEH *A tasty, versatile salad from the Middle East.*

TABBOULEH

THIS IS A VARIATION of the Lebanese salad served as a starter with other Middle Eastern dishes. It is also suitable as a side dish to accompany cold meats or fish.

PREPARATION TIME: 1 HOUR
CHILLING TIME: overnight

INGREDIENTS FOR SIX
180 ml (6 fl oz) boiling water
175 g (6 oz) fine burghul, millet or
   couscous
4 medium-sized onions, peeled and
   finely chopped*
4 tablespoons chopped parsley
½ green cucumber, chopped
3 tablespoons chopped mint
225 ml (8 fl oz) olive oil
2 tablespoons lemon juice
Salt and freshly ground black
   pepper
6 firm, ripe tomatoes
2 medium-sized onions, peeled and
   finely sliced*
½ green cucumber, diced
75 g (3 oz) black olives

1 green pepper, seeded and
   coarsely chopped
60 ml (2 fl oz) wine vinegar
Lettuce leaves, well washed

Pour the boiling water over the burghul millet or couscous, allow to cool, then add the finely chopped onion, parsley, chopped cucumber, mint, 90 ml (3 fl oz) of the olive oil and the lemon juice, and season to taste. Refrigerate overnight.

Next, coarsely dice the tomatoes. Add the sliced onions, diced cucumber, olives, green pepper, vinegar and remaining olive oil. Gently toss the ingredients and season with salt and pepper.

Line a platter with the lettuce leaves. Mound the grain mixture on top, pile on the tomato mixture and serve.

SERVING SUGGESTION Tabbouleh makes the ideal centrepiece for a buffet. Serve with kebabs. Thread chunks of lamb, red pepper, onion and mushrooms onto skewers. Baste with olive oil, sprinkle with herbs and grill or barbecue.

VARIATION Toss the grain mixture with the tomato mixture and add 300 g (11 oz) diced feta cheese.

COUSCOUS

COUSCOUS IS THE STAPLE of North Africa, as rice is to the Chinese. The word has two meanings – the completed dish, and the cereal from which it is made, which is usually semolina but might also be barley, wheat or millet. Couscous made from semolina pellets is available from some speciality food shops as well as many health food stores.

PREPARATION TIME: 30 MINUTES
SOAKING TIME: OVERNIGHT
COOKING TIME: 1¾ HOURS

INGREDIENTS FOR SIX

250 g (9 oz) couscous, millet or burghul
125 g (4½ oz) haricot beans
125 g (4½ oz) chick-peas
500 g (1 lb 2 oz) chicken pieces
500 g (1 lb 2 oz) lamb leg (chump) chops
*1 large onion, peeled and sliced**
1 teaspoon salt
12 black peppercorns
25 g (1 oz) butter
½ teaspoon freshly ground black pepper
2 medium-sized carrots, scraped and diced
4 courgettes (zucchini) sliced
2 medium-sized tomatoes, skinned and quartered*
1 small green pepper, seeded and finely chopped
½ teaspoon celery salt
½ teaspoon cayenne pepper
½ teaspoon chopped thyme
½ teaspoon chopped parsley

Place the couscous, millet or burghul, the beans and the chick-peas in separate basins, cover with cold water and leave to soak overnight.

Next day, drain the beans and place in a very large saucepan with the chicken, lamb, onion, salt and peppercorns. Cover with water, bring to the boil and remove the scum. Lower the heat and stew gently for 1 hour.

Meanwhile, drain the couscous, millet or burghul and pour it into a separate saucepan containing 500 ml (17 fl oz) salted boiling water, stirring the grain frequently as it boils to prevent lumps from forming; it will absorb almost all the liquid. After 15 minutes, reduce the heat to very low and stir in the butter and freshly ground pepper. Cover closely with a lid, or with aluminium foil, and leave it over the heat to soften and swell while you continue preparing the stew. Make sure that it does not burn.

When the chicken and lamb have cooked for 1 hour, lift them from the pan and slice off all the meat, discarding the skin, fat and bones. Return the meat to the pan. Drain the chick-peas and add to the meat with the carrots, courgettes (zucchini), tomatoes and green pepper. Add the celery salt, cayenne pepper, thyme and parsley. Boil gently for a further 35 minutes. Taste and adjust the seasoning if necessary.

Just before serving, increase the heat under the couscous, millet or burghul and stir until it is very hot.

POTATO GNOCCHI

SERVED WITH TOMATO SAUCE, potato gnocchi make a light dish on their own. They can also be served with any kind of grilled or fried meat.

PREPARATION TIME: 45 MINUTES
STANDING TIME: 1 HOUR
COOKING TIME: 20 MINUTES

INGREDIENTS FOR SIX

2 large, floury potatoes
Salt
15 g (½ oz) butter
1 egg yolk
250-300 g (9-11 oz) flour

Boil the potatoes in salted water until tender. Drain well and peel. Push the cooked potatoes through a metal sieve over a bowl. Add the butter, which will melt from the heat of the potatoes.

Stir in the yolk and a pinch of salt. Add 250 g (9 oz) flour gradually until the dough has a firm consistency – if necessary, add a little more flour. (You can mash the potatoes and mix the dough in a food processor.)

Break off small pieces of the dough and shape into sausage-like rolls, each about 2.5 cm (1 in) long and 1 cm (½ in) thick. Traditionally each piece is pressed with the thumb against the concave surface of a cheese grater to give the gnocchi the appearance of shells with ridged patterns on their backs. Place the gnocchi on a floured surface to prevent them from sticking together. Flour lightly and leave to dry for an hour or more.

Cook the gnocchi in batches (so that they do not stick together) in a large saucepan of boiling, salted water for about 20 minutes. The gnocchi will rise to the top as soon as they are cooked. Remove with a slotted spoon.

SERVING SUGGESTION Serve with a meat sauce sprinkled with grated Parmesan.

SPINACH GNOCCHI

ALTHOUGH THIS ITALIAN favourite makes a very good starter, it is often served as the main course of a light meal.

PREPARATION TIME: 30 MINUTES
CHILLING TIME: 1 HOUR
COOKING TIME: 30 MINUTES

INGREDIENTS FOR SIX

250 g (9 oz) frozen spinach
250 g (9 oz) ricotta
2 eggs, beaten
120 g (¼ lb) flour
15 g (½ oz) butter
Salt and pepper
Grated nutmeg
1 tablespoon grated Parmesan cheese
60 ml (2 fl oz) melted butter
Grated Parmesan cheese for sprinkling

Cook the spinach over a medium heat, stirring often, until all the moisture has evaporated. Stir in the ricotta and cook briefly over a gentle heat.

Remove from the stove and mix in the beaten eggs, flour, butter, seasoning, nutmeg and the Parmesan. If the mixture seems too sloppy, add a little more flour. Chill for 1 hour.

Shape into tiny balls with a spoon and drop them, a few at a time, into barely simmering water for about 5 minutes. When cooked, they rise to the top. Remove with a slotted spoon and drain.

Pour the melted butter over the gnocchi and serve hot. Pass around a bowl of grated Parmesan to sprinkle over each serving.

SERVING SUGGESTION Serve the gnocchi with ratatouille*.

VARIATION Gnocchi can also make an unusual topping for a stew or a dish with plenty of sauce. Serve your stew in a deep dish and arrange the cooked gnocchi close together on top.

EGGS
AND
CHEESE

Eggs and cheese are among the most versatile and nutritious ingredients in the kitchen. Both are rich in animal protein, fats, minerals and vitamins, and are popular in family meals as less expensive – but equally beneficial – substitutes for meat and poultry.

The egg is seen by many cultures as a symbol of life and fertility. Early Christians, borrowing from pagan tradition, regarded it as a symbol of rebirth and made hard-boiled, decorated eggs as Easter gifts – the precursors of today's chocolate eggs.

Eggs are perfect for breakfast or light meals, whether poached, boiled, fried, coddled, baked or scrambled. They can also be made into omelettes, soufflés and quiches, and are useful for coating fried food, thickening or emulsifying sauces, binding rissoles, glazing, and using in a host of baked foods.

Cheese is almost as universally useful and is included in all types of dishes, from starters to desserts. It is ideal for a snack, served with fruit, wine, bread or crackers, and combines particularly well with pasta and rice dishes.

EGGS BENEDICT

THIS INTERNATIONAL FAVOURITE consists of poached eggs and ham on toasted soft rolls, topped with Hollandaise sauce.

PREPARATION TIME: 15 MINUTES
COOKING TIME: 40 MINUTES

INGREDIENTS FOR SIX

6 extra-large eggs
3 English muffins or soft, round rolls, or 6 slices bread
Butter for spreading
6 slices cooked ham

For the Hollandaise sauce:
175 g (6 oz) butter
1 tablespoon white wine vinegar
2 tablespoons lemon juice
3 egg yolks
$\frac{1}{4}$ teaspoon caster sugar
Salt and freshly ground pepper

First make the sauce. Put the butter into a small saucepan over a gentle heat and leave it to melt slowly. Put the vinegar and lemon juice into a second saucepan and bring to the boil. Process the egg yolks, sugar and a little salt in a blender or food processor, gradually adding the lemon juice and vinegar, and pepper.

When the butter starts to boil, pour it very slowly (with the blender still switched on) into the yolk mixture until all the butter has been added and the sauce has thickened. Turn the sauce into a basin and keep it warm by standing the basin in a saucepan of hot water.

To poach the eggs, bring a frying pan of water to the boil. Reduce to a simmer and slip in 3 eggs for poaching, one at a time. When they are set to your liking (about 3 minutes), lift them out with a slotted spoon and leave to drain well on a plate lined with paper towels. Poach the remaining eggs in the same way. Meanwhile, split and toast the muffins, rolls or bread and spread them with butter. Top each with a slice of ham and a poached egg. Spoon over the warm Hollandaise sauce and serve.

VARIATION Before assembling the eggs Benedict, cover the ham with 2 tablespoons sherry or Marsala, top with aluminium foil and warm it through in a 120°C (250°F, mark $\frac{1}{2}$) oven for about 10 minutes.

If you do not have a blender, use a conventional Hollandaise sauce*.

INDA NU SAKH *A perfect blend of spices goes into these curried eggs.*

INDA NU SAKH

THIS SIMPLE INDIAN DISH consists of hard-boiled eggs doused with a curry sauce with onions and tomatoes. It is a superb light meal.

PREPARATION TIME: 30-40 MINUTES
COOKING TIME: 30 MINUTES

INGREDIENTS FOR FOUR TO SIX

8 eggs
2 tablespoons chopped coriander leaves for garnish

For the sauce:
4 tablespoons sunflower oil
1-1$\frac{1}{2}$ green chillies, chopped
8 curry leaves, fresh or dried (optional)
2 onions, peeled and grated or finely chopped*
4 tomatoes, halved and finely chopped
$\frac{3}{4}$ teaspoon turmeric
1 teaspoon cumin seeds, crushed
2 teaspoons coriander seeds, crushed
1 teaspoon salt

Boil the eggs for 10-12 minutes, cool under cold running water, and shell. Set them aside.

To make the sauce, heat the oil in a shallow pan and add the chopped chillies and curry leaves (if used). Brown for 10 seconds, then add the grated or chopped onion to the pan and stir the mixture well. Cook for 3 minutes.

Pour the chopped tomato into the pan and add the remaining spices and salt. Stir, cover the saucepan and simmer for 20 minutes, or until the vegetables are soft and blended with the spices. Cut the eggs in half lengthways and arrange in the saucepan. Cook for 3 minutes.

Transfer to a heated serving dish, garnish with the coriander leaves and serve immediately.

SERVING SUGGESTIONS Serve with a helping of rice or chapati and fresh pickle.

EGGS FLORENTINE

Quick and easy to prepare, this light lunch dish consists of a bed of spinach topped with eggs and covered with a cheese sauce.

PREPARATION TIME: 40 MINUTES
COOKING TIME: 20 MINUTES
PREHEAT OVEN TO 190°C (375°F, MARK 5)

INGREDIENTS FOR FOUR
1 kg (2¼ lb) fresh spinach
Salt and freshly ground black
   pepper
45 g (1¾ oz) butter
8 eggs
40 g (1½ oz) grated Parmesan cheese

For the sauce:
55 g (2 oz) butter
40 g (1½ oz) flour
500 ml (17 fl oz) milk
Salt and pepper
150 g (5 oz) Cheddar or Gruyère
   cheese, grated
1 teaspoon French mustard
   (optional)

Cook the spinach with about 100 ml (3½ fl oz) water until tender, then drain well. Chop it roughly and season.

Melt 30 g (1¼ oz) of the butter, stir in the spinach and allow to heat through. Turn the spinach and butter mixture into a buttered, shallow gratin or baking dish and spread evenly over the base.

To make the sauce, melt the butter, stir in the flour and cook for 1-2 minutes without browning. Gradually beat in the milk and bring to the boil, stirring all the time to make a smooth sauce. Season and stir in the grated cheese and mustard (if used). Cook over a gentle heat for 1 more minute.

Make 8 depressions in the spinach with the back of a spoon. Gently break an egg into each one, season and spoon over the sauce.

Sprinkle with Parmesan cheese and dot with the remaining 15 g (½ oz) butter. Bake for 15-20 minutes.

SERVING SUGGESTIONS This dish is especially good when served with crusty bread or rice tossed in butter.

VARIATIONS Use poached or hard-boiled eggs, cover with a cheese soufflé* mixture and bake at 200°C (400°F, mark 6) for 30 minutes. Although not 'Florentine', you can use lettuce instead of spinach.

QUICHES – QUICK AND TASTY SAVOURY TARTS

Quiches – open tarts with savoury fillings based on egg custard – make simple and thoroughly delicious meals served hot or cold. They also take very little time to prepare and bake.

The first step is to line a quiche tin: roll out unsweetened shortcrust pastry so that it fits a 23 cm (9 in) loose-bottomed quiche tin. Prick the base.

Next make an egg custard: beat 3 eggs with 250 ml (9 fl oz) cream or sour cream or half cream and half milk and 4 tablespoons grated Cheddar or Gruyère cheese, salt and freshly ground pepper.

Place the filling of your choice in the pastry case, pour over the custard, then bake the quiche at 180°C (350°F, mark 4) for 35-45 minutes until set but not overcooked. The centre may be a little soft, but will settle further as the quiche cools slightly.

Asparagus quiche Fill the pastry case with egg custard and the contents of a 425 g (15 oz) tin of drained asparagus cuts.

Smoked haddock quiche Sprinkle the pastry case with 250 g (9 oz) cooked, flaked smoked haddock. Pour over egg custard, seasoned with salt, freshly ground black pepper and 1 teaspoon finely grated lemon rind, if desired.

Leek quiche Simmer 2 bunches (6-8) well-washed, sliced leeks in 50 g (2 oz) butter until they are soft (but not brown). Spoon this into the pastry case and cover with well-seasoned egg custard. Sprinkle the top with grated cheese.

Mushroom quiche Fill the pastry case with 300 g (11 oz) sliced mushrooms fried in 30 g (1¼ oz) butter. Top this with egg custard and sprinkle with grated cheese.

Onion quiche Fry 3-4 large sliced onions* in 50 g (2 oz) butter and 1 tablespoon sunflower oil until they are very soft. Spread the onions over the pastry case and top with egg custard, with or without grated cheese.

Prawn or crayfish quiche Fill the pastry case with 200 g (7 oz) cooked, de-veined* prawns or roughly chopped cooked crayfish or lobster. Cover with egg custard, flavoured with a hint of grated nutmeg.

Quiche Lorraine Coarsely chop 6 thin rashers streaky bacon and fry them for a minute so that the fat begins to run. Sprinkle the bacon in the pastry case, cover with egg custard and sprinkle the top with cheese. Add to the bacon 2-3 chopped spring onions sautéed in butter, if desired.

Smoked salmon quiche Arrange 175-200 g (6-7 oz) sliced smoked salmon in the pastry case. Cover with egg custard, flavoured with a little freshly chopped dill, if liked. Alternatively, garnish with sprigs of dill once baked.

Smoked trout quiche Flake 250 g (9 oz) smoked trout into the pastry case. Add a thinly sliced onion* (optional) sautéed in butter, then pour over egg custard and sprinkle with grated cheese, if desired.

Spinach quiche Cook 500 g (1 lb 2 oz) spinach in 2 tablespoons water. Drain the spinach well, season and chop coarsely. Beat in 3 eggs, 125 ml (4 fl oz) cream, 250 g (9 oz) cottage cheese and a sprinkling of grated nutmeg. Spoon this into a pastry case and bake until firm.

Tuna quiche Drain and flake a 200 g (7 oz) tin of tuna. Sprinkle the fish over a pastry case with 2 teaspoons capers or 3-4 chopped anchovies, if liked. Cover this with egg custard and bake.

PIPERADE

THIS DISH originates in the Basque region of Spain. It combines creamy scrambled eggs with simmered onions, peppers and tomatoes – ingredients which provide a wonderful combination of flavours.

PREPARATION TIME: 10 MINUTES
COOKING TIME: 30 MINUTES

INGREDIENTS FOR FOUR
3 tablespoons olive oil
2 medium-sized onions, peeled and thinly sliced*
2 cloves garlic, crushed
2 large sweet red peppers, thinly sliced
4 ripe red tomatoes, skinned* and chopped
½ teaspoon oregano
Salt and freshly ground black pepper
6 eggs, lightly beaten

Heat the oil in a frying pan and add the onions. Cook very gently until barely soft, then add the garlic and sliced peppers, and continue to cook gently until very soft. Add the tomatoes, oregano and seasoning.

Cook (covered) very gently for another 5-10 minutes. Pour in the beaten eggs and cook over a gentle heat, stirring, until the eggs are barely set and very creamy. Season to taste and serve.

STUFFED EGGS

Hard-boiled eggs can be stuffed with a variety of fillings to make tasty snacks.

Shell 6 hard-boiled eggs and slice in half lengthways. To make the basic filling, remove the yolks and mash them with 2 tablespoons mayonnaise* and seasoning. Spoon or pipe the filling into the whites. If you like, mix in a little whipped cream.

Devilled stuffing Mash the yolks with 50 g (2 oz) unsalted butter, and season with nutmeg and cayenne pepper.

Anchovy stuffing Pound 8 (drained) anchovy fillets to a paste and mix thoroughly with the basic egg filling.

Ham stuffing Dice 4 slices ham very finely and add to the basic egg filling. Use a good smoked ham or gammon to enhance the flavour further.

SCOTCH EGGS

IN THE LAND of their origin, Scotch eggs are part of the traditional and, to foreigners, staggering Scots breakfast, which also includes porridge, bacon, fried eggs, flat sausage, black, white and fruit puddings and hot scones and jam. Elsewhere, Scotch eggs are served hot with gravy, or cold with salads.

PREPARATION TIME: 20 MINUTES
COOKING TIME: 10 MINUTES

INGREDIENTS FOR SIX
7 eggs
350 g (¾ lb) sausage meat
4 teaspoons finely chopped parsley or sage
Finely grated rind of 1 lemon
¼ teaspoon grated nutmeg
¼ teaspoon dried marjoram, basil or savory
Salt and freshly ground black pepper
120 g (¼ lb) dried breadcrumbs
Refined peanut or sunflower oil for deep-frying

Boil 6 of the eggs for 10-12 minutes, then allow them to cool under cold running water. Shell carefully, and put the whole eggs on one side.

Put the sausage meat into a bowl with the finely chopped parsley or sage, the lemon rind and nutmeg. Add the marjoram, basil or savory (these herbs greatly improve the flavour).

Season the mixture with salt and freshly ground black pepper, and work all these ingredients well into the sausage meat with your hands.

Make a coating for each hard-boiled egg out of the sausage meat, working it round the eggs with wet hands to form an even layer.

Roll the covered eggs in the remaining egg (beaten), and then in the dried breadcrumbs.

Heat the oil in a deep frying pan. When the oil has just started to smoke – at 180-190°C (350-375°F) – carefully put in 3 coated eggs and fry for 4-5 minutes, or until they turn deep golden.

Turn the eggs as they cook so that they brown evenly. Remove with a slotted spoon, drain on paper towels, and repeat with the remaining 3 eggs.

SERVING SUGGESTIONS Eat hot with gravy or serve cold, halved lengthways, with a green salad*.

VARIATIONS For a cheesy version of Scotch eggs, mix 250 g (9 oz) grated Cheddar with 30 g (1¼ oz) flour, 1 teaspoon salt, 1 teaspoon Worcestershire sauce, a beaten egg and 2 tablespoons milk. Using wet hands, coat 6 hard-boiled eggs with the cheese mixture, then roll in dried breadcrumbs. Refrigerate the crumbed eggs for an hour or so to allow the crumbs to set. Fry in hot oil until golden.

To make baked Scotch eggs, rather than deep-fried ones, place the prepared eggs on an oiled baking sheet. Drizzle with oil and bake at 200°C (400°F, mark 6) for 30 minutes, or until golden-brown and the meat is cooked through.

OEUFS MEULEMEESTER

THIS DISH, which derives its name from a family of restaurant owners in Bruges, is a traditional north Belgian method of serving eggs. It has long been a favourite with Belgian families, and has now become popular further afield.

PREPARATION TIME: 20 MINUTES
COOKING TIME: 10 MINUTES
PREHEAT OVEN TO 200°C (400°F, MARK 6)

INGREDIENTS FOR FOUR
8 eggs
15 g (½ oz) butter
1½ teaspoons chopped chervil
1½ teaspoons chopped parsley
½ teaspoon French mustard
100-125 g (about ¼ lb) prawns, shelled and de-veined*
300 ml (½ pint) cream
Salt and freshly ground pepper
2 tablespoons grated Cheddar cheese

Boil the eggs for 10-12 minutes. Hold them under cold running water until cool. Shell them, chop both white and yolk coarsely and set aside.

Put the butter, chopped chervil and parsley, mustard, prawns and cream into a medium-sized saucepan. Season and stir well with a wooden spoon. Stir in the chopped eggs and heat through, stirring.

Grease an ovenproof dish and pour in the mixture. Sprinkle with the grated cheese and bake in the top of the preheated oven for about 10 minutes, or until the top is golden-brown. Serve very hot with a green vegetable.

SPANAKOPITTA *This classic Greek spinach and feta cheese pie makes an excellent meal on its own.*

SPANAKOPITTA

THIS TRADITIONAL Greek recipe has become popular throughout the world. Now that filo pastry is available in supermarkets, even the novice can tackle it with confidence.

This dish may be made in advance, since it freezes well. If frozen, allow it to thaw before baking.

PREPARATION TIME: 40 MINUTES
COOKING TIME: 40 MINUTES
PREHEAT OVEN TO 180°C (350°F, MARK 4)

INGREDIENTS FOR SIX
1 kg (2¼ lb) spinach
2-3 bunches spring onions
1 tablespoon salt
150 g (5 oz) butter
2 medium-sized onions, peeled and finely chopped*
2 extra-large eggs, beaten
200 g (7 oz) feta cheese, crumbled
Freshly ground black pepper
10 sheets filo pastry

Wash, dry and finely chop the spinach (use a food processor if you have one).

Chop the spring onions and place them in a colander in alternate layers with the spinach, sprinkling each layer with a little salt. Leave for 20 minutes.

Heat half the butter in a frying pan and add the chopped onions. Cook until they are transparent but not brown.

Squeeze out most of the moisture from the spinach and spring onion mixture. Place the vegetables in a mixing bowl and add the sautéed onion. In a separate bowl, add the crumbled feta cheese to the egg and season with black pepper. Blend the spinach and the cheese mixtures.

Melt the remaining butter. Grease a dish 25 cm × 25 cm × 4 cm (10 in × 10 in × 1½ in), and lay one sheet of filo pastry in it, allowing the ends to overlap the dish. Brush with melted butter.

While you are doing this, make sure that the rest of the pastry is covered all the time with a slightly dampened cloth or a sheet of plastic wrap to prevent it from drying out. Repeat the process until you have used 5 sheets of filo pastry.

Fill the pastry-lined dish with the spinach filling. Cover with a further 4 sheets of the pastry (remember to brush each

layer with butter), cutting each piece of pastry to fit the exact size of the dish.

Fold the bottom layers of pastry over the top layers to tidy the edge. Brush the last piece of pastry with butter and overlap with the folded pastry. Make a diamond pattern, if desired, by cutting through the first 2-3 sheets of pastry with the tip of a sharp knife. Bake for 40 minutes in the preheated oven.

SERVING SUGGESTION Serve with a fennel, tomato and mushroom salad*, or accompany with another Greek dish. Try butter beans with tomato* or aubergines (eggplants) à la Grecque*.

VARIATIONS Spanakopitta may also be made in a rectangular dish or a round cake tin. If you use the latter, do not cut the pastry into a round shape, as the leaves must still overlap.

If fresh spinach is not available, use 1.5 kg (3 lb 3 oz) frozen spinach, thawed.

Fresh dill makes a refreshing difference to the flavour, and 50 g (2 oz) of freshly grated Parmesan cheese added to the spinach mixture also tastes good.

ROULADES – FLUFFY SOUFFLÉ ROLLS

Roulades are light, fluffy soufflé rolls that lend themselves well to imaginative fillings. This recipe is for the basic roulade and three fillings, but any other savoury vegetable or seafood mixture, folded into a cream or white sauce, is also suitable for a filling. Roulades can be reheated successfully and make good starters.

First make the soufflé base: melt 60 g (2 oz) butter in a saucepan, stir in 60 g (2 oz) flour and cook for 1 minute without browning. Gradually add 500 ml (17 fl oz) milk and cook, stirring constantly, in order to make a thick sauce.

Remove from the heat, stir in 1 teaspoon sugar, and season with salt and pepper. Lightly beat together 4 egg yolks, then beat them into the sauce. Whisk 4 egg whites until they are stiff, then fold them into the sauce.

Spread the soufflé mixture evenly into a greased, lined Swiss roll tin about 33 cm × 23 cm (11 in × 9 in). Bake at 160°C (325°F, mark 3) for 40-45 minutes, or until golden.

Turn out the roulade on a sheet of wax or greaseproof paper, then peel off the lining paper. Keep warm.

Prepare the filling of your choice, then spread it over the roulade. Roll up the roulade from the long side and, if necessary, reheat it for 10-15 minutes at 160°C (325°F, mark 3). It should be served hot.

Fillings for roulades

Mushroom roulade Fry 1 large chopped onion* in 2 tablespoons sunflower oil and 30 g (1¼ oz) butter until soft. Add 400 g (14 oz) sliced mushrooms, and cook until the liquid has evaporated.

Remove from the heat, and stir in 2 tablespoons lemon juice and 125 ml (4 fl oz) sour cream. Season the mixture with salt and pepper. Serve the completed roulade with a further 125 ml (4 fl oz) sour cream for spooning on top of each of the individual servings.

Spinach roulade Heat 500 g (1 lb 2 oz) cooked and chopped spinach with 30 g (1¼ oz) butter in a large saucepan. Stir in 2 teaspoons flour and cook, stirring constantly, for 1 minute. Slowly add 250 ml (9 fl oz) cream or milk, and heat gently. Season well, then stir in a pinch of freshly grated nutmeg and 3 chopped hard-boiled eggs (optional).

Haddock roulade Toss 500 g (1 lb 2 oz) cooked and flaked smoked haddock in 2 teaspoons butter and 2 teaspoons flour, and cook, stirring constantly, for 1 minute.

Slowly add 250 ml (9 fl oz) cream or milk, and heat gently, stirring. Season well with salt and pepper, and stir in 2 tablespoons freshly chopped parsley. Garnish the completed roulade with a further 2 tablespoons fresh parsley.

CHEESE SOUFFLÉ

THIS IS A BASIC soufflé recipe which can be adapted to almost any fish or vegetable filling. A soufflé makes an inexpensive starter, or a light lunch dish. Many people are intimidated by the idea of making soufflés, but they are, in fact, easy to prepare.

PREPARATION TIME: 30 MINUTES
COOKING TIME: 25 MINUTES
PREHEAT OVEN TO 200°C (400°F, MARK 6)

INGREDIENTS FOR FOUR

30 g (1¼ oz) butter
2 tablespoons flour
250 ml (9 fl oz) hot milk
Salt and freshly ground black pepper
4 egg yolks
A good pinch of dry mustard
A pinch of cayenne pepper
100 g (3¾ oz) mature Cheddar or Gruyère cheese, grated
5 egg whites
1 tablespoon fine dry breadcrumbs
1 tablespoon grated Parmesan cheese

Melt the butter, stir in the flour and cook for 1-2 minutes without browning. Add the milk and bring the mixture slowly to the boil, stirring continuously to make a smooth, thick sauce.

Remove from the heat and beat in the seasoning, followed by the egg yolks, one at a time. Beat in the mustard and cayenne pepper with the grated Cheddar or Gruyère cheese.

Whisk the egg whites until they are stiff but not dry, and fold them into the soufflé mixture. Spoon the mixture into a 750 ml (26 fl oz) buttered ovenproof dish dusted all over with the breadcrumbs and grated Parmesan cheese. Bake the soufflé for about 25 minutes.

SERVING SUGGESTION Serve with a fresh green salad*.

If you are serving the soufflé as the main course of a vegetarian meal, accompany with a substantial vegetable dish, such as stuffed aubergines (eggplants) or leeks in vinaigrette*.

VARIATIONS Pour the soufflé mixture into half-baked pastry or tartlet shells and bake at 200°C (400°F, mark 6) for 15 minutes until puffed and golden.

Pour the soufflé mixture over fillets of sole and bake until well-risen.

HINTS ON MAKING SAVOURY SOUFFLÉS

A soufflé is simply a highly flavoured sauce or purée mixed with stiffly whipped egg whites which expand and puff in a really hot oven.

There is no mystery to making a good soufflé. Simply follow three easy rules: the basic sauce or purée must be fairly thick (like whipped cream), but soft enough to drop from a spoon; the egg whites must be stiffly whipped but not over-beaten and dry; and the whites should be folded, not beaten in.

A savoury soufflé dish need not have a paper collar, and the soufflé mixture can be left in the refrigerator for up to 2 hours before baking.

Bake at a high heat (200°C, 400°F, mark 6) so that it rises quickly and is soft inside but crisp and brown outside.

When ready, a soufflé should have increased by a half to two-thirds in volume, and should have risen above the edge of the dish. Shake it gently: if it wobbles all over, it is not done, and if just the middle wobbles, it is done to suit the French preference (a further 2-3 minutes' cooking will give slightly firmer results).

Even if the soufflé does not rise as high as you had hoped, it will still taste wonderful. The presentation trick is just to call it a savoury mould, and your guests will be none the wiser.

Soufflé Fillings

Asparagus soufflé Make a cheese soufflé using 75 g (3 oz) grated cheese. Spoon half the soufflé mixture into a prepared dish. Add 125 g (4¼ oz) cooked, chopped tender asparagus. Top this with the remaining soufflé mixture and bake it.

Salmon or tuna soufflé Flake or pound 225 g (½ lb) cooked fresh (or a tin of drained) salmon or tuna. Add this to the basic egg yolk sauce of the cheese soufflé recipe, with or without cheese. Season it well, then fold in the egg whites. Turn into a dish and bake it.

Smoked fish soufflé Flake or pound 225 g (½ lb) cooked smoked fish and stir this into the egg yolk mixture of the cheese soufflé. Fold in the remaining ingredients with a pinch of ground nutmeg, if liked. Turn this mixture into a soufflé dish and bake until golden.

Blue cheese soufflé Use 100 g (3¾ oz) blue cheese in the cheese soufflé recipe.

If liked, you can add chopped walnuts which will give additional texture.

SPANISH OMELETTE *Potatoes and onions set in golden egg.*

SPANISH OMELETTE

THIS LIGHT but solid-textured Spanish omelette makes a fine lunch dish with a simple salad of lettuce, tomato and onion tossed at the table (Spanish-style) with a generous sprinkling of olive oil and a little vinegar. Serve with a slice of crusty bread and a glass of wine.

PREPARATION TIME: 15 MINUTES
COOKING TIME: 20 MINUTES

INGREDIENTS FOR FOUR

2 medium sized onions, peeled and finely chopped*
4 medium-sized potatoes, peeled and finely chopped
60 ml (2 fl oz) olive oil
6 eggs, beaten
Salt and freshly ground black pepper
Finely chopped parsley for garnish

Use a very wide, heavy frying pan. Sauté the onions and potatoes very gently in the heated oil until they are soft but not browned. Pour in the beaten eggs and then cook until set.

Place a large ovenproof plate or baking tray over the frying pan and invert the omelette onto it. Then slip the omelette carefully back into the pan to brown the other side.

Season lightly, sprinkle with parsley and serve immediately.

SERVING SUGGESTION Cut the omelette into individual wedges and then serve either hot or cold.

VARIATIONS Add any of the following ingredients to the softened onions and potatoes: peas, sliced mushrooms, spinach, tinned asparagus or fresh cooked asparagus, fresh or tinned artichoke hearts, chopped ham, anchovies, sliced chorizo sausage, salami or garlic.

For a big buffet, make three Spanish omelettes. When cool, sandwich them together with cream cheese (mixed with chives or onion) and cut into wedges.

131

FRENCH TOAST

THE FRENCH NAME for this popular snack is *pain perdu*, literally 'lost bread', for it is a delicious way of making use of slightly stale leftover bread.

PREPARATION TIME: 10 MINUTES
COOKING TIME: 10 MINUTES

INGREDIENTS FOR FOUR
8 slices French bread, or 4 slices of
*   a larger loaf*
3 eggs
125 ml (4 fl oz) milk
Butter for frying
Cinnamon sugar* for garnish

Prick the bread well with a fork. Beat the eggs and milk together and pour the mixture over the bread. Keep pricking and turning with a fork until the bread is saturated with the liquid.

Fry the slices in hot butter until golden-brown and serve immediately, sprinkling the toast with cinnamon sugar (or offer the sugar separately).

SERVING SUGGESTION Serve the toast American-style, with maple syrup and crisply grilled bacon.

POTTED STILTON

THE VILLAGE OF STILTON in England gave its name to this most noble of cheeses. During the 18th century a number of cheeses were potted with spices and a 'glass of sack' (sherry). Although sherry benefits a mild cheese it is not the best for Stilton: if the Stilton is very dry, add a little port.

PREPARATION TIME: 10-15 MINUTES

INGREDIENTS TO YIELD ABOUT 275 G
(10 OZ)
225 g (½ lb) mellow Stilton
50 g (2 oz) unsalted butter,
*   softened*
¼ teaspoon ground mace or
*   nutmeg*
½ teaspoon freshly made English
*   mustard*
Clarified butter* or ghee
*   (optional)*

Mash the cheese with the butter, add the mace or nutmeg and mustard, and work to a cream. Press into earthenware or china pots. The cheese will keep well if sealed with clarified butter.

OEUFS EN COCOTTE Eggs baked in cream make excellent breakfast fare.

OEUFS EN COCOTTE
À LA CRÈME

THERE ARE MANY WAYS of serving *oeufs en cocotte* – eggs baked in small dishes. When *à la crème* is added to the name, this indicates the classic version, which consists simply of eggs baked with cream.

This recipe for a perfect light breakfast dish can easily be varied.

PREPARATION TIME: 5 MINUTES
COOKING TIME: 8 MINUTES
PREHEAT OVEN TO 200°C (400°F, MARK 6)

INGREDIENTS FOR FOUR
15 g (½ oz) butter
Salt and freshly ground pepper
4 eggs
4 tablespoons cream
Boiling water

Put a dab of butter and a tiny pinch of salt and pepper in the bottom of each of 4 small ovenproof dishes. Break an egg into each and season the tops with more salt and pepper. Pour 1 tablespoon cream over each egg and add a further dab of butter to finish.

Place the 4 *cocottes* in a baking dish, and then pour round them enough boiling water to come halfway up the sides of the dishes.

Place in the preheated oven and bake for 7-8 minutes, until the white has just set (shake a *cocotte* to see if the white is still liquid) and the yolks are still runny. Eat this dish as soon as possible to avoid overcooking the eggs.

VARIATIONS Instead of using cream in this dish, try adding cooked asparagus tips, prawns, cooked chicken breast or chopped mushrooms (fried with a pinch of thyme) under the eggs.

OMELETTE ARNOLD BENNETT

THIS PERFECT MARRIAGE of haddock and Parmesan cheese took place in London's Savoy Grill. The name is a salute from one great artist to another – from Jean Baptiste Virlogeux, then the Savoy Hotel's *chef de cuisine*, to Arnold Bennett, the novelist who had immortalised Virlogeux as 'Roho' in his novel *Imperial Palace*, which was based on life at the Savoy Hotel.

Serve this dish as a light lunch or as a snack before an evening at the theatre.

PREPARATION TIME: 15 MINUTES
COOKING TIME: 5 MINUTES

INGREDIENTS FOR ONE
*75 g (3 oz) cooked smoked
  haddock, flaked
1 teaspoon grated Parmesan cheese
Salt and freshly ground pepper
2 eggs
1 tablespoon water
1¼ teaspoons butter
1 tablespoon cream*

Mix together the flaked haddock and cheese, season with salt and pepper, and then set aside.

Break the eggs into a bowl, add the water and season with a little pepper. Beat lightly with a fork.

Melt the butter in an omelette pan and, when it has become frothy, pour in the beaten eggs.

Cook over a medium heat until the omelette is only just set and still liquid in the middle. Salt lightly and transfer (unfolded) to an ovenproof plate.

Spread the haddock and cheese mixture over the top of the omelette and pour on the cream.

Grill under very high heat for a few minutes, until it is slightly browned and bubbling. Serve immediately.

SERVING SUGGESTIONS To make a more substantial meal, serve with grilled tomatoes or creamed spinach and follow with a green salad.

VARIATION For a more luxurious version substitute smoked trout or salmon for the haddock.

The omelette would also be good with a small quantity of prawns added. Use 25 g (1 oz) prawns and reduce the smoked haddock to 50 g (2 oz) per person.

MINTED EGG PIE *makes a special meal at a low cost.*

MINTED EGG PIE

THIS RECIPE is not only delicious, but also extremely economical. The minted pie makes an ideal dish for a light lunch served with a salad.

PREPARATION TIME: 15 MINUTES
COOKING TIME: 40 MINUTES
PREHEAT OVEN TO 220°C (425°F, MARK 7)

INGREDIENTS FOR FOUR
Shortcrust pastry using 225 g
  (½ lb) flour
225 g (½ lb) cream cheese
50 g (2 oz) Cheddar cheese, finely
  grated
¼ teaspoon grated nutmeg
Salt and freshly ground pepper
4 eggs
4 teaspoons chopped fresh mint*

Place a baking tray in the middle of the preheated oven to get really hot.

Butter a deep pie plate (19 cm/7½ in)

and line it with half the shortcrust pastry. Thoroughly mix the cream cheese, grated Cheddar, nutmeg and seasoning, and spread the mixture over the pastry.

Make 4 little nests and break the eggs into these hollows. Sprinkle thickly with the mint, and season again lightly. Cover with the rest of the pastry. Stand the plate on the baking tray in the oven so that the bottom crust cooks, and bake for about 40 minutes. After 25 minutes, cover lightly with greaseproof paper to prevent over-browning. Cool before serving.

SERVING SUGGESTION Make a salad accompaniment by mixing together 3 coarsely sliced heads of chicory with the inner hearts of 2 lettuces and ½ finely chopped onion*. Serve this salad with 150 ml (¼ pint) homemade mayonnaise*.

VARIATION Substitute another herb for the mint. Freshly chopped basil would be particularly suitable, or try 2 teaspoons of chopped fresh thyme.

CRUSTLESS SAVOURY TART *A scrumptious choice for those watching their figures.*

CRUSTLESS SAVOURY TART

THIS DISH has been evolved for the weight-conscious who love quiches – or for people who cannot eat pastry but love the filling. It can be cut as a normal tart since it sets firmly.

PREPARATION TIME: 15 MINUTES
COOKING TIME: 45 MINUTES
PREHEAT OVEN TO 180°C (350°F, MARK 4)

INGREDIENTS FOR FOUR
4 slices cooked meat (such as ham,
  bacon or beef), diced
250 g (9 oz) cottage cheese
25 g (1 oz) flour
1 teaspoon salt
Freshly ground black pepper
1 teaspoon dry mustard
1 tablespoon chopped parsley, or 1
  teaspoon dried parsley
1 tablespoon dried onion or 1
  onion, peeled, finely chopped*
  and cooked
4 large eggs
375 ml (13 fl oz) milk
1 teaspoon Worcestershire sauce
A dash of paprika for the garnish

Grease a shallow ovenproof dish, which has a capacity of 1.5 litres (about 3 pints). In a large bowl, mix together the meat, cottage cheese, flour, salt, pepper, mustard, onion and parsley. Beat in the eggs, milk and Worcestershire sauce and combine the ingredients thoroughly. Pour into the greased dish and sprinkle with paprika. Bake for 45 minutes.

SERVING SUGGESTION Serve with a salad of finely grated carrot, dressed with lemon juice and freshly chopped dill.

VARIATION Replace the meat with smoked trout and bake in small patty pans for a cocktail snack.

EGGS MORNAY

SLICED OR WHOLE hard-boiled eggs are quickly baked in a creamy cheese sauce. This is a wonderfully easy dish that will be enjoyed by the whole family.

PREPARATION TIME: 40 MINUTES
COOKING TIME: 30 MINUTES
PREHEAT OVEN TO 200°C (400°F, MARK 6)

INGREDIENTS FOR FOUR
8 extra-large eggs

For the sauce:
50 g (2 oz) butter
50 g (2 oz) flour
500 ml (17 fl oz) milk
Salt and freshly ground black
  pepper
250 g (9 oz) mature Cheddar
  cheese, grated
1 teaspoon prepared mustard
25 g (1 oz) breadcrumbs

Boil the eggs in water for 10-12 minutes. Drain, cool under cold running water and shell the eggs. Halve them lengthways and arrange them, cut side down, in a shallow ovenproof or gratin dish.

To make the sauce, melt the butter, stir in the flour and cook for 1-2 minutes without browning. Gradually stir in the milk and bring to the boil, stirring continuously to make a smooth sauce. Season well with salt and freshly ground black pepper.

Remove from the heat and add half the cheese and the mustard. Stir until the cheese has melted, and pour the sauce over the eggs. Sprinkle with the crumbs (mixed with the remaining cheese) and bake for 30 minutes.

SERVING SUGGESTIONS Serve with crusty bread or a green vegetable: spinach is particularly good.

VARIATIONS Instead of baking, grill until golden and bubbling.

Make a bed of mashed potato or creamed spinach. Lay the halved eggs on top, then spoon over the sauce.

Although the expression 'mornay' refers specifically to a cheese sauce, there is no reason why hard-boiled eggs cannot be served with other sauces.

Celery sauce* would be a particularly good choice, with a some grated Cheddar sprinkled over the eggs before you grill them. For a spicier dish, try curry sauce* and accompany with rice or Bhaji Masoor ni Dhal*.

WELSH RAREBIT

THERE ARE ALMOST as many recipes for Welsh rarebit as there are cookbooks. This recipe is slightly more complicated than some, but it combines all the traditional ingredients, and produces a very tasty result.

PREPARATION TIME: 15 MINUTES
COOKING TIME: 15 MINUTES

INGREDIENTS FOR SIX
30 g (1¼ oz) butter
250 ml (9 fl oz) beer
500 g (1 lb 2 oz) Cheddar cheese, grated
1 egg, lightly beaten
1 teaspoon Worcestershire sauce
1 teaspoon salt
¾ teaspoon paprika
¼ teaspoon dry mustard, or a pinch of cayenne pepper
¾ teaspoon curry powder (optional)
6 slices hot, buttered toast

Melt the butter in the top of a double boiler and add the beer. When the beer is warm, slowly add the cheese and stir until melted. Beat slightly with a wire whisk, then add the egg and Worcestershire sauce, stirring until well mixed.

Season to taste with the salt, paprika, mustard or cayenne pepper and curry (if used). Turn at once onto the hot, buttered toast and arrange the slices in a hot serving dish. Serve immediately with grilled tomatoes or crisply cooked cauliflower and follow with a fresh green salad* garnished with spring onion.

CHEESE BOUREKITAS

THIS EASY AND UNUSUAL recipe will win many admiring comments. Try experimenting with different fillings and textures to suit your own tastes and availability of ingredients.

PREPARATION TIME: 1 HOUR
COOKING TIME: 15-20 MINUTES
PREHEAT OVEN TO 180°C (350°F, MARK 4)
INGREDIENTS FOR SIX TO EIGHT
250 ml (9 fl oz) sunflower oil
250 ml (9 fl oz) iced water
¾ teaspoon salt
480 g (1 lb 1 oz) flour (or enough to make a firm dough)

CHEESE BOUREKITAS *Spinach and potato fill these pastry crescents.*

For the potato filling:
4 large potatoes, peeled, boiled and mashed
3 eggs, beaten
120-150 g (4-5 oz) grated Parmesan cheese
Salt and pepper

For the spinach filling:
1 bunch spinach, stalks removed, washed, dried and finely shredded
1 tablespoon flour
2 eggs, beaten
100 g (3¾ oz) mozzarella cheese, finely chopped
Salt and pepper

For the garnish:
1 egg, beaten
Parmesan cheese

Mix the oil, water and salt in a deep mixing bowl. Add the flour slowly and knead vigorously, then shape the dough into 4 cm (1½ in) balls. Allow the balls to rest for 15 minutes before rolling them out into thin discs on a floured board.

Mix the ingredients of each filling until smooth, and place 1 teaspoon of filling in the centre of each disc. Fill half of the discs with the spinach mixture and fill the rest with the potato mixture. Fold the discs into crescent shapes, brush the tops with beaten egg and sprinkle with the Parmesan cheese.

Bake until golden (about 15-20 minutes) and serve immediately.

SERVING SUGGESTION This dish makes a tasty teatime snack or light snack before a midday or evening meal.

PUDDINGS
AND
DESSERTS

M AN HAS PROBABLY always had a sweet tooth, but it is only in recent centuries that the idea of a sweet 'finale' to a meal has come about. In many countries, sweet and savoury dishes were served as part of the same course in the past. Early pies often contained sweet and savoury fillings under the same pastry crust, a combination still found, but which is now less common than separate pies for savoury main courses and sweet desserts. You should always try to avoid serving a pie for both the main course and dessert. Wherever possible, select a dessert that complements your meal and is also suited to the weather.

Appearance is often the key to the success of a dessert. Even at the end of the heartiest meal, few people are able to resist a beautifully presented dessert. Glass bowls are ideal if the dish itself is very pretty – for example, caramel oranges or trifle. Garnishes of citrus peel, fresh fruit, mint leaves or piped rosettes of cream can also do much to give a lift to something which is usually a little less decorative.

TARTE AUX POMMES

THE FOLLOWING apple tart recipe from France combines the incomparable taste and texture of the cooking apple with a tasty, sweet shortcrust pastry.

PREPARATION TIME: 40 MINUTES
CHILLING TIME: AT LEAST 2 HOURS
COOKING TIME: 30-35 MINUTES
PREHEAT OVEN TO 180°C (350°F, MARK 4)

INGREDIENTS FOR SIX TO EIGHT
1 portion sweet shortcrust pastry*
  using 225 g (½ lb) flour

For the filling:
3 medium-sized cooking apples,
  peeled, cored and sliced
2 tablespoons sugar
1 tablespoon water
3-4 crisp eating apples, peeled,
  cored and thinly sliced in
  crescents

For the glaze:
3 tablespoons apple jelly, apricot
  jam or honey – melted with 2
  teaspoons lemon juice

First make the pastry, then wrap it in greaseproof paper and chill for 2 hours in the refrigerator.

Meanwhile, cook the prepared cooking apples gently with the sugar and water in a covered pan until the fruit makes a thick purée.   Roll out the pastry to line a 25 cm (10 in) flan ring. Prick the pastry base in several places with a fork.

Spread the apple purée over the base, and on it arrange a circle of closely overlapped slices of eating apple. One tip of each apple slice should touch the rim of the crust, and the other tip should point towards the centre of the flan. Fill the centre of this circle with a smaller circle of slices radiating from the centre of the flan.

Bake the tart in the centre of the preheated oven for 30-35 minutes, or until the crust is crisp and golden-brown and the apple slices are soft. When the tart is cooked, remove it from the flan ring and stand it on a wire rack.

Warm the jelly, jam or honey with the lemon juice. Strain and brush over the fruit. Cool before serving.

VARIATION Instead of the crisp eating apples, arrange greengages, apricots or small plums (halved and stoned) on top of the apple purée before baking.

APPLE STRUDEL

CONTRARY TO the popular belief that *apfelstrudel* is an Austrian dish which originated in Vienna, it actually comes from Hungary. It was the Hungarians who first took their incredibly thin strudel dough from the great Turkish delicacy baclava and filled it with spiced apples.

Today, however, the making of strudel has become an almost sacred rite in the city of Vienna, where it is said that a good strudel dough is one through which you can read a newspaper.

PREPARATION TIME: 1 HOUR FOR THE
FILLING; 50 MINUTES FOR THE PASTRY
STANDING TIME: 30 MINUTES
COOKING TIME: 30-35 MINUTES
PREHEAT OVEN TO 200°C (400°F, MARK 6)

INGREDIENTS FOR TEN TO FIFTEEN
Strudel pastry* using 225 g (½ lb)
  flour
8 large apples (Granny Smith)
170 g (6 oz) sultanas
4 tablespoons breadcrumbs
100 g (3¾ oz) sugar
2 teaspoons ground cinnamon
120 g (4 oz) chopped almonds or
  other nuts
50 g (2 oz) butter, melted
2 tablespoons vanilla sugar*

First prepare the strudel pastry, then peel, core and thinly slice the apples. Wash the sultanas in hot water and dry them well.

Sprinkle the breadcrumbs over the entire surface of the pastry. Pile the sliced apples along the top of the pastry to within 5 cm (2 in) of each side.

Sprinkle the sultanas, sugar, cinnamon and nuts over the apples, and fold in the edges of the pastry.

Picking up two corners of the tablecloth on which you stretched the strudel pastry, allow the pastry to roll gently over onto itself, repeating this process until you have a cylinder resembling an elongated Swiss roll.

Gently slide it onto a greased baking tray, and shape it into a horseshoe curve. Brush with melted butter and sprinkle with a little water.

Bake for 20 minutes. Brush once more with butter, lower the temperature to 180°C (350°F, mark 4) and bake for a further 10 minutes, or until the strudel is golden and crisp.

Remove from the oven and dust with vanilla sugar.

SERVING SUGGESTION Cut into wide, diagonal slices and serve with lightly whipped cream flavoured with a little caster sugar and some brandy.

VARIATIONS Using the apple filling, simplify the whole procedure by using filo pastry*, instead of strudel dough.

A sweet cream cheese or cherry filling is also delicious. If you use a cherry filling, flavour the accompanying cream with Kirsch instead of brandy.

SCOTTISH FLUMMERY

ALL HUSKED CEREALS, if soaked and boiled, will set to make a kind of jelly. A traditional Scottish flummery made with oatmeal has a smooth, jellied texture, a very white colour, and a delicious and distinctive flavour.

PREPARATION TIME: 10 MINUTES
SOAKING TIME: 48 HOURS
COOKING TIME: ABOUT 15 MINUTES
SETTING TIME: 1 HOUR

INGREDIENTS FOR SIX TO EIGHT
4 tablespoons fine oatmeal, or 5
  tablespoons cracked wheat
Juice of 2 oranges, strained
2 tablespoons caster sugar
150 ml (¼ pint) cream
Finely grated rind of 2 oranges
60-80 ml (2-2½ fl oz) honey, brandy
  or whisky
150 ml (¼ pint) whipped cream for
  garnish

Soak the oatmeal or cracked wheat (in enough cold water to keep it covered) for 24 hours. Pour off the water, and cover the grain with about 1 litre (1¾ pints) fresh, cold water. Leave to stand for another 24 hours.

Stir well, strain the liquid into a pan and discard the oatmeal. Add the strained orange juice and the sugar, and boil, stirring frequently, for about 10 minutes, or until very thick. Allow to cool a little before stirring in the cream.

Pour into one large dish or into individual dishes, sprinkle with the grated rind and set aside until set.

To serve, top each dish with 2 teaspoons honey, brandy or whisky and a spoonful of whipped cream.

AMERICAN CHEESECAKE *The tart taste of black cherries is a perfect foil for the creamy, savoury filling.*

AMERICAN CHEESECAKE

A MERICAN CHEESECAKE differs from the continental cheesecakes in that it has a biscuit crust, as opposed to a pastry one, and a filling of cream cheese rather than one made from curds.

PREPARATION TIME: 50 MINUTES
COOKING TIME: 1 HOUR
COOLING AND CHILLING TIME: 2 HOURS
FOR THE CRUST; 4 HOURS FOR THE
FILLING
PREHEAT OVEN TO 180°C (350°F, MARK 4)
INGREDIENTS FOR SIX TO EIGHT
For the crust:
*1 packet (200 g/7 oz) wheatmeal,
   digestive or plain sweet biscuits
2 tablespoons caster sugar
100 g (3¾ oz) butter, melted*

For the filling:
*250 g (9 oz) cottage cheese and
   250 g (9 oz) cream cheese, or
   500 g (1 lb 2 oz) cream cheese
125 g (4¼ oz) caster sugar
2 eggs, separated
125 ml (4 fl oz) sour cream
2 tablespoons flour*

*1 teaspoon vanilla essence
1 teaspoon grated lemon rind*

For the topping:
*1 tin (425 g/15 oz) stoned black
   cherries in syrup
2 tablespoons cornflour
1 teaspoon lemon juice
1 tablespoon caster sugar
   (optional)*

To prepare the crust, reduce the biscuits to crumbs in a food processor, or put them in a paper bag or between 2 sheets of greaseproof paper and crush them into crumbs with a rolling pin.

Put the crumbs in a bowl, mix in the sugar and gradually blend in the melted butter until it is fully absorbed.

Spread the mixture over the base and sides of a well-greased 5 cm (2 in) deep 24 cm (9½ in) flan dish, springform cake tin or flan ring set on a baking tray. Use the back of a wooden spoon to press the crumbs into an even layer. Leave to set in the refrigerator for 2 hours.

For the filling, blend the cottage cheese (if used) to a smooth consistency with the cream cheese. Beat in the sugar and egg yolks, one at a time.

Stir in the sour cream, flour, vanilla essence and lemon rind, and then beat thoroughly until the mixture is smooth and glossy. Whisk the egg whites until stiff but not dry, and fold them into the cheese mixture, using a metal spoon.

Spoon the filling into the prepared pie crust and bake in the centre of the pre-heated oven for 1 hour. Leave to cool at room temperature.

For the topping, put the cherries in a pan with their juice; if necessary, make this up with cold water to 175 ml (6 fl oz). Reserve 2 tablespoons of the liquid and use it to blend the cornflour to a paste.

Add the lemon juice to the pan of cherries and bring to the boil over gentle heat. Stir in the cornflour paste and continue boiling for 5 minutes, stirring constantly until the mixture clears and thickens. Add caster sugar to taste.

Let the cherries cool slightly before spreading them over the top of the cheesecake. Chill in the refrigerator for at least 3 hours before serving.

VARIATIONS Top with crushed strawberries, pineapple or apricots, or with grated chocolate or split almonds.

A SELECTION OF CHOUX PASTRY FAVOURITES

Choux pastry can be used for both savoury and sweet dishes. It puffs up to 3 or 4 times its original size, and must be placed straight into a hot oven so that the puffing up starts immediately. Only after about 10 minutes should the heat be reduced to prevent over-browning. The pastry must be baked until it is quite dry or else it will collapse when it is removed from the oven.

GÂTEAU SAINT-HONORÉ

Make a sweet shortcrust pastry* from 225 g (½ lb) flour, roll it out to a thickness of 5 mm (¼ in) and cut a circle 23-25 cm (about 9 in) in diameter to form the base of the gâteau. Place this on a greased baking tray. Brush a little cold water on the perimeter of the crust base, and then, using a piping bag fitted with a plain round nozzle, make a border of choux pastry*, about as thick as a man's thumb, around the edge of the pastry circle. Brush the choux pastry with an egg yolk mixed with a little water.

Bake the tart at 220°C (425°F, mark 7) for 20-25 minutes, or until the choux edge is brown. After removing from the oven, quickly cut a few slits in the choux ring to allow the steam to escape.

Meanwhile, make 18-20 profiteroles. When these are cool, make a hole in each of them and fill it with whipped cream.

Heat 75 g (3 oz) caster sugar in a small saucepan over a gentle heat until it turns golden. Dip the bottom of the profiteroles in this warm caramel syrup and arrange them around the edge of the gâteau. Drip the caramel over the puffs, working quickly before the syrup hardens. Fill the centre of the cake with whipped cream sweetened with caster sugar. Decorate with crystallised flowers.

LEMON ÉCLAIRS

Pipe choux pastry* mixture onto a greased baking tray in lengths of 8 cm (3¼ in). Bake and fill with whipped cream or cream cheese, and lemon curd.

PROFITEROLES WITH ICE CREAM AND HOT CHOCOLATE SAUCE

To make profiteroles, force choux pastry* through a piping bag fitted with a plain nozzle onto a greased baking sheet, leaving enough space for the puffs to expand. The portions should each be about the size of a walnut. Bake them at 200°C (400°F, mark 6) for 10 minutes, then reduce the heat to 180°C (350°F, mark 4) and bake for a further 15-20 minutes, depending on size. Make sure they are firm to the touch. When they are cool, and just before serving, fill them with small scoops of vanilla ice cream. Serve them piled up on a serving dish – each serving consisting of two or three profiteroles, covered with hot chocolate sauce.

To make the chocolate sauce mix a large tin (about 400 g/14 oz) evaporated milk with 350 g (¾ lb) sugar and 2 tablespoons cocoa, and bring to the boil over a medium heat. Cook the mixture for 3 minutes, stirring all the time. Remove from the heat and add 1 teaspoon vanilla essence and a pinch of salt. Beat for 1-2 minutes.

The sauce may be kept in a jar in the refrigerator and reheated before use.

MINCE PIES

SMALL PIES FILLED with spicy fruit mincemeat and coated with sugar have been traditional Christmas fare for centuries. It was customary in the past to eat one for each of the twelve days of Christmas, to ensure twelve happy months ahead.

Mincemeat is better if it matures for at least a week or two before use and it is convenient if you make several jars at once. The recipe below is for about 6 jars containing 500 ml (17 fl oz). Mincemeat will remain fresh and juicy for up to six months if covered with a plastic top or screw-on lid to prevent it drying out.

PREPARATION TIME: 45 MINUTES FOR THE MINCEMEAT; 50 MINUTES FOR THE PIES
COOKING TIME: 20 MINUTES FOR THE PIES
PREHEAT OVEN TO 220°C (425°F, MARK 7)

For the mincemeat:
750 g (1 lb 10 oz) cooking apples
500 g (1 lb 2 oz) seedless raisins
500 g (1 lb 2 oz) sultanas
250 g (9 oz) currants
250 g (9 oz) chopped candied peel
500 g (1 lb 2 oz) soft brown sugar
500 g (1 lb 2 oz) shredded suet, finely chopped
50 g (2 oz) flaked or chopped almonds
Juice and grated rind of 2 lemons
½ teaspoon ground mixed spice
¼ cup brandy, whisky or rum

For 18-20 mince pies:
Shortcrust pastry* using 335 g (¾ lb) flour, or puff pastry* using 450 g (1 lb) flour
450 g (1 lb) fruit mincemeat
1 egg white
Caster sugar for sprinkling

Wash, peel, core and chop the apples. Combine with the raisins, sultanas, currants and candied peel. Mince coarsely and place in a mixing bowl.

Add the sugar, suet, almonds, lemon juice, lemon rind and spice. Mix well.

Cover the bowl with a tea towel and leave for 2-3 days. Stir the mixture well 2-3 times a day. Add the brandy or other spirit and then bottle.

To make the mince pies, first roll out the prepared pastry thinly and cut out 18-20 rounds, about 8 cm (3¼ in) across, for the bases. Line patty tins (about 6 cm/2½ in wide) with these, and fill to about half their depth with the fruit mincemeat.

Cut out slightly smaller rounds for the pie covers. Dampen the rims of the pie bases with cold water and place the covers on top, pressing the edges together lightly to seal them. Make a small slit in the top of each pie, brush with the egg white and sprinkle with caster sugar.

Put the pies in the preheated oven and bake for about 20 minutes, or until they are a light golden-brown.

Remove from the oven and let them stand for 3-5 minutes before lifting them from the tins with a round-bladed knife. Put them on a wire rack to cool. Serve with cream or brandy butter*.

TREACLE TART

TREACLE IS THE SYRUP remaining after sugar has been crystallised. The blackest treacle, or molasses, is treacle which has had the most sugar removed from it.

The idea for this crumb and syrup tart may have developed from the old method of making gingerbread (mixing breadcrumbs with honey and spice). Treacle was used in tarts until the late 1800s, when golden syrup – a refined, diluted type – became available.

PREPARATION TIME: 15 MINUTES
COOKING TIME: 25 MINUTES
PREHEAT OVEN TO 190°C (375°F, MARK 5)

INGREDIENTS FOR FOUR TO SIX
225 g (8 oz) shortcrust pastry*
8 tablespoons golden syrup
2 tablespoons lemon juice
50 g (2 oz) fresh white
    breadcrumbs
¼ teaspoon ground ginger

Roll out the pastry and line a greased 20 cm (8 in) shallow pie plate with it. Trim the edges and reserve the excess pastry. Mix the breadcrumbs and ginger together and sprinkle evenly over the pastry base.

Warm the syrup over a very low heat and stir in the lemon juice. Pour the mixture over the breadcrumbs. Decorate with a lattice pattern of strips cut from the rolled trimmings.

Bake in the preheated oven for 25 minutes. Serve hot or cold with cream or scoops of ice cream.

CRÊPES SUZETTE *have long been popular for the citrus tang of the sauce.*

CRÊPES SUZETTE

THESE PANCAKES with their citrus and liqueur sauce offer a delightful and surprisingly simple way to end a dinner party. The pancakes and the sauce can be made early, then baked in the oven just before they are served. Flame them at the dinner table for a special effect.

One of the secrets of making really good crêpes Suzette is to keep the pancakes as thin and as light as possible.

PREPARATION TIME: 15 MINUTES
CHILLING TIME: 1 HOUR FOR THE
PANCAKE BATTER
COOKING TIME: 15 MINUTES
PREHEAT OVEN TO 180°C (350°F, MARK 4)

INGREDIENTS FOR FOUR TO SIX
75 g (3 oz) butter
1 teaspoon finely grated orange
    rind
4-6 teaspoons caster sugar
175 ml (6 fl oz) strained orange
    juice
2-3 tablespoons Grand Marnier or
    other citrus-based liqueur
12 pancakes*
2 tablespoons brandy

To make the sauce, melt the butter with the grated orange rind and the caster sugar. Add the orange juice and the Grand Marnier.

Make the 12 pancakes, fold each of them in quarters and then arrange them neatly in an ovenproof dish. Heat the prepared sauce very gently and then pour it over the laid-out pancakes.

Cover the dish and bake in the preheated oven for 15 minutes.

Warm the brandy, light it as you pour it over the crêpes and serve immediately.

VARIATION Place skinned, thinly sliced segments of orange (marinated in brandy) onto each pancake before folding and baking.

BREAD AND BUTTER PUDDING

SLICES OF BUTTERED BREAD are layered with fruit, then topped with a rich custard and baked until crisp and golden on top, yet meltingly soft inside. Made this way, with a dash of rum or brandy, the bread and butter pudding is suitable for any dinner party.

PREPARATION TIME: 30 MINUTES
STANDING TIME: AT LEAST 30 MINUTES
COOKING TIME: 55 MINUTES
PREHEAT OVEN TO 160°C (325°F, MARK 3)

INGREDIENTS FOR FOUR
8 thin slices of buttered bread
45 g (1¾ oz) currants or sultanas, soaked for 15 minutes in 4 teaspoons rum or brandy
2 tablespoons candied peel, chopped
4 extra-large eggs
300 ml (½ pint) milk
125 ml (4 fl oz) cream
100 g (3¾ oz) brown sugar
¼ teaspoon ground cinnamon
A pinch of freshly grated nutmeg

Trim the crusts from the buttered bread and cut the slices in half (diagonally).

Arrange the bread slices in a buttered baking dish or soufflé dish, layering them with the currants or sultanas, any remaining rum or brandy and the chopped candied peel.

Beat together the eggs, milk, cream, sugar and cinnamon with a little freshly grated nutmeg. Pour over the bread in the dish and leave to stand for at least 30 minutes (or overnight).

Bake the dish for 55 minutes, or until set and golden-brown.

SERVING SUGGESTIONS For a richer dish, pass around extra cream for spooning over each serving.

Accompany the pudding either with a compote of dried fruits, using apricots, peaches, prunes and pears, or a salad of fresh fruits in season.

VARIATIONS Spread the bread with marmalade, apricot jam or lemon curd as well as butter, or put sliced bananas between the layers.

For a family pudding, you could make the custard less rich: use 3 eggs to 500 ml (17 fl oz) milk and leave out the cream and candied peel.

BANANA FRITTERS

THE BASIC DIRECTIONS for cooking and serving fritters were recorded some 500 years ago, and they still apply, although today we are more adventurous with the fillings. One of the most popular types of fritter has a banana filling – this particular recipe is given a slightly exotic flavour through the use of rum.

PREPARATION TIME: 25 MINUTES
STANDING TIME: 1 HOUR
COOKING TIME: 15-20 MINUTES

INGREDIENTS FOR FOUR TO SIX
3 large ripe bananas, peeled
2 tablespoons sugar
60 ml (2 fl oz) rum
1 teaspoon vanilla essence
115-125 g (4-4¼ oz) flour
1 teaspoon baking powder
¼ teaspoon salt
2 tablespoons melted butter
175 ml (6 fl oz) milk
1 egg white, whisked until stiff
Sunflower oil for frying

Cut the bananas in half lengthways, then cut each half in three or four pieces. Arrange the pieces in one layer in a shallow dish. Mix together the sugar, 3 tablespoons of the rum and the vanilla essence, and pour over the bananas. Leave for 1 hour, turning the fruit occasionally.

To prepare the batter, sieve the flour, baking powder and salt into a large bowl. Stir in the melted butter and the remaining 1 tablespoon rum. Add the milk a little at a time, beating well after each addition until the batter is perfectly smooth. Leave to stand for 1 hour. Fold in the whisked egg white to give the batter the consistency of thick cream.

Dip the banana pieces into the batter a few at a time and allow to drain until only thinly coated. Pour a 5 cm (2 in) layer of oil into a deep pan and heat it to 190°C (375°F) – a cube of bread should turn golden-brown in about a minute. Fry the pieces 4-5 at a time until golden-brown. Drain on paper towels and keep hot until all are ready.

SERVING SUGGESTIONS Serve sprinkled with vanilla sugar*. The hot fritters are delicious with vanilla ice cream.

VARIATION Leave out the rum for an everyday family dessert.

QUEEN OF PUDDINGS

THIS RICH LAYERED PUDDING of fresh breadcrumbs, thick jam and golden meringue wears its title easily, for there are many who claim that it is the most delicious and royal of puddings.

PREPARATION TIME: 30 MINUTES
COOKING TIME: 40 MINUTES
PREHEAT OVEN TO 180°C (350°F, MARK 4)

INGREDIENTS FOR FOUR TO SIX
150 g (5 oz) fresh white breadcrumbs
1 tablespoon caster sugar
Grated rind of 1 lemon
575 ml (1 pint) milk
50 g (2 oz) butter
4 large egg yolks
2 tablespoons raspberry or apricot jam

For the meringue:
4 large egg whites
115-125 g (4-4¼ oz) caster sugar

Put the breadcrumbs, caster sugar and lemon rind into a mixing bowl.

Heat the milk and butter in a saucepan over a low heat until the butter has melted and the milk is lukewarm.

Pour the warm milk and butter onto the breadcrumb mixture and leave to stand for 10 minutes to absorb the milk. Beat in the egg yolks.

Grease a 1 litre (1¾ pint) pie dish and pour in the crumb mixture. Bake in the centre of the preheated oven for 30 minutes, or until just firm on the top.

Warm the jam so that it spreads easily, and very gently spread it over the pudding without breaking the surface.

To make the meringue topping, whisk the egg whites until they form stiff peaks and, using a metal spoon, gently fold in the caster sugar.

Pile the meringue over the pudding and return to the oven for a further 10 minutes, or until the meringue is lightly browned and crisp.

SERVING SUGGESTION Serve the pudding hot with cream.

UPSIDE-DOWN WINTER PUDDING *Golden pear halves set with cherries decorate this hearty cold-weather pudding.*

UPSIDE-DOWN WINTER PUDDING

GLISTENING RED CHERRIES nestling in a wheel of pears give a festive air to this delicious baked pudding. Properly turned out, the pudding is a credit to the cook, yet is easy to make.

PREPARATION TIME: 25 MINUTES
COOKING TIME: 45 MINUTES
PREHEAT OVEN TO 180°C (350°F, MARK 4)

INGREDIENTS FOR SIX
Melted butter
3 tablespoons brown sugar
3 pears, peeled, halved and cored
6 glacé cherries, rinsed
115-125 g (4-4¼ oz) butter
5 tablespoons golden syrup
4 tablespoons black treacle
1 egg, beaten
150 ml (¼ pint) lukewarm milk
1 teaspoon bicarbonate of soda
225 g (½ lb) flour
1 teaspoon ground cinnamon
1 teaspoon ground ginger
75 g (3 oz) brown sugar

Line the base and side of a deep (20 cm/8 in), round cake tin with a layer of greaseproof paper, and brush over with melted butter. Sprinkle the base with the sugar.

Place the pears, cut side down, on the sugar, radiating from the centre of the tin. As you do so, tuck a cherry into the cavity of each pear half, where the core has been removed.

Put the 115-125 g (4-4¼ oz) butter, syrup and treacle in a small pan over a low heat until the butter has melted. Set to one side. Stir together the beaten egg, milk and bicarbonate of soda until they are thoroughly mixed.

Sieve the flour, cinnamon and ginger into a mixing bowl and stir in the 75 g (3 oz) brown sugar.

Make a well in the centre of the dry ingredients and pour in the melted butter mixture and the egg mixture. Stir together and beat thoroughly. Then pour the mixture into the prepared cake tin.

Bake in the centre of the preheated oven for about 45 minutes, or until well risen and firm to the touch. Turn out the pudding onto a warmed plate and peel away the paper.

SERVING SUGGESTION Serve hot, cut in wedges, with cream or custard.

VARIATIONS Tinned or fresh pineapple rings, or rings of apple (cored) would be just as delicious as pears for the upside-down pudding. Remember to use a firm, dessert variety of apple which will not break up during cooking.

143

CHRISTMAS PUDDING

A MEAT STEW called 'girout', a dish served at every coronation from that of William the Conqueror to George V, is the ancestor of Christmas pudding, though it has gone through many changes since William's day.

Gradually the meat was phased out, prunes and sultanas were substituted for plums, and the modern Christmas pudding evolved.

Christmas puddings need to mature, and are all the better for being prepared several weeks or even months in advance. Store them in a well-ventilated, dry place, and steam a second time before serving.

This well-tried recipe makes three medium-sized puddings, light-textured, dark and delicious.

PREPARATION TIME: 1 HOUR
FIRST COOKING TIME: 7 HOURS
(2¾ HOURS IN A PRESSURE COOKER)
MATURING TIME: AT LEAST 6 WEEKS
SECOND COOKING TIME: 3 HOURS
(30 MINUTES IN A PRESSURE COOKER)

INGREDIENTS FOR THREE 700 G (1½ LB)
PUDDINGS
225 g (½ lb) self-raising flour
225 g (½ lb) shredded suet
225 g (½ lb) fresh white
    breadcrumbs
225 g (½ lb) currants
350 g (¾ lb) sultanas
350 g (¾ lb) seedless raisins
225 g (½ lb) brown sugar
1 teaspoon salt
1-2 teaspoons ground mixed spice
125 g (4¼ oz) chopped mixed peel
125 g (4¼ oz) glacé cherries, rinsed
    and chopped
1 small carrot, peeled and grated
1 small apple, peeled and grated
6 eggs, beaten
Grated rind and juice of 1 orange
Grated rind and juice of 1 lemon
300 ml (½ pint) stout

Grease three 1 litre (1¾ pint) pudding basins. Mix the flour, suet, breadcrumbs, dried fruit and sugar together in a large bowl. Stir in the salt, mixed spice, mixed peel, glacé cherries, carrot and apple.

Mix together the eggs, orange and lemon juice, rind and stout, and add to the dry ingredients to give a soft, dropping consistency. Add more stout if the mixture seems too dry.

Divide the mixture between the prepared basins, leaving 5 cm (2 in) headspace to allow for rising. Prepare each basin for steaming. Fold a pleat in a square of greaseproof paper (or foil). Place the paper over the pudding and cover with a cloth, tying securely with string below the rim. Knot the ends of the cloth over the top. Place each in a saucepan of boiling water. Cover the saucepans with lids and steam for 7 hours. Top up with more boiling water as necessary to maintain the level.

Remove the basins from the pans and leave to cool. Re-cover and store in a cool, dry place for as long as possible.

Before serving, cover with fresh greaseproof paper, foil or cloth again and steam for another 3 hours. Remove the covering, invert the pudding onto a warmed plate and decorate with holly.

If using a pressure cooker, cook each pudding for 15 minutes without pressure (pre-steaming), then for a further 2½ hours at high pressure. Before serving, steam at high pressure for 30 minutes.

SERVING SUGGESTION Warm a small wineglassful of brandy in a saucepan and, at the last moment, pour it over the pudding and set it alight. Serve with brandy butter.

BRANDY BUTTER

B RANDY BUTTER has become a traditional Christmas side dish to serve with Christmas pudding and warm mince pies.

PREPARATION TIME: 10 MINUTES

INGREDIENTS FOR FOUR
115-125 g (4-4¼ oz) soft, unsalted
    butter
2 tablespoons caster sugar
60 ml (2 fl oz) brandy

Cream the butter and sugar together thoroughly until fluffy and pale. Work in the brandy, a few drops at a time, beating well after each addition, until completely absorbed.

SERVING SUGGESTIONS Serve the brandy butter well chilled, either piled into a small dish or formed into small balls. Apart from being served with Christmas pudding and mince pies, it is also good with other steamed puddings.

CARAMEL ORANGES

T HIS SIMPLE yet attractive dessert calls for few ingredients, and can be prepared well in advance of the meal. The syrup, flavoured with Grand Marnier liqueur, adds a delicious taste.

PREPARATION TIME: 30 MINUTES
COOKING TIME: 45 MINUTES
CHILLING TIME: 3 HOURS

INGREDIENTS FOR SIX
6 oranges
310 ml (11 fl oz) water
150 g (5 oz) sugar
180 ml (6 fl oz) golden syrup
2 tablespoons lemon juice
2 tablespoons Grand Marnier
    liqueur
Sprigs of mint for garnish
    (optional)

Remove the rind from 2 of the oranges with a vegetable peeler, avoiding any of the white pith. Cut the rind into long, thin strips and bring to the boil in 125 ml (4 fl oz) of the water. Drain well.

In a fairly large saucepan, mix together the sugar, golden syrup and remaining water, then bring to the boil, stirring until the sugar has dissolved completely.

Boil (uncovered) for 10 minutes, then add the rind and continue to cook on a very low heat for another 30 minutes, or until the syrup has slightly thickened.

Remove from the stove and stir in the lemon juice and liqueur.

Peel all the oranges, including the 2 rindless ones, and remove any white membrane adhering to the fruit. Place them in an ovenproof bowl.

Pour the hot syrup over the oranges and stir them around from time to time while the syrup cools down. When the syrup is quite cool, pack the oranges into a jar, pour over the syrup and store in the refrigerator (the oranges taste better when chilled).

Serve in individual glass bowls and garnish with the caramelised orange rind. Alternatively, heap the oranges on a tall pedestal dish, decorating them with the peel and sprigs of mint.

VARIATIONS Slice the oranges into discs, pour over the syrup and serve with scoops of vanilla ice cream.

Other varieties of citrus fruit, grapefruit or tangerines, for example, can be sliced and served in the same way.

CHINESE TOFFEE APPLES *Their appeal goes further than sheer visual delight – both flavour and texture are memorable.*

CHINESE TOFFEE APPLES

THIS IS A TRUE Pekinese dessert, more correctly named Drawn Thread Apple, which refers to the thin threads of toffee which form as the apple pieces are removed from the pan. This spectacular course is worth the last-minute preparation involved; if you can cook it over a portable gas burner it is a fascinating and dramatic operation which your guests will enjoy watching.

PREPARATION TIME: 15 MINUTES
COOKING TIME: 20 MINUTES

INGREDIENTS FOR SIX
*2 medium-sized green apples,
   peeled and cored
Sunflower oil for frying*

*For the batter:
115 g (¼ lb) flour
1 tablespoon cornflour
250 ml (9 fl oz) water
2 teaspoons sunflower oil*

For the toffee:
*2 teaspoons sunflower oil
400 g (14 oz) sugar
250 ml (9 fl oz) warm water
2 tablespoons sesame seeds*

Cut the apples into quarters and then into eighths.

To make the batter, sieve the flour and cornflour into a bowl, and then gradually add the water and oil. Stir until the mixture is smooth.

Drop the apple pieces into the batter, then drain off the excess batter and fry them in deep, hot oil for 3-4 minutes until they are golden-brown. Drain the pieces on paper towels.

To make the toffee, heat the oil in a pan or wok, add the sugar and warm water, and stir until the mixture boils. Continue stirring rapidly.

After about 5 minutes the mixture will foam and look as if it is going to crystallise. Stir it for another 2-3 minutes until the toffee turns a light golden-brown.

Remove the saucepan from the heat immediately and add the sesame seeds and apple slices, making sure that the slices are completely coated. Transfer the apples to lightly oiled serving dishes and place them quickly on the table.

SERVING SUGGESTIONS Place a glass bowl filled with iced water and ice cubes on the table. Using chopsticks, each guest should pull the apple slices apart, then plunge them into the iced water. The syrup will turn into a brittle glaze which cracks easily when bitten into.

Make sure you have plenty of ice cubes in the bowl or else the hot toffee will soon warm the water.

Try serving the toffee apples with a jug of chilled cream. Scoops of homemade vanilla ice cream would also complement the hot dessert.

VARIATIONS You may use 2 large bananas, cut into chunks, instead of the sliced apples.

Alternatively, make the dessert from 1 apple and 1 banana.

145

ZABAGLIONE

ITALIANS REGARD this hot, golden froth, imbued with the distinctive flavour of Marsala, as a dessert as well as a restorative. Zabaglione originated in Sicily, where the local grapes are used to make the fortified Marsala wine.

If the dessert is to be eaten hot, it should be served immediately after being made. It can, however, be eaten cold if it is prepared slightly differently.

PREPARATION TIME: 10 MINUTES
COOKING TIME: 5 MINUTES

INGREDIENTS FOR FOUR
4 egg yolks
1 tablespoon caster sugar
90 ml (3 fl oz) Marsala, warmed to
  body temperature

Put the egg yolks and sugar in the top of a small double boiler, and whisk with a balloon whisk (or use an electric mixer) until the mixture thickens enough to fall from the whisk in a broad ribbon.

Set the pan over the bottom half of the double boiler, in which water is just simmering over a low heat. Make sure that the base of the top pan does not touch the hot water, or crusty grains will form in the mixture.

Add the warm Marsala and whisk the mixture continuously over a low heat until it rises and forms a creamy foam that has noticeably thickened. Serve the zabaglione at once.

SERVING SUGGESTION Pour the mixture into warmed individual glasses and serve with sponge finger biscuits.

The zabaglione would make an unusual accompaniment for Christmas pudding or other steamed puddings.

VARIATIONS For a cold zabaglione, not quite authentic but nevertheless delicious and able to be kept for up to 3 days in a refrigerator, make as above, but take the top pan from the double boiler as soon as the mixture has thickened. Set it immediately in a large pan already half filled with ice cubes. Keep whisking the mixture vigorously until the zabaglione is quite cold, then fold into it 150 ml ($\frac{1}{4}$ pint) thick cream, whipped but not stiff. Chill in a refrigerator until serving time.

This cream version can also be made with sweet wine instead of the Marsala and used as a sauce with fresh strawberries, raspberries or sliced peaches.

STUFFED APPLES *are baked with a choice of fillings and a sherry syrup.*

BAKED STUFFED APPLES

BAKED APPLES are a popular dish that can be combined with a number of different fillings. The sherry syrup adds an elegant touch to them all.

PREPARATION TIME: 10 MINUTES
COOKING TIME: 1 HOUR
PREHEAT OVEN TO 180°C (350°F, MARK 4)

INGREDIENTS FOR SIX
6 large cooking apples
25 g (1 oz) butter
75 g (3 oz) caster sugar
100-125 ml (3½-4 fl oz) sherry

Fillings (one of the following):
125 g (4¼ oz) dried apricots,
  chopped and mixed with
  2 tablespoons clear honey
125 g (4¼ oz) fruit mincemeat
125 g (4¼ oz) dried dates, chopped
  with 75 g (3 oz) nuts, and the
  juice of 1 lemon
75 g (3 oz) soft brown sugar mixed
  with 2 teaspoons ground nutmeg

Core the apples and score the skin round the middle of each. Stand them in a buttered, deep ovenproof dish. Fill the cavities with your chosen filling, put a knob of butter on each apple, and sprinkle thickly with caster sugar. Pour the sherry around the apples.

Bake in the preheated oven for 1 hour. Baste the apples occasionally with the sherry syrup.

SERVING SUGGESTIONS Serve hot or cold with cream or custard.

VARIATION Stuff the apples with chopped stem ginger and almonds or use dried peaches and pine nuts (kernels).

SUMMER PUDDING

STRICTLY SPEAKING, summer pudding is a way of using up excess bread. But the pudding is such a favourite that nowadays it may be necessary to set a few slices aside deliberately to let them go stale. A liberal sprinkling of fruit juice transforms the bread into a cover as rich as any pastry.

Most soft fruits can be used: raspberries, stoned cherries, blackberries, black currants, red currants, loganberries or blueberries, and preferably a mixture of two or three. But be sparing with blackberries and black currants – they can give the pudding too dark a colour, and dominate the flavour.

Remember to prepare summer pudding the day before it is needed.

PREPARATION TIME: 30 MINUTES
STANDING TIME: 8 HOURS

INGREDIENTS FOR SIX
7-8 slices day-old bread from a large white loaf, with crusts removed
900 g (2 lb) mixed soft fruit
About 125 g (4¼ oz) caster sugar

Prepare and wash the fruit and place in a heavy-based saucepan with the sugar, which should be added according to taste, taking into account the tartness of the fruit. Cook over a low heat until the sugar has dissolved and the juices flow.

Line the base and side of an 850 ml (1½ pint) pudding basin with just over two-thirds of the bread, making sure that the slices overlap slightly and fit tightly with no gaps for the fruit to fall through. Pack in the fruit and sugar mixture, adding just enough juice to soak the bread. Cover with the remaining slices of bread – cut to fit exactly – and sprinkle with a little juice. But do not saturate to the point that the bread is soggy, or it will not mould well enough for the pudding to stand on its own. Set aside the rest of the juice to serve with the pudding.

Cover the top of the pudding with a saucer, curved side down, that just fits inside the top of the basin. Place a 450 g (1 lb) weight, or a heavy tin or jar, on top of the saucer to compress the pudding. Leave to stand overnight in a cool place.

To turn out, remove the weight and saucer carefully and ease round the side of the pudding with a round-bladed knife. Then invert onto the serving plate.

SOUFFLÉ JAM OMELETTE *A simple dessert that is bound to please.*

SOUFFLÉ JAM OMELETTE

SWEET OMELETTES were very popular in English manor houses in Edwardian times. The cook could make them while the family and guests were eating the previous course.

PREPARATION TIME: 10 MINUTES
COOKING TIME: 5 MINUTES

INGREDIENTS FOR FOUR TO SIX
4 egg yolks
2 tablespoons caster sugar
6 egg whites
¼ teaspoon salt
30 g (1¼ oz) butter
Caster sugar for sprinkling
1 tablespoon jam, warmed

Beat the egg yolks and caster sugar together. Whisk the egg whites with the salt until they have become stiff enough to stand up in peaks (this can be done well before the meal).

Just before cooking, quickly whisk the egg whites and salt again, and then stir them lightly into the beaten yolks while the butter melts in a large omelette pan.

When the butter is very hot, pour in the egg mixture and cook for 3 minutes. Finish cooking the top by grilling under fierce heat for about 2 minutes, or until the omelette is well risen and golden.

Slide it onto aluminium foil sprinkled with caster sugar, carefully spread the warmed jam over it, and fold it in half by folding over the foil.

Slide the omelette from the foil onto a warm dish and serve at once, cut into wedges. Accompany with a jug of cream.

SERVING SUGGESTION A variety of jams can be used, such as apricot, strawberry, raspberry or black cherry jam.

ICE CREAM *Fill parfait glasses with scoops of praline and dark chocolate ice cream for a treat with broad appeal.*

DARK CHOCOLATE ICE CREAM

THIS RICH ICE CREAM can be the basis for many a delicious pudding, and is also very appealing on its own. Buy a good-quality dark chocolate to achieve the optimum results.

The ice cream will hold its shape very well and is therefore ideal for setting in differently shaped moulds.

PREPARATION TIME: 45 MINUTES
COOKING TIME: 10 MINUTES
FREEZING TIME: 5 HOURS

INGREDIENTS FOR SIX
50 g (2 oz) sugar
125 ml (4 fl oz) water
250 g (9 oz) dark chocolate
3 egg yolks
400 ml (14 fl oz) cream
2 tablespoons chocolate or coffee liqueur
Sunflower oil, safflower oil or non-stick spray

Combine the sugar and water in a saucepan and bring to the boil, stirring all the time. Boil for 3 minutes, then remove from the heat and leave the syrup to cool for 15 minutes.

Grate the chocolate into the syrup and pour into a blender. Cover and blend at high speed for 10 seconds, or until smooth and well mixed. Set the blender at a medium-high speed and add the egg yolks, one by one, blending until the mixture is smooth.

Beat the cream until it forms soft peaks and fold into the chocolate mixture with the liqueur.

Lightly coat a lidded mould with the oil or non-stick spray and pour in the ice cream. Cover and freeze for 5 hours before serving.

Remove the ice cream from the freezer and leave to stand for 10 minutes to soften before turning out onto a plate. If you wish, you can turn out the ice cream well in advance, cover with foil, then return it to the freezer. This will save time for last-minute decorating.

SERVING SUGGESTIONS Decorate with chopped nuts (pecans, walnuts or flaked almonds are suitable) or rosettes of cream. Serve with more liqueur.

Alternatively, instead of unmoulding the ice cream, form it into scoops and serve it on its own or with scoops of other homemade ice creams in tall parfait glasses. Decorate with wafers.

VARIATIONS Instead of the liqueur, add 2 teaspoons vanilla essence to the ice cream and fold 50 g (2 oz) chopped pecans or walnuts into the mixture before freezing.

Add Grand Marnier liqueur to the ice cream in place of the coffee or chocolate liqueur, decorate with rosettes of cream flavoured with Grand Marnier and top with pieces of preserved orange peel.

Use rum instead of the liqueur and fold in 50 g (2 oz) chocolate chips with the cream before freezing the mixture. Decorate the completed ice cream with rosettes of cream studded with chocolate chips or sprinkle with finely grated dark or milk chocolate.

PRALINE ICE CREAM

MAKE THIS NUTTY ice cream a day ahead to allow it time to set properly. The lemon juice adds an interesting tang to the mixture.

PREPARATION TIME: 30 MINUTES
COOKING TIME: 30 MINUTES
FREEZING TIME: 8 HOURS

INGREDIENTS FOR SIX TO EIGHT
For the praline:
125 g (4¼ oz) sugar
2 tablespoons lemon juice
125 g (4¼ oz) almonds, blanched*
    and coarsely chopped

For the custard:
4 extra-large egg yolks
125 g (4¼ oz) sugar
A pinch of salt
500 ml (17 fl oz) pouring cream
250 ml (9 fl oz) cream
2 teaspoons almond-flavoured
    liqueur or brandy

To make the praline, place the sugar and lemon juice in a saucepan over medium heat and stir until the sugar has dissolved completely. Boil gently until the sugar caramelises to a light brown colour.

Add the almonds and stir until they are well coated with caramel and slightly browned. Do not allow it to get too brown, or the praline will be bitter.

Pour the mixture onto a baking tray that has been well coated with a non-stick spray or lined with baking parchment and leave to cool. When the praline is cold and hard, pound it finely.

To make the custard, whisk the egg yolks with the sugar and salt until light and lemon-coloured. Scald* the pouring cream and whisk it into the egg mixture. Pour this custard into the top of a double boiler and stir over a medium heat until the mixture thickens sufficiently to coat a wooden spoon. Add the praline to the custard, pour it into a bowl and leave the mixture to cool.

Cover and freeze until half set (about 2 hours), then whip the remaining cream and beat it into the semi-frozen custard, together with the liqueur. Pour into a well-greased mould, and freeze for 4-6 hours until firm.

SERVING SUGGESTION Turn out the mould, or scoop balls of ice cream into a chilled bowl, and garnish with flaked almonds or grated chocolate.

VANILLA ICE CREAM

A TIME-HONOURED FAVOURITE throughout the world, this ice cream lends itself to variation and may be flavoured with any one of dozens of tasty extras.

PREPARATION TIME: 10 MINUTES
COOKING TIME: 20 MINUTES
FREEZING TIME: 5 HOURS

INGREDIENTS FOR FOUR TO SIX
4 extra-large egg yolks
125 g (4¼ oz) sugar
A pinch of salt
500 ml (17 fl oz) thin cream
2 teaspoons vanilla essence

Whisk the egg yolks with the sugar and salt until light and lemon-coloured. Scald* the cream and whisk it into the egg mixture. Pour this custard into the top of a double boiler and stir over a medium heat until the mixture thickens sufficiently to coat a wooden spoon.

Strain into a bowl and add the vanilla essence. Cover with aluminium foil or plastic wrap and freeze for 2 hours, then remove the ice cream from the freezer and whisk with a hand beater or electric beater until light and mushy. Pour it into a mould well greased with oil, or into an ice cream container. Cover and freeze for 2-3 hours.

VARIATIONS For a coffee ice cream, dissolve 1 tablespoon pure instant coffee in the hot custard and reduce the vanilla essence to 1 teaspoon.

For a chocolate ice cream, grate 4-6 squares dark chocolate into the hot custard and stir until completely dissolved.

For a strawberry ice cream, add 250 ml (9 fl oz) strawberry purée (use a blender or food processor) to the ice cream before freezing. Add more sugar to taste.

To make honey and nut ice cream, substitute 125 ml (4 fl oz) honey for the sugar and add 125 g (4¼ oz) chopped mixed nuts (unsalted).

To make banana ice cream, blend 3 ripe bananas with 1 tablespoon lemon juice to a smooth purée and then beat well into the semi-soft ice cream (made without vanilla essence.)

For a banana split, slice bananas lengthways and sandwich together with scoops of 2 or 3 different flavoured ice creams, then smother with piped whipped cream and sprinkle with flaked toasted nuts.

KHULFI

KHULFI-WALLAHS or professional ice cream makers of India are second to none. They use fresh tropical fruits, nuts of all kinds, and flavourings such as rose petals, saffron and cardamom to make deliciously unusual ice creams.

PREPARATION TIME: 30 MINUTES
COOKING TIME: 45 MINUTES
FREEZING TIME: 3 HOURS

INGREDIENTS FOR FOUR TO SIX
1.5 litres (52 fl oz) milk
1 tin (400 g/14 oz) condensed milk
2 tablespoons cold milk
2 tablespoons cornflour
80 g (3 oz) sugar
2 tablespoons water
5 teaspoons slivered almonds
1 tablespoon pistachios or other
    nuts, chopped
2 tablespoons crushed cornflakes

Using a heavy-bottomed saucepan, bring the 1.5 litres (52 fl oz) milk and the condensed milk to boiling point. Simmer for about 20 minutes – stir continuously because the mixture burns very easily.

Make a smooth paste with the 2 tablespoons cold milk and cornflour, then add 100 ml (3½ fl oz) of the warm milk to it. Stir and then add to the milk in the saucepan.

Stir again and simmer the mixture for about 30 minutes, until it is thick. A thin film of milk may form at the top – simply stir it into the mixture as this occurs. Remove the pan from the heat.

In a small pot heat the sugar and water, and boil rapidly until the syrup turns light brown. Remove from the heat, allow to cool slightly and then stir it into the milk mixture while it is still liquid. Pour into a freezer container and allow to semi-freeze. Stir well again, mixing in half the nuts and half the cornflakes. Freeze until solid and serve in individual bowls. Decorate with the remaining nuts and cornflakes.

SERVING SUGGESTION Serve the khulfi at the end of an Indian meal, accompanied by sliced mangoes.

CASSATA

MANY OF TODAY'S classic ice cream recipes, like cassata, originated in Italy. This impressive dessert combines chocolate and vanilla ice cream with glacé fruit and nuts. You can change the character of the dessert by experimenting with different flavours of ice cream.

PREPARATION TIME: 50 MINUTES
FREEZING TIME: 10 HOURS

INGREDIENTS FOR EIGHT TO TEN
175 g (6 oz) mixed glacé fruit, finely chopped
6 glacé cherries, halved
80 g (3 oz) mixed unsalted nuts, coarsely chopped
2 tablespoons brandy or Grand Marnier (optional)
Non-stick spray, sunflower or safflower oil
1 litre (1¾ pints) vanilla ice cream*
500 ml (17 fl oz) chocolate ice cream*
1 teaspoon vanilla essence
250 ml (9 fl oz) cream whipped to soft peaks
1 tablespoon caster sugar

For the garnish:
Whipped cream
A few whole hazelnuts

Combine the glacé fruit, cherries and nuts in a bowl and pour over the brandy or liqueur (if used). Leave to stand while assembling the cassata.

Coat a 2 litre (3½ pint) loaf tin or 2 smaller tins with non-stick spray or oil. Spread a thick layer of vanilla ice cream evenly around the tin(s). Return immediately to the freezer to harden (this will take about 1 hour).

Layer the chocolate ice cream evenly on the vanilla ice cream. Return to the freezer again until firm (about 1 hour).

Mix the fruit and nuts with the vanilla essence, cream and caster sugar to taste. Fill the centre of the cassata with the cream mixture, cover with foil and freeze for 8 hours, or until very firm.

To unmould, turn the container over onto a dish and cover the loaf tin with a cloth which has been wrung out in hot water, to help ease the cassata out. Decorate with cream rosettes and hazelnuts. Serve sliced like a loaf of bread in 2 cm (¾ in) slices. Allow to soften slightly before slicing.

LEMON SORBET

THIS IS A VERY refreshing dessert with a sweet-sharp flavour. It is ideal for serving at an elegant dinner between courses to freshen the palate.

PREPARATION TIME: 20 MINUTES
STANDING TIME: 30 MINUTES
FREEZING TIME: 5 HOURS

INGREDIENTS FOR FOUR TO SIX
4 large juicy lemons
130 g (4½ oz) sugar
2 tablespoons Grand Marnier (optional)
60 ml (2 fl oz) water

Peel the fruit, removing all the pith and pips, and dice. Purée in a food processor with the rest of the ingredients, then leave to stand for 30 minutes.

Pour into a shallow, freezer-proof container. Freeze until mushy, then process again until smooth. Re-freeze until set. If frozen very hard, allow to soften at room temperature for 10 minutes before serving in individual dishes.

SERVING SUGGESTIONS Decorate this lemon sorbet with some candied peel or fresh mint leaves.

CHOCOLATE MOUSSE

WITH A LITTLE CARE, you can make a chocolate mousse that beats any you may be served in a restaurant.

PREPARATION TIME: 30 MINUTES
CHILLING TIME: 3 HOURS

INGREDIENTS FOR SIX
150 g (5 oz) dark chocolate
3 eggs, separated
1 tablespoon caster sugar
250 ml (9 fl oz) cream
1 tablespoon cognac or coffee liqueur

Break the chocolate into a bowl and set it over another bowl of hot water. Stir until it melts, then leave to cool to room temperature. Beat the egg whites until stiff, then (using the same beater) lightly whisk the sugar and cream together.

Lastly, whisk the egg yolks lightly and add to the chocolate with the cognac or liqueur. Mix the ingredients until well blended and smooth.

Stir a quarter of the beaten egg white into the chocolate mixture and fold the chocolate mixture into the rest of the egg white, then fold in the cream which has been whisked until it forms soft peaks. Spoon the mousse into dessert glasses or bowls and chill (covered with plastic wrap) for 3 hours.

SERVING SUGGESTIONS Decorate with chocolate curls, a rosette of cream and flaked almonds or chopped pecan nuts.

VARIATIONS Make the mousse with an orange-flavoured liqueur and add the grated rind and strained juice of 1 orange. Decorate with rosettes of cream topped with pieces of preserved orange peel or chopped crystallised ginger.

Use white chocolate instead of dark.

LEMON MOUSSE

THIS IS A RICH and extravagant dessert in the old-fashioned tradition. For the best results, choose lemons that are fresh and firm. Using fruit that is past its prime will spoil the effect.

PREPARATION TIME: 35 MINUTES
SETTING TIME: 4-5 HOURS

INGREDIENTS FOR FOUR
2 teaspoons gelatine
3 tablespoons water
3 eggs, separated
150 g (5 oz) caster sugar
Juice and grated rind of 2 lemons
250 ml (9 fl oz) cream, lightly whipped
3 tablespoons flaked almonds

Put the gelatine and water into a small saucepan and leave to soak for 10 minutes. Combine the egg yolks and sugar in a bowl and beat until light, lemon-coloured and thick, and then beat in the strained lemon juice and rind.

Slowly warm the gelatine mixture and stir until the gelatine is completely dissolved. Add it to the egg mixture, mixing gently but well. Leave until it starts to set.

Beat the egg whites until stiff but not too dry, and then fold into the egg yolk mixture with half the whipped cream.

Turn into a serving dish, cover with plastic wrap and leave to set in the refrigerator (about 4-5 hours). Decorate with the rest of the cream, perhaps piped into rosettes, and the flaked almonds.

PAVLOVA

THIS DISH IS ONE of Australia's most popular desserts. It consists of a crispy meringue crust with a thick marshmallow texture inside. The centre of the meringue case is filled with a mixture of whipped cream and a selection of fruit in season. To give the Pavlova an extra special touch, you may lightly frost the fruit with egg white and a generous dusting of caster sugar.

PREPARATION TIME: 45 MINUTES
COOKING TIME: 1 HOUR
PREHEAT OVEN TO 140°C (275°F, MARK 1)

INGREDIENTS FOR SIX
For the meringue:
4 egg whites
175 g (6 oz) caster sugar
60 g (2 oz) granulated sugar
1 tablespoon cornflour
¾ teaspoon lemon juice

For the filling:
250 ml (9 fl oz) cream, whipped until soft peaks form
100 g (3¾ oz) fresh strawberries, washed and hulled, or 100 g (3¾ oz) seedless grapes
100 g (3¾ oz) stoned cherries or plums
4 ripe apricots, or 2 nectarines, peeled, stoned and cut into slices
Pulp of 2 passion fruit

Beat the egg whites until soft peaks form, then gradually add the caster sugar, beating the mixture well until all the sugar has dissolved. Fold the combined granulated sugar and cornflour into the meringue with the lemon juice.

Mark a 23 cm (9 in) circle on greaseproof paper, grease it with butter and dust it with cornflour. Shake off the excess cornflour and fill in the circle with about one-third of the meringue mixture.

Place the rest of the meringue in a piping bag fitted with a star nozzle. Pipe the mixture decoratively around the edge of the Pavlova to form a rim. Bake the meringue for 1 hour.

If you would prefer a crisp texture throughout the meringue ring, then bake for an extra 45 minutes.

Fill the meringue case with most of the whipped cream and the prepared fruit, and then decorate it with the remaining cream and a few strawberries or small clusters of grapes.

SERVING SUGGESTION Garnish with frosted grape clusters and plums. Dip the fruit in beaten egg white, then into caster sugar and allow to dry.

VARIATIONS You can make a simpler yet still traditional Pavlova by topping the baked meringue shell only with whipped cream and sliced kiwi fruit.

A mixture of ice cream and fruit makes an excellent filling for the meringue. Try a combination of raspberries and praline ice cream*. Serve immediately.

PAVLOVA *Fresh fruit in season and whipped cream nestle in a delectable case of chewy meringue.*

151

SUMMER FRUIT BOWL *The pick of the season's crop in one dish.*

SUMMER FRUIT BOWL

THIS FRUIT SALAD is particularly attractive as well as being delicious. The Kirsch is an important ingredient because it enhances and melds together the flavours of the various fruits.

PREPARATION TIME: 30 MINUTES

INGREDIENTS FOR SIX

3 oranges
1 pear
2 peaches
¼ Honeydew melon
1 slice watermelon
¼ Ogen melon (rock melon)
½ mango
12-16 grapes (preferably seedless)
115 g (¼ lb) strawberries (optional)
1 tablespoon Kirsch
Caster sugar (optional)
Fresh mint for garnish

Wash and dry the fruits where necessary. Squeeze the juice from 2 oranges and pour into a bowl. Peel and slice the pear and peaches, and toss gently in the orange juice, using two wooden spoons.

Use a small scoop to cut out balls from the melons (or slice them) and add to the bowl. Next, peel the last orange and slice it into thin segments. Add to the bowl with cubes of mango, then add the grapes (halved and seeded if not the seedless variety) and the strawberries (if used).

Pour in the Kirsch and gently toss the fruit salad. If you think it necessary, add a light sprinkling of caster sugar (although the natural sweetness of the fruits should be sufficient).

Cover the bowl and chill until serving. Garnish with fresh mint and a few of the best strawberries (with their stalks) set aside for decoration.

SERVING SUGGESTION Serve with a bowl of sweetened whipped cream.

VARIATIONS Add stoned fresh cherries when available, a sliced kiwi fruit, or some fresh raspberries instead of the strawberries.

The summer fruit bowl would be a refreshing accompaniment for a rich crème brûlée.

SYLLABUB

TO THE ELIZABETHANS, the syllabub was a frothy drink made by milking directly from the cow into a cup of ale, wine or cider. By the 18th century the name had come to be applied to a number of creamy whips, often thickened with a variety of fresh fruit juices.

One of the most popular was this confection of sweetened wine laced with brandy and whipped cream (sharpened by the juice of a lemon or a Seville orange), which can be eaten as a pudding in its own right, or used as a topping for trifle in place of plain cream.

PREPARATION TIME: 25-30 MINUTES
STANDING TIME: OVERNIGHT (8 HOURS)
CHILLING TIME: 2 HOURS

INGREDIENTS FOR SIX

150 ml (¼ pint) sweet white wine
1 tablespoon medium-sweet sherry
2 tablespoons brandy
1 lemon, or 1 Seville (bitter)
  orange (or a sweet orange if
  preferred)
150 ml (¼ pint) water
4 tablespoons caster sugar
275-300 ml (9½-10 fl oz) cream

Pour the wine, sherry and brandy into a large basin.

Remove the rind of the lemon or orange, leaving the white pith intact, and reserve half the rind for a garnish.

Squeeze the juice from the lemon or orange and add it to the wine, with the remaining half of the rind. Leave this mixture to stand overnight, then remove and discard the rind.

Boil the reserved rind in the water, simmering for 2 minutes to remove its bitter taste. Drain off the water, then cut the rind into shreds.

Stir the sugar into the wine mixture until it dissolves, then add the cream and whip with a hand whisk until the mixture forms soft peaks. Spoon it into 6 wine glasses, or small glass bowls.

Stand the finished syllabub in the refrigerator for 2 hours. Before serving, decorate each syllabub with the shredded lemon or orange rind.

SERVING SUGGESTIONS The syllabub may also be used as a topping for fruit – fresh, poached or stewed dried fruit.

Serve with sponge fingers, homemade macaroons* or brandy snaps*.

CRÈME BRÛLÉE *Crunchy caramel conceals a rich, creamy custard.*

CRÈME CARAMEL

THIS IS ONE of the most popular desserts in homes and restaurants alike. It is simple to make and can keep for 3-4 days in the refrigerator.

PREPARATION TIME: 25 MINUTES
COOKING TIME: 30-45 MINUTES
CHILLING TIME: 4-6 HOURS
PREHEAT OVEN TO 140°C (275°F, MARK 1)

INGREDIENTS FOR SIX
5 tablespoons sugar
1 tablespoon water
3 eggs
500 ml (17 fl oz) milk
A pinch of salt

Melt 4 tablespoons of the sugar with the water in a pan over a hot plate until the mixture melts and turns light brown. Do not stir the mixture or disturb it in any way until it has turned a good caramel colour. Be careful not to let it become too dark, however, as it will be bitter.

Pour the caramel into a straight-sided ovenproof dish or deep 20 cm (8 in) cake tin. Swirl it around so that it coats the bottom and sides of the container, then set aside and allow time for it to cool.

Beat the eggs and mix with the milk. Add the salt and remaining sugar, and pour this mixture into the caramel-lined container. Stand the container in a *bain-marie** making sure that the water in the larger dish is warm.

Bake for 30-45 minutes, depending on the depth of the dish. It is done when a knife inserted in the centre comes out clean. Do not allow the water in the *bain-marie* to boil as this will make the custard watery.

Allow the crème caramel to cool, adding cold water to the *bain-marie* during the cooling period. Chill in the refrigerator until the custard is quite firm – say, 4–6 hours, but overnight is even better.

Crème caramel can be served at room temperature directly from the dish. Run a knife around the edge to loosen the caramel and turn it out onto a dish which has a rim at least 1 cm (½ in) high.

VARIATION Add 2 tablespoons strong coffee to the egg and milk mixture to make a delicious coffee custard.

To make a richer, firmer crème caramel to serve ten people, use 9 eggs, 1 litre (1¾ pints) milk and sugar to taste.

CRÈME BRÛLÉE

THIS IS A RICH RELATION of crème caramel: being made with cream it is not only more expensive but is also very rich and filling. The custard dessert with its crunchy caramel topping is fairly simple to make but is always considered to be something special.

PREPARATION TIME: 15 MINUTES
COOKING TIME: 40-50 MINUTES
CHILLING TIME: 4-6 HOURS
PREHEAT OVEN TO 140°C (275°F, MARK 1)

INGREDIENTS FOR SIX
600 ml (21 fl oz) cream
70 g (2½ oz) white sugar
A 2 cm (¾ in) piece of vanilla pod,
or 1¼ teaspoons vanilla essence
4 egg yolks
100 g (3¾ oz) brown sugar for
topping

Heat the cream in a double boiler and stir in the sugar. If using the vanilla pod, add it to the cream. Continue to stir until all the sugar has dissolved.

In a large mixing bowl, beat the egg yolks until they are thick and light in colour. Pour the hot cream over the yolks, stirring vigorously.

If using vanilla essence, add it after the cream and yolks are mixed.

Strain the mixture into an ovenproof dish measuring 23 cm × 15 cm × 5 cm (9 in × 6 in × 2 in) – or 6 individual dishes – and place in a larger pan containing a 3 cm (1¼ in) depth of hot water.

Bake for about 40-50 minutes. Allow to cool before placing the custard in the refrigerator to chill properly (allow about 4-6 hours).

Before serving, cover the entire surface with a thin layer of the brown sugar. Set the dish on a bed of cracked ice to prevent the custard from being reheated, then grill until the sugar has melted and caramelised.

This dish can be served immediately or kept in the refrigerator until it is needed – not more than 2-3 hours.

VARIATION Stewed or fresh fruit may be added before the dish is baked to make an even more exotic dessert.

Place a layer of sliced peaches, sprinkled with a little cinnamon sugar*, under the cream, or use a mixture of soft fruits (raspberries, redcurrants and blackcurrants) sweetened with sugar.

TRIFLE *Layered in a glass dish, this traditional feast of a dessert is a temptation to the eye as well as the tastebuds.*

TRIFLE

RICH CREAM DISHES were the delight of the 18th century. Among them was a frivolous confection of biscuits or cake, soaked in dry white wine or sherry, topped with custard or syllabub, and decorated with almonds, macaroons, jelly or crystallised fruits and flowers. This was known as a trifle.

Preparation needs to begin the day before so that the flavours in both the base and the syllabub can blend fully.

PREPARATION TIME: 40 MINUTES
COOKING TIME: 25 MINUTES
SETTING TIME: OVERNIGHT
CHILLING TIME: 2 HOURS
INGREDIENTS FOR EIGHT TO TEN
For the base:
115 g ($\frac{1}{4}$ lb) macaroons, or 8-10
   slices of sponge cake
3 tablespoons brandy
150 ml ($\frac{1}{4}$ pint) dry white wine
   or sherry

3-4 tablespoons thin raspberry or
   strawberry jam
600 ml (21 fl oz) cream
2 eggs, beaten
2 egg yolks, beaten
2 tablespoons caster sugar

For the topping:
Syllabub* and prepared shreds of
   orange or lemon rind
75 g (3 oz) blanched* almonds
   slivered and lightly toasted
   (optional)

Arrange the macaroons or slices of sponge cake on the bottom of a large glass dish. Spoon over the brandy and as much of the wine as they will soak up. Then carefully spread the macaroons or slices of sponge cake with the jam.

Bring the cream almost to boiling point, and stir it well into the beaten eggs and egg yolks. Pour into the top pan of a double boiler and set this over the bottom pan of hot water, taking care that the water does not touch it.

Keep the double boiler simmering and stir the custard until it thickens (about 15-20 minutes). Remove from the heat and stir in the sugar until dissolved.

Leave until almost cold before pouring over the macaroons or slices of sponge cake. Set in a cold place overnight. Begin making the syllabub, which also needs to stand overnight.

The next day, spread the syllabub carefully over the trifle and chill for 2 hours. Just before serving, sprinkle the blanched almonds (if used) and shredded lemon or orange rind on top.

VARIATION Top the trifle with whipped cream instead of the syllabub and decorate the top with crystallised flowers or halved glacé cherries.

Fresh strawberries or sliced peaches can be used instead of jam, and sherry or rum would make good substitutes for the brandy.

If you have used sponge cake for the bottom layer of the trifle, decorate the top with tiny macaroons*.

PINEAPPLE ROMANOFF

GENEROUS FLAVOURINGS of Kirsch, Cointreau and rum make this dessert rich enough to serve in small portions. Make sure that it has been properly chilled before serving.

PREPARATION TIME: 20 MINUTES
CHILLING TIME: AT LEAST 4 HOURS

INGREDIENTS FOR SIX
1 large pineapple (or 2 small ones), peeled and cut into 1 cm ($\frac{1}{2}$ in) cubes
100 g (3$\frac{3}{4}$ oz) icing sugar
3 tablespoons Cointreau
3 tablespoons white rum
250 ml (9 fl oz) cream
3 tablespoons Kirsch
Grated rind of 1 orange

Place the pineapple cubes in a bowl and sprinkle 60 g (2 oz) of the icing sugar over them. Add the Cointreau and rum, and cover with plastic wrap. Chill for at least 4 hours (or overnight).

About 1 hour before serving, whip the cream lightly with the rest of the icing sugar and flavour with the Kirsch. Pour over the pineapple pieces and toss gently to coat them evenly.

Spoon the mixture into a glass serving bowl, cover and chill until ready to serve. Sprinkle the grated orange rind over the dessert just before serving.

VARIATIONS This dessert is equally delicious if you substitute strawberries (carefully wiped) for the pineapple cubes, and Grand Marnier for the Cointreau. Try mixing the two fruits and adding flaked almonds as a decoration.

MACAROONS

THESE DELICIOUS little almond biscuits are often used as a base for trifles or served with syllabub.

PREPARATION TIME: 20 MINUTES
COOKING TIME: 15-20 MINUTES
PREHEAT OVEN TO 180°C (350°F, MARK 4)

INGREDIENTS FOR 26 MACAROONS
200 g (7 oz) ground almonds
250 g (9 oz) sugar
$\frac{1}{2}$ teaspoon vanilla sugar* or
$\frac{1}{4}$ teaspoon vanilla essence
2 egg whites

Water for brushing
Icing sugar for dusting

Place the almonds in a bowl, pounding them with a pestle as the sugar is gradually added (or use a food processor). Add the vanilla sugar or essence and, little by little, the egg whites. The dough should be firm enough to knead.

Mix or knead well and divide the dough into small balls (about 3 cm/1$\frac{1}{4}$ in across is ideal, but size can be varied).

Oil a sheet of greaseproof paper (or use non-stick baking paper) and place on a biscuit tray. Put the almond balls on the paper and flatten them slightly, allowing room for them to spread.

Brush the surface of each macaroon with water. Dust with a little icing sugar. Bake in the middle of the preheated oven for 15-20 minutes. If using greaseproof paper, place the paper on a well-dampened tea towel as the macaroons come out of the oven. As soon as the paper is moist, remove the biscuits.

SERVING SUGGESTION Macaroons are delicious served with fruit fools.

BRANDY SNAPS

CHILDREN AND ADULTS alike tend to find these gingery, crunchy snaps irresistible, whether served plain to accompany a rich syllabub, or filled with whipped cream.

PREPARATION TIME: 20 MINUTES
COOKING TIME: 8-10 MINUTES
PREHEAT OVEN TO 180°C (350°F, MARK 4)

INGREDIENTS FOR 20 BRANDY SNAPS
65 g (2$\frac{1}{4}$ oz) butter
50 g (2 oz) caster sugar
2 tablespoons golden syrup
65 g (2$\frac{1}{4}$ oz) flour, sifted
A pinch of salt
$\frac{3}{4}$ teaspoon ground ginger
1 teaspoon grated lemon rind
1 tablespoon brandy

For the filling (optional)
250 ml (9 fl oz) cream
30 g (1$\frac{1}{4}$ oz) icing sugar, sifted
1 tablespoon brandy

Melt the butter, sugar and syrup over a moderate heat, stirring until the sugar dissolves. Allow the mixture to cool and then gradually beat in the flour, salt, ginger, lemon rind and brandy.

Drop teaspoonfuls of the batter on a well-greased baking tray – they tend to spread, so keep them well spaced. Bake for 8-10 minutes, or until golden-brown. Roll each brandy snap around the buttered handle of a wooden spoon, doing so as quickly as possible.

If the snaps harden before you are able to curl them, return them briefly to the oven until soft. Once you have curled the snaps around the handle, leave them there and place on a wire rack until cool. It is advisable to have 3-4 wooden spoons handy.

To make the filling, beat the cream until thick, add all the icing sugar and beat to form stiff peaks. Fold in the brandy. Carefully pipe the cream into the brandy snaps and serve immediately.

LEMON PUDDING

CENTURIES AGO, lemons were valued especially for their 'zest' – the aromatic oil obtained from the peel – which was used in perfumes and as a flavouring. The zest is used in this pudding. As the dessert is cooking, it separates to give a layer of sponge over a base of tangy lemon curd.

PREPARATION TIME: 25 MINUTES
COOKING TIME: 45 MINUTES
PREHEAT OVEN TO 170°C (340°F, MARK 3$\frac{1}{2}$)

INGREDIENTS FOR FOUR TO SIX
120 g ($\frac{1}{4}$ lb) sugar
50 g (2 oz) butter
1 tablespoon boiling water
50 g (2 oz) flour
Juice and grated rind of 1 large lemon
2 eggs, separated
225 ml (8 fl oz) milk

Cream together the sugar and butter, adding the boiling water to make the mixture workable. Stir in the flour, lemon juice and rind. Whisk the egg yolks in the milk and add to the creamed mixture, a little at a time. Beat the egg whites until stiff and fold them into the mixture.

Pour the pudding into a buttered 1 litre (1$\frac{3}{4}$ pint) pie dish and stand it in a roasting tin half filled with warm water. Bake in the preheated oven for 45 minutes.

SERVING SUGGESTION Serve hot on its own, or cold with a little cream.

BAKED BANANA ALASKA

EASY TO PREPARE, this version of the classic Baked Alaska makes an ideal family treat for a special occasion.

PREPARATION TIME: 45 MINUTES
COOKING TIME: 2-3 MINUTES
PREHEAT OVEN TO 220°C (425°F, MARK 7)

INGREDIENTS FOR SIX
A 12 cm × 20 cm (about 5 in × 8 in)
  trifle sponge
4 tablespoons medium sherry
3 medium-sized, ripe bananas
3 extra-large egg whites
80 g (3 oz) caster sugar
¾ teaspoon cream of tartar
1 litre (1¾ pint) block vanilla ice
  cream frozen hard
100 g (3¾ oz) pecans or walnuts,
  coarsely chopped, or flaked
  almonds, toasted

Slice the sponge cake in half horizontally and place half on a wooden board (keep the rest of the sponge for use on another occasion). Sprinkle with the sherry.

Peel the bananas and slice in half lengthways. Beat the egg whites until they begin to stiffen, then fold in the caster sugar and cream of tartar. Beat the mixture until it is very stiff.

Place the ice cream neatly on the sponge cake, trimming the sponge to fit. Working swiftly, arrange the bananas neatly on the ice cream and sprinkle with the nuts and a little more sherry if you wish. Using a rubber spatula, cover the ice cream and sides of the sponge base completely with the egg white mixture, making sure there are no holes in this covering. Sprinkle with a little caster sugar and place immediately in the pre-heated oven. Bake for 2-3 minutes until the peaks are just browned (you can also grill the meringue). Serve the Alaska immediately.

SERVING SUGGESTION This dessert needs no accompaniment and is served sliced like a loaf of bread. A garnish of toasted almonds would be attractive if you have used almonds in the dish.

VARIATIONS Tinned apricots marinated in a little rum (in this case, sprinkle the sponge with rum instead of sherry) are a good substitute for the bananas, as are pears (with a combination of chocolate and vanilla ice cream as the base) or even sliced peaches (tinned or fresh).

SPICED PEACHES

GLOWING AMBER PEACHES in a spicy, brandied syrup make a very grand sweet to serve at a dinner party.

This recipe is an adaptation of an 18th-century one. It is quick and simple to prepare. Keep the dish for three days before serving; by then the syrup will have fully penetrated the fruit. If you want to keep it longer, double the amount of brandy.

PREPARATION TIME: 15 MINUTES
COOKING TIME: 20 MINUTES
STANDING TIME: 3 DAYS

INGREDIENTS FOR SIX
6 ripe peaches
6 cloves
450 ml (¾ pint) water
350 g (¾ lb) sugar
1 cinnamon stick (5 cm/2 in), or
  1 teaspoon ground cinnamon
¼ teaspoon ground mace or nutmeg
100-125 ml (3½-4 fl oz) brandy

Put the peaches in boiling water for 2-3 minutes. Drain and peel them carefully.

Stud each with a clove.

Put the water, sugar, cinnamon stick and mace or nutmeg in a deep pan, and bring to the boil, stirring until the sugar has dissolved completely.

Add the peaches to this syrup and cook them gently for about 15-20 minutes, making sure that they are completely covered by the syrup during that time. The cooking ensures that the fruit will not discolour while it matures in the jar.

Lift the peaches carefully into a wide-mouthed, screw-top jar.

Remove the cinnamon stick from the syrup and stir in the brandy. Pour the syrup over the peaches and leave them to cool before covering tightly with the screw top. Stand in a cool place and keep for 3 days before using.

SERVING SUGGESTION Serve the spiced peaches in individual glass bowls and pass around a jug of pouring cream or a bowl of whipped cream.

SPICED PEACHES *need time to absorb the heady brandy and spice flavour.*

FRUIT CRUMBLE

PERHAPS THE CRUMBLE was considered too lowly to be awarded a place in standard cookery books, for though it has been a firm family favourite for many years, the first recorded appearance of this crumbled pastry is in an American recipe dating back only to the 1940s. There it is described as a 'crunch' which is used as a topping for a 'candy pie' containing either apples or peaches.

PREPARATION TIME: 20 MINUTES
COOKING TIME: 45 MINUTES
PREHEAT OVEN TO 180°C (350°F, MARK 4)

INGREDIENTS FOR SIX
700 g (1½ lb) fruit of your choice
75 g (3 oz) granulated or brown
  sugar
2 tablespoons water

For the crumble:
175 g (6 oz) flour
¼ teaspoon salt
75 g (3 oz) butter
75 g (3 oz) caster sugar

Prepare the fruit. Put it in layers in an 850 ml (1½ pint) pie dish and sprinkle each layer with the sugar; then add the water.

Sieve the flour and mix it with the salt in a large mixing bowl. Rub in the butter lightly with your fingertips until the mixture resembles fine breadcrumbs. Stir in the caster sugar and mix well.

Spread the flour mixture over the fruit, covering it completely. Immediately place the dish in the oven and cook for 45 minutes, or until golden-brown.

SERVING SUGGESTIONS Serve with fresh whipped cream and custard.

VARIATIONS Instead of all flour in the recipe, use half wholewheat and half porridge oats, or half flour and half muesli breakfast cereal.

For a nut crumble, use three-quarters flour and one-quarter chopped nuts.

Vary the fruit, using poached apricot halves, lightly cooked rhubarb segments, thinly sliced apples flavoured with cinnamon, or poached plums.

If you are using fruit that has been cooked and sweetened already, you will not need to add water or sugar before covering with the crumble topping. Try flavouring the fruit filling with wine or port (very good with plums).

ORIENTAL FRUIT SALAD

THIS IS AN IDEAL DESSERT for a Chinese menu. The ginger gives this fruit salad a refreshing tangy flavour.

PREPARATION TIME: 10 MINUTES

INGREDIENTS FOR SIX
1 tin (about 575 g/1¼ lb) lychees
1 tin (about 350 g/11 oz) mandarin
  oranges (or tangerines)
Juice of 1 lemon
Juice of 1 orange
2 tablespoons chopped ginger in
  syrup

Drain the tinned lychees and mandarin oranges (or tangerines) well, and place the fruit in a bowl with the lemon juice, orange and ginger. Chill before serving.

RUM AND CHOCOLATE GÂTEAU

THIS DELICIOUS, RICH fridge cake is appealing to both the eye and palate, and has the advantage of being easy to make.

PREPARATION TIME: 45 MINUTES
CHILLING TIME: OVERNIGHT

INGREDIENTS FOR SIX
50 g (2 oz) sugar
3 tablespoons water
2 tablespoons rum
100 g (3¾ oz) plain dark chocolate
100 g (3¾ oz) butter
100 g (3¾ oz) icing sugar, sifted
4 egg yolks
18 sponge fingers

For the garnish:
Grated chocolate
Chopped walnuts (optional)

Dissolve the sugar in the water, then simmer for 5 minutes. Take off the heat and add the rum. Melt the chocolate in a bowl over a basin of gently simmering water, stirring from time to time.

Cream the butter with the icing sugar, then beat in the egg yolks, a little at a time. Stir in the melted chocolate.

To assemble the cake, divide the sponge fingers into three lots of 6 each. Dip the biscuits (one or two at a time) into the warm syrup, letting them soak for a moment.

Arrange a neat row of 6 biscuits on a serving dish and spread with a layer of the chocolate cream. Cover with a second layer of soaked biscuits and another of chocolate cream. Top with a final layer of biscuits and any remaining syrup.

Spread the rest of the chocolate cream over the top and around the sides of the cake. Decorate with grated chocolate and chopped walnuts (if used), and chill overnight. Cut into thin slices and serve with cream. The slices will have a pretty striped appearance. As this is a rich dessert, serve with a fresh fruit salad.

NECTARINE FOOL WITH PISTACHIO NUTS

ALTHOUGH THIS RECIPE calls for nectarines, you may replace them with other fruit in season, such as strawberries, peaches or apricots.

PREPARATION TIME: 20 MINUTES
CHILLING TIME: 2 HOURS

INGREDIENTS FOR FOUR
4-5 large, very ripe nectarines
1 tablespoon lemon juice
¼ teaspoon ground cinnamon
250 ml (9 fl oz) cream
2 tablespoons caster sugar
50 g (2 oz) pistachio nuts, chopped
  (preferably unsalted)

Place the nectarines in a bowl, cover with boiling water and leave for 30 seconds to loosen the skins. Drain the fruit and cover with cold water: the skins will now peel off easily.

Quarter the fruit and mix immediately with the lemon juice (to prevent discoloration) and cinnamon. Blend the fruit to a smooth purée, and pour into a glass bowl. Cover with plastic wrap and chill for at least 2 hours.

Whip the cream with the sugar until it holds soft peaks, then fold the cream into the fruit purée, mixing gently.

Spoon the nectarine fool into individual serving dishes and sprinkle with chopped unsalted pistachio nuts.

Unsalted pistachio nuts are sometimes hard to obtain. If you are able to buy only salted ones, shell them and allow to stand in boiling water for 10 minutes. Then peel off the skins and dry the nuts in a 120°C (250°F, mark ½) oven for 15 minutes or longer, if necessary.

PECAN PIE

THIS DISH, with its buttery, sweet filling, is sometimes referred to as 'Southern pecan pie', because it was invented in the southern part of the United States, where pecan nuts are in plentiful supply.

PREPARATION TIME: 15 MINUTES FOR THE PASTRY; 10 MINUTES FOR THE FILLING
CHILLING TIME: 30 MINUTES FOR THE PASTRY
COOKING TIME: 50 MINUTES
PREHEAT OVEN TO 180°C (350°F, MARK 4)

INGREDIENTS FOR SIX TO EIGHT
Shortcrust pastry* using 225 g
   (½ lb) flour
125 ml (4 fl oz) melted butter
200 g (7 oz) sugar
250 ml (9 fl oz) golden syrup or
   maple syrup
A pinch of salt
4 eggs, lightly beaten
100 g (3¾ oz) pecan nuts

Line a 26 cm (10½ in) pie dish with the pastry, fluting the edges, and chill the pastry case for 30 minutes.

To make the filling, combine the butter, sugar, syrup and salt. Stir in the eggs and nuts and pour the mixture into the prepared pie shell.

Bake for 50 minutes, or until a knife inserted in the centre comes out clean.

SERVING SUGGESTION Serve at room temperature with unsweetened cream, or with a scoop of vanilla ice cream*.

BABA AU RHUM

THIS FAMOUS FRENCH dessert has found favour the whole world over. It is said to have been the creation of a Polish king who named it after his favourite hero in the Tales of a Thousand and One Nights. More precisely, what the creator of this dish did was to invent a new way of serving kugelhupf, an old, well-established central European cake, by soaking it in a rum syrup.

PREPARATION TIME: 25 MINUTES
RISING TIME: 1½ HOURS
COOKING TIME: 20 MINUTES FOR THE BABAS; 40 MINUTES FOR THE SYRUP
PREHEAT OVEN TO 200°C (400°F, MARK 6)

BABA AU RHUM A French favourite redolent with rum.

INGREDIENTS FOR EIGHT TO TEN
1 tablespoon dried yeast, or 25 g
   (1 oz) fresh yeast
60 ml (2 fl oz) lukewarm milk
A pinch of sugar
250 g (9 oz) flour, sifted
4 eggs, lightly beaten
¾ teaspoon salt
1 tablespoon sugar
180 g (6 oz) soft butter
120 g (¼ lb) currants

For the rum syrup:
200 g (7 oz) sugar
375 ml (13 fl oz) water
125 ml (4 fl oz) rum

Mix the yeast with the milk and add the pinch of sugar. Allow to stand for 10 minutes, or until frothy.

Place the flour in a large mixing bowl and make a well in the centre. Add the eggs, salt, the 1 tablespoon sugar and the yeast mixture. Mix this well and then beat it in the bowl for a few minutes. Cover and allow to rise in a warm place until it is double in bulk. This will take

about 45 minutes or a little longer.

Stir down the mixture and add the butter and currants. Beat it in the bowl for another 4 minutes. Fill 8-10 well-greased muffin or dariole moulds to one-third full and allow to rise until the batter doubles again in bulk (about 45 minutes).

Bake for 15 minutes. Reduce the heat to 180°C (350°F, mark 4) and bake until the babas are golden-brown. Turn them out onto a wire rack and cool them until they are lukewarm.

While they are cooling, make the rum syrup. Simmer the sugar and water together for 35-40 minutes, or until the liquid is syrupy. Add the rum.

Place the babas in a deep dish, prick them all over with a skewer and pour the hot rum syrup over them. Baste them until most of the syrup is absorbed.

SERVING SUGGESTION Serve at room temperature with whipped cream.

VARIATION Omit the currants and bake the dough in a round-bottomed ring mould – the dish is then called a savarin.

THE PRACTICAL COOK

COOKING IS NOT SO MUCH a science as it is an art. As with any artistic endeavour, the success of one's efforts depends on skill, ability, and the mastery of basic techniques. Here you will find useful information on those important basics: advice on selecting the freshest of ingredients, preparing essential stocks and soups, perfecting sauces and pastry – even making your own pasta and growing bean sprouts. There is also a guide to the herbs and spices most commonly used in the recipes and there are charts giving the appropriate cooking times for cuts of meat, poultry and game birds. The following pages will act as a useful reminder, whatever your level of experience.

STOCKS

Whatever soup you are making, it will taste better if its base is a homemade stock. Stock is the liquid in which meat and vegetables have been cooked, and which has taken in their flavour. Sauces and gravies are also improved when made with good stock.

Making your own stock is simple and straightforward: you can use scraps of meat, bones, poultry carcasses, vegetable trimmings and leftovers that might otherwise be thrown away.

Most stock needs long simmering to produce the best flavour. Make it in a large, heavy-based saucepan with a well-fitting lid. A pressure cooker will reduce the amount of time and fuel needed to make the stock, while a slow-cooking pot will reduce the amount of electricity used.

MAIN TYPES OF STOCK

Choose the stock that best suits the dish you are making. Many ingredients will give your stock flavour, but its greatest nutritional value comes from gelatine. The best source of this is bones: there is eight times as much gelatine in bone as in meat. To extract the most goodness, break up the bones to expose as much of their surface to the liquid as possible. Break them yourself with a hammer, or ask a butcher to do it for you. Simmer the bones until they are pitted with small holes. They will give an even better flavour if they are roasted for half an hour before being simmered.

Household stock

For use as an economical all-round base in family soups and dishes. Use cooked and uncooked scraps of meat, bones and poultry carcasses, giblets, meat juices, gravy and pieces of fresh vegetables or clean peelings.

Chicken and other poultry stock

For use in soups and casseroles. Use a raw or cooked carcass, the trimmings and giblets. Do not use the liver, however, as it can impart a bitter flavour.

For making small amounts of stock, use the giblets alone, barely covered with water and flavoured with onion and seasonings. Simmer for 1 hour.

Chinese chicken stock

This distinctively flavoured stock is used in a variety of Chinese soups and other dishes.

PREPARATION TIME: 15 MINUTES
COOKING TIME: 2¼ HOURS

INGREDIENTS TO YIELD 2 LITRES (3½ PINTS)
1 chicken
3 litres (5½ pints) cold water
2 or 3 slices fresh green ginger
6 spring onions, sliced

Place the well-washed chicken in a large pot. Add the water and quickly bring to the boil on high heat. Remove any scum, then reduce the heat, add the ginger and spring onions and allow to simmer (covered) for at least 2 hours. Strain and reserve the chicken meat for another use.

If you prefer, concentrate the stock by boiling to reduce it by half – allow the stock to cool before refrigerating. Remove any fat and impurities before using. The fat will settle on the surface as the stock cools and any other impurities will sink to the bottom.

Fish stock

For use in fish soups and sauces. Use fish heads, skins and trimmings, or cheap white fish. Do not use oily fish.

PREPARATION TIME: 15 MINUTES
COOKING TIME: 40 MINUTES

INGREDIENTS TO YIELD 1.5 LITRES (52 FL OZ)
1 kg (2¼ lb) fish heads, bones and trimmings
1 onion, peeled and sliced*
1 carrot, sliced
1 stalk celery, chopped
Bouquet garni*
1.5 litres (52 fl oz) water
125 ml (4 fl oz) dry white wine (optional)
1 teaspoon salt

Rinse the fish bits and pieces very well before placing in a saucepan with the vegetables, herbs, water and wine. Add the salt. Bring gently to the boil.

Remove the scum as it rises. When there is no scum left, half-cover the saucepan and simmer for about 30 minutes. Strain the stock and leave it to cool completely before refrigerating or freezing. If stored in small quantities, the stock will dissolve more easily.

Clear stock

For use as a clear soup. Use only fresh uncooked meat and vegetables. Simmer the meat (such as shin of beef or chicken) for 3 hours before adding the vegetables. It is essential to make this stock in advance so that every particle of fat can be removed when it has set.

Brown stock

For use in brown meat or vegetable soups, and in casseroles and sauces. Use the same ingredients as you would for a basic household or vegetable stock, but fry the solid ingredients lightly in a little butter or dripping until golden-brown before adding to the liquid. Heat the fat first, so that the surface of the meat or vegetables is sealed as soon as it touches the pan, and does not absorb too much fat.

White stock

For use as the basis of a white cream soup, or in chicken, rabbit and veal dishes. White stock is also used in dishes that require jellied stock. Use the knuckle and feet of veal (first plunge them into boiling water for 2-3 minutes to ensure that they are thoroughly clean) and, if possible, some chicken meat to add extra flavour.

A basic stock

You can vary what type of bones and meat you use in the following recipe to suit what you have available and which dish you are making. Keep the proportions of roughly 500 g (1 lb 2 oz) solid ingredients to 2 litres (3½ pints) liquid. This will make about 1 litre (1¾ pints) stock. For a larger amount, increase all the ingredients keeping the same proportions.

PREPARATION TIME: 15 MINUTES
COOKING TIME: 5¼ HOURS

INGREDIENTS TO YIELD 1 LITRE (1¾ PINTS)
500 g (1 lb 2 oz) bones and meat (beef, poultry and so on)
2 litres (3½ pints) cold water
1 teaspoon salt
2 large carrots, well scrubbed and cut into large pieces
1 large onion, peeled* and halved
2 stalks celery, well washed

If you wish to intensify the flavour and colour of the stock, roast the bones before use.

Cut the meat into large even-sized cubes. Place the meat and bones in a large, heavy-based saucepan with water and salt. Bring slowly to the boil and remove any white scum that forms on the surface. Cover with a well-fitting lid and simmer gently for 3 hours. Add the carrots, onion and celery, cover again and simmer for another 2 hours.

Strain through a sieve, taste, and if the stock lacks flavour, boil it rapidly to reduce its volume and concentrate its flavour. Pour into a bowl, and allow to get quite cold. Remove any fat from the surface with a slotted spoon. Cover the bowl and store in a refrigerator. Use the stock within 1 week, or freeze it.

Vegetable stock
To make this simple vegetable stock, use well washed stalks and vegetable peelings which you would normally throw away. Avoid cabbage and cauliflower leaves and stalks, as these impart a very strong flavour when boiled. Store vegetable trimmings and offcuts in a plastic bag in the refrigerator until you have 1 kg (2¼ lb) or more. The stock provides a good base for delicious soups and sauces. Store it in convenient-sized quantities in the freezer.

PREPARATION TIME: 20 MINUTES
COOKING TIME: 1 HOUR

2 *medium-sized onions, cut in half but not peeled*
2 *medium-sized carrots, scrubbed and cut in half lengthways*
2 *stalks celery, broken into short lengths (and a few celery leaves)*
2 *teaspoons salt*
2 *teaspoons black peppercorns*
Large bouquet garni* which includes 2 bay leaves
2 *tablespoons soy sauce*
Vegetable trimmings such as:
Tips of green beans and courgettes (zucchini)
Pea pods
Spinach and parsley stems
Carrot ends (especially green tops)
Trimmed ends of leeks
Brussels sprout trimmings
Turnip, swede or parsnip trimmings
Potato peelings

Place the onions, carrots, celery and vegetable trimmings in a large saucepan

and cover generously with water. Add the salt, peppercorns, bouquet garni and soy sauce, cover and simmer for 45 minutes. Cool and strain; the stock is now ready for use or for freezing.

STORING STOCK
Most stocks can be kept covered in a refrigerator for up to 1 week. If you have a freezer you can prepare any kind of stock in bulk and divide it into suitable quantities for freezing. Stock loses flavour if stored in a freezer for more than 2-3 months. Never freeze a fish stock for longer than 2 months. If your freezer space is limited, reduce stocks by half before you freeze them

and make up with water when you want to use them in a recipe. Always bring all stocks to the boil before they are used, no matter which way they have been stored.

REMOVING THE FAT
If you intend to cook and use the stock on the same day, try to make it a few hours in advance to give it time to cool so that any fat that has risen to the top can solidify: it is then easy to lift off the layer of fat. If you wish to use the stock immediately, let it stand for a few minutes so that the fat rises to the surface, then draw paper towels across the surface to absorb the fat.

ESSENTIAL POINTS IN STOCK-MAKING

- All ingredients must be fresh and well-cleaned.
- Use a heavy-based saucepan with a well-fitting lid.
- Cook bones and meat for 2-3 hours before adding vegetables. Once the vegetables are cooked they will start absorbing the flavour from the liquid, so do not leave them in the liquid for too long either during or after cooking.
- Do not cook fish stock for more than 45 minutes.
- Use a balanced mixture of vegetables so that none predominates.
- Cook vegetables in large pieces.
- Do not use too many green vegetables, or the stock will have a bitter taste.
- Use herbs and spices in very small amounts. If you add too much, the stock

is almost certain to taste bitter.
- Avoid starchy ingredients, such as potato or thickened gravy, which can make the stock cloudy and can give it a sour taste.
- Do not use the liquid in which bacon or salt beef has been cooked for stock, because it is much too salty.
- Remove any white scum that rises during cooking, but do not remove brown scum; this is nourishing protein that has set in the hot liquid.
- As soon as the stock is cooked, strain it into a clean china or plastic bowl. Leave it to cool and skim off the fat before storing in a refrigerator or freezer.
- Never keep stock standing in a saucepan. It will develop a sour flavour and stain the saucepan.

SOUPS

Choose your soup to complement the rest of the meal. A hearty soup would be welcome before a light main course, but not before a substantial casserole. Avoid serving a fish soup before a main fish dish, for example, or a tomato soup before a dish flavoured with tomatoes. Soups can also provide satisfying low-fat meals for slimmers.

THIN SOUPS
Among the variety of thin soups are some which are absolutely clear liquids; this type of soup is usually called a consommé. Chicken and beef are the ingredients most used as a base. A clear

soup should have a clean, sparkling quality, and should be free of fat. Its clean, pure flavour and lightness make it an excellent beginning to a rich or heavy meal.

The Japanese are particularly fond of thin, clear soups, served with delicate garnishes. Try a light fish stock garnished with a single butterflied prawn and a few shavings of lemon rind for decoration.

To prepare the prawn for the garnish, first remove the head and shell the prawn, leaving the last tail section intact. Now turn the prawn into a butterfly by running a sharp knife down the middle (without cutting right through the flesh) and opening it out. Salt the prawn, dip it lightly in cornflour, then drop it into rapidly boiling water until just cooked. Dip into iced water and pat dry before adding the prawn to the soup.

Thin soups are not always clear. Even a consommé sometimes has a few spoons of cooked peas or carrot added to it. Others are broths in which the liquid is unthickened, but has pieces of vegetable or meat in it. Cock-a-leekie, Borshch and onion soup are all thin soups, even though they are not clear. If you find this kind of soup is not thin enough when cooked, add clear stock or a little wine.

THICK SOUPS

There are many more thick soups than thin – perhaps because their satisfying and substantial nature gives them a broad appeal.

Thickened broths have pieces of vegetable and meat in a liquid thickened with flour or a grain such as pearl barley. Thick vegetable soups include those based on fresh vegetables and dried pulses.

Most thick soups need a thickening or binding agent; without this the solid ingredients would sink to the bottom. A thickener is known as a liaison, from the French verb *lier* which means 'to bind'. Liaisons include:

Some form of starch, such as flour, cornflour, arrowroot, sago, pearl barley, semolina, oatmeal or potato.
Fat and flour in equal quantities heated gently together and mixed to a thick, smooth paste called a roux.
Egg yolks mixed with cream, a little stock, or milk.
Cream, which is usually added to smooth, rich or white soups.

If using flour (or cornflour) as the liaison, mix it first to a smooth, thin cream with a little of the soup liquid, milk or water. Then stir it into the soup in the pan and continue to stir while cooking gently for at least 5 minutes.

A liaison of egg yolks should be added to the soup just before serving. Beat the yolks well in a cup or small basin, and stir in several spoons of liquid from the soup. Remove the soup from the heat while you stir in the egg mixture.

Return the soup to the heat to make sure that it is heated through for serving; stir continuously and take great care not to let the soup boil again, or it will curdle.

Cold soups are popular during the summer and can be made from raw ingredients. Gazpacho, for example, is made from raw cucumbers, peppers, garlic and onions and tomato juice.

Many hot soups can successfully be served cold, though small modifications in preparation may be required. For instance, when serving a cold purée it is often a good idea to add cream: this will enrich the purée and will also help to dilute it.

Fatty soups should not be served cold, however, since the fat will congeal when the liquid cools.

Texture

Aim for an even texture in thick soups other than broths, but take care not to make the soup too smooth. A blender will save time in preparing a thick soup, but can give a rather bland, emulsified result. Rubbing through a sieve or passing through a food mill produces a more interesting, slightly grainy texture in the soup. If using a food processor, strain the soup, then process the vegetables to form a thick purée. Mix with the reserved liquid until smooth.

When you make a fish soup, do not overcook it, or the delicate texture of the fish will be spoiled.

Flavour

An appetising taste and aroma are a soup's most important features. The best guarantee of these is to start with a well-flavoured stock, but if your finished soup is a little short of flavour you can add some reduced stock or meat glaze, small amounts of herbs or spices, tomato paste, or use concentrated onion.

Peel and slice an onion, dust it with some flour and then fry it in a little butter until it is well browned. Rub the slices through a sieve and add to the soup, a little at a time, until the flavour is correct.

Some soups benefit from the addition of soy sauce (either during the cooking time or swirled into each serving) or of a little sherry or other liquor. Experiment by removing a small amount of the soup from the pot and adding the flavouring to that, rather than ruin the entire pot with an ingredient that you find does not work.

Pistou can be served as a flavour-enhancing accompaniment to chunky, hot vegetable soup. Pound 4 fat cloves of garlic with 6 tablespoons chopped basil leaves, 4 tablespoons tomato paste and 4 tablespoons grated Parmesan cheese to a paste. Gradually add 60-125 ml (2-4 fl oz) olive oil. Add a spoonful or two of pistou to each serving at the table.

The flavour of fish soup can be enhanced by adding a spoonful of aïoli* to each serving. Alternatively, make a paste by pounding together $\frac{1}{4}$ tinned pimiento or a cooked red pepper with a red chilli, 4 fat cloves of garlic (crushed) and a cooked potato. Once it forms a smooth, thick paste, gradually add 60 ml (2 fl oz) olive oil and seasoning. Just before serving, thin the mixture down with a few spoonfuls of the hot fish soup. Again, add a spoonful or two of this spicy sauce to each serving at the table.

If you over-salt a soup by mistake, cook a peeled potato in it until tender (not broken), then lift the potato out – it will have absorbed much of the salt. If you make a soup which you wish to freeze, do not season it. Salt and pepper increase in strength when frozen, so it is preferable to add them when you reheat the soup.

SERVING SOUPS

A hot soup will lose flavour as it cools, and any fat in it will float to the top, so always serve in heated bowls.

A cold soup, such as gazpacho, should be thoroughly chilled to achieve a refreshing effect. In hot weather add one or two ice cubes to the soup before you serve it.

More seasoning is usually needed in a cold soup, because cold foods tend to have less flavour than hot foods. Add a little lemon juice to sharpen the taste.

Try a tablespoon of cream swirled on each serving and sprinkle with a pinch of cayenne pepper or paprika to add extra colour. Freshly chopped herbs also make good garnishes.

SOUP GARNISHES

Garnishes are added to soups either as an embellishment to improve the flavour or appearance or to provide a contrasting texture.

There is virtually no end to the type of ingredient which you can use for garnishing. Sometimes the garnish is integral to the recipe, but it is often just a matter of taste.

Consommé julienne, for example, is garnished with julienne strips of carrot, celery, leek and turnip. These strips are boiled until soft in lightly salted water, then rinsed in cold water and added to hot consommé before serving.

Vegetable and fruit garnishes

Vegetable and fruit garnishes add colour to plain cream soups. Celery leaves, watercress and parsley should be trimmed and washed before floating them on top of the soup.

Cucumber may be cut into julienne strips as a garnish for chilled soups. For hot soups, sauté cucumber strips or thin rounds of leeks in a little butter.

A garnish of thinly sliced mushrooms lends additional texture and flavour to cream soups. Fry the sliced mushrooms in a little butter until soft, but not coloured. Drain thoroughly before spooning them over the soup.

Thin onion rings add flavour to soups. Sauté or, alternatively, coat them in milk and flour, and deep fry until crisp and golden.

Add texture to a clear, homemade consommé by shredding lettuce or spinach and simmering in the soup for barely a minute to soften the vegetable slightly. Serve immediately.

Egg garnishes

Consommé royale is a garnish of firm savoury egg custard cut into tiny fancy shapes. Beat an egg with 1 tablespoon clear stock and pour into a small bowl or dariole moulds. Bake the moulds in a pan of water for 20 minutes (or until firm), in the centre of an oven preheated to 180°C (350°F, mark 4).

Another egg garnish for a clear consommé can be made as follows: beat an egg and pour it into a lightly oiled omelette pan. Cook until lightly browned, turn and lightly brown the other side. Roll the omelette up loosely, cut into thin ribbons and scatter them over the soup just before serving.

For a threadlike egg garnish in consommé, beat 1 or 2 eggs and pour into the boiling soup through a strainer. The egg threads will float when they are cooked. Do not overcook after the egg has been added or the egg will become rubbery.

Noodle garnishes

Pasta is used to garnish many thin soups. Macaroni, tagliatelle and spaghetti can be broken into short pieces and added to soup purées for the last 20 minutes of cooking. For hot consommés, the pasta should be cooked separately so that the starch will not cloud the soup.

Bread and cheese garnishes and accompaniments

Cheese makes a pleasant accompaniment to most vegetable soups. Choose a well-flavoured cheese, and serve it, grated, in a separate dish.

Bread croûtons are a classic garnish with thick soups. Remove the crusts from 1 cm ($\frac{1}{2}$ in) thick slices of white bread; cut into 1 cm ($\frac{1}{2}$ in) cubes and toast or fry in a little butter until crisp and golden. Serve in a separate dish or sprinkled over the soup.

Cheese toasts not only make a good garnish for a vegetable soup, they also turn it into an adequate meal in itself. Slice a French loaf and brush both sides of the slices with melted butter. Slowly toast the slices under the grill until golden. Sprinkle them with grated cheese and float the toasts on the soup. They can also be returned to the grill for a few minutes until the cheese melts.

For a fish soup, try hard-toasted French bread: slice a French loaf and bake the slices in a single layer at 160°C (325°F, mark 3) for 20-30 minutes until pale golden and dried out. You can drizzle the slices with olive oil half-way through the baking time. After baking, rub the slices with cut cloves of garlic.

For consommé, you could cut a few pancakes into thin shreds and add them to the simmering soup for a few minutes until they are heated through. If you like, add some chopped fresh herbs to the pancake batter.

Melba toast is made by toasting thin slices of white bread, splitting them through the middle, and then toasting them again on the uncooked surfaces. Alternatively, cut stale bread into very thin slices. Place them on a baking tray and dry them in the bottom of the oven until crisp and curling at the edges.

Dumplings

Dumplings are ideal for turning a meat or vegetable soup into a substantial family meal. The variety of dumplings is almost endless. The following basic recipes can be changed by simply adding herbs or spices to complement the flavour of your soup. Enhance a vegetable soup by adding a little finely chopped bacon to the dumpling dough.

Mix 100 g ($3\frac{3}{4}$ oz) self-raising flour with 50 g (2 oz) shredded suet and a sprinkling of salt and pepper. Bind the mixture with sufficient cold water to make a soft dough. Shape the dough into 16 balls and drop them into the simmering soup for the last 15-20 minutes of cooking.

For another simple dumpling soup, cream a little butter, beat in 1 or 2 eggs and add nutmeg, salt and a small quantity of breadcrumbs. Next, add just enough flour to bind the dough, which should have the consistency of pancake batter. Place the dumplings in the soup with a teaspoon. (This would be suitable for bean or pea soup).

SAVOURY SAUCES

Sauces have been used for many centuries – although the reasons for their use have changed through the ages. In the past rich sauces were often employed to disguise the flavour of meat or fish that was less than fresh.

Some sauces are traditionally served with certain dishes because they naturally complement each other: apple sauce tempers the sweetness of pork; mint sauce counters the fattiness of lamb. Sauces can also be used as a foundation – to bind croquettes or rissoles, for example.

The most common sauces are those thickened with a roux – a blend of fat and flour – but they can be thickened in other ways using cornflour or arrowroot, eggs, butter or oil, or by reducing over heat.

Flavour sauces carefully so that they do not overpower the individual taste of the dish but retain their own distinctive taste.

SAUCES THICKENED WITH A ROUX

A roux consists of equal quantities of fat and flour, blended together and cooked for a few minutes over a gentle heat. The length of cooking depends on whether you want a white or brown sauce for your recipe.

The proportion of fat and flour to liquid varies according to the consistency required – thin enough for pouring or thicker for coating and binding ingredients together.

The recipes for basic brown, Espagnole, white and béchamel sauces are for pouring sauces.

Basic Brown Sauce

A basic brown sauce is used to accompany many dishes. Gravy can also be made in this way.

INGREDIENTS TO YIELD 600 ML
(ABOUT 1 PINT)
40 g (1½ oz) butter
40 g (1½ oz) flour
600 ml (21 fl oz) brown stock*

Melt the butter in a heavy-based saucepan, then draw the pan off the heat and mix in the flour smoothly with a wooden spoon or spatula.

Stir continuously over a gentle heat for 2-3 minutes until you have a thick paste. Cook for a further 3-4 minutes to a light chestnut-brown.

Remove the pan from the heat and add the warm, strained stock, stirring all the time. When the mixture is thoroughly blended, return the saucepan to the heat and bring to boiling point, stirring continuously.

Cook gently for 5-7 minutes, stirring from time to time, until the sauce is smooth and well-blended.

Espagnole Sauce

This rich, brown sauce is the basis of many other sauces to accompany meat. Different versions can include mushrooms, onions, red wine, Marsala, tomatoes, brandy or jellied veal stock.

INGREDIENTS TO YIELD 500 ML (17 FL OZ)
1 rasher bacon, diced
1 tablespoon sunflower oil
1 small onion, peeled and finely chopped*
1 carrot, scraped and diced
1 stalk celery, diced
2 teaspoons flour
1 teaspoon tomato paste
500 ml (17 fl oz) brown stock*
1 bouquet garni*, or ½ teaspoon dried mixed herbs
Salt and pepper

Gently fry the diced bacon in the oil. Add the onion, carrot and celery. Stir in the flour and cook the mixture for 6-8 minutes, or until golden-brown.

Remove from the heat and stir in the tomato paste and stock. Bring to the boil, add the bouquet garni and season to taste. Reduce the heat to a simmer and cook, covered, for 15-20 minutes. Strain and skim off any fat.

White Sauce

This basic recipe can be used with various flavourings to make sauces for vegetables, poultry, fish or egg dishes.

INGREDIENTS TO YIELD 600 ML
(ABOUT 1 PINT)
40 g (1½ oz) butter
40 g (1½ oz) flour
600 ml (21 fl oz) warm milk, or white* or chicken stock*

Melt the butter in a heavy-based saucepan, then draw the pan off the heat and mix in the flour smoothly with a wooden spoon or spatula. Stir continuously over a gentle heat for 2-3 minutes until it becomes a thick paste. Do not allow the roux to brown.

Remove the pan from the heat again and add the warm, strained liquid, stirring all the time. When the mixture is thoroughly blended, return the saucepan to the heat and bring it to boiling point, stirring continuously. Cook gently for 5-7 minutes, stirring from time to time, until the sauce is smooth and creamy.

Béchamel Sauce

Use the basic white sauce recipe, but before preparing put a small, peeled onion, a bay leaf, 2-3 cloves and peppercorns and a blade of mace in the saucepan with the milk. Heat gently, put the lid on the pan and leave to infuse for 5-10 minutes. Strain through a sieve before using.

Cream Sauce

Make a basic béchamel replacing part of the milk with cream, or enrich a velouté sauce with cream. Alternatively, use the pan in which you have sautéed meat or fish, add cream and stock or wine (off the heat), then reduce over a high heat until slightly thickened.

A cream sauce would go well with poached chicken or fish.

Binding Sauce

A binding sauce, also referred to as a panada, is used to bind meat, fish or poultry into croquettes. It is also the basis of many hot soufflés. Make a binding sauce in the same way you would a white sauce, but use about 120 g (4 oz) fat and about 120 g (4 oz) flour to 575 ml (1 pint) milk, or white or chicken stock.

Velouté Sauce

INGREDIENTS TO YIELD 150 ML (¼ PINT)
25 g (1 oz) butter
25 g (1 oz) flour
300 ml (½ pint) white stock*
Salt and freshly ground black pepper
1-2 tablespoons cream (optional)

Melt the butter in a heavy-based saucepan, then draw the pan off the heat and mix in the flour smoothly with a wooden spoon or spatula. Stir continuously over a gentle heat for 2-3 minutes until it becomes a thick paste. Do not allow the roux to colour.

Remove the saucepan from the heat once again and gradually stir in the hot stock until the sauce has become quite smooth. When the mixture is thoroughly blended, return the saucepan to the heat and bring it up to boiling point, stirring continuously. Lower the heat, and allow the sauce to simmer gently for about 1 hour (or until it has reduced by half).

Stir the sauce occasionally. Strain through a sieve, season to taste, and stir in the cream (if used).

Suprême Sauce

This rich sauce is made by adding eggs and cream to 300 ml (½ pint) velouté sauce. Beat 2 egg yolks with 2 tablespoons thick cream. Add a little of the warm velouté sauce to the egg mixture, then add this blend to the remaining velouté sauce (off the heat). Stir in 25 g (1 oz) butter, cut into pieces, and serve immediately.

Coating Sauce

To make a coating sauce for dishes such as cauliflower cheese, use 50 g (2 oz) fat and 50 g (2 oz) flour to about 575 ml (1 pint) milk, or white or chicken stock. Make in the same way as white sauce.

Rescuing a roux-based sauce that has gone wrong

Too thick Dilute with a little milk, water or stock. Bring to the boil, stirring or whisking continuously, then remove from the heat.

Too thin Reduce by cooking rapidly, uncovered, for a few minutes. Stir or whisk continuously until the consistency is correct, then remove the pan from the heat.

Lumpy Remove the pan from the heat and beat the sauce vigorously with a whisk for a few seconds. Alternatively, rub the sauce through a sieve or else put it through a blender.

OTHER THICKENINGS FOR SAUCES

Sauces thickened with cornflour
Like flour, cornflour is a reliable thickener. It is often used in Chinese stir-fried dishes and gives an attractive, glossy sauce. Use in small quantities and cook well so that the sauce is not dominated by a starchy taste. Add 1 teaspoon to 2 tablespoons cold water for 275-300 ml (9½-10 fl oz) liquid. Blend into a smooth paste and stir into the hot cooking liquid. Boil for 2-3 minutes, stirring all the time.

Sauces thickened with arrowroot
Arrowroot gives a clear thickness to a sauce. Use in the same way as cornflour but, after you bring the sauce to the boil, simmer for 2-3 minutes, remove from the heat and serve immediately. Arrowroot liquefies easily, and sauces and glazes incorporating it cannot be reheated.

Sauces thickened with beurre manié (kneaded butter)
This is a quick and easy way to thicken a sauce or soup. Use equal quantities of butter and flour – about 15 g (½ oz) of each to 275-300 ml (9½-10 fl oz) liquid. Soften the butter, blend with the flour and, just before serving, add in small pieces to the cooking liquid, whisking the sauce continuously.

Sauces thickened with eggs, butter or oil
Eggs, butter or oil are used as thickeners for sauces such as Hollandaise and mayonnaise. The ingredients are blended by whisking and beating. Make sure that all the ingredients are at room temperature before you start, or the sauce may curdle and separate.

Should mayonnaise curdle while you are adding the oil to the eggs, you may beat an egg yolk in a clean bowl, then beat the curdled mixture into the yolk, drop by drop.

When adding eggs or egg yolks to hot sauces – velouté, for example – first lightly beat the eggs (with the cream, if using) in a bowl. Add a little of the hot sauce to the egg to bring it to the same temperature as the sauce.

Remove the sauce from the heat and stir in the egg mixture with a wooden spoon. Return the sauce to the heat and heat gently over low heat until the sauce has thickened. Be careful not to boil or overcook the sauce, as the eggs will curdle.

Egg-based sauces should not be frozen, as they may separate when thawed. Most egg sauces – apart from mayonnaise – will not keep for longer than three days in the refrigerator.

Sauces thickened by reduction
A well-made sauce contributes flavour, texture and colour to a meal. The trend in nouvelle cuisine is to make sauces which depend on reduced liquids for concentrated flavour and thickening, rather than on the classic haute cuisine methods which use starchy thickeners such as flour.

Rich stocks with added cream are cooked until their flavours are concentrated and their consistency has thickened.

Supplementary thickening from puréed vegetables, eggs, nuts or butter may also be used.

TIPS FOR KEEPING AND REHEATING ROUX-BASED SAUCES

- Remove the sauce from the heat as soon as it is cooked.
- If the sauce is one that contains herbs, do not add them until the sauce is reheated, or their distinctive flavour will be reduced or lost.
- If a recipe specifies adding knobs of butter at the end of the cooking time, do this when reheating the sauce.
- A sauce which is being kept for reheating a little later can remain in the saucepan with a circle of wet greaseproof paper on top to prevent a skin from forming on the surface. Cover the pan with a lid.
- To reheat, remove the paper and put the pan over a gentle heat, or put the sauce in the top of a double boiler or in a bowl placed over simmering water. Stir or whisk the sauce continuously as it heats through, to avoid lumps.
- An alternative method of keeping a thick, roux-based sauce for a short time is to reserve about 50-100 ml (1½-3½ fl oz) of the liquid when making it. Once the sauce is cooked, carefully pour the reserved liquid on top of the sauce to prevent contact with air. When reheating the sauce, simply stir well to blend in the extra liquid.
- White sauces may be refrigerated or alternatively frozen in airtight containers or plastic bags. If the white sauce has been frozen, thaw it completely before reheating gently in the top of a double boiler or in a bowl placed over simmering water. Stir continuously to prevent lumps from forming. If lumps do form, follow the tips for rescuing a roux-based sauce that has gone wrong.

FATS AND OILS

Fats and oils play an important part in cooking, as they contribute to and sometimes alter the flavour of food – particularly when frying.

Fats
These are derived from animal tissue (for example, from meat, dairy products or oily fish) and also from nuts, seeds and vegetables.

Cooking fats that are commonly used include butter, blended fats, dripping, lard, margarine and suet.

Butter Made from the fatty substances skimmed from full-cream milk. It is churned, then pressed to squeeze out water, and salt is often added.

Butter is suitable as a cooking medium for egg dishes, sautéed vegetables and shallow-frying. Cakes and biscuits also benefit from being cooked with butter.

Melted butter Usually served as a sauce with poached fish or boiled vegetables. Heat the butter over low heat and season lightly with salt, freshly ground pepper and a few drops of lemon juice.

Beurre noisette (noisette butter) Melted butter which is allowed to brown lightly before being seasoned. It is served with eggs, brains, poached fish, fish roe or boiled vegetables.

Beurre noir (brown butter) Melted butter in this instance is heated until it becomes nut-brown, but not black. Add 2 tablespoons finely chopped parsley, 1 tablespoon wine vinegar and 1 tablespoon chopped capers to every 100 g (3¾ oz) butter. Serve with the same types of food as a *beurre noisette*.

Ghee This is a form of clarified butter, which is sometimes used in Indian cooking. Since it can be heated to a high temperature, ghee makes frying less troublesome, as butter in its conventional form burns rapidly. Another advantage is that it can be stored at room temperature for over six months; this is vital in India, where the heat can quickly make butter rancid.

Use 500 g (1 lb 2 oz) butter; this will yield about 350-400 g (12-14 oz) ghee. Put the butter in a deep saucepan, place it on the stove and bring to a gentle boil. Keep at a medium to low temperature and boil the liquid butter slowly for 15-20 minutes. The butter will bubble audibly as the water evaporates (however, once all the water has evaporated, the sound will cease).

At this stage a layer of scum will rise to the surface, the salt will settle at the bottom, and the clarified butter will settle in the middle. Place a steel, enamel or glass container on a flat surface nearby. Remove the ghee from the heat and blow the scum to one side of the saucepan.

Pour the clarified butter into the container, leaving the salt at the bottom of the saucepan. The ghee should be crystal-clear. Cool and store.

Commercially prepared ghee can be found in specialist shops, but may contain unwanted extra flavourings.

Clarified fat or dripping Add water to fat or dripping – about one-third as much water as fat. For example, for 250 g (9 oz) fat, use 80 ml (2½ fl oz) water. Bring the mixture to the boil, then strain it into a bowl and leave it to cool and solidify.

When cold and set, remove the cake of clarified fat and scrape any scum from the bottom.

Store in a dry bowl or jar. It will keep for up to three weeks in a refrigerator. Heat again to use for sealing dishes such as potted meats.

Crème fraîche To make crème fraîche, beat 250 ml (9 fl oz) cream with 250 ml (9 fl oz) sour cream in a bowl. Cover the mixture loosely with plastic wrap and leave it to stand overnight, or until it has thickened. Then refrigerate it for at least four hours to thicken it even further. The tart flavour of this sauce will intensify the longer it remains in the refrigerator.

Clarified butter Sometimes used in recipes for frying or grilling, or for sealing potted food. It is an expensive cooking medium, because 250 g (9 oz) butter only produces about 175 g (6 oz) clarified butter.

Put the butter in a saucepan and place the saucepan over a low heat to melt the butter completely. Skim off the foam as the butter heats.

The sediment will sink to the bottom. To make sure that it stays there, remove the pan from the heat and leave it to stand for 5 minutes. Then strain the butter through a double layer of scalded cheesecloth or fine cotton into a bowl.

If you are using the butter to seal potted meat or fish, allow to cool a little before pouring it over the surface.

Store clarified butter in pots marked with the date of preparation. It will keep for 3-4 weeks in a refrigerator or up to six months in a freezer.

Oils

There are several types of oil, differing in flavour and colour, and used for different purposes. Some commercial oils are blends sold as 'cooking oil' or 'salad oil'. The price varies considerably, depending on the demand and the cost of the refining process.

All-round oils, which can be used for cooking and salad dressings, are made from corn (maize), olives, peanuts (groundnuts), sesame seeds, soya beans or sunflower seeds.

Walnut and wheatgerm oil are particularly expensive. Both are used in small quantities in salad dressings for their distinctive flavours.

Making herb oils

Herb oils are delicious for use in salad dressings. Use a good-quality oil – preferably olive oil. Place sprigs of fresh herbs in an attractive glass jar. Thyme, tarragon and marjoram work particularly well. Pour the oil into the container, seal and leave for at least two months before using.

FISH

Fish is an excellent and still relatively inexpensive food, which will appeal to the health-conscious because it is easily digested, low in fat, and rich in high-grade protein, vitamins and minerals. Even fatty fish, such as mackerel, are rich in polyunsaturates, which inhibit cholesterol formation.

BUYING FRESH FISH

There is no mistaking the plumpness and firmness of really fresh fish. Scaly fish should have a sequin-like iridescence, and the eyes should be clear, bright and bulging. As a general rule, fresh fish are bright, with firm, springy flesh and tight skin. Stale fish – no matter how often they are hosed down – look grey, dull and limp, with blurred eyes, flabby flesh and often a tell-tale smell.

These guidelines are easy to apply to whole fish, but because much of the fish sold is already cut up or filleted, look for firm flesh and no more than a 'seaweedy' smell (a stronger smell means that the fish is past its prime).

Smoked fish should be plump and moist, with a glossy skin. There should be no unpleasant smell or traces of mould or mildew in the pack.

Shellfish are best bought alive, but as this is often impractical only buy from a reliable source. Choose crayfish, lobster and crabs that feel heavy and firm for their size. To check the freshness of a crayfish or lobster, ensure that the tail springs back sharply when it is flexed.

Oysters and mussels should always be tightly closed – a sign that they are alive. Never be tempted to buy oysters or mussels with half-open shells, and avoid shellfish with heavily encrusted shells (this is usually a sign of old age).

Frozen fish should be clean, neatly prepared and sealed into dry, 'frost-free' packets. Do not buy packets that are partly thawed.

PREPARING FISH

All fish, with the exception of anchovies and other very small fish, should be gutted and cleaned (most fishmongers will happily do this).

Cut off the spiky fins and, if the fish has scales, lay it on a few sheets of newspaper on a work-surface. Then, holding it by the tail with one hand, scrape away the scales with a short, blunt knife (working from the tail towards the head). Rinse the fish well under cold water.

If you prefer to do it the easy way, cook the fish with scales and skin intact, and carefully remove the skin before serving the fish.

The next step is to gut the fish. In a round fish, the entrails are in the belly, but in flat fish they lie in a cavity behind the head.

To gut a round fish, such as mackerel or pilchard, slit the fish with a sharp knife along the belly from behind the gills to just above the tail. Scrape out the entrails.

Rinse the fish in cold water and scrape away any traces of blood with a small, sharp knife. Cut off the head and tail (optional).

Flat fish, such as sole, are gutted by making a semicircular slit just behind the head on the dark skin side. Scrape out the entrails, then cut off the fins and skin, or fillet before cooking.

Skinning

Round fish are best cooked with the skin left intact: this keeps the flesh moist and tender (the fish are skinned and garnished before serving).

Alternatively, you can fillet the fish and, with the skin side of the fillet down, hold the tail end in one hand while easing the flesh carefully from the skin with a small, sharp knife (starting at the tail end).

A flat fish is also skinned from tail to head, but with the dark skin facing up. Make a slit just above the tail, then hold the tail while pulling the skin off (towards the head).

BONING AND FILLETING FISH

A fish cannot be completely boned without first being divided into fillets. When boning and filleting fish, it is advisable to use a special fish-filleting knife with a thin flexible blade. In the case of a round fish, start by scaling the fish, cutting off the fins, and removing the entrails. When boning and filleting a flat fish, scaling is unnecessary.

ROUND FISH

To fillet a round fish, hold the knife horizontal and slice down the backbone, from head to tail, so that the backbone is exposed. To remove the upper fillet, slice it just behind the gills, then, using stroking motions, cut the fillet carefully away from the ribs. Turn the fish over and repeat this process for the bottom fillet. If the fillets contain small bones near the centre, remove them with tweezers. Trim away any discoloured flesh and, if desired, skin the fillet.

To fillet a firm-fleshed round fish after cooking, place it on a serving board or platter and strip off the skin from just below the head to just above the tail. Using a pair of kitchen scissors, snip the backbone just behind the head and above the tail. With a sharp knife separate the flesh from the backbone, and carefully ease out the bone without damaging the shape of the fish.

FLAT FISH

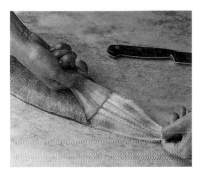

To fillet a flat fish, lay the fish dark side up on a board and cut a slit just above the tail. Carefully prise a flap of skin away from the flesh with a knife and pull the whole skin firmly away from the flesh all the way up to the head. Pull the skin over the head and then cut through the exposed flesh and bone, just behind the head, so that the head comes away but remains fully attached to the skin on the other side. Turn the fish over, and holding the head, continue pulling away the skin until you reach the tail, loosening with a knife if necessary.

Lay the skinned fish on a board and, holding the knife almost flat, cut down both sides of the backbone. With a stroking motion cut away the fillets on both sides of the backbone keeping the knife in contact with the bone. Turn the fish over and repeat the process. Remove any small bones.

COOKING METHODS FOR FISH

Coating

Always coat the fish before frying, to prevent it becoming greasy and soggy instead of crisp and delicious.

First dip the fish in a light coating of seasoned flour, oatmeal, batter, or egg and crumbs. Allow about 2 minutes' frying for each side, or fry until the fish is golden outside and opaque all the way through.

Shallow-frying

Choose a small whole fish or fillets for this cooking method and fry in a mixture of half sunflower oil and half butter. There should be about 5 mm ($\frac{1}{4}$ in) of fat in the pan – make sure that it is really hot before adding the fish.

It is best to thaw frozen fish before frying (unless it is already coated in crumbs or batter).

Deep-frying

Before adding the fish, test the oil by cooking a small cube of bread in it for 1 minute. The bread should turn golden-brown in this time – if it burns, the oil is too hot; if it becomes soggy, the oil is not hot enough.

The fryer should be only one-third full of oil. The fish should be at room temperature before frying; if colder, it will reduce the oil temperature too much and the fish will absorb oil.

Coat the fish portions with batter or egg and crumbs, and cook until golden. Before serving, lift out and drain well on crumpled paper towels to remove any excess oil.

Grilling

Line the pan with aluminium foil to prevent the fish flavour from clinging to the pan and preheat before starting.

Small, whole fish of about 250 g (9 oz) are best slashed 2-3 times on each side, then brushed with butter or sunflower oil and grilled for about 7 minutes on each side.

Whole sole and fillets should be brushed with butter, sprinkled with lemon juice and grilled for 2-6 minutes on each side.

Fish steaks of about 250 g (9 oz) should be buttered and grilled for 5-6 minutes on each side, basting once.

Leftover juices can be stirred with a little extra butter and a small glass of dry white wine or cream to make a delicious sauce. Garnish the fish with finely chopped parsley.

Poaching

Poaching means slowly simmering the fish in just enough liquid to cover it.

To make a basic cooking liquid (known as a court-bouillon), add the following peeled and chopped vegetables to a mixture of 250 ml (9 fl oz) dry white wine and 750 ml (26 fl oz) water: 2 carrots, 1 onion and 2 stalks celery. Add 3 parsley stalks, 2 sprigs thyme, 2 tablespoons lemon juice or vinegar, a bay leaf, salt and pepper.

Bring the court-bouillon to the boil, cover and simmer over a low heat for about 15 minutes. Leave to cool slightly and strain before using as a poaching liquid for the fish.

Alternatively, poach the fish in milk and water. Place the fish in a large saucepan or special fish kettle and cover completely with the poaching liquid. Bring to the boil over moderate heat, then cover the pan or kettle, lower the heat and simmer until done. The fish is ready as soon as it becomes opaque and flakes away from the bone.

To eat hot, drain and serve immediately with herb butter. For cold dishes, cool the fish completely in the poaching liquid before garnishing.

Steaming

Sprinkle the fish with lemon juice (this prevents discoloration on white fish) and wrap loosely in aluminium foil before lowering into a steamer. Alternatively, arrange the fish on a buttered dish set over a saucepan of boiling water, cover loosely and steam for 10-15 minutes – depending on the thickness of the fish.

Baking

To bake a whole fish, stuff the gutted fish with a mixture of sliced tomato, fresh herbs, lemon juice and a few breadcrumbs. Brush well with butter and bake at 190°C (375°F, mark 5) for about 30 minutes (cooking time depends on the size of the fish – allow less time for smaller, unstuffed fish).

Cooking in parcels

Fish cooked in aluminium foil retains its own juices and gives maximum flavour. Season well, dab with butter, wrap loosely in buttered foil and bake at 220°C (425°F, mark 7) for 15-40 minutes, depending on the size and thickness of the fish. Try sprinkling with herbs before baking.

TIPS FOR COOKING FISH

- To eat fish at its best, cook it the day you buy it. If this is not possible, sprinkle it with coarse salt and refrigerate to ensure it remains firm. Before cooking fish, rinse it quickly and wipe all surfaces with a clean damp cloth.
- Never overcook fish – it will toughen the flesh and destroy the flavour. Short, gentle cooking over a low heat gives the best results.
- Test for readiness by inserting a skewer. The fish is cooked when the flesh separates easily from the bone, or if boned, when a soft white liquid similar to curd oozes out.

- If you need to reheat fish that has already been cooked, it must be thoroughly heated through – to a temperature of 80°C (175°F). Finely slice, chop or mince the fish to allow the heat to penetrate. Reheat only once.
- Line the pan with aluminium foil when grilling fish. This prevents smells from clinging to the pan.
- When grilling fish whole, make two or three deep cuts on each side to help the heat penetrate.
- To prevent fish from sticking to the rack, brush with melted fat, butter or sunflower oil on both sides.

- Fried fish should be crisp, and free from grease. To prevent fat soaking into the fish always coat before frying.
- Do not overfill the pan when frying fish. The cold fish reduces the temperature of the cooking oil.
- When baking fish without foil, use moderate heat and baste occasionally to prevent it from drying out.
- Roll stuffed fillets of flat fish from head to tail with the skin side innermost before you bake them. This prevents the flesh from breaking.
- Simmer fish gently when poaching. Cooking too rapidly will break the skin before the flesh near the bone is cooked.

MEAT

Meat is the food richest in body-building proteins. The proteins are in the lean part of the meat – the muscle fibre and tissues of the animal. The fat in meat provides energy, while offal (the internal organs), particularly liver, is rich in vitamins.

The grade of meat does not affect its nutritional value, only its relative tenderness. The less tender parts of the carcass – the coarse-fibred meat – take longer to cook. Meat from older slaughter animals also tends to be tougher, but has generally developed a better flavour.

Fat provides both juiciness and flavour, but too much fat does not improve either quality. Lean meat has a protective layer of fat around it, and in mature animals the fat is distributed among the muscle fibres, giving a flecked appearance known as marbling.

Beef, lamb and mutton are best if allowed to ripen before being eaten. This allows the fibres in the meat to soften, making it more tender. If your butcher has not hung the meat, you can ripen it yourself in the refrigerator for 5-10 days for beef, 2-5 days for lamb and 5-7 days for mutton. Pork and veal are never ripened.

HINTS ON BUYING MEAT
Good beef is cherry red, lamb and mutton lighter red, and pork greyish-pink. The fat should be firm to the touch and creamy-white. Bone surfaces should be red and porous where they have been sawn, and rib bones should have red flecks. The cartilage between the vertebrae should be white, soft and elastic to the touch.

Meat is sold on or off the bone. If you want your butcher to prepare a special cut for a dinner party, such as a crown roast or saddle of lamb, give a few days' notice.

BEEF
The best beef is from slaughter animals at least 18 months old.

When buying beef, allow about 250-350 g (9-12 oz) per person if it contains bone, about 200-250 g (7-9 oz) boned joints, and 150-200 g (5-7 oz) steak. For an expensive fillet steak, however, allow about 115 g ($\frac{1}{4}$ lb).

Steaks
Steaks are small portions of the rump and sirloin of beef. They are tasty and tender, and suitable for grilling, barbecuing or frying. Steaks are among the more expensive cuts.

Chateaubriand About 3 cm (1$\frac{1}{4}$ in) thick, cut from the centre of the fillet or undercut of the sirloin.

Filet mignon Small, triangular pieces cut from the end of the fillet.

Fillet Slices from the fillet or undercut of the sirloin.

Minute steak Thin cuts of tenderised steak for pan frying.

Porterhouse About 2-2.5 cm ($\frac{3}{4}$-1 in) thick slice from the sirloin, which contains a small proportion of the fillet.

Rump Most people regard this as the most tasty steak. It is a cut, up to 3 cm (1$\frac{1}{4}$ in) thick, from the rump.

Sirloin or entrecôte About 2.5 cm ($\frac{3}{4}$ in) thick slice from the upper sirloin.

T-bone This steak takes its name from the small, T-shaped piece of bone in the cut, which is from the fillet end of the sirloin of beef.

Tenderising steak
To tenderise steak before grilling or barbecuing, place it between two sheets of wax paper and pound it with a wooden hammer for about a minute on each side. This breaks down the tissue.

Alternative methods are marinating or brushing the steak with lemon juice or a little wine vinegar.

VEAL
Veal is the meat from young calves. Because of the youth of the slaughter animal, the meat contains little fat, and the proportion of bone to meat is high. Veal bones are ideal for making aspics, as they contain large amounts of gelatinous matter.

Veal generally needs long cooking to make it tender, and has a bland flavour. Milk-fed veal is the most tender, but is very expensive and therefore sold mainly to restaurants.

Allow about 250 g (9 oz) veal per person if it contains bone, or 175 g (6 oz) if it is off the bone. Cook the meat as soon as possible after you buy it, as it does not keep well.

LAMB AND MUTTON
Lamb is the meat of a sheep 3-12 months old; mutton comes from older sheep. Lamb, the more tender, is also the more expensive but mutton has more flavour.

Buy 350 g ($\frac{3}{4}$ lb) lamb or mutton per person if it contains bones, or 200-250 g (7-9 oz) if it is boned.

PORK
Pork is the meat of young pigs. It has more fat than other meats and does not keep well. Pork must be cooked thoroughly, otherwise it can be dangerous to health.

Most pork is tender, and suitable for roasting. Ask your butcher to trim the fat layer to your preference and to score the fat (make cuts that penetrate it) of joints for roasting.

Allow 225-350 g ($\frac{1}{2}$-$\frac{3}{4}$ lb) per person of pork on the bone, 175 g (6 oz) if boned.

BACON, GAMMON AND HAM
Bacon pigs are larger than pork pigs and have less fat. Gammon and ham both come from the hindquarters of the bacon carcass.

Bacon is made by curing the meat in brine. Various methods can be used – salting the carcass, laying the meat in a brine bath, or injecting the meat with the brine. After brining, the meat is a greyish colour.

The bacon can then be heat-treated at 50°C (120°F) to develop a pink colour without cooking the meat. This unsmoked bacon is known as 'green bacon'. The meat may also be smoked, which gives it a darker colour and stronger flavour.

Gammon is cured and smoked in much the same way as bacon. Follow the cooking instructions that come with the gammon, as preparation depends on the method of curing used.

Ham is cured in a similar way. Commercial curers massage or tumble the meat in a drum to enhance its absorption of brine. Cooked and smoked ham is usually sold pre-packaged but special varieties (Parma ham or prosciutto) can be bought sliced to order, from delicatessens.

SAUSAGES
Sausages are made from minced beef, mutton or pork, mixed with fat, cereal, herbs and flavourings. The recipes for

the meat mixtures vary considerably from butcher to butcher.

The sausage meat is encased in animal intestines or casings made from synthetic material.

Some butchers will sell you sausage casings so that you can make your own sausages. Wash them carefully before you stuff them.

Sausage mixtures can also be formed into patties or meatballs and cooked without a skin.

Allow 125-150 g (4-5 oz) per person.

OFFAL

Offal refers to the internal organs of animals – the liver and kidneys, for example – which are rich in nutrients. Other parts, such as the head, tail and feet, are also often sold as offal. It is usually cheap compared to other meat.

Avoid buying discoloured offal, and use the meat on the day you buy it, since it does not keep well. If you have frozen offal make sure it is thoroughly thawed before you cook it.

Using offal

Liver Buy 120-175 g (4-6 oz) per person. Cut away any fat, gristle and tubes before cooking; clean with a damp cloth and dry. To reduce the strong flavour of ox liver, soak it in milk for 20-30 minutes. Liver is best fried, except ox liver, which will need to be braised or stewed.

Kidney Buy two per person, except for ox kidney (allow 120-175 g/4-6 oz per person). Peel off the outer skin of the kidney before cooking. Cut the kidney in half lengthways and remove the white core. Drop the kidney halves in hot water for 2 minutes, then cold water for 30 seconds to prevent them from curling during cooking.

Ox and calf kidneys may be soaked in milk or water for 2 hours before cooking if you wish to reduce the strong flavour.

Lamb kidney is best for frying or grilling. Grill, fry or stew calf and pig kidney. Stew ox kidney, or use it with steak in pies.

Tongue One ox tongue serves six. Allow one lamb tongue per person.

Soak tongue for 1-2 hours in cold water; soak salted tongue overnight. To boil tongue, simmer gently in fresh water for 2-3 hours or until tender.

To remove the skin after boiling, plunge the tongue into cold water, then slit the skin at the tip with a sharp knife and peel. Remove any bones or gristle at the root, and trim.

Serve tongue hot with sauce, or press and serve cold in slices.

Marrow bones Beef marrow from the large thigh and shoulder bones of the animal is regarded as a delicacy by many. Ask your butcher to saw the bones into manageable lengths.

Scrape and wash the bones, then seal the ends with a paste of flour and water. Tie each bone in cheesecloth or muslin and simmer gently in court-bouillon for 1½-2 hours. Drain, extract the marrow, and spread it on toast.

RABBIT AND HARE

Rabbits and hares are sometimes available at butchers or supermarkets, either whole or jointed, and some people still hunt them.

The meat should be hung before it is eaten – hare for 7-10 days, rabbit for up to 24 hours. If buying the meat, check how long it has already been hung. Allow about 250 g (9 oz) meat for each person.

To joint rabbit or hare, cut away the skin flaps below the rib cage with a sharp knife and discard. Slice the carcass in half lengthways, cutting down the backbone. Cut off the hind legs at the thigh, slicing through the joint. Remove the forelegs, cutting through the shoulder joints.

Divide the carcass in half along the backbone and cut each half into two serving portions. If you intend to use the saddle for roasting, joint as above but leave the backbone complete.

Rabbits should be fresh, with firm, plump flesh. Wild rabbits are smaller than domesticated animals, but have a better flavour. Roast young rabbit, or use it in a fricassee, stew or pie.

Young hares are very good when stuffed and roasted whole, but you can roast the saddle or use the hare jointed in a casserole. An old hare will benefit by being marinated before it is cooked.

COOKING MEAT

There are several methods of cooking meat: some concentrate flavour, others ensure tender results with a tough cut of meat. It is important to use the correct method for the meat you have bought, otherwise you could ruin what is probably the most expensive item on your menu.

Meat may be marinated for 3-4 hours before cooking to make it more tender or to give it a variety of flavours. Oil, wine, vinegar and lemon juice are most often used in a marinade.

Roasting

Roasting is cooking by radiant heat. The meat shrinks in the heat, which brings the juices to the surface. The juices dry out, sealing the meat and concentrating the flavour. Roast only tender cuts of meat, otherwise the result will be tough and dry. Roast your joint with the fat side uppermost and baste the meat with the cooking juices or, if it has been marinated, with heated marinade.

To ensure crisp crackling on pork, rub the rind with olive or sunflower oil and coarse salt and roast, with the rind uppermost.

Cover very lean meat, such as veal or venison, with strips of pork or similar fat during cooking (this is known as barding) to prevent the meat from drying out as it cooks.

When roasting boned and rolled meat, place the bones in the roasting tin with the meat to add flavour to the basting juices and gravy. The bones can later be used for making basic stock.

When roasting in aluminium foil, wrap the meat with the shiny side inside. Since foil reflects heat, use a higher roasting temperature than you would otherwise use.

Tie aluminium foil around the tip of each rib of a crown roast to prevent them from burning, and before serving decorate the individual ribs with bought paper frills.

To check whether roasted meat is done, stick a skewer into it (near the bone if there is one). The juice should run pink for underdone, clear for more thoroughly cooked meat.

Always rest roasts for 15 minutes after cooking for juicier results and easier carving. Follow the chart (right) as a guide to oven temperatures and required cooking times.

For the most tender results when carving a joint, slice across the grain of the meat. The exception is with leg of lamb, which may be carved either at a

90 degree angle to the bone or almost parallel to the bone.

Carving a boned and rolled joint presents no problem – simply secure the meat with the carving fork and cut downwards across the grain. When it comes to a joint which contains bone, however, it helps to know the shape and in what position it is lying.

The thickness of carved slices is largely a matter of personal preference, but roast beef and ham are usually sliced very thinly, pork slightly thicker, and veal and lamb fairly thickly.

Grilling and frying
Both methods of cooking should be used only for tender cuts of meat.

Grilling is cooking by radiant heat, similar to roasting. Frying is fast cooking in hot fat.

Leave some fat on the meat when grilling to keep it moist. Slash any borders of fat on steak or chops to prevent them curling during cooking.

Before grilling the meat, brush the rack or pan with sunflower oil or

COOKING TIMES FOR MEAT

As ovens vary in accuracy, refer to this chart as a guideline, adjusting roasting times to your oven. Always rest roast meats for 15 minutes under aluminium foil or in a warming oven for juicier results and easier carving.

	Roasting	Boiling	Grilling or frying
Beef	*High-heat roasting* On the bone: 10 minutes at 220°C (425°F, mark 7), then 15 minutes per 500 g (1 lb 2 oz) for rare, 18-20 minutes for medium, 25 minutes for well-done. Off the bone: 10 minutes at 220°C (425°F, mark 7); then 12 minutes per 500 g (1 lb 2 oz) at 180°C (350°F, mark 4) for rare, 15 minutes for medium, 20 minutes for well-done. *Slow-roasting* On or off the bone: 20-25 minutes at 160°C (325°F, mark 3) per 500 g (1 lb 2 oz) for medium, 30-35 minutes for well-done. *Stuffed joints* Add 5-10 minutes per 500 g (1 lb 2 oz). *Whole fillet* 8 minutes at 230°C (450°F, mark 8) per 500 g (1 lb 2 oz) for rare, 10 minutes for medium.	*Unsalted* 20 minutes per 500 g (1 lb 2 oz) + 20 minutes *Salt Beef* 25 minutes per 500 g (1 lb 2 oz) + 25 minutes	*Steaks* (2.5 cm/1 in thick) Sear the steaks for 1 minute on each side at high heat, then cook for 2-3 minutes each side for rare, 3-4 minutes a side for medium, 5 minutes a side for well-done. *Sausages* 5-8 minutes each side.
Veal	Roast veal must be fully cooked but still juicy. 15 minutes at 190°C (375°F, mark 5), then 25-30 minutes at 180°C (350°F, mark 4) per 500 g (1 lb 2 oz). *Stuffed joints* Add 5-10 minutes per 500 g (1 lb 2 oz).	20 minutes per 500 g (1 lb 2 oz) + 20 minutes	*Chops* 6-8 minutes each side. *Escalopes* 2-3 minutes each side. *Calf liver* 2-4 minutes each side.
Lamb and mutton	*High-heat* 10 minutes at 230°C (450°F, mark 8), then 10 minutes at 180°C (350°F, mark 4) per 500 g (1 lb 2 oz) for pink meat, 15 minutes for medium, 20 minutes for well-done. *Slow-roasting* 25 minutes at 160°C (325°F, mark 3), then 25 minutes per 500 g (1 lb 2 oz). *Stuffed joints* Add 5-10 minutes per 500 g (1 lb 2 oz).	*Mutton* 20 minutes per 500 g (1 lb 2 oz) + 20 minutes	*Chops* Sear chops for 1 minute each side at high heat, then cook 2-3 minutes a side for 1 cm ($\frac{1}{2}$ in) thick chops, 5-7 minutes for 2.5 cm (1 in) thick. *Liver* 2-4 minutes each side. *Sausages* 5-8 minutes each side.
Pork	30 minutes at 190°C (375°F, mark 5), then 30 minutes per 500 g (1 lb 2 oz). *Stuffed joints* Add 5-10 minutes per 500 g (1 lb 2 oz).	20 minutes per 500 g (1 lb 2 oz) + 20 minutes *Cured bacon and ham* 25 minutes per 500 g (1 lb 2 oz) + 25 minutes (weigh after soaking)	*Chops* 8-10 minutes each side. *Sausages* 5-8 minutes each side. *Bacon* 3-5 minutes each side. *Gammon steaks* 5-8 minutes each side. *Loin chops* 5-7 minutes each side.

melted butter to prevent the meat from sticking to it. You may also brush the meat lightly with oil.

The pan, grill or coals should be very hot before you begin. Sear the meat quickly on both sides to seal in the juices, then cook according to your preference at a slightly lower temperature. (This can be achieved by turning down the heat or moving the meat further from the source of heat.)

For frying, a vegetable oil such as sunflower or peanut oil is most suitable, since it can reach a high temperature without burning. Cook small amounts at a time so that the temperature of the fat is not lowered too much. Meat will become greasy in an overcrowded pan.

Fry liver slices quickly to prevent toughness. To test whether the liver is cooked, pierce with a skewer – the juice should be slightly pink.

Braising, pot-roasting and boiling
These methods use low, moist heat to soften the fibres of the meat, and are ideal for tenderising lower grades of meat.

Pot-roasting and braising are done mostly in steam in a covered pan with a tightly fitting lid. The meat is browned first in hot fat to seal in the juices. Basic stock, wine, beer, vinegar or fruit juice are all good sources of liquid, since they impart additional flavour.

In pot-roasting, the base of the pan is covered with liquid and the meat raised above it on a rack.

Braised meat is cooked on top of a bed of lightly fried vegetables with enough liquid to cover them. Make sure the pot is large enough for the meat not to touch the edge, which may cause scorching.

Boiled meat is either cooked in water or stock. Bring the liquid just to the boil, then reduce the heat to keep it simmering (constant boiling at high heat should be avoided as it toughens the meat).

Parboiling ham before roasting helps to keep it moist. To get rid of excess salt before parboiling, soak a whole ham for 12-24 hours, changing the water twice.

Alternatively, cover the ham with cold water and bring it to the boil, then drain and replace the water before cooking the meat.

Pot-roast of beef
For four to six people, brown a 1-1.5 kg (about 2-3 lb) topside or silverside on all sides in 50 g (2 oz) butter, then set it aside.

Lightly fry 2 large peeled and quartered onions, 2 large scraped and sliced carrots and 1 medium-sized peeled and sliced turnip or swede in the butter until they just begin to brown, then put them into a large casserole.

Place the meat on a rack over the vegetables, sprinkle with 1 teaspoon fresh thyme or ¼ teaspoon dried thyme and 1 clove crushed garlic, and salt and freshly ground pepper.

Pour in 300 ml (½ pint) basic stock and 125 ml (4 fl oz) red wine, and cover the casserole tightly. Place in an oven preheated to 180°C (350°F, mark 4) for at least 1½ hours, or until tender, removing the lid for the last 20 minutes to brown the meat. (You can also use beer instead of the wine.)

Pot-au-feu
To make pot-au-feu for four people, tie a 1 kg (2¼ lb) topside of beef with string (so that it keeps its shape during cooking). Place it in a large pan with 3 litres (5¼ pints) cold brown stock, bring slowly to the boil, covered, then remove any scum that rises to the top.

Add 2 large scraped and sliced carrots, 2 large peeled and coarsely chopped onions, 2-3 cleaned and sliced leeks, 1 peeled and chopped turnip and 1 chopped stalk of celery, and simmer gently for 1½ hours.

Add a set of cleaned chicken giblets and cook for a further 30 minutes.

Add 1 small washed and quartered cabbage, and cook until the cabbage is tender (about 15-20 minutes).

Lift out the meat, slice it and serve with the drained vegetables. The cooking liquid makes an excellent soup.

Stews and hotpots
Stews (or casseroles) are made from small pieces of meat cooked slowly in liquid that forms part of the final dish. They are usually flavoured with onions and diced vegetables, and can be thickened with flour or pearl barley. Hotpots are similar to stews, but traditionally have potato toppings.

Brown stews are usually made with beef, mutton, lamb or rabbit; white stews with veal, chicken or rabbit. Any meat is suitable, but the long, slow cooking is excellent for tougher cuts, such as shin of beef.

Very tough meat may need up to 4 hours' cooking, but generally beef stews should be cooked for 2½-3 hours, mutton for 2 hours, lamb and veal for 1-1½ hours.

Cook stews and hotpots in a tightly covered ovenproof dish on top of the stove or in the oven. For hotpots, remove the lid for the last 30 minutes and brown the potatoes.

The flavour of most stews is better the day after cooking – simply reheat to just boiling point. Marinating the meat for between 4-12 hours before cooking will also enhance the flavour, as well as making the meat more tender.

To make a stew, trim the fat from the meat, cut into bite-sized pieces, and fry on all sides to brown.

For brown stews, fry the vegetables lightly to improve the colour. Remove the vegetables, then add flour (if used) and cook it gently until it is light brown. Use 25 g (1 oz) flour per 500 g (1 lb 2 oz) meat.

Add cold liquid – stock, water, fruit juice, beer or wine – to the meat (350-500 ml/12-17 fl oz per 500 g/1 lb 2 oz meat), and increase the heat gently to boiling point.

As soon as the boiling point is reached, reduce the heat until the stew is just simmering. Add the vegetables and any other flavourings to the stew as directed in the recipe. Skim off excess fat while the stew is simmering.

For a white stew, drain off the stock after the meat has cooked, and use it to make a white sauce. Pour the sauce back onto the meat, and reheat.

REHEATING MEAT
When reheating cooked meat, you must take care to do so properly in order to avoid a potential health hazard. Heat the meat to a temperature of at least 77°C (170°F); or, if it is covered by sauce, cook until the sauce bubbles.

MAKING GRAVY
Gravy is best made from the meat juices left in the pan after roasting. It can be thickened by the addition of flour or cornflour.

To make a thin gravy, spoon off the fat from the roasting pan, leaving only the meat juices.

For thick gravy, leave about 1 tablespoon of the fat in the juices, and stir in 1 tablespoon flour (use cornflour for a smoother result) over a gentle heat. Stir until the flour has become golden-brown.

Add 300 ml (½ pint) hot stock or boiling water to both types of gravy, stir in any meaty residue from the bottom of the pan, and concentrate the flavour by boiling – 2-3 minutes for thin gravy, 3-4 minutes for thick gravy.

Stir thick gravy constantly to prevent lumps forming. (If it does become lumpy, pass the gravy through a sieve, beat it for a few seconds with a whisk or blend in a food processor.)

If you find excess fat gathering on the surface of the gravy draw a paper towel across it, then season to taste.

If you prefer a dark gravy, add a little gravy browning or meat extract. A little yeast or meat extract will improve a flavourless gravy.

DRIPPING

Dripping is made from leftover fat which is rendered down. The fat that has dripped from roast meat can be used, or you can make dripping from fat trimmed from raw meat.

Mince or chop the fat finely and place it in a heavy saucepan. Cover and place over low heat, shaking the pan from time to time until the fat has melted well. Be careful to prevent the fat from burning.

When the fat has melted completely, strain carefully, add salt to taste and allow the dripping to cool slightly. Pour into glass jars and store in the refrigerator or a cool place.

POULTRY AND GAME

Poultry is defined as birds bred especially for the table: chickens, turkeys, ducks, geese, and now guinea fowl – formerly regarded as game.

Methods of breeding and rearing have changed dramatically over the past fifty years, so that chicken, in particular, is cheap, plentiful and almost entirely intensively reared. Although freshly killed poultry is far superior in flavour and texture, frozen birds, properly thawed and cooked, can be very good.

CHOOSING POULTRY

Almost all poultry is now sold oven-ready. If you are offered a bird in feather or one that has been rough-plucked, it will need to be hung, plucked and drawn before you prepare it for the oven.

Fresh, oven-ready birds

Look for a soft, flexible breastbone and a plump breast in a roasting bird. If the breastbone is rigid, the bird may be old and suitable only for casseroling, boiling or making soup.

Frozen poultry

Always buy birds from a reputable source of supply.

Make sure that the bag covering the bird is unbroken and that there are no marks of 'freezer burn' – discoloured dried-up patches on the skin caused by faulty or damaged packaging. If this occurs the flavour will be poor.

It is absolutely essential that frozen poultry is completely thawed before cooking. Incomplete thawing can lead to the risk of salmonella poisoning. Allow the chicken to thaw out overnight at room temperature or in the main compartment of your refrigerator. Remove the giblets before cooking and make sure that the inside of the bird is fully thawed, as well as the outside.

Trussing

Place the bird, breast down, on a table or chopping block. Close the neck cavity by folding the loose skin over the back. Fold back the wings, and hold the skin in place with a poultry skewer or with a trussing needle and string.

Turn the bird over. Make a horizontal slit in the skin above the tail vent, and push the parson's nose (tail) through it.

Draw the thighs close to the body and cross the legs over the tail end. Loop the string around the legs and parson's nose, and tie securely.

Jointing

Pull the bird's leg away from the body and, using a sharp knife, slice down to the thigh joint. Break at the joint and cut away the whole leg. Repeat with the other leg.

Slice through the outer breast meat towards the wing joint. Sever the wing

from the body. Fold the breast meat over the wing joint. Repeat with the other wing.

There is a natural division in the rib cage. Slice along it to separate the breast from the lower carcass.

Cut the breast meat into serving portions. If jointing a large bird, separate the drumstick (the lower leg joint) from the thigh.

Use the rest of the carcass and the giblets to make stock.

Stuffing

As a general rule, use about 125 g (4½ oz) of stuffing for each 500 g (1 lb 2 oz) of bird.

Most poultry and game birds are stuffed from the crop (neck) cavity. Do not fill too tightly: the stuffing needs room to expand. Duck and goose are commonly stuffed from the body (tail) end. Turkey traditionally has two stuffings: a bread and herb one spooned into the neck, and a sausage meat filling for the body.

COOKING POULTRY

Poussin (Spatchcock) A chicken 3-4 weeks old weighing up to 575 g (1¼ lb). Roast, spit-roast or grill. If roasting, place a nut of butter inside the bird. If spit-roasting, first brush all over with melted fat or sunflower oil and sprinkle with dried herbs.

Roasting chicken or broiler The most widely sold bird, 6-8 weeks old, weighing on average 1.5 kg (3 lb 3 oz). Roast, spit-roast, grill or fry.

Boiling fowl Usually 12 months old or more. It can weigh up to 3.2 kg (7 lb) and is well flavoured and meaty, but tougher than a roasting bird. Boil, casserole or use it to make soup. A pressure cooker speeds up cooking.

Turkey Choose a turkey of medium size (4.5-5 kg/10-12 lb). The best choice is a hen bird 6-8 months old. Turkey is usually dry, so bard it (lay bacon rashers across the top) or spread with softened butter and cover in aluminium foil or greaseproof paper for most of the cooking time.

Duck Oven-ready ducks on sale usually weigh 1.75-2.75 kg (3¾-6 lb). The proportion of meat to bone is less generous than in chicken – a 1.75 kg (3¾ lb) duck will just serve four people.

A duck is fatty so prick the skin before cooking in order to allow some of the fat to escape.

Goose A fresh bird will have yellow, soft, pliable feet. Roast or braise. Goose can be bought frozen all the year round, but for fresh birds it is sensible to order well in advance of requirements. The average mass is 2.75-5.5 kg (6-12 lb), but the proportion of meat to bone is less than for chicken.

Testing whether poultry is cooked
Never serve poultry undercooked. To see if a roasted bird is ready, push a skewer into the thickest part of the thigh. If clear juices run out, the bird is ready; if the juices are pink, it needs longer cooking.

A bird which is being boiled or casseroled will be ready when a skewer penetrates the thigh easily.

Carving poultry
First, cut off both legs. Hold the leg in position with a fork while you use a sharp knife to sever the thigh joint. Remove both wings. Carve the meat from the breast downwards, in thin or thick slices as you prefer.

Poultry shears, or a stout pair of kitchen scissors can be a great help for cutting a raw or cooked bird into neat serving portions, as they will cut through the bones.

GAME
Game birds are generally available only to the families and friends of hunters, but are sometimes to be found in butchers and speciality shops.

Choosing and preparing game birds
Look for smooth, pliant legs, with rounded or short spurs on the male. If unplucked, turn the feathers back to see if the breast is plump and firm.

The plumage of a young bird will not be as bright as that of an older bird. Be careful with a bird that shows signs of having been badly shot (its skin will be 'peppered' with shot marks). Some parts will start decomposing before the rest is tender.

ROASTING POULTRY AND GAME BIRDS
For stuffed poultry, allow an extra 15-20 minutes for birds weighing up to 1.6 kg (3 lb); 30-40 minutes for birds weighing 1.8-4.5 kg (4-10 lb). These are general guidelines only. See individual recipes for specific cooking times.

Type of Bird	Weight	Time	Temperature	Servings
Chicken	450 g-3.6 kg (1-8 lb)	15-20 minutes per 450 g (1 lb) + 20 minutes	180°C (350°F, mark 4)	1 kg (2¼ lb) serves 4 people
Duck	1.4-2.7 kg (3-6 lb)	20 minutes per 540 g (1 lb) + 20 minutes	190°C (375°F, mark 5)	2 kg (4½ lb) serves 4 people
Goose	2.7-4.5 kg (6-10 lb)	20 minutes per 450 g (1 lb) + 20 minutes	190°C (375°F, mark 5)	4.5 kg (10 lb) serves 6-8 people
Guinea Fowl	575 g-1.8 kg (1¼-4 lb)	20 minutes per 450 g (1 lb) + 20 minutes	180°C (350°F, mark 4)	1 kg (2¼ lb) serves 4 people
Turkey	2.7-4.5 kg (6-10 lb)	20 minutes per 450 g (1 lb) + 20 minutes	180°C (350°F, mark 4)	4 kg (8¾ lb) serves 8-10 people
	4.5-8.1 kg (10-18 lb)	15 minutes per 450 g (1 lb) + 20 minutes	180°C (350°F, mark 4)	
Grouse		30-40 minutes	190°C (375°F, mark 5)	1 young bird serves 1 person
Partridge		30-45 minutes	190°C (375°F, mark 5)	1 young bird serves 1 person
Pheasant (hen)		45 minutes-1 hour	190°C (375°F, mark 5)	1 bird serves 2 people
Pheasant (cock)		1-1½ hours	190°C (375°F, mark 5)	1 bird serves 3-4 people
Quail, Pigeon and Poussin (spatchcock)		20 minutes	200°C (400°F, mark 6)	1 bird serves 1 person

Hanging

Hang birds by the neck, unplucked and undrawn, in an airy, cool larder or pantry. Do not hang two or three together: there should be a free circulation of air around each bird.

If flies are a nuisance, dredge the birds with pepper or enclose in a loose muslin bag.

Small birds should be hung for 24 hours, and large ones for 3-4 days. But hanging time depends on age, condition, and the weather. If the weather is warm and humid, the bird will decompose faster.

Plucking

Hold the bird firmly on a large sheet of paper, in a draught-free space. Have a large bag handy for the feathers as you pluck them.

Start with the legs and wings, drawing the feathers out with a slight, backward pull against the lie of the feathers.

Pluck the breast last. Do not try to pluck too many feathers at one time, and take care not to tear the skin.

After plucking, get rid of remaining down and hairs by singeing. Use a lighted taper, or pour a little methylated spirit into a dish, set alight and turn the bird over the flame. Be careful not to scorch the skin.

Wipe the bird thoroughly with a clean cloth. If any long hairs or quills still need to be removed, you can pluck them out with a pair of tweezers.

Drawing

Cut off the head, leaving about 8 cm (3¼ in) of neck. Slit the skin on the underside of the neck and pull it towards the body. Cut the neck again close to the body. (Set the neck aside to use for stock.)

Put your hand, knuckles upwards, into the neck cavity. Remove the crop, windpipe and any fat present. Keeping your hand high under the breastbone, gently loosen and dislodge the entrails.

Turn the bird on its back. Make a slit with a sharp knife to enlarge the vent at the tail end.

Loosen the fat and the skin, then, holding the bird firmly with one hand, put the other hand inside and gently draw out the entrails.

Clean the giblets, washing away any blood, and cut the bitter, green gall bladder away from the liver.

Put the liver, heart and gizzard (the bird's second stomach) with the neck to make stock.

Wipe the bird thoroughly, inside and out, with a damp, clean cloth.

Break the legs at the lower joint, at the base of each drumstick, to expose the tendons. Use a skewer to pull out one tendon at a time, taking care not to tear the flesh.

Bend the joint backwards, then twist and break the bone. Cut through the skin. Scald and scrub the feet and remove the scales. Put the feet with the rest of the giblets to make stock.

COOKING

Young birds are best roasted. Lay bacon rashers across the breast to keep the flesh moist. If you have an older, tougher bird, braise or casserole it to keep the flesh tender.

In general, small birds such as quail and pigeon provide a meal for one person. After roasting they are often served on a slice of crustless fried bread or hot buttered toast.

If you are not using a stuffing, one or two small pieces of butter, a few pieces of juicy steak, a peeled, cored apple or a whole, peeled onion placed in the body will keep the bird moist.

About 10 minutes before serving, remove the strips of bacon covering the breast. Baste well with butter and pan juices, dredge with seasoned flour, baste again and return to the oven. This gives a good, golden-brown, crispy finish. Use the leftover bacon in stock.

To give a distinctive flavour to game birds and counteract any fattiness, flame them with brandy when almost cooked. Heat 1-2 tablespoons in a ladle, light it and pour over the bird.

VEGETABLES

Vegetables, both raw and cooked, form an indispensable part of our diet since they are a vital source of a wide range of minerals and vitamins.

STORING VEGETABLES

Where large quantities of vegetables need to be stored for some time, it is important to consider the temperature and relative humidity of your storage space. The ideal storage temperature for most vegetables is 4°C (39°F). However, some – such as onions, potatoes, marrows, squashes and pumpkins – can tolerate room temperature storage.

The basic principle in vegetable storage is to limit moisture loss. To help retain moisture the vegetables should be covered or stored in perforated plastic or paper bags, or individually wrapped in newspaper.

However, few vegetables keep well for longer than about 10 days.

PREPARING VEGETABLES

Wash vegetables just before using. Most vegetables can be used in their skins – which helps to retain vitamins. Should they need peeling, do so as thinly as possible or use a pot-scourer or brush to remove dirt.

Vegetables can be sliced, diced or chopped by hand. Food processors, however, can be very useful for preparing vegetables because they have fittings that regulate the size of slice or dice and produce uniform shapes.

Shredding and grating can also be done manually or with the help of specialised equipment.

COOKING VEGETABLES

Vitamins A, B and, particularly, C are present in most vegetables. Vitamin C is, however, unstable and much of it can be lost with wrong storage and preparation. Prolonged soaking or cooking, or the addition of bicarbonate of soda, destroys Vitamin C.

Blanching

Vegetables are blanched by being dunked into boiling water for 2-3 minutes. This is usually done prior to freezing or if tough vegetables are to be used in salads, stir-fried or braised.

Boiling

Roots and tubers These include potatoes, carrots, turnips, parsnips, swedes, celeriac, beetroots, salsify, Jerusalem artichokes and the bulbous roots of onions, shallots and leeks.

Put the cleaned and prepared vegetables into a saucepan and add sufficient cold water to cover. For each 275-300 ml (½ pint) of water add ½ teaspoon of salt. Cover the pan, bring the water to the boil and boil until tender, but firm.

THE PRACTICAL COOK
Green vegetables These include cabbages, kale, Brussels sprouts, cauliflowers, broccoli, spinach, and globe artichokes.

Use only a small amount of water for boiling green vegetables. About 150 ml (¼ pint) of water to every 450 g (1 lb) of vegetables is sufficient. Bring the salted water to the boil before adding the vegetables. Cover the pan and boil at a moderate heat until the vegetables are tender but firm. Drain the vegetables well and finish according to the recipe.

Steaming
The flavour and food value of vegetables is successfully retained when they are steamed.

Prepare the vegetables and place them in a perforated vegetable steamer or wire colander, and fit this in a pan over rapidly boiling water. Make sure the water is not deep enough to reach the vegetables. Sprinkle with salt, allowing 1 teaspoon to each 450 g (1 lb) of vegetables. Cover the pan with a tightly fitting lid and steam until the vegetables are just tender. This will take at least 5 minutes longer than cooking vegetables by boiling.

Braising
This method is suitable for vegetables such as carrots, celery or fennel. Vegetables are braised by being lightly fried in butter, oil or fat. A liquid or stock is added and the vegetables are then cooked until tender. The juices may be reduced by rapid boiling. Braised vegetables are usually brownish in colour and cooked until soft.

Roasting
This method is suitable for root vegetables such as potatoes, onions and parsnips. They are often roasted round a meat joint. They can also be roasted separately in an ovenproof dish in which you have heated a 5 mm (¼ in) layer of dripping.

Parboil the vegetables first for 5 minutes, then drain. Turn them in the hot fat to coat them. Roast at 220°C (425°F, mark 7) for 30 minutes.

Baking
This cooking method is used mostly for potatoes. Scrub the vegetables well and prick to prevent bursting. Brush the vegetables with melted butter or oil and cook in an oven preheated to 200°C (400°F, mark 6) until they feel tender when pinched between your forefinger and thumb.

If you stick a metal skewer into each potato, they will cook more quickly.

Frying
Shallow frying or sautéing Suitable vegetables for frying are courgettes (zucchini), tomatoes, mushrooms, aubergines (eggplants), onions and other tender vegetables. In a heavy-based frying pan heat enough butter or oil to cover the base thinly. Add the vegetables and fry gently until tender and golden-brown, turning over from time to time during cooking. Salt lightly after cooking. Less tender vegetables must be precooked or boiled for 5 minutes before shallow-frying.

Deep-frying For deep-frying chipped potatoes, see the recipe for Fish and Chips (page 37). Many other vegetables can be deep-fried, usually coated with batter or egg and breadcrumbs before being cooked.

Stir-frying When vegetables are stir-fried they keep their texture and flavour. Chop the vegetables into small pieces of even size so that they will all be ready at the same time. Heat a thin layer of oil in a heavy frying pan until sizzling, and add the vegetables. Stir continuously with a wooden spoon or spatula and turn down the heat. The vegetables are done when their colour has brightened and although softer, they still should be crunchy.

Serving
Serve vegetables as soon as possible after they are cooked. They can be served plain, tossed in butter, sprinkled with chopped parsley and other herbs, or coated with a sauce.

Making use of pulses
The more common pulses are peas (green and yellow), beans (haricot, butter and kidney) and lentils (green, yellow and red).

To prepare pulses pick over the seeds, discarding any black or discoloured ones, and wash the pulses under cold running water. Place in a large bowl and cover with cold water. Leave them to soak for several hours, and if possible overnight. Lentils can be cooked without soaking. Dried beans contain lectin, a poisonous chemical destroyed by rapid boiling. Soak the beans, drain and rinse them under running water, cover with fresh cold water, bring slowly to the boil and keep boiling rapidly for 10 minutes.

To cook, drain the pulses and place in a saucepan. Cover with plenty of fresh cold water. Do not add salt at this stage as it makes the pulses hard. Bring to the boil and simmer gently until soft. Cooking time varies, depending on the type and age of the pulses, and can be anything from 30 minutes to 2 hours.

SEEDS FOR SPROUTING
Any of the pea, lentil or bean varieties can be used for sprouts. Some – such as alfala, mung beans, chick-peas and lentils – sprout more easily than others. When seeds sprout, the nutrient concentration changes and they become a source of Vitamin C. Only seeds that have the potential to germinate will sprout – seeds that have been heat-treated will not do so.

There are various sprouting methods. In general, the seeds need to be washed daily with tepid water and left in a cool moist atmosphere to germinate. This may take 3-4 days.

Sprouts can be kept in a sealed container or plastic bag in the refrigerator for up to two weeks.

Stir-frying is a particularly good cooking method for sprouts.

Mung beans should be soaked continuously for 12-24 hours, until the skins just start to burst. Drain off and sprout as described above. Husks can be removed by hand after sprouting.

Soya beans are difficult to sprout and must be soaked well beforehand. The best temperature is 20-25°C (about 70–77°F) and the beans must be continuously dunked in water to avoid mouldiness. Check once a day and remove those going mouldy. In 3-4 days the sprouts should be long enough. Rinse and steam gently for a few minutes to remove the raw 'beany' taste.

Alfalfa produces fine 2 cm (¾ in) sprouts in 3-4 days. They have a delicate nutty flavour.

Whole dried peas give sprouts 5 cm (2 in) long that have a pleasant flavour of peas.

Lentils are ready for use when they reach a length of 2 cm (¾ in).

PASTA, RICE AND CEREALS

Pasta or rice can supply the starchy part of a main course in place of potatoes, dumplings or pastry.

PASTA

Pasta simply means the paste or dough from which Italian noodles are made. The basis of pasta is flour from hard durum wheat, which grows particularly well in Italy. The flour is mixed with oil and water, and sometimes spinach purée and egg are added. The pasta is then moulded into various shapes and dried before being sold.

The commonest shapes are long threads (spaghetti and vermicelli), tubes (macaroni), narrow strips (tagliatelle) and sheets (lasagne). Pasta is also moulded into broad ribbons, short thin threads, butterflies, shells and several other fancy shapes.

Cooked pasta can be served as a simple side dish (tossed with a light coating of butter or olive oil) made into a composite dish such as lasagne, or served with any one of an almost endless variety of special accompanying sauces. These sauces are mostly tomato-based, such as Napolitana sauce (a simple, homemade tomato sauce flavoured with herbs) or Bolognese sauce (tomatoes and meat). Cream is also a popular base for a pasta sauce.

Grated Parmesan cheese is an almost indispensable part of most pasta meals; use it for sprinkling over the top, or incorporate it into your sauce.

Cooking pasta

Allow 75-125 g (3-4¼ oz) uncooked pasta for each person. All pasta is boiled, but cooking time depends on size and freshness. Pasta should be just firm to the bite, or al dente as the Italians say.

For every 125 g (4¼ oz) pasta use 1 litre (1¾ pints) water and 2 teaspoons salt. Bring the water to the boil in a large saucepan, add the salt and put in the pasta. Do not break up the long strands of spaghetti, but hold them at one end and curl the strands gradually into the boiling water as they soften. Cook the pasta at a steady boil,

uncovered, until just tender. Drain thoroughly in a colander and return to the pan with a large knob of butter or 1 tablespoon olive oil. Season with salt and pepper, and toss the pasta until it is well coated. Remember that fresh pasta will take only a fraction of the cooking time for dried pasta.

MAKING HOMEMADE PASTA

Although a large variety of pasta is available pre-packed, it is much tastier if made at home.

These basic recipes are for making pasta by hand or with a pasta-making machine, and can be varied easily.

Basic pasta

PREPARATION TIME: 45 MINUTES 1 HOUR
RESTING TIME: 30 MINUTES
COOKING TIME: 3-5 MINUTES

INGREDIENTS FOR FOUR TO SIX
250 g (9 oz) flour
1 teaspoon salt
2 eggs, lightly beaten
60 ml (2 fl oz) warm water

To mix by hand, sift the flour and salt into a bowl. Lightly beat the eggs and water together, and pour into the middle of the flour. Mix together, then knead to make a stiff dough. Wrap well with plastic wrap and allow to rest for 30 minutes before rolling.

To mix in a food processor, place the flour and salt in the bowl of the food processor, and spin around to aerate. Add the eggs through the funnel and process together. Then gradually pour in the water and process until well mixed. If the dough seems to need it, add a little more water, but add it drop by drop as it is easier to work with the dough if it is slightly dry. Wrap well and leave to rest for 30 minutes.

To roll out the pasta by hand, work with a small amount at a time. Divide the dough into 4 pieces and keep each piece well wrapped in plastic or a damp tea towel.

Roll out one piece very thinly, then roll up loosely like a Swiss roll, and cut across to form ribbons of noodles. Repeat with the other pieces. If using a pasta machine follow the manufacturer's instructions.

You can cook the pasta ribbons fresh, or allow them to dry out, well

separated, on tea towels so that they do not stick together during cooking. You can also freeze the pasta, well dusted with flour, in plastic bags.

Cook the pasta in a large, uncovered saucepan of salted boiling water. Homemade pasta cooks very quickly. Within a matter of minutes it will float to the top and be ready.

Drain thoroughly and toss the noodles in oil or butter. Serve immediately with a sauce. Pasta is also very good made with wholemeal flour.

Spinach pasta

Spinach pasta is particularly tasty with cream-based sauces. Use for making lasagne noodles.

Follow the basic recipe, substituting 100 g (3¾ oz) spinach leaves for one of the eggs.

Wash the spinach very well and remove any tough stalks and ribs. Cook the wet leaves in a saucepan until they have wilted.

Drain and rinse under cold running water. As soon as the spinach is cool enough to handle, squeeze out the excess moisture by hand. Chop and purée the spinach.

Follow the method for basic pasta and add the spinach at the same time as you add the egg.

Lasagne noodles

Use the spinach pasta recipe and cut the rolled-out sheets of pasta into squares. Cook in plenty of salted boiling water and drain well, separating the noodles on tea towels to prevent sticking. Use the prepared noodles for the classic baked lasagne.

Cannelloni cases

Use the basic pasta recipe and cut the rolled-out sheets of pasta into 12 cm (4¾ in) squares. Cook until barely tender and drain well, separating the squares on tea towels to prevent sticking. These are then wrapped around a filling, covered with sauce and baked.

Ravioli

Ravioli are small pasta 'parcels' containing a filling of meat or spinach and cheese. For the pasta use the basic recipe. Divide the dough, roll out into two sheets and trim them to the same size. Place tiny spoonfuls of filling on one of the sheets at 5 cm (2 in) intervals, leaving a 2.5 cm (1 in) margin around the edge of the pasta.

Brush the dough with water around the spoonfuls of filling. Carefully place the second sheet of dough on top. Press it down well between the heaps of filling, so that the sheets of dough stick to each other.

Cut between the rows of filling into neat squares. Place them well apart on floured tea towels until you are ready to cook them.

RICE

There are several kinds of rice. Polished rice is usually white, while unpolished rice (from which the bran has not been removed) is brown. Wild rice, grey-brown in colour, has a nutty taste and is the seed of an aquatic grass, not a grain. For savoury dishes, long-grain rice is best. Round-grain rice is suitable for risottos and puddings.

Cooking plain boiled rice
Allow 50-60 g (about 2 oz) uncooked rice for each person. Put the rice in a fine sieve and wash well in plenty of cold running water. Drain and put in a pan. Pour in enough cold water to cover the rice by 2.5 cm (1 in). Add salt to taste and cover the pan. Bring to the boil, stirring occasionally, and simmer undisturbed for 10-12 minutes, or until all the water is absorbed. Remove from the heat and leave, covered, for 10-12 minutes. It should be dry and fluffy.

Cooking yellow rice
Heat 40 g (1½ oz) butter and 5 teaspoons sunflower oil, and add 200 g (7 oz) long-grain rice. Cook, stirring constantly, for about 10 minutes, or until transparent. While the rice is cooking, mix together the following ingredients: 750 ml (26 fl oz) boiling water, 2 teaspoons turmeric, 1 teaspoon salt, 2 teaspoons caster sugar.

Pour this mixture onto the rice when it has become transparent, mix well with a fork, cover the pan lightly and turn the heat to low. After 15 minutes, scatter 50 g (2 oz) seedless raisins on top of the rice. Cover the pan again and cook for 10-15 minutes more, or until all the water has been absorbed. Then lightly stir the rice and raisins together.

Instead of cooking on the stove, the rice and boiling water mixture can be cooked in a casserole in a 160°C (325°F, mark 3) oven for about 1 hour, or until the water has been absorbed. The raisins should be added 15 minutes before the end of the cooking time.

CEREALS

Oats are an important breakfast food, but fine oatmeal can also be used to coat fish for frying, or in flummery.

Wheat has been the principal cereal grain of Europe and the Near East for thousands of years and is high in gluten-forming protein. Wheat is the principal grain from which bread flour is milled. A hard variety, durum wheat, is used for making pasta.

Pearl wheat is the whole grain from which some of the bran has been removed to allow better penetration of water, so that the wheat can be cooked and eaten in a similar way to rice. Cracked wheat has been milled in such a way that the whole grain is broken but the kernel is left intact, whereas crushed wheat, or burghul as it is sometimes known, is similarly milled into finer pieces. Semolina is also a wheat product, consisting of the hard part of the wheat, sifted out and used in its fine form or made into pellets known as couscous.

CHOOSING, STORING AND COOKING EGGS

With the exception of Vitamin C, eggs contain all the vitamins, including the rare sunshine-growth Vitamin D, as well as 13 minerals, including iron, phosphorus and calcium. The yolk of an egg is about 33 per cent fat, while the white is mainly water. The shell is porous and can be penetrated by air, water or odours. The air chamber between the shell and the inner lining at the larger end gets bigger with age.

Cooked on their own, eggs thicken and solidify at 60-68°C (140-155°F) – temperatures considerably lower than the boiling point of water. When mixed with other ingredients, however, they solidify at higher temperatures.

CHOOSING EGGS
The nutritive value of all eggs of like grade and size is the same – size and colour do not affect quality. Eggs are checked for cleanliness, soundness of shell, thickness of albumen and size of air cells. Size is based on minimum mass per dozen.

Very fresh eggs have small air cells, a large amount of thick white and a firm, upstanding yolk. Out of the shell, they cover a small area. Older eggs will spread a bit more, the white is not as thick nor the yolk as high.

STORING EGGS
Store eggs in a clean, cool place with the pointed end down. Do not wash unless absolutely necessary, and keep away from strong-smelling foods whose flavour might permeate the porous shell and taint the eggs.

Eggs up to 1 week old when bought will keep for 2 weeks at normal room temperature – about 18°C (64°F) – or up to 5 weeks in a refrigerator.

Store separated whites and yolks in a refrigerator in different containers. Pour a thin layer of milk or water over the yolks to prevent them from drying out and hardening.

Yolks are best used within 2 days; whites can be kept up to 4 days.

Take eggs out of the refrigerator and leave them at room temperature for 45 minutes before using. Very cold eggs will crack when boiled, and chilled whites cannot be whisked easily.

Egg whites freeze well, but egg yolks must first be beaten with a little salt or sugar before they are frozen.

HOW TO TELL A FRESH EGG
If you put a fresh egg in a solution of salt and water (10 per cent salt), it will sink to the bottom. If the egg floats, it is stale.

When broken into a bowl, a fresh egg has a rounded yolk and a firm white. A stale egg has a flat yolk and a runny white.

TIPS FOR COOKING EGGS
The following are the five most popular methods of preparing eggs. The cardinal rule that applies to all of them is never to overcook eggs and never to use too high a temperature – doing so will make them hard, rubbery and unpleasant to eat.

Boiled eggs
Although this is the simplest method of preparing an egg, it still has its pitfalls.

Eggs frequently crack while being boiled. This can usually be prevented by pricking a tiny hole in the broad end of the egg which will allow the air bubble within the egg to escape during boiling. Remember that an egg at room temperature is less likely to crack than one that comes straight out of the refrigerator.

Boil eggs by warming up the water and eggs together, or introducing the eggs to the water when it is already simmering. In the first method, there is less chance of the eggs cracking.

If you warm up the water and eggs together, start timing from the moment the water boils, then simmer for 3 minutes for soft boiled eggs, 4 minutes for firm whites with soft yolks, and 10 minutes for hard-boiled eggs.

If you introduce the eggs when the water is simmering the following cooking times will apply: 3¾ minutes for soft-boiled eggs, 7 minutes for firm whites with soft yolks, and 12 minutes for completely hard-boiled eggs.

Avoid cooking eggs in rapidly boiling water; doing so makes the whites hard and tough before the yolk is cooked.

Plunge hard-boiled eggs into cold water immediately after taking them out of the boiling water. Peel them underwater and allow to cool to prevent an unattractive dark ring from forming around the yolk.

Fried eggs

Butter is the most recommended medium for frying eggs – it imparts a light-golden colour and a pleasant taste. Cooking oil is relatively tasteless and bacon fat will give the eggs a slight bacon flavour.

Always fry eggs over a medium heat in hot but not smoking fat. When you slip the eggs in, the white should solidify but not bubble and burn at the edges. If it does, lower the heat. Baste the eggs with fat from the pan while they are frying, which will give the yolk a shiny appearance.

Fry eggs for 1-2 minutes and when cooked, lift them out of the pan with a fish slice. Place the eggs briefly on paper towels to drain off excess fat, then serve within two to three minutes.

Scrambled eggs

Scrambled eggs are very versatile, being suitable for breakfast, a light lunch, or a modest supper.

The basic recipe for scrambled eggs is 2 eggs to which 5 teaspoons milk or water has been added, and some seasoning. Whisk the mixture and pour into a heavy-based frying pan in which 2 teaspoons butter has been melted. (The butter should be sizzling.)

Never cook scrambled eggs at high temperatures, otherwise they will become dry and crumbly. The right ratio of eggs to liquid is important because too much liquid will separate and stop the eggs from congealing.

Cook until the mixture is firm but not dry. Well-prepared scrambled eggs should consist of big soft chunks.

For variety, fry tomatoes and onions, leftover meat or vegetables, pasta or rice in the pan before adding the eggs.

Omelettes

For each person, use 2 eggs, 1 tablespoon water, ½ oz butter, salt and freshly ground pepper.

Use a pan with a rounded side and of a suitable size to allow about 5 mm (¼ in) depth of egg.

Butter gives omelettes a very characteristic flavour and colour. It is best to use unsalted or clarified butter since salted butter can cause the omelette to stick to the pan.

Let the butter in the frying pan bubble and be slightly brown before you pour in the egg mixture. The darker the butter, the darker the final omelette will be.

It is best to fry a number of smaller omelettes instead of making one big one. The smaller they are, the lighter their texture will be. Season the omelette before folding and ensure that any warm filling has been sufficiently heated before being folded in. Omelettes can be served with a wide variety of fillings – cooked meat, vegetables, cheese – or beat a spoonful of freshly chopped herbs into the egg mixture before cooking.

Poached eggs

When poaching eggs, boil about 5 cm (2 in) of liquid in a saucepan, then lower to simmering before you break the eggs and slide them in. Eggs are normally poached in water, but you can also use tomato juice, milk, stock or soup. If you are using water, the addition of lemon juice or vinegar will enhance the flavour, but do not add salt.

USING EGGS IN COOKING

● The capacity that eggs have to coagulate when heated makes them ideal for binding loose, crumbly ingredients together – for example, poultry stuffing and croquettes. Mixed with breadcrumbs or flour, eggs form a crisp coating that protects fried foods from very hot fat. Fritters that are dipped in beaten egg before frying absorb virtually no oil.

● Beaten eggs are invaluable as a thickening agent, being used to thicken custards, sauces, soups, fruit curds and tart fillings. A useful rule of thumb is that one medium-sized egg will thicken 275-300 ml (about ½ pint) liquid. Take care not to heat the mixture to which the egg has been added for too long or the liquid will tend to separate out, with the egg forming a tough clot.

● A particularly useful quality of egg yolks is that they act as emulsifiers – blending oil and other liquids, as in mayonnaise. The addition of vinegar or lemon juice stabilises the emulsion.

● A beaten egg will give a pleasing gloss to pastries and prevent raw pie crusts from becoming soggy from the moisture in the filling.

● Whisked egg whites are the main ingredient of meringues, soufflés and light sponge cakes.

● Because eggs are rich in many nutrients, they are ideal for increasing the nutritional value of other foods. They can be mixed with vegetables, pastas, grain and bread, and even a fruit drink becomes a complete meal with the addition of a raw egg.

● Lightly beaten egg white or crushed egg shells can be added to broths and jellies to remove solids and to clarify the liquid. The whites solidify in the warmed liquid, trapping small particles, and this white solid is strained off. Similarly, food particles will also adhere to crushed egg shells added in the same way.

● Hard-boiled eggs are widely used as an attractive and nutritious garnish. They may be used halved or quartered, or the yolk may be rubbed through a sieve, and the white cut into strips.

PASTRY

Some people shy away from making their own pastry, believing it to be too difficult an art to master. There is a knack to making pastry, but if you follow the general rules and are meticulous about measuring out proportions of ingredients, the results will be very rewarding.

PIES AND TARTS

A pie is made of two pastry layers enclosing a filling – or a filling in a deep container covered by a pastry lid. A tart or flan is a flat pastry case containing a sweet or savoury filling.

Tips for making pies and tarts

Hard fruit which will take longer to cook than the pastry can be softened a little by cooking it gently for 5-6 minutes before filling the pie or tart.

Do not place a pastry lid on a hot pie filling. Allow the filling to cool first, or the pastry will become soggy.

Do not leave a final layer of sugar on top of any pie or tart filling but mix it in with the fruit. Otherwise the pastry lid or decorations will become soggy.

For tarts or flans with a custard filling, brush the base well with egg white before you add the filling. This seals the pastry and stops the custard mixture from leaking through.

Preparing savoury fillings

To prepare meat, trim off any gristle or excess fat and cut the meat into bite-sized pieces or mince.

For pies with added liquid, first coat the meat in seasoned flour. Put 1 tablespoon flour and a good pinch of both salt and pepper into a plastic bag, add the pieces of meat and shake well. The flour also helps to thicken the liquid in the pie.

A filling made from less tender cuts of meat will take longer to cook and should be made in advance. Cool your pie filling well, before covering with the prepared pastry.

Coat small chunks of fish with seasoned flour and add freshly chopped parsley or other herbs if liked.

Vegetables can also be used as a savoury filling. Cut into cubes of about 2.5 cm (1 in), as they need to cook over the same period of time as the pastry.

Blanch hard vegetables first to ensure even cooking. A pie containing mainly vegetables needs to be well seasoned, and will benefit greatly from the addition of herbs and spices.

Assessing the amount of pastry

Most pie and tart recipes stipulate making pastry with a particular quantity of flour. If this is not identical to the amount given in the following pastry recipes, simply adjust all the pastry ingredients in proportion.

For example, if a recipe calls for 'flaky pastry using 450 g (1 lb) flour', double all the ingredients listed in the flaky pastry recipe.

The final quantity of the pastry will be roughly the total of flour and fat.

Pastry ingredients

Pastry consists of flour and fat mixed with a little liquid. Other ingredients are added as flavouring or to ensure that the pastry rises.

The proportions of the basic ingredients and the method of mixing are crucial to the texture of the pastry. Flour contains a sticky, elastic substance called gluten, which holds the dough together. Different mixing methods are used to control the gluten and vary the pastry texture. The type and amount of fat determines the richness and flavour.

Another vital ingredient is air, introduced during mixing and rolling. When the pastry is heated, the air expands, causing the pastry to rise and helping to make it light.

Flour Use soft plain (or cake) flour to make sure the pastry has a fine, short texture and rises only a small amount when heated. Strong (or bread) flour is not usually suitable, because it is high in gluten and would make the pastry rise too much and be too elastic, but it can be used in puff pastry.

Sieve the flour before use to make sure it is fresh, dry and free from lumps. If it has become damp, dry it in a warm place before using. Damp flour can make pastry heavy.

Fat Always use fresh fat. If it is stale and has a slightly 'off' flavour, this will be even more pronounced in the pastry after it has been cooked.

Butter, lard, good dripping, clarified fat, margarine, vegetable fat and suet can all be used. Butter produces a rich pastry, but for an economical, well-flavoured, short pastry, use a mixture of lard and margarine, or margarine and vegetable fat. Lard used on its own can give a flavour that many people find unacceptable.

Salt A pinch of salt helps to develop the flavour of the pastry.

Lemon juice Flaky, puff, strudel and rough puff pastries are rich; adding lemon juice counteracts the richness.

Egg yolk Adding an egg yolk enriches pastry and gives it a very short (crumbly) texture.

Hints for making pastry

When mixing and rolling pastry, the aim is to introduce as much air as possible so that the pastry will rise well when heated. The colder the air, the more it will expand during cooking.

Keep all utensils and ingredients as cool as possible, and wash your hands in cold water before you mix pastry. The exception to this rule is when you are making strudel pastry which requires slightly warmer conditions.

Mixing the dough

Sieve together the dry ingredients. This not only sifts out lumps but also ensures even distribution.

Weigh out the correct amount of fat. Too much will make the pastry break easily; too little could make it hard and tough. Whichever method you use, the fat must be properly incorporated and distributed as evenly as possible, otherwise it will melt and run before it is absorbed into the flour during baking, giving tough, streaky pastry.

Mix in cool water or other liquid with a broad-bladed knife. Add the water gradually. Too much can spoil the texture of the pastry.

When the dough is properly mixed it should be soft and elastic, and leave the side of the bowl clean.

Do not rub off any little pieces from your fingers into the pastry. This can result in rough spots and flecks when the pastry is rolled out.

Rolling pastry

If time allows, leave the pastry to rest in a cool place for 10-20 minutes before rolling it out, particularly in hot weather. Pastry that gets overheated during handling will be tough.

Dredge the board and rolling pin with flour, but not the pastry. Too much flour rolled in can alter the ratio of flour to fat, particularly if you are making only a small quantity.

When rolling pastry, use short, quick, light strokes with even pressure from both hands. Always roll in a forward direction and lift the pin between strokes. Stop rolling just short of the edges to ensure a uniform thickness and avoid squeezing out air. Lift the edges lightly to check that the pastry is not sticking to the board. If it is, lightly dust beneath it with flour.

Do not handle pastry unless necessary. To move it or lift it onto a dish, turn it over a floured rolling pin. Unroll it onto a freshly dredged surface or across the surface of the dish. The rolled side of the pastry is the smoothest, and should be used for the pie surface.

Storing uncooked pastry

Pastry can be stored after mixing until ready for use. If sealed in a plastic bag, it will keep in a refrigerator for up to 3 days, whether in a lump or rolled out. It can be frozen for up to 3 months, but roll and shape it before freezing.

Shortcrust pastry, mixed to a crumb stage but with no liquid added, can be stored in a plastic bag or covered container in a refrigerator for up to 4 weeks. Use portions as required. It can also be frozen for up to 6 months.

Lining a shallow dish or flan ring

Grease the dish or ring, using sunflower oil, butter or margarine. Be particularly careful if using cheese pastry, which is likely to stick.

Roll out the pastry to the thickness required and a size large enough to allow for the depth as well as the width of the container, adding an extra 5 mm ($\frac{1}{4}$ in) to allow for shrinkage during the cooking process.

Lift the pastry on a floured rolling pin and place it over the dish or ring. Press it into the container gently with your fingertips and give a clean finish to the edges, rolling across the top of the container, so that the surplus bits of pastry drop off.

Use the pastry offcuts to decorate the pie with leaves or other shapes.

Baking blind

A pastry case is baked blind – without a filling – if the filling needs little or no cooking or will be added later.

Prick the base of the pastry lining with a fork to let out the air. Cover the base with a circle of greaseproof paper or aluminium foil, and put in a temporary filling of dried beans or rice to prevent the pastry from rising.

Bake in the centre of an oven preheated to 190°C (375°F, mark 5) for about 15 minutes. When the pastry is cooked, take out the greaseproof paper or foil and the beans or rice (which can be used again), and put the case back into the oven for 2-3 minutes to dry out. Once the case is ready, proceed with the filling.

Covering and filling a pie

Roll out the pastry to the thickness required – usually no more than 5 mm ($\frac{1}{4}$ in) – and an area roughly 2 cm ($\frac{3}{4}$ in) larger all round than the top of the dish you are covering.

Invert the pie dish onto the pastry and cut away the spare pastry. Roll these trimmings into a strip about 2.5 cm (1 in) wide.

Distribute the filling evenly in the dish. For a covered pie, pile the filling up in the centre to support the lid or put an egg cup or pie funnel in the middle of the dish, to raise the filling. For savoury pies, use a large onion.

Dampen the rim of the dish with a wet pastry brush, and line the moistened rim with the pastry strip. This forms the base of a double rim that provides a good seal and lessens the risk of liquid boiling out of a pie.

Brush the rim with water, lift the lid on a floured rolling pin and lay it over the top of the dish. Gently press the two edges together.

Trim off any excess pastry with a sharp knife. Hold the knife handle at a slight angle so that the trimmed edge slopes outwards from the rim. This allows for any shrinkage which may occur during cooking.

Make two slits in the centre of the lid to let steam escape.

Decorate the pie with pastry leaves made from the offcuts of pastry and glaze the lid with beaten egg if desired.

Seal or 'knock up' the edge of the pastry with the back of a floured knife blade held horizontally. Tap all round

the edges with a slight lifting movement. Scallop the edges by drawing towards the centre at intervals.

Shortcrust pastry

Shortcrust pastry should have a crisp, short (melt-in-the-mouth) texture. The pastry is usually baked at 190-220°C (375-425°F, mark 5-7), depending on richness and size.

PREPARATION TIME: 10 MINUTES

INGREDIENTS TO LINE A 23 CM (9 IN) FLAN RING, TO LINE AND COVER AN 18 CM (7 IN) PIE PLATE, OR COVER A 1 LITRE (1¾ PINT) PIE DISH

225 g ($\frac{1}{2}$ lb) flour
$\frac{1}{2}$ teaspoon salt
50 g (2 oz) lard
50 g (2 oz) margarine
60 ml (2 fl oz) cold water

Sieve the flour and salt into a bowl. Cut the fat into small cubes and distribute them evenly over the flour.

Rub the fat lightly into the flour with your fingertips, lifting up the mixture while rubbing to keep it as cool and aerated as possible. Continue rubbing until the mixture resembles fine breadcrumbs.

Make a well in the centre of the mixture and add the water gradually while you stir it in with a knife. Use just enough of the water to produce a soft (but not sticky) dough.

Turn out the dough on a floured surface and roll to the thickness required for your pie or flan.

Sweet shortcrust pastry

Flans and tarts to serve cold are sometimes made with sweet, enriched shortcrust pastry that can be rolled out very thinly. It is usually baked at 180°C (350°F, mark 4).

PREPARATION TIME: 15 MINUTES

INGREDIENTS TO LINE TWO 18 CM (7 IN) FLAN RINGS

225 g ($\frac{1}{2}$ lb) flour
$\frac{1}{2}$ teaspoon salt
100 g (3¾ oz) butter
25 g (1 oz) caster sugar
2 extra-large egg yolks
2 tablespoons water

Sieve the flour with the salt, and mix in the fat as for shortcrust pastry. Add the sugar and mix well.

Beat the egg yolks together and mix in the cold water, then make a well in the centre of the flour and stir in the egg and water mixture with a knife to produce a soft dough.

Turn out the dough onto a floured board and knead gently until it is pliable and free from cracks. Roll out to the required thickness.

Puff pastry

Puff pastry is rich and very light. It is similar to flaky pastry, but lighter and with more layers, and is used for vol-au-vent cases. Strong bread flour can be used instead of soft cake flour.

This pastry is baked at a higher temperature than either flaky or rough puff – usually 230°C (450°F, mark 8).

It is worth buying puff pastry ready mixed and frozen; the pastry will be ready for rolling once thawed. Note that the amount of pastry specified in recipes in this book is based on the quantity of flour; you will need more than 225 g (½ lb) frozen pastry for a recipe that specifies puff pastry using 225 g (½ lb) flour.

PREPARATION TIME: 40 MINUTES
STANDING TIME: 1 HOUR

INGREDIENTS TO LINE TWO 23 CM (9 IN) FLAN RINGS, OR COVER A 1 LITRE (1¾ PINT) PIE DISH
225 g (½ lb) unsalted butter or firm margarine
225 g (½ lb) flour
¼ teaspoon salt
1 teaspoon lemon juice
60-100 ml (2-3½ fl oz) cold water to mix

Pat the fat into a square and put it in a cool place to get firm, but not hard.

Sieve the flour and salt into a bowl. Make a well in the centre and add the lemon juice. Stir in enough water, using a knife, to form an elastic dough.

Turn out the dough on a floured board and knead it gently for 5-10 minutes until it is smooth and does not stick to your fingers.

Roll out the pastry to a strip large enough to enclose the fat. Place the fat in the middle of the pastry and fold the ends over it one at a time. Flatten the lump in 1 or 2 places with the rolling pin, then roll it out evenly and lightly into a long strip, taking care that the fat does not break through. Do not roll beyond the top and bottom edges.

Fold one-third of the length into the middle and press it down gently, then fold the other end over to form 3 layers, and again press down gently. Do not seal the edges, as this could trap large air bubbles and cause the pastry to rise unevenly. Leave the pastry to rest in a cool place for 15 minutes.

Place the dough on the floured board so that an unsealed edge is towards you, then roll and fold again. Each rolling and folding is known as a turn, so this completes the second turn. Make two more turns, then leave the pastry to cool again for another 10 minutes.

Make three more turns – to give 7 turns in all. Roll out the pastry to the size and thickness required. Leave it in a cool place for 10 minutes before baking in a preheated oven.

Rough puff pastry

Rough puff pastry is similar to flaky pastry, but has larger flakes and is not as light. It is usually baked at 220°C (425°F, mark 7).

PREPARATION TIME: 20 MINUTES

INGREDIENTS TO COVER AN 850 ML-1 LITRE (1½-1¾ PINT) PIE DISH
225 g (½ lb) flour
¼ teaspoon salt
175 g (6 oz) firm margarine or butter, or a mixture of both
1 teaspoon lemon juice
100-125 ml (3½-4 fl oz) cold water

Sieve the flour and salt into a mixing bowl. Add the fat in one lump, cover it with flour and then, with a knife or pastry blender, cut it into cubes – each about the size of a hazelnut.

Make a well in the centre of the mixture and add the lemon juice, then stir in the water gradually with a knife, mixing lightly so that you do not break down the fat. Continue until the mixture is a firm, elastic dough.

Turn out the pastry on a floured board and press it into a lump, but do not knead it. Roll the pastry lightly into a strip about 3 times as long as it is wide and about 5 mm (¼ in) thick.

Fold one-third of the length into the middle, then the other end over the top to make 3 layers. Seal the open edges by pressing firmly with a rolling pin to enclose as much air as possible.

Turn the pastry so that a sealed edge is facing you, and make ridges in 2 or 3 places with a rolling pin. This distributes the air and stops it from collecting in a large bubble that will be difficult not to break when rolling.

Roll the pastry into a strip again, but be careful not to roll beyond the top and bottom edges, as this will press out air. Fold the pastry in three as before, then seal, turn and ridge again.

Repeat the process twice more, then roll out the pastry to the size and thickness required. Be very careful not to stretch it, as this will cause the pastry to shrink.

Strudel pastry

Strudel pastry is made with warm ingredients – unlike most other pastries, which require cool ingredients and utensils. It is usually baked at 180-200°C (350-400°F, mark 4-6).

PREPARATION TIME: 50 MINUTES
STANDING TIME: 30 MINUTES

INGREDIENTS FOR A STRUDEL
40 CM × 15 CM (16 IN × 6 IN)
225 g (½ lb) flour
A pinch of salt
2 eggs
¾ teaspoon lemon juice or vinegar
2 teaspoons butter
80-125 ml (2½-4 fl oz) lukewarm water
60 ml (2 fl oz) melted butter

Warm all the utensils you will be using.

Sieve the flour and salt into a bowl. Make a well in the centre of the flour and add the eggs and lemon juice or vinegar. Cut in the butter with a knife or rub it into the mixture with your fingertips until a crumb consistency is reached. Add just enough water to make a soft dough. Knead the strudel dough well.

Bang the pastry on a board about 50 times (until it blisters). Sprinkle the dough with flour, cover with a warmed pot, and allow it to rest for 30 minutes.

Prepare the filling for the strudel. When it is complete, proceed with the dough as follows.

Cover a table with a clean tablecloth. Work on a table which is easily accessible from all sides. Sprinkle the cloth with flour and rub it in with your hands. Roll out the pastry on the board, then transfer it to the tablecloth.

Brush the dough with a little melted butter, then, working under the sheet of dough with hands lightly clenched, stretch it with your knuckles, from the centre outwards. Work very gently, going around the table. Try not to tear the dough. It should stretch to about 1 metre (3 ft 3 in) square.

A fairly thick border will form and this must be cut off before you spread the filling onto the dough. Use the off-cuts to patch any holes you may have made. Brush the dough again with melted butter.

Flaky pastry
Flaky pastry is made up of thin, crisp layers with air in between. It is particularly suitable for pies to be served cold. It is usually baked at 220°C (425°F, mark 7).

PREPARATION TIME: 30 MINUTES
STANDING TIME: 45 MINUTES

INGREDIENTS TO COVER A 1 LITRE (1¾ PINT) PIE DISH
225 g (½ lb) flour
½ teaspoon salt
175 g (6 oz) butter or firm margarine, or a mixture of both
1 teaspoon lemon juice
100-125 ml (3½-4 fl oz) cold water

Sieve the flour and salt into a bowl. Divide the fat into 4 equal portions.

Take one portion of fat, cut it into small pieces and rub it into the flour with your fingertips, lifting up the mixture while rubbing to keep it cool and aerated. Continue until the mixture resembles fine breadcrumbs.

Make a well in the centre of the mixture and add the lemon juice and just enough water to mix, with a knife, to a firm, elastic dough. Turn out the dough on a floured board and knead it until it is free from cracks.

Roll the dough into a strip 3 times as long as it is wide and about 2.5 cm (1 in) thick. Take a second portion of the fat and, with a knife, flake it in even rows along two-thirds of the strip of pastry. Leave a clear strip about 2 cm (¾ in) wide at the edge. If the fat is too close to the edge, it will be squeezed out when you roll the pastry.

Fold one-third of the strip (the end with no butter) over to the middle. Then fold the other end (covered with butter) over that, so that the pastry is folded into 3 layers.

Leave the pastry to rest for 15-20 minutes in a cool place, then turn it so that an open edge is towards you.

Press the open edges together with a rolling pin to enclose the air. Then make ridges in 2 or 3 places by pressing with the rolling pin. This distributes the air and stops it from collecting in a large bubble that is difficult not to break when rolling.

Roll out the pastry again to a strip 3 times as long as its width, then flake on the third portion of fat in the same way as the second. Fold, rest, seal and ridge as before.

Repeat the whole process using the fourth portion of fat. Then roll out to the thickness required.

Choux pastry
Choux pastry is usually shaped through a forcing bag to make both sweet and savoury dishes, such as éclairs or cheese puffs. (For a cheese choux, beat in 75 g/3 oz grated cheese after the eggs.)

The pastry is very light and airy, and has a hollow centre.

During cooking – usually at 180-220°C (350-425°F) – choux pastry puffs up to about three times its original size.

PREPARATION TIME: 15 MINUTES

INGREDIENTS TO MAKE 16-18 ÉCLAIRS OR ABOUT 20 CREAM PUFFS
65 g (2½ oz) flour
¼ teaspoon salt
50 g (2 oz) butter
150 ml (¼ pint) water
2 eggs, beaten

Sieve the flour and salt onto a sheet of greaseproof paper. Put the butter and water in a heavy-based saucepan and place over a low heat until the butter melts, then increase the heat and bring rapidly to the boil.

Remove the pan from the heat and pour in all the sifted flour, stirring quickly with a wooden spoon until the flour has been absorbed into the liquid.

Return the pan to a gentle heat, then cook for 2-3 minutes until the mixture is smooth and comes away from the side of the saucepan.

Cool the mixture for a few minutes, then beat in the eggs gradually. The pastry must be firm enough for piping, but not too stiff. If you are not going to use the pastry immediately, closely cover the saucepan with a sheet of moist greaseproof paper under the lid. This keeps the dough pliable.

Do not open the oven door while the pastry is cooking, otherwise it will be flat. If making éclairs or puffs split them open when cooked and leave in the oven for 30-60 seconds to dry the insides thoroughly.

TIPS FOR COOKING PASTRY

● Always preheat the oven before baking pastry. If you put it into a cool oven, the fat will melt and run out before it is absorbed into the flour. This will make the pastry tough, greasy and of poor texture.
● Make sure the oven is not too hot, otherwise the pastry surface will set too quickly and form a crust that prevents full expansion of steam and air. This makes the pastry hard and biscuit-like. Place the pie or flan dish on a baking tray before you put it in the oven. It is then easier to remove when hot.

● The top of the oven is the hottest part and the bottom the coolest. It is usual to bake in the centre, but this may vary according to the make of oven. Follow the manufacturer's instructions for the baking position.
● If you have to open and close the oven door during baking, do it very gently because cold air may make pastry drop, particularly if it is light. Puff pastry needs a very hot oven; do not put anything else in the oven at the same time.
● If the pastry starts to brown too

quickly, wait until it has finished rising, then cover it with aluminium foil.
● When baking a large pie in a small oven (or a pie that needs long cooking, such as a game pie), once the pie has reached the desired colour put a stiff collar of cardboard or a double collar of aluminium foil round the dish, and secure it with string. Lay foil or grease-proof paper on top of the collar.
● After cooking, leave the pudding or pie to cool slowly in a warm kitchen. If it cools too quickly in a draught or a cold room, it will be heavy.

BATTERS

A batter is a mixture of flour, liquid and eggs. It is used for a number of purposes, including pancakes, puddings and fritters. The following recipe is suitable for pancakes. For fritters, make a coating batter by halving the liquid content and using only 1 egg.

Basic batter

PREPARATION TIME: 10 MINUTES
CHILLING TIME: 1 HOUR
COOKING TIME: 15 MINUTES

INGREDIENTS FOR 12 PANCAKES
100 g (3 oz) flour
A pinch of salt
3 eggs
250 ml (9 fl oz) milk, or half milk
  and half water
1 tablespoon melted butter or
  sunflower oil (optional)
Melted butter and oil for frying

Sift together the flour and the salt. Beat in the eggs and the milk to make a smooth batter. Chill for an hour.

Pancakes

Heat a frying pan until very hot and brush quickly with melted butter and oil before pouring in a thin layer of batter. Once browned and set, flip the pancake over to lightly brown the other side. Transfer to a plate and keep warm while making the rest of the pancakes. They may be made a day or two ahead of time and refrigerated (well-covered), or frozen for later use.

Serve the basic pancakes with honey, syrup and lemon juice, or scoops of ice cream. Alternatively, fill them with fresh fruit and serve with cream.

Pancakes can also be rolled up round a wide variety of savoury fillings, placed in a buttered ovenproof dish, topped with a cheese sauce* and extra grated cheese. Sprinkle with dry breadcrumbs, dot with butter and bake for 20 minutes at 200°C (400°F, mark 6) until bubbly and golden.

Fritters

Coat chunks of fruit or thin slices of vegetables with batter and deep-fry until golden. Apples and bananas would be suitable for sweet fritters, while aubergines (eggplants), courgettes (zucchini) and carrots make very good vegetable fritters.

HERBS

The judicious use of herbs is one of the most important culinary skills. Although most herbs are best used fresh, they can be dried or frozen. Process as soon as possible after picking, and wash if necessary.

If the weather is warm, herbs can be left to dry naturally. Alternatively, spread the herbs on a rack, heat the oven to its lowest temperature, then switch off and wait for the temperature to drop to 40-50°C (105-120°F) before placing the herbs inside. Leave them in the oven overnight.

When substituting dried herbs for fresh, use much smaller quantities, since the flavour is more concentrated.

Delicate-tasting herbs that do not dry well – such as borage, tarragon, parsley and basil – are suitable for freezing.

Freeze clean, dry herb sprigs in aluminium foil or plastic bags. If the leaves are large, wash and chop as desired. Use within six weeks or if longer storage is required, blanch for 45 seconds. If using in cooked dishes, there is no need to thaw frozen herbs.

Bouquet garni is the name given to a muslin sachet of fresh herb sprigs (or a bundle of herbs tied with string), which is used to flavour stocks and stews.

The traditional bouquet garni consists of parsley, thyme and bay leaves, but other flavourings, such as celery or rosemary, may be added.

Basil Often known as the 'tomato herb', basil will enhance the flavour of all tomato dishes. Use also as a pungent addition to eggs, fish, shellfish and pasta dishes.

Bay leaves Use the leaves alone or in a bouquet garni. Add them to soups, fish chowders and meat casseroles.

Borage The foliage has the aroma and flavour of cucumber. Chop the leaves into soups in the place of parsley. Cook young leaves with green peas or beans and use fresh borage in salads.

Chervil Blends well with veal, pork, chicken or lamb. Serve with potato salad or cooked aubergine (eggplant).

Chives Garnish cold soups and salads with chives. Scatter chopped chives over omelettes just before serving.

Dill Goes well with fish or poultry. Leaves and seeds are excellent combined with cheese or eggs and a few seeds will improve the taste of cauliflower and cabbage.

Fennel The leaves can be used in salads or as a garnish. Use the stems as a bed on which to grill fish. Spice fish, egg, meat and vegetable dishes with the seeds. Fennel bulbs (also known as Florence fennel) can be used raw in salads or cooked.

Lemon balm Use freshly chopped leaves in fruit salad, sorbet, or with lemon desserts. Garnish fruit drinks with whole leaves.

Lovage Lovage has a celery-like taste and can be used if celery is not available. Use in soups and stews.

Marjoram Add chopped marjoram to fresh avocados or mushrooms, and use to flavour meat pot-roasts.

Mint Chop and serve fresh with fruit salad (try with sliced peaches in wine) or crush into fruit drinks. A handful of mint leaves, very finely chopped, to which boiling hot vinegar and sugar (to taste) have been added, forms mint sauce – the classic English accompaniment to roast lamb.

Oregano This pungent herb is often used with Italian food and for stuffings.

Parsley A very versatile herb, rich in iron, parsley is widely used as a garnish, and is a good seasoning for most dishes.

Rosemary Use sprigs in casseroles or when roasting lamb, beef, mutton or game. Bake with fish or sauté with fresh mushrooms.

Sage The flavour of poultry and pork dishes is brought out by sage, which is particularly good in stuffings.

Summer savory Use freshly chopped in lamb, veal, or pork stew. It makes an unusual combination stewed with pears.

Tarragon The delicate aniseed flavour of fresh tarragon suits fish and poultry.

Thyme Use a bouquet garni. Sprinkle into soups and stews, or use in game pies for meat loaves.

Winter savory Add sprigs to sautéed chicken livers and mincemeat dishes. Boil with lentils and dried beans.

SPICES

Spices have been prized for thousands of years for their qualities as preservatives and digestives, as well as for their appetising flavour. They mainly consist of the fruits, seeds, bark or roots of a wide variety of plants, and they may be used fresh or dried.

Whenever possible, buy spices in small quantities and preferably whole because they tend to lose their flavour once they have been ground or powdered. Store spices in small, airtight containers in a cool, dry place.

The following is a list of the spices most commonly used in cooking.

Allspice The small, unripe berries of the tropical allspice tree are sun-dried and used in many spice mixtures. Allspice derives its name from its versatile nature and taste, which is like a mixture of cinnamon, cloves and nutmeg. It is used in baking and pickling, and to flavour sauces, fish, meat, vegetables and desserts.

Aniseed The liquorice-flavoured seed of the anise plant (not to be confused with star anise) is used in confectionery and sometimes in curries.

Caraway seeds The seed-like fruits of a plant similar to parsley can be used to flavour bread, cheeses and pork dishes.

Cardamom The straw-coloured or pale green cardamom pod, which contains several tiny black seeds, is the most expensive spice in the world after saffron. The pungent flavour is particularly suitable for curries, and can also be used to flavour khulfi (Indian ice cream).

Cassia This reddish-brown bark of a type of cassia tree is often confused with cinnamon, which it resembles.

Cayenne pepper This red pepper is derived from a fiery hot pepper pod. Use sparingly with eggs, cheese, soups, curries, sauces, stews and seafood.

Celery seeds The tiny seeds of the annual celery plant have a bitter flavour. They are used in soups, stews, vegetables or curries. Crush the seeds and add to salt for celery salt.

Chilli powder Made from ground, dried chillies, it can be as mild or hot as the chillies, from which it is made, and is one of the basic ingredients of curry.

Cinnamon A pungent, sweet spice sold in sticks of curled bark from the cinnamon tree or in ground form. It is a popular flavouring for both sweet and savoury dishes.

Cloves The dried, unopened flower buds of a tropical tree, cloves have a pungent, aromatic flavour. The oil is used for relieving toothache, and the spice is used to flavour apples, bread sauce and ham.

Coriander (dhania) This hardy annual, cultivated widely for both its leaves and aromatic seeds, is related to the carrot. The leaves and seeds taste totally different, but both are very popular curry ingredients. The seeds are also useful for flavouring soups, eggs, fish, meat, marinades, vegetables, pickles and chutneys, and are a basic ingredient in many curries.

Cumin The small, aromatic, seed-like fruit of an Indian and North African plant, this spice is available whole or ground, and looks like caraway. It is used in Mexican and Indian dishes, and also as a flavouring for meat, poultry, rice, eggs, cheese and pickles.

Curry leaves The leaves of the curry bush (a relative of the lemon tree) give a pungent flavour to various Indian dishes. They are available dried from speciality spice shops.

Dill seeds The seed-like fruits of the dill plant, with their mild aniseed flavour, are used particularly for pickling cucumbers. The fresh or dried leaves of the plant are also used as a herb. Use to flavour soups, sauces, fish dishes and salad dressings.

Fennel seeds These seeds, with their slight aniseed taste, are used in Malay and Indian curries, in fish or egg dishes, and in liver, pork or lamb stews. The seeds can also be used to stud bread or rolls, and to spice cabbage.

Fenugreek This is the pod of an annual, heavily scented legume. The seed is used in curry powder.

Ginger The rhizome or rootstock of a tropical plant, ginger is frequently used fresh (peeled) in Oriental dishes. It is also preserved in syrup or crystallised, or dried and sold whole or ground.

Mace see Nutmeg

Mustard The whole seeds, called rai in India, are used in pickles, soused herring and salted meat. They can also be sprouted for use in salads and sandwiches. Prepared mustards add zest to a large range of dishes (which are often referred to as 'devilled').

American mustard is mild and yellowish; French mustards are stronger and sometimes have whole seeds and other spices added; and English mustard is very hot.

Nutmeg and mace Mace is the amber, fibrous network surrounding the brown nutmeg, the fruit of a tropical tree. Both have a sweet, delicate taste.

Paprika This sweet and mild spice, which is ground into a bright red powder, comes from the same family as cayenne. Paprika is used to flavour goulashes, soups, eggs, cheese, rice, chicken, meat and fish dishes.

Pepper The dried berries from a tropical vine provide the most widely used seasonings of all. Berries which have been picked just before they are ripe produce black pepper, which is aromatic. If they are left to ripen and then dried, they yield white pepper, which has a hotter flavour.

Saffron This spice, made from the stigmas of the purple-flowering saffron crocus, takes its name from the Arabic for yellow (za'faran). It is the most expensive spice in the world, and is used to colour and flavour soups, cakes and savoury rice dishes. Because of the price, many people substitute turmeric in recipes calling for saffron.

Tamarind The acid fruit of the tropical tamarind tree is sold dried for use in Indian and Malay cooking. It is soaked in boiling water, then strained to produce tamarind water.

Turmeric A dried, ground root of a plant of the ginger family, it is aromatic and mild. Turmeric is used to flavour and colour curries, pickles, sauces and rice dishes.

Vanilla The pod or bean of a tropical climbing orchid, it is used in pâtisserie and ice cream. Vanilla essence is more commonly used in the kitchen.

185

GLOSSARY

A

à la grecque In the Greek style. Vegetables, particularly mushrooms and artichokes, cooked in olive oil and/or stock, with coriander seeds and other seasonings, and served cold.

al dente The phrase refers to the texture of food, particularly pasta, which is properly cooked but still firm to the bite.

antipasti Italian starters, which often consist of marinated vegetables and seafoods and slices of salami or other cold meats.

arrowroot A starch made from the root of a plant of the same name. It is used to thicken sauces.

aspic A clear jelly made from the cooking juices of meat, poultry or fish. It is used to coat or mould cold food, and as a garnish.

au gratin A method of finishing a cooked dish by covering it with sauce, and sprinkling over breadcrumbs and/or grated cheese, then grilling it or cooking it in the oven until it is browned.

B

bain-marie A large pan of hot water in which a smaller pan or other container is placed for cooking food or keeping it warm. It can also refer to a double boiler: a two-part saucepan with a top pan fitted to a lower one that holds simmering water.

bake blind To bake a pastry case without its filling.

bard To wrap lean meat, game or poultry with strips of pork fat or fatty bacon to prevent the flesh from drying out during cooking.

baste To spoon juices over food during cooking to prevent it from drying out.

beurre manié (kneaded butter) Flour and butter worked to a paste, used to thicken soups, sauces and stews.

beurre noir A sauce for fish or brains made by frying butter until dark brown (not black) and adding parsley, vinegar, capers and seasoning.

beurre noisette A sauce of melted butter, cooked until nut-brown, and seasoned.

bind To add egg, fat or liquid to a pâté, rissole or stuffing, to hold it together.

biriani An Indian dish of meat, fish or chicken with rice, lentils, eggs and spices.

blanch To immerse food briefly in boiling water for any of the following reasons: to soften it (for example, vegetables); to skin it (as with tomatoes or nuts); to rid it of excess salt or very strong flavours; or to kill enzymes before freezing.

blanquette A white stew, made of veal, poultry or rabbit, with a creamy sauce.

blini A pancake made of buckwheat flour, often served with caviar and sour cream.

boil To cook in liquid at boiling point, that is, the temperature at which the liquid evaporates when bubbling.

bouchée A small puff pastry case, baked blind and filled with a savoury or sweet filling.

bouquet garni A small bunch of herbs (often consisting of thyme, parsley, marjoram and a bay leaf) tied together with string or placed in a small muslin bag. It is used to flavour soups and stews and is removed and thrown away before serving.

braise To cook food slowly, covered, in a minimum of liquid after it has been browned in fat.

brown To sear the outer surface of meat so that the juices are sealed. Also used to refer to cooking other foods until they are brown.

brûlé(e) Applied to dishes such as cream custards that are finished with a caramelised sugar glaze.

C

canapé An appetiser made of biscuits or small slices of fresh, fried or toasted bread topped with a savoury mixture.

cannelloni Large pasta tubes stuffed with savoury fillings.

capers The pickled flower buds of the Mediterranean caper bush, used in sauces and as a garnish.

caramelise To heat sugar until it turns brown and syrupy.

casserole A cooking pot with a lid, made of ovenproof material. It also refers to a slow-cooking stew of meat, poultry, fish and/or vegetables.

chutney An Indian relish, cooked or uncooked, of fruits or vegetables and spices, served with curries or other foods.

cinnamon sugar Sugar flavoured by the addition of ground cinnamon: use 1-2 teaspoons for every 200 g (7 oz) sugar.

clarified butter Butter that has been cleared of impurities or sediment by melting and straining.

clarify To clear fat by heating and filtering. Alternatively, clearing consommés and jellies with beaten egg white or broken eggshell.

cocotte A small ovenproof dish used for baking individual mousses, soufflés or egg dishes.

coddle To cook food, particularly eggs, slowly in simmering water.

colander A perforated metal or plastic basket used for draining away liquid.

compote Fresh or dried fruit cooked in syrup, often flavoured with spices such as cloves or cinnamon.

conserve Whole fruit preserved by boiling in sugar. It is used like jam.

coral Orange shellfish roe.

court-bouillon Liquid used for poaching fish, made from water and wine or vinegar, flavoured with herbs and vegetables.

crackling Crisp skin of pork obtained by frying, rendering or roasting.

cream To work together a mixture such as fat and sugar with a wooden spoon until light and fluffy, like whipped cream.

crème fraîche Cream that has been allowed to mature but not sour.

crêpe A thin pancake.

croûtons Small cubes of fried bread used to garnish soups and dishes that have sauces.

crudités Raw vegetables or fruit, served as an appetiser or snack, often with sauces for dipping the food into.

curd The semi-solid part of curdled milk.

curdle To cause fresh milk or a sauce or other liquid to separate into solids and liquids by overheating or by adding acid (such as lemon juice or vinegar). Alternatively, to cause creamed butter and sugar in a cake recipe to separate by adding the eggs too rapidly.

D

Danish caviar Lumpfish roe.

deglaze To scrape browned, solidified cooking juices off the bottom of a roasting or frying pan with the help of a liquid such as wine, stock, cream or brandy.

demerara A soft brown sugar produced in the West Indies and nearby countries.

dice To cut into small cubes.

dough A mixture of flour, water, milk and/or egg, sometimes enriched with fat, which is firm enough to knead, roll and shape.

draw To disembowel.

dredge To coat food lightly with flour, icing sugar or other fine powders.

dress To pluck, draw and truss poultry or game birds. Alternatively, to pour salad dressing over a salad.

dripping Fat that runs from meat or poultry during roasting, or rendered animal fat.

dumplings Small balls of dough, stuffing or vegetable mixture, which are steamed or poached. They are used to garnish soups and stews.

dust To sprinkle flour, sugar, spice or seasoning lightly over food.

E

éclair A light, oblong of choux pastry split lengthways and filled with cream, usually topped with chocolate icing.

en croûte Food encased in pastry.

escalope A thin slice of meat, usually veal, which is beaten flat and shallow-fried, often after being coated with breadcrumbs.

F

filo pastry Very thin sheets of pastry dough (available from specialist grocers or delicatessens), used for both sweet and savoury dishes.

fines herbes A mixture of finely chopped fresh herbs: parsley, chervil, tarragon and chives.

flake To separate cooked fish into individual flaky slivers. Alternatively, to grate chocolate or cheese into small slivers.

flambé Flamed, for example food tossed in a pan to which burning brandy or other alcohol is added.

flan An open pie or tart filled with fruit or a savoury mixture.

florentine Of fish and eggs: served on a bed of buttered spinach and coated with a cheese sauce.

fluff To fluff with a fork, as for cooked rice: lift the rice lightly with the fork and toss to separate the grains.

fold in To envelop one mixture or ingredient into another with a metal spoon or spatula, so that air does not escape. Cut through the mixture with the spoon or spatula, slide it along the bottom of the bowl, then lift and turn the mixture over the ingredient to be folded in. Continue until blended.

fool An English cold dessert made of fruit purée folded into whipped cream.

French dressing A mixture of oil, vinegar (or lemon juice), salt and pepper, sometimes flavoured with herbs and garlic. (Also known as vinaigrette.)

fricassee A white stew of chicken, veal or rabbit and vegetables, first fried in butter and cooked in stock, then completed with cream and egg yolks.

G

galantine A dish of boned and stuffed poultry, game or meat glazed with aspic and served cold.

garam masala A mixture of hot spices and herbs lightly sprinkled over Indian food at the end of cooking.

ghee Clarified butter used in Indian cooking.

giblets Edible internal organs of poultry and game birds, including the liver, heart, gizzard and neck.

glaze A glossy finish given to food by coating it with beaten egg, milk, sugar syrup or aspic after cooking.

gnocchi Small dumplings made from semolina, potato, spinach or choux pastry.

gratin The French term for a crust.

H

haricot A variety of green bean or the dried seed of this plant. Alternatively, a casserole of lamb or mutton and dried haricot beans.

hoisin sauce A thick, soy-based barbecue-type sauce used in Chinese cooking.

hors d'oeuvre Hot or cold appetisers served at the beginning of a meal.

hull To remove the green leafy cup (calyx) and stalk from berries.

I

infuse To extract flavour through immersion and soaking in hot water (such as spices, herbs or tea). The resulting liquid is called an infusion.

J

joint A prime cut of meat for roasting. Alternatively the word means to divide meat, poultry or game into individual pieces.

julienne Thin, matchstick strips of vegetables, often used as a garnish or in clear soup.

K

kebab Meat cubes marinated and grilled on a skewer. Also refers to fish, poultry, fruit and/or vegetables prepared in the same way.

kneaded butter See beurre manié.

L

lard To thread strips of fat (lardons) through lean meat, using a special larding needle, to prevent it from becoming too dry during roasting.

lardons Strips of fat threaded through lean meat to keep it moist during roasting (see lard). Anchovies can also be used as lardons.

legumes Vegetables from plants with seed pods, such as beans and peas.

lentils The small seeds of a legume. They are used in soups, stews, curries and salads.

liaison A thickening for sauce or soup, for example egg yolk and oil in mayonnaise, or a starch such as flour or cornflour in a sauce.

M

macerate To soften food by steeping it in liquid.

marinade A blend of oil, wine or vinegar, herbs and spices used to tenderise and flavour meat, poultry or fish. Other ingredients are often added or substituted.

marinate To soak foods in liquid to make them more tender or to flavour or preserve them. See marinade.

marinière Of mussels: cooked in white wine and herbs, and served on the half shell. Of fish: cooked in white wine and garnished with mussels.

Marsala A sweet Italian wine drunk as an apéritif or used in cooking.

masala A mixture of spices and herbs used in curries.

mask To cover food with sauce.

melba toast Very thin, crisp toast made by splitting a freshly toasted slice of bread horizontally and grilling the two inner surfaces until the corners curl up.

meringue Whisked egg white and sugar, which is spooned or piped on top of sweet pies or into shapes and baked at a low temperature until crisp.

mornay A cheese sauce used to coat fish, egg or vegetable dishes.

mousse A smooth sweet or savoury mixture, enriched with cream, lightened with beaten egg whites, and, if necessary, stiffened with gelatine.

mushrooms, dried Chinese Dehydrated mushrooms used in Chinese cooking.

N

noodles Pasta made from flour, water and egg.

O

offal Edible internal organs of animals.

P

paella A Spanish dish of saffron rice, chicken and shellfish, which is named after the shallow round pan in which it is cooked.

parboil Partially cooking food by boiling it for a short while.

pasta A paste made of flour and water, sometimes with eggs or other ingredients added, from which macaroni, spaghetti and other Italian noodles are made.

pastry Dough made from flour, fat and water (sometimes with other ingredients), which is baked or deep-fried until crisp.

pâté A savoury mixture of finely chopped meat, game or poultry which is baked in a casserole or terrine, and served cold. The name is also used for some mixtures that are not baked, such as fish pâtés.

pearl barley De-husked barley grains used in soups.

pesto A sauce made from pine nuts, basil garlic and olive oil, served with pasta.

petit pois Tiny, young, green peas.

pickle To preserve meat or vegetables in brine or vinegar mixtures.

pimento The spice called allspice.

pimiento Sweet green or red peppers.

pipe To force cream, meringue, icing, savoury butter, mashed potato or other pastes through a forcing bag fitted with a nozzle to decorate various dishes.

piquant Pleasantly sharp and appetising.

pith The white fibrous part of citrus peel, situated under the rind.

pitta bread See unleavened bread

poach To cook gently by immersing food in simmering liquid.

pot-roast To cook food in steam, raised on a rack above a small amount of liquid in a covered pot.

praline Hot, caramelised sugar and browned

almonds mixed together and left to set into a brittle sheet, which is then pounded in a mortar or broken into pieces for use as a flavouring.

preserve To keep food in good condition by treating it with chemicals, heat, refrigeration, pickling in salt or vinegar or boiling in sugar. It also refers to pieces of fruit suspended in a sugar syrup.

prove Causing dough to rise in a warm place before baking.

provençale In the Provence style, cooked with garlic and tomatoes.

pulp The soft, fleshy tissue of fruit or vegetables. Alternatively, to reduce food to a soft mass by crushing or boiling.

purée Raw or cooked food crushed to a very smooth texture by passing it through a sieve or blending in a blender or food processor. Alternatively, thick vegetable soup which is passed through a sieve or blended.

Q

quiche An open tart with a savoury filling based on an egg and milk or cream custard.

R

ramekin A small baking dish for individual servings.

ravioli Small squares of pasta stuffed with a savoury filling.

reduce To concentrate or thicken a liquid by rapid boiling. To 'reduce by half' means to boil until half the liquid has evaporated.

refresh To freshen food, such as boiled or blanched vegetables, by placing it under cold running water.

relish A sharp or spicy sauce made with fruit or vegetables, which adds a piquant flavour to hot or cold foods.

render To melt animal fat slowly to a liquid. It is then strained to eliminate any residue.

rind The coloured, outer oily skin of citrus fruit which, when grated or thinly peeled, is used as a flavouring.

risotto Italian savoury rice, fried and then cooked in stock or tomato juice, with or without other ingredients added.

roast To cook in the oven with radiant heat, or on a spit over or under an open flame.

roe Milt of the male fish, called soft roe; eggs of the female fish, called hard roe; or shellfish roe, called coral because of its colour.

roti Flat Indian bread, alternatively called chapati.

rotisserie A rotating spit used for roasting or grilling meat or poultry.

roulade A roll of meat, vegetables, chocolate cake, soufflé omelette or pastry.

roux Melted fat (usually butter) and flour mixed together and cooked to form the basis of savoury sauces.

rub in To mix flour or other dry ingredients with fat (usually butter) using the fingertips to give a crumbly result.

S

saddle The undivided loin from a meat carcass.

salami Spiced Italian pork sausage, which is sold fresh, smoked or cooked.

sambals Side dishes served with Indian or Malay dishes.

sauté Frying food rapidly in a small amount of fat until it is evenly browned, shaking the pan to toss and turn the contents. The food is either just browned or cooked through.

savoury rice The term refers to a number of different rice dishes, particularly risottos, or rice flavoured with fried onion, tomato and green pepper, or other ingredients. Commercially packaged savoury rice is also available.

scald To heat liquid, usually milk, to just below boiling point, until bubbles form around the edge of the pan. The word is sometimes used as an alternative to blanch.

schnitzel A slice of veal, often coated with crumbs before being cooked. See escalope.

score To make shallow cuts, preferably with a heavy knife, over the surface of fish or meat, such as steak, to tenderise it or to allow better penetration of heat.

sear To brown meat rapidly with fierce heat to seal in the juices.

seasoned flour Flour flavoured with salt and pepper.

seasoning Salt, pepper, spices or herbs, which are added to food to improve flavour.

sift To pass flour or sugar through a sieve to remove lumps.

simmer To cook in liquid which is just below boiling point, with only a faint ripple showing on the surface.

skewer A metal or wooden pin used to hold meat, poultry or fish in shape during cooking, or to hold small pieces of food together during cooking.

skim To remove cream from the surface of milk, or fat or scum from broth, stews or jam.

slake Adding water (or other liquid) to a powder, such cornflour.

sorbet Water ice made with fruit juice or purée.

sour(ed) cream A commercially prepared product made from half cream and half skim milk which has been cultured sour (therefore lower in fat than cream).

steam To cook food in the steam rising from boiling water.

steep To soak in liquid until saturated, or to remove an ingredient such as salt.

stock Liquid that has absorbed the flavour of the fish, meat, poultry and/or vegetables cooked in it.

strain To separate liquids from solids by passing them through a metal or nylon sieve or through muslin.

strudel Thin leaves of pastry dough, filled with fruit, nuts or savoury mixtures, which are rolled and baked.

stuffing A savoury mixture of bread or rice, herbs, fruit or minced meat, which is used to fill cavities in poultry, fish, meat or vegetables.

suet Fat around beef or lamb kidneys.

syrup A thick, sweet liquid made by boiling sugar with water and/or fruit juice.

T

tagliatelle Thin, flat ribbons of pasta.

terrine An earthenware pot used for cooking and serving pâté. It also refers to the food cooked in the pot.

thickening A preparation such as flour, butter, egg yolks or cream used to thicken and bind sauces and soups.

truss To tie a bird or joint of meat in a neat shape with skewers and/or string before cooking.

U

unleavened bread Bread made without a raising agent which, when baked, is thin, flat and round. Frequently sold as pitta bread.

V

vanilla sugar Sugar flavoured with vanilla by enclosing it with a vanilla pod in a jar.

velouté A basic white sauce made with chicken, veal or fish stock. It also describes a creamy soup.

vermicelli Very fine strands of pasta.

vinaigrette A mixture of oil, vinegar (or lemon juice), salt and pepper, sometimes flavoured with herbs and garlic.

W

whey The watery liquid that separates out when milk or cream curdles.

Y

yeast Fungus cells (*Saccharomyces cerevisiae*) used to cause dough to rise. Available fresh – in the form of a putty-like block, or dried – in the form of granules.

yoghurt Curdled milk which has been treated with harmless bacteria.

Z

zest The coloured, outer oily skin of citrus fruit which, when grated or thinly peeled, is used as a flavouring. It is also referred to as the rind.

INDEX